50170
18.99
(1)

The Nutritional Psychology of Childhood

The Nutritional Psychology of Childhood

Robert Drewett

CAMBRIDGE
UNIVERSITY PRESS

CAMBRIDGE UNIVERSITY PRESS
Cambridge, New York, Melbourne, Madrid, Cape Town, Singapore, São Paulo

Cambridge University Press
The Edinburgh Building, Cambridge CB2 8RU, UK

Published in the United States of America by Cambridge University Press,
New York

www.cambridge.org
Information on this title: www.cambridge.org/9780521535106

First published 2007

Printed in the United Kingdom at the University Press, Cambridge

A catalogue record for this publication is available from the British Library

ISBN 978-0-521-82787-4 hardback
ISBN 978-0-521-53510-6 paperback

To J, K & L

Contents

Illustrations and Table

Table

Preface

Feeding, like breathing, is central to our survival. I do not mean to the survival of 'our species' but literally to the survival of each one of us. Yet, unlike breathing, it has never been very clear to what discipline the study of feeding belongs. In respect of children it is the province of midwives and health visitors, of paediatricians and specialist nurses, of speech therapists, of dieticians and nutritionists, of child psychiatrists, of psychologists, and of others, no doubt, as well. To some extent this may reflect the rather uncertain academic position of the study of nutrition more generally. Whatever the reason, published research concerning psychological aspects of nutrition in childhood is very widely scattered, and this is, I believe, the first attempt that has been made by a single author to gather it together in one place in the form of a book. No doubt the attempt will leave a lot to be desired, but I hope that it will provide at least an initial source and a reasonably useful framework for those who need them in first approaching this area.

Tastes will differ, but speaking for myself I do not enjoy reading reviews that report findings without giving any indication of the nature or quality of the research that gave rise to them, so I have tried to say enough about the research I cite at least to give a flavour of the methodology used in it. This is, of course, a big field, and I have left out much more than I have included, as is inevitable in a book of this size.

1 Introduction

1.1 Introduction

My aim in this book is to summarise recent research dealing with psychological aspects of nutrition in childhood. Broadly speaking, these psychological aspects involve two kinds of problem – those concerned with the development of behaviour that is related to food intake, and those concerned with the later consequences of malnutrition, or more generally with the later consequences of different types of nutrition. The overall organisation of the book is developmental. I deal in turn with problems that arise before or around the time of birth, with problems associated with infancy and the weaning period, and with problems which are more characteristically associated with later childhood and adolescence. These are the major transitions. Birth is a major transition because although malnutrition can arise before or after birth (and malnutrition in both periods can have effects on the child's development), its causes before and after birth are obviously different: only malnutrition after birth can result from problems with the child's own feeding behaviour, for example. Weaning is a major transition between two quite different kinds of feeding behaviour. Adolescence and the period preceding it involve transitions of a different kind, characterised by changes in the meaning and significance of food and body weight rather than in the nature of eating behaviour and the foods that are eaten. But although the overall organisation of the book is developmental, some departure from this order is necessary, and there cannot, of course, be any strict demarcations between the different stages of life. Important questions about infancy, for example, concern the later effects of early nutritional experiences, and important questions about adolescence concern the early precursors of the eating disorders that characteristically develop over the teenage years. So when we deal with problems in infancy we shall often also be looking forward, and when we deal with later problems we shall often also be looking backwards.

Here is a handful of questions that arise in this area. Does it matter if young infants gain weight very slowly, and if so why? Are infants who gain weight quickly more likely to be too fat as children, or even as adults? Does it matter whether infants are breast-fed or bottle-fed, and if so, in what ways? Does it matter if an infant is born very small? How should an infant born before term be fed? Does the way they are fed affect their subsequent development, and if so, how? How common is iron deficiency in infants? Does it have adverse effects on the child's intellectual development? Do other forms of malnutrition have adverse effects? What should we do about children who are picky eaters? Does it matter that their choice of foods is narrow, and if so why? How can we encourage healthy eating, especially the eating of fruit and vegetables by children? Are some children born to be fat? Are children who are fat more likely to suffer from low self-esteem, or in other ways? Is there an epidemic of obesity in children, and if so why has it arisen and how should we deal with it? Can schools help? How common is dieting in children and adolescents? Which children diet and why? Does dieting put a child at risk of the development of eating disorders? What other characteristics put children at risk of an eating disorder? In what kinds of family are we likely to find a child with an eating disorder, and how can we bring up our children so that they can steer the right course between the Scylla of obesity and the Charybdis of the eating disorders?

Some of these problems are wholly psychological in nature, and some are partly psychological. Health psychology is not very good at keeping within its academic boundaries, and nor, in my view, should it be – the human world was not organised to conform to the academic structures of British universities. They are all practical rather than theoretical problems, and my aim in this book is practical too: it is to offer a somewhat sceptical appraisal of recent research on psychological issues that arise in connection with nutrition in childhood. For reasons which will, I hope, become clear, I have concentrated on areas in which we can call upon a reasonably substantial body of research of reasonably good quality. It is difficult enough to arrive at clear conclusions even in these areas.

Before we embark on our developmental journey, there are some necessary preliminaries to deal with, and they take up the remainder of this chapter (Chapter 1). Chapters 2 and 3 deal with feeding behaviour in infancy, and then with the development of eating in older children. Chapter 4 deals with the growth of infants before birth, and with the nutritional problems of infants born too small, which may reflect malnutrition before birth, or born too soon, which can be associated with nutritional problems after birth. In Chapter 5 we turn to specific nutritional deficiencies, especially iron deficiency and protein-energy malnutrition. Much of the best research on these topics comes out of an interest in the health and welfare of children in less developed countries; perhaps surprisingly, though, both kinds of malnutrition are also quite common in infants and young children in more affluent countries. Chapter 6 deals with physical illnesses or disabilities. This is a big topic, and I have tried to do no more than sample one or two examples that have important nutritional aspects. In Chapter 7 I deal with infants who for no obvious medical reasons gain weight very slowly. Traditionally these are described as infants who 'fail to thrive'. This chapter might seem out of sequence, and it is, but dealing with this calls for some prior knowledge of the issues dealt with in Chapters 5 and 6. Chapter 8 deals with the opposite problem – children whose excessive weight gain puts them on the path to obesity. Finally, in Chapter 9, we consider the development of the major eating disorders of later childhood and adolescence, especially anorexia nervosa and bulimia nervosa. There's nothing much in Chapter 10.

1.2   Growth and development

A particular reason for considering the issues involved in childhood nutrition separately from those involved in adult nutrition is that childhood is the period of growth. When we talk in an everyday sense of a child's growth, we are generally referring to skeletal or *linear* growth, as it is reflected in their height. But every organ system in a child is growing, including their reproductive system and their central nervous system. The growth of all these is dependent on adequate nutrition, so nutrition and malnutrition in infancy and childhood can affect a child's development in ways that it does not in adults.

A useful overall framework for considering linear growth in childhood is provided by the infancy-childhood-puberty (ICP) model (Karlberg, 1987; 1989). This considers a child's growth as made up of three components. The infancy component is continuous with fetal growth (growth before birth), and lasts through the first year. This is a period of very rapid growth. Then follows a period of steady but slower growth, the childhood component, which lasts through to the beginning of puberty. In the pubertal component there is a growth spurt, together with a rapid maturation of secondary sexual characteristics, and skeletal growth then stops with the attainment of adult height. We meet different kinds of psychological problems over these different periods. The special feeding problems associated with nursing and weaning are characteristic of the infancy period. A key milestone in the development of obesity is the 'adiposity rebound' which develops from about 3 years of age, in the childhood period, when many eating habits are also formed. Eating disorders such as anorexia nervosa commonly develop over the pubertal

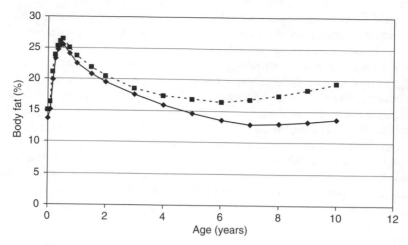

Figure 1.1 Body fat of the 'reference child' at different ages. The data represent the proportion of body fat in an average child at each age, and were derived from a variety of sources by Fomon *et al.* (1982). Males: ♦ Females: ■.

period, and important questions arise concerning their relationship to sexual development and the other somatic changes that occur over puberty.

Unlike the skeletal system, which develops particularly rapidly early in life, much reproductive development is rather late, though critical aspects of reproductive development also occur before birth. Males and females differ initially only in their chromosomes. The female has two large X chromosomes, and the male one large X and a one small Y chromosome. The presence of the Y chromosome leads by about eight weeks after fertilisation to the development of a testis, which begins a few weeks later to secrete the male sex hormone, testosterone. Testosterone leads to sexual differentiation of the body into that characteristic of a male; in its absence a female body develops. One obvious consequence of this process of sexual differentiation is the development of different external and internal genitalia in males and females, but there are other more subtle consequences. Girls mature faster than boys, for example (Tanner, 1989). They reach half their adult height by 1.75 years, compared with 2 years in boys, and they go into puberty earlier. It is principally because puberty is earlier in girls that they tend to be shorter than boys, who continue to grow for longer. As well as skeletal growth, there are important growth-related changes in fat deposition over infancy, childhood and puberty. The general pattern of fat deposition over the first ten years is reported by Fomon *et al.* (1982) and by Fomon and Nelson (2002) and is shown in Figure 1.1. At birth a typical boy's body is about 14% fat but this rapidly increases to about 25% at 6 months. This period of early infancy over which so much fat is stored corresponds to the period of exclusive or largely exclusive milk feeding, during which the mother's lactation provides a store of energy that the infant can call upon as they learn to feed independently. After 6 months body fat slowly declines again to a minimum of about 13% at about 7 years of age, from which point it starts to rise again (this is the 'adiposity rebound'). A generally similar pattern is seen in girls, though there is an important sex difference here too. Girls have stored noticeably more fat by the time they go into puberty.

The growth of the brain takes place principally before birth and in the early childhood period. The weight of the whole body of a child at birth is about 5% of the weight of a young adult's, and at 10 years it is about 50%; but the weight of a child's brain at birth is about 25% of the weight of a young adult's, and at 10 years it is about 95% (Tanner, 1989). Of course different components of the nervous system develop at different times. Neurones in the cerebral cortex, for example, are initially generated between day 42 and about day 138 of embryonic life (Kolb, 1999). They migrate towards their final positions up to about seven months of gestation. The production of axons, dendrites and synapses begins then, but continues after birth. Synaptogenesis mostly takes place after birth (Huttenlocher, 1999). Its exact timing is different in different areas of the brain: in the visual cortex, for example, it takes place largely over the first four months, and in the prefrontal cortex over the first year (Huttenlocher, 1999). In speech-related areas it occurs first in the primary auditory cortex, then in Wernicke's area, which is concerned with receptive language, and then in Broca's area, which is concerned with speech production (Huttenlocher, 1999). One general ground for concern about effects of nutrition early in life on subsequent psychological development lies in the fact that vulnerability to malnutrition may be particularly acute then (both before and after birth) as a result of the very rapid development of the brain.

Although there has been some direct anatomical and physiological work on the effects of malnutrition on the human brain, and extensive work on its effects on the brains of animals of other species, structural and physiological information concerning the effects of malnutrition on the brain can only be interpreted in a way that is of importance in practice if it can be related to functional effects of malnutrition. These functional effects are mostly psychological, and can be examined in a number of different ways. One possibility is to examine effects of malnutrition on particular psychological functions – for example, its effects on perceptual capacities, on different types of memory functions or on anxiety or other emotions. Another is to examine its effects on aspects of the child's development known to be of importance in their future lives. Learning to read, for example, is the foundation of educational success, and it would be important to know whether malnutrition delayed reading development – which it might do through an effect on a variety of basic perceptual or cognitive skills, or, for example, if it leads to absence from school.

In practice, though, much of the available research in this area has involved standardised developmental or intelligence tests. Whether an infant is showing a normal rate of developmental progress can be assessed informally by parents, by monitoring the attainment of different 'milestones' – taking the first step, speaking the first word and so on. In research and other contexts that call for more formal measures a number of tools are available to assess development in infancy in the same general way (Wyly, 1997). The most widely used have been the Bayley Scales of Infant Development, which were initially developed by Nancy Bayley in the 1930s. They were published in a standardised form in 1969 (Bayley, 1969) and in a revised and restandardised form in 1993 (Bayley, 1993). The original version covered the period from 2 to 30 months, and the revised version the period from 1 to 42 months. They assess infant development using a 'mental' scale, which is summarised as a mental development index (MDI), and a 'motor' scale, which is summarised as a psychomotor development index (PDI). Scores on these indices provide a measure of overall developmental progress, tested using a range of tasks that test skills of different kinds at different ages.

Studies that have investigated older children have generally used intelligence (IQ) tests. IQ tests can be used from 4 or 5 years of age, and involve a sample of tasks that reflect intellectual abilities, especially abilities of a kind that are important in an educational context. IQ tests use well-standardised procedures and have high reliability, and when IQ tests (or the standard developmental tests such as the Bayley Scales) have been used in research, it has been relatively easy to compare and combine the results of different studies, which is important in trying to arrive at firm generalisations. In unselected populations IQ tests show reasonably stable correlations with adult IQ from about 8 years of age, and they predict later educational and occupational success, even after other characteristics of the child's family have been taken into account (Fergusson, Horwood & Ridder, 2005; McCall, 1977). There are, however, difficult problems with the use of IQ tests in cultures other than those for which they were first developed (Baddeley, Gardner & Grantham-McGregor, 1995). Apart from language problems, the sample of intellectual skills that are appropriate in a Western educational context may not be appropriate elsewhere. Even in Western cultures, the *validity* of IQ tests is difficult to determine. A striking example of this problem is the remarkable rise in IQ over the last century, documented by Flynn (1987). There is no doubt that there has been a large rise in measured IQ in every country in which we have data, but there is considerable uncertainty about its meaning. We know children have got better at doing IQ tests, but it is much less certain what other intellectual tasks they have got better at.

Early developmental tests such as the Bayley Scales were developed as practical tools for the detection and assessment of delayed development, and some children whose development is delayed also have a relatively low intelligence when they are older, as is typically found in Down syndrome and other forms of learning disability. It does not follow that there is a general correlation between scores on a developmental scale such as the Bayley Scales and later intelligence. Bornstein *et al.* (1997) point out that many of the items on the Mental Scales tested in the first year involve perceptual-motor skills, for example 'eyes follow rod', 'uses eye–hand coordination in reaching' and 'picks up cube' at 4 months, and 'turns pages of a book', 'fingers holes in pegboard' and 'builds tower of three cubes' at 12 months. There is no reason to think that success at these tasks would reflect the sort of intellectual abilities required for success in intelligence tests at later ages, and the extent to which these and similar scales used in infancy actually do predict subsequent intellectual abilities in typically developing children is very limited (Kopp & McCall, 1982). Combining different studies, the median correlation Kopp and McCall found with IQ at 8 to 18 years if the infants were tested between 1 and 6 months was .06; tested from 7 to 12 months it was .25; tested from 13 to 18 months it was .32; and tested from 19 to 30 months it was .49.

Attempts to develop more specific measures of cognitive performance in infancy of a kind that might relate better to later intelligence have had some success. McCall and Carriger (1993), for example, review the relationship between performance on habituation and recognition memory tasks in infancy and later intelligence. Habituation tasks can be carried out from birth, and even before birth. They can use a variety of sensory stimuli; after birth visual stimuli have generally been used. If the same visual stimulus is presented repeatedly the time spent looking at it by the infant decreases over time. Controls involving the presentation of a changed stimulus show that this decrease is not due to tiredness or simple sensory adaptation. It involves, rather, the encoding of the stimulus into memory so that it becomes familiar and no longer attracts attention. A closely related task involves visual recognition memory, in which a pair of standard visual stimuli are presented together over a series of trials, and one of the two is then replaced with a novel stimulus. The higher proportion of time spent looking at the novel stimulus provides a measure of the extent to which the earlier standard stimuli have become familiar, something which again depends on the encoding of the stimulus into memory. McCall and Garriger (1993) summarised the results of a large number of studies of the relationship between habituation or recognition memory in the first year and later intelligence as measured with IQ tests. They found overall correlations of .39 for habituation and .35 for recognition memory studies. These are higher than the correlation found between traditional infant developmental scale scores in the first year and later intelligence. There is, however, also a worryingly high correlation ($-.56$) reported in this paper between the size of the correlation found in each study and the size of the sample in the study. The reason this is worrying is that a correlation of this kind is typically found when there is a publication bias in favour of larger effect sizes, which are more likely to be statistically significant (Sutton *et al.*, 2000). A publication bias of this kind would mean that the correlations of .39 and .35 could not be taken at face value.

In any case, any correlation between a test given in infancy and a test given later that is less than perfect ($r < 1$) implies that some children are changing their relative position over time – improving or getting worse – and no currently available test carried out in infancy shows a correlation with later intelligence of more than about .4. Children might recover from effects of malnutrition measured early in life, just as they recover from effects of other kinds of early adversity (Clarke & Clarke, 2000). So whether there are tests available in infancy that assess the same cognitive skills as intelligence tests in older children or not, it will always be necessary to examine both short-term and longer-term effects of malnutrition if its implications for the development of children are to be properly understood. There is no substitute for the long-term follow-up of the children involved. It would even be possible in theory for some kinds of adverse effects of early malnutrition only to become apparent for the first time late in life. Malnutrition may reduce structural and functional brain reserves in a way that comes to matter only in old age; and indeed, a number of recent studies do suggest that the time at which the cognitive impairments in the elderly first develop is related to their nutrition early in life (Abbott *et al.*, 1998; Graves *et al.*, 1996). Essentially, then, we need to examine effects over the whole lifespan if we are to know how abilities in later life are affected by malnutrition early in life. We are a long way from being able to do so. The best that is available in most of the areas we shall deal with is follow up into the middle school years.

1.3   Energy balance

All the activities of a child depend upon energy. So too does their growth, in which energy is stored in the tissues of the body. Many of the nutritional problems of children that we shall deal with involve energy balance. The problem of slow weight gain in infancy ('failure to thrive') is principally a problem of insufficient energy intake. Anorexia nervosa is principally an elective energy deficit that leads to weight loss in adults, and to poor growth and failure to gain weight adequately in children. Obesity is principally a problem of energy intake that is not being balanced by a comparable energy expenditure, leading to a storage of fat.

Energy is not an altogether straightforward concept. In its standard physical sense, it is the capacity to do work. But the term 'energy' is also used in a more figurative sense, in which it refers to the temporary or more lasting motivational characteristics of individuals, and it is important not to confuse the physical and motivation senses of the term. The decimal system of units currently used internationally in scientific work is the SI system, and in the SI system the unit of energy is the joule (J). So in nutritional research measurements of energy are now usually expressed as kilojoules (kJ) or megajoules (MJ). A megajoule is about as much energy as a croissant provides. A child 4 years old consumes and expends in the region of 5 MJ in a day (Davies *et al.*, 1994). In everyday nutritional contexts, however, the *calorie* is still widely used as the unit of energy. People on diets, for example, generally talk about 'counting calories'. A nutritional calorie is 4.184 kJ (slight differences in this value reflect the fact that the calorie can take five slightly different values). The use of calories in this area is hallowed by a long tradition, which predated our understanding of the interchangeability of heat and mechanical energy. But the use of a single decimal unit of energy must be simpler once we have got used to it, so in the interests of our children I have generally used joules as the appropriate unit for energy in this book, in accordance with the SI system. I hope this will not cause undue difficulty for grown-ups.

Energy consumed as food by a child can either be stored in body tissues as part of the growth process, or it can be utilised. The energy required for growth in infancy is quite small. According to one recent calculation (Butte, 1996) infant girls store on average 0.740 MJ (177 kcal) a day in the second month of life; this reduces rapidly to 0.150 MJ (36 kcal) a day from 9 months to 1 year. The figures are similar in boys but slightly higher, reflecting their faster growth. Soon after birth the growth of the child uses up about 40% of the energy they take in; at about a year this is reduced to about 5%. Very small amounts of energy are needed

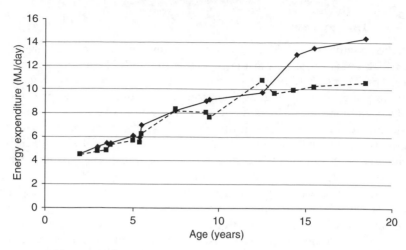

Figure 1.2 Energy expenditure of children of different ages. The data were derived from a variety of sources summarised in Torun *et al.* (1996). Males: ♦ Females: ■.

for growth thereafter. The utilisation of energy involves oxidative metabolism, in which oxygen is converted to carbon dioxide. This allows energy expenditure to be assessed via measurement of the extent of carbon dioxide production. There are a number of ways in which this can be done, which involve varying degrees of interference with normal behaviour. The one that interferes least is the doubly labelled water method. In this a small amount of water is drunk, labelled with two stable isotopes, deuterium ($^2H_2$) and oxygen-18 (^{18}O). The labelled oxygen is used in the production of both carbon dioxide (CO_2) and of water (H_2O), but the labelled hydrogen is used only for the production of water. So the difference in the rate at which the two isotopes disappear provides a measure of oxidative metabolism which very accurately reflects energy expenditure over extended periods of time (Prentice, 2002). This recently developed method has no known adverse effects, and has allowed the measurement of energy expenditure in children from birth (Davies *et al.*, 1994; Wells *et al.*, 1997; Wells & Davies, 1996). Energy expenditure in infancy has been measured in a longitudinal study by de Bruin *et al.* (1998). At 1 month of age average energy expenditure in girls in a day was 1.19 MJ. It rose to 1.78 MJ at 4 months, 2.56 MJ at 8 months and 3.08 MJ at a year. In boys these figures were 10–25% higher. Data summarising later energy expenditure up to the age of 19 are summarised in Turun *et al.* (1996) and are shown graphically in Figure 1.2.

An irreducible minimal level of energy expenditure is needed to maintain the basic physiological processes of life, and this is measured as the basal metabolic rate. Energy is also used for physical activity, and as physical activity varies from person to person and from time to time, this component of energy expenditure also varies. At the extremes, adolescents who are physically handicapped and use wheelchairs expend in the region of 6 MJ per day, while cyclists in the Tour de France expend in the region of 34 MJ per day, which is nearly five times their basal metabolic rate; physical activities of the kind more commonly encountered in everyday life are unlikely to more than double energy expenditure, except over short periods (Black *et al.*, 1996).

All these energy needs have to be met from the energy taken in as food, and it would be very helpful for research purposes if we were able to make equally accurate measurements of energy intake. Unfortunately we aren't. Over a single meal it is possible to weigh each individual food eaten, and then calculate overall energy intake provided the energy content of the individual foods taken is known. But for most purposes it is the child's average energy intake over more extended periods of time that it important, rather than energy intake over a single meal, and this is much more difficult to determine.

In theory it is most easily determined in infants in the first few months of life, when their diet is restricted to milk. If an infant is bottle-fed it is reasonably straightforward to measure the amount of milk they take in by weighing the bottle before and after the feed (Fomon *et al.*, 1975; Fomon, Owen & Thomas, 1964). If this is done reliably at every feed, day and night, for a number of days (easier said than done) the energy intake of the infant can then be calculated precisely provided the composition of the milk is known. If an infant is breast-fed, however, their energy intake is not so easy to determine. The amount taken can be measured by weighing the infant before and after the feed, and using the best available electronic balances these difference weighings can be done accurate to about 5 g. An alternative is to use a method related to the method described above for the measurement of energy expenditure (Butte *et al.*, 1991; Coward *et al.*, 1979). A small dose of heavy water ($^{2}H_2O$) is given to the infant, and the rate at which it is lost from the body measured. The heavy water is replaced by water in the milk, and provided the infant is not given any other water its loss from the body is proportional to the infant's milk intake. These methods allow accurate measurement of the amount of milk taken, but breast milk does not have a uniform composition: it varies from woman to woman, with the stage of lactation, and from the beginning to the end of a feed (Hytten, 1954; 1959). The fat content of breast milk, for example, can be up to ten times higher at the end of a feed.

Accurate measurements of the energy intake of breast-fed infants therefore also require samples of milk to be taken so that their energy content can be determined.

Although easy in theory, then, the measurement of energy intake is quite complex in practice even in infants. But in older children (and adults) it is even more complex, principally because after weaning the foods we eat are much more variable. The most accurate method for measuring food intake again involves the weighing and recording of all foods eaten over an extended period (Bingham, 1987). How long the extended period needs to be depends on the age of the person and the degree of precision required. To classify people into thirds of a distribution for energy intake (i.e. into those whose intake is in the top, middle and bottom third) with an acceptable degree of confidence needs weighed records for two or three days in infants and toddlers but a week or more in adults (Black et al., 1983). Collecting such records is difficult and time consuming, and a variety of other ways to determine food intake have been utilised, involving records of estimated rather than weighed food intake, or the recall of food intake at interview. There is, unfortunately, good evidence that all these methods can be seriously inaccurate, including, in practice, methods involving food weighing. This evidence has come particularly from studies in which energy intake has been compared with energy expenditure, measured using the very accurate doubly labelled water technique (Black et al., 1993). If body weight is not changing, energy intake must match energy expenditure. Black et al. reviewed a series of different studies in which this comparison had been made with a range of different participants. When food intake was recorded by observers, in a hospital or metabolic unit, there was indeed good agreement between the estimates of energy intake and energy expenditure. When food intake was measured in highly motivated volunteers using food weighing, there was also good agreement. But when it was measured in randomly selected men and women, who would be more representative of the general population, weighed records underestimated energy intake by about 20%, and in studies of obese and previously obese women the underestimation of energy intake was even greater.

These are systematic biases, not simply random errors, and these biases are also present in dietary intake reporting by children (Champagne et al., 1998). These authors found that the bias was greater in centrally fat children, that is, in those with fat concentrated in the abdomen, and also, interesting enough, in older children, over the range 9–12 years. Self-reported energy intakes are also biased in 12–18-year-old adolescents. Bandini et al. (1990) measured their energy expenditure over a two-week period and their energy expenditure over exactly the same period using food diaries. Reported energy intakes were substantially lower than measured energy expenditure, but the participants gained weight, and as it is not possible to take in less energy than is spent over an extended period and to gain weight, the conclusion has to be that the diary records systematically underestimated energy intake. Clearly self-reported energy intakes of this kind are of limited value. Our inability to measure energy intake accurately is one of the major current impediments to research in this area.

Essentially the sole source of energy available to the body is food, so food intake must provide for all the energy that is utilised. The link between energy expenditure and food intake is provided by eating, and by the motivational systems that control it. Although eating serves a number of different purposes, and is motivated in a number of different ways, for life to be possible at all it needs to be at least partly linked to the physiology of the body in such a way that our basic needs for energy are met. So the motivational systems that give rise to hunger and stimulate food intake are at least partly homeostatic systems, organised so as to preserve the 'constancy of the internal environment'. Other homeostatic systems control body temperature, plasma calcium levels and water balance.

Energy intake, however, is regulated much less precisely than any of these, and body weight is only moderately stable over time. Nonetheless, there is some homeostatic control over energy intake, and so over fatness. A striking illustration of this can be seen when one of the homeostatic controls on hunger and food intake does not operate. Figure 1.3 shows the weight gain of a child who completely lacked a hormone, leptin (Farooqi et al., 1999; Montague et al., 1997). 'Leptin' comes from the Greek leptos, meaning 'thin'. It is produced in adipocytes (fat cells), and suppresses hunger. As fat stores get larger more leptin is produced and hunger is suppressed – a homeostatic system involving negative feedback. The weight of this little girl who lacked leptin was normal at birth, but from 4 months of age she began dramatically gaining weight. She was constantly hungry and as a result ate excessive amounts of food, storing the excess energy she took in as fat. By the age of 5 she weighed over 50 kg, about three times as much as an average 5 year old. By 9 she weighed about 95 kg. Clearly when hunger is not regulated in the usual way, energy intake can go quite out of control. The control of energy balance therefore normally involves some matching of energy intake to energy expenditure.

How can this matching be achieved? In general terms there are two possibilities. Firstly, energy intake could be monitored and matched directly to energy expenditure, so that if energy intake is below what is required for energy expenditure food intake is stimulated, and if it is

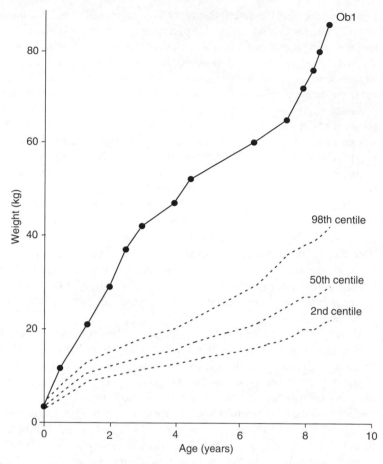

Figure 1.3 Weight gain of a leptin-deficient child (Ob1). The weight of the child, a girl, is plotted against centiles for weight: the 50th centile shows the average weights of girls at different ages. From Montague *et al.*, 1997. Reproduced by permission from Macmillan Publishers Ltd.: *Nature*, *387*, 903–8. Copyright 1997.

above what is required food intake is reduced. But if energy intake does not match energy expenditure the energy stored in the body (principally as fat) is reduced or increased. So a second possibility is that the energy stores themselves are monitored. We do not have a complete explanation of the mechanisms involved in the control of food intake even in human adults, but we know enough to be able to give an outline of some of the key mechanisms likely to be involved.

One important source of energy in cells is glucose, a simple sugar formed by the digestion of carbohydrates. Indeed, nerve cells in the brain depend entirely on glucose for their energy needs, though skeletal muscles can use either glucose or fatty acids, depending on their availability. Energy is used all the time, but food intake is clumped into *meals*. When rats are allowed to feed freely, meals tend to follow a small decline in blood glucose levels (Campfield, 1997). A similar association is found in adult humans (Campfield *et al.*, 1996). In this study 18 healthy adults were fitted with a cannula in a vein so that blood glucose levels could be continually measured. Ratings of hunger were completed about every half an hour by the participants in the study, and they could ask for a meal whenever they wanted to. The requests for meals tended to be preceded by small reductions in blood glucose levels, of about 10%. These results might indicate the existence of an energy-related signal that stimulates the onset of meals, namely a reduction in blood glucose. There is, however, an alternative explanation. Woods *et al.* (2000) note that this is only one of a series of different changes that immediately precede the onset of meals, which include an increase in body temperature, a decrease in metabolic rate and an increase in activity. They suggest that the meals might not themselves be responses to these changes; rather that when the meals are about to begin for other reasons, these changes take place as part of a process preparing the body to receive the food – so the decline in blood glucose, for example, functions to dampen the rise in glucose levels that will result from the meal. On this view, the onset of meals is normally determined by temporal habits or by environmental circumstances, rather than being a response to energy-related internal stimuli.

Whatever it is that leads to the onset of meals, stimuli associated with food intake do lead to their termination. When we refer to feeling 'full' it is natural to think that it is simply the amount of food in the stomach that is responsible, acting through gastric tension or stretch receptors. Although receptors of this kind are involved in satiation (Woods *et al.*, 2000), there are also more complex mechanisms involved. Food is digested in the stomach and the small intestine, and the products of digestion are transported from the intestine to the liver in the hepatic portal vein. This means that monitoring the contents of the hepatic portal vein is a useful way of monitoring foodstuffs coming into the body. There is a good deal of evidence that glucose is monitored in the liver, where there are sensory neurons in the hepatic portal vein which are sensitive to glucose levels (Toates, 2001). Infusions of glucose into the hepatic portal vein induce satiety, and infusions of 2-deoxy-D-glucose, a glucose analogue which competes with glucose to cross cell membranes and prevent its metabolism, stimulate feeding. These findings indicate that food intake leads to the cessation of feeding partly as a result of internal stimuli associated with glucose coming into the body via the liver. But humans consume a wide variety of foods of different chemical composition, and they use a wide variety of enzymes and other secretions to digest them (Woods *et al.*, 2000). The identification of other components of food involves sensors in the mouth and gut that respond to the chemicals involved. A hormone in the gut, *cholecystokinin*, is secreted in response to partly digested proteins and fats in the duodenum. Its role in digestion is to release bile from the gallbladder into the gut, and to release digestive enzymes from the pancreas. But there is now good evidence that cholecystokinin is also involved in satiation, and has a role in the termination of meals. Other gastric hormones act in similar ways.

Satiation is not, however, simply an unlearned response to characteristics of foods. It also involves learning mechanisms, so that foods acquire satiating properties as a result of experience. This learned ('conditioned') satiety was first demonstrated by Booth (1972; Booth, Lee & McAleavey, 1976; Booth, Mather & Fuller, 1982; Sclafani, 1997), initially in rats and subsequently in humans. An example of a study in which learned satiety was demonstrated involved measuring the intake of yoghurt-based desserts of different flavours. To establish the learning, experimental meals were preceded by high or low energy drinks. The yoghurt dessert was given two different flavours, and the high energy drink was paired with one flavour and the low energy drink with the other. During the testing phase, identical drinks of intermediate energy content were given before desserts of either flavour. Nonetheless, more of the yoghurt with the flavour that had followed the low energy drinks was consumed than of the yoghurt with the flavour that had followed the high energy drinks, showing that the yoghurt that had followed high energy drinks had acquired satiating properties partly by association between its flavour and the energy content of the drink with which it had been associated. It seems very likely that memory processes have a still more extensive role in controlling meal times and food intake. Rozin *et al.* (1998) have shown that two adults with dense amnesia would eat a normal lunch and then, within half an hour, eat a second complete lunch and even start on a third. Behaviour of this kind was not seen in either of two controls with brain damage that did not affect memory, and suggests that much of the information that controls food intake is information about recent meals that is stored in memory.

Leptin, the hormone that suppresses food intake, was first discovered in mice, and then rapidly identified in humans. Rather than providing a signal relating to energy intake or energy expenditure, leptin provides a signal related to the level of the fat stores. Considine *et al.* (1996)

measured leptin levels in blood in people of normal weight and others who were obese. The mean level was over four times as high in those who were obese. Seven of the obese people lost weight on a low energy diet, and their leptin levels fell. Leptin levels are quite highly correlated with hunger, as rated through the day on a visual analogue scale, with higher leptin levels associated with lower hunger ratings (Keim, Stern & Havel, 1998). The girl whose history is shown in Figure 1.3 came from a family with a single gene defect that led to very low leptin levels. The two affected children both developed severe obesity from a very early age. It is now possible to replace the missing leptin, and results of this treatment have been reported for this girl. The effect of the treatment with leptin was dramatic. She ate less rapidly, her food intake at a daily test meal dropped by 42%, and she lost a total of 16.4 kg of weight over a 12 month period.

Although energy intake is of central importance in many of the areas we shall deal with, food is more than a source of energy and comprises complex mixtures of important nutrients. Carbohydrates and fats are the principal sources of energy. Other important components are proteins, vitamins and micronutrients, which include iron and zinc. But even the behavioural regulation of energy balance is very complex, and I have done no more in this section than outline one or two of the mechanisms that are likely to be responsible. A recent comprehensive review can be found in Woods (2000). We are a long way from a comprehensive understanding of the details of this regulation in adults, and in dealing with infants and young children there is an added problem that different mechanisms may be involved. It would be surprising if they were not, since in mammalian infants energy intake and water intake cannot be separately regulated, as milk from the mother is the source of both. We now turn to consider the feeding of infants on milk more specifically.

2   The development of feeding behaviour: infancy

2.1   Human lactation and the structure of infant feeding

Much human behaviour has characteristics that we share with other species among the primates, the order to which *Homo sapiens* belongs. But we share the way we feed our young much more widely with other species of mammals, the class to which the primates belong. Indeed, the defining characteristic of this class is the feeding of their young on milk, and the class is named for the mammary glands that make this possible. Because infant mammals are initially fed exclusively on milk, it contains a large number of different nutritional constituents. The largest is water. It also contains energy-yielding components, which include a sugar, lactose, and fats, which provide a particularly dense source of energy, and it contains protein, in the form of casein and whey protein. These constituents of milk provide for the initial growth and energy expenditure of infants after birth. A range of immunological constituents help protect the infant against disease.

Feeding their young on milk has been a very successful adaptation for mammals; indeed, Caroline Pond has argued that it has been a major determinant of their ecological role (Pond, 1977; 1983). Although some reptiles guard their young as a form of parental care, reptiles do not bring food to the nest. The young must forage for themselves, and reptiles must therefore reproduce in environments that provide a supply of food suitable for infants as well as for adults. In mammals food for infants comes via the mother, and this allows the reproduction of mammals in a much wider range of environments. It also allows very rapid growth after birth. The newborn mammal does not need initially to develop foraging skills, and the milk provided by the mother is adapted to their needs. Even the mother is to some extent less dependent on a nutritionally adequate environment, since the milk can be formed from fats and other materials stored in advance in the mother's own body.

The basic biology of lactation is common to all mammals, but the details differ from species to species. The concentration of the major nutritional components in the milk of mammals is related to their ecology, and to the frequency with which the infant is fed, which is very variable (Blurton Jones, 1972). Rabbits and hares secrete milk with high concentrations of fats and proteins and nurse their infants only once in 24 hours, for a period of about 5 minutes (Blurton Jones, 1972). Apes and monkeys tend to have milk with rather low concentrations of these components (Wolff, 1968b), and to nurse their infants rather frequently. The stump-tailed macaque, *Macaca arctoides*, for example, nurses about every half an hour. Fats and proteins are similarly low in concentration in human milk, suggesting that we are also adapted to frequent nursing. A classic study among the !Kung hunter-gatherers found that in the daytime nursing bouts averaged four per hour (Konner & Worthman, 1980). In a study of infant feeding in Northern Thailand, female observers were present in village households throughout the day and night, and recorded and timed all nursing episodes in infants over the first year; most infants were nursed between 20 and 40 times over a 24 hour period (Drewett *et al.*, 1993).

In initiating feeding for the first time newborn human infants show a systematic sequence of behaviour which has been carefully described by Matthiesen *et al.* (2001) and Ransjö-Arvidson *et al.* (2001). About 6 minutes after birth, they open their eyes. Then they start using their hands, firstly using rhythmic massage-like milking movements on the mother's breast, and then moving their hands to their mouths, and sometimes licking or sucking them. About 20 minutes after the birth they show 'rooting' movements, in which the head is turned towards the nipple and the mouth opened. Olfactory cues guide the infant to the breast (Marlier & Schaal, 2005; Varendi, Porter & Winberg, 1994). Soon after, they start licking the areola and nipple, and after about 80 minutes take the nipple into the mouth and start to suck. The first sucking episode lasts about 10 minutes. Thereafter the infant feeds (or is fed) frequently through the day and night. These patterns of behaviour presuppose, of course, a system of obstetric care in which the nursing of the infant is allowed to follow on immediately from the birth.

The sucking of an infant on a bottle serves one function, the ingestion of milk. The sucking of an infant on the breast also serves another: it provides an afferent stimulus to endocrine reflexes acting via the central nervous system to release hormones into the mother's blood stream. The infant's sucking stimulates receptors in the nipple sensitive to touch, pressure or warmth. Sensory stimuli are relayed from the nipple to the mother's central nervous system, and eventually to neuroendocrine neurones in the hypothalamus that project to the posterior pituitary gland. Neuroendocrine neurones act both as neurones and as endocrine glands.

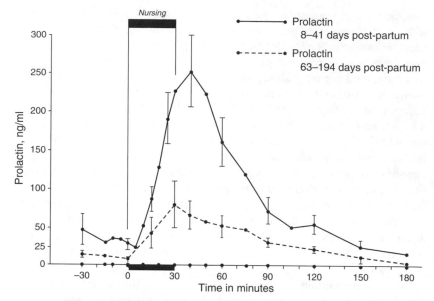

Figure 2.1 Release of prolactin in response to the sucking of infants nursed early and late in lactation. Adapted by permission from Noel, Suh and Frantz (1974). Copyright, 1974, The Endocrine Society.

They transmit action potentials like other neurones, but also secrete peptide hormones into the mother's blood stream. The hormones are vasopressin (antidiuretic hormone), which causes water retention by the kidney, and oxytocin, which stimulates myoepithelial (smooth muscle) cells surrounding the alveoli in the mammary gland to contract. The alveoli contain milk, and their contraction causes the 'milk ejection', in which milk is released through the nipples into the infant's mouth. The dilation of the milk ducts that results from a milk ejection can be seen under ultrasound, and the more milk ejections there are during the feed the more milk is transferred to the infant (Ramsay *et al.*, 2004).

In addition, the sucking of the infant stimulates a hormone from the anterior pituitary gland, prolactin, which is responsible for milk production, as shown in the data of Noel *et al.* (1974) in Figure 2.1. These effects of the stimulus from the infant's sucking on the release of prolactin from the pituitary gland of the mother mean that milk production in the mother is stimulated by the sucking stimuli provided by the infant. Although infants who suck for longer at a feed do stimulate the release of prolactin over a longer period (Amatayakul *et al.*, 1987), quantitatively milk production is more closely related to the number of feeds in a day than it is to the duration of the feeds (Drewett *et al.*, 1989a; 1989b). Milk production is also controlled in a separate way by the removal of milk from the breast by the infant, probably as a result of the removal of a milk protein that inhibits milk secretion within each breast (Wilde, Prentice & Peaker, 1995). When the breast is more completely emptied, milk synthesis generally increases (Daly, Owens & Hartmann, 1993). So we have here a form of 'inter-personal homeostasis'.

During a feed the milk ejection reflex changes the rate at which milk flows from the breast, and changes in the milk flow rate in their turn change the infant's sucking rate. An infant sucking on an empty bottle characteristically sucks in bursts, at a rate of about two sucks per second within the bursts. If milk is supplied, the sucking slows to about one suck per second, and rather than sucking in bursts the infant sucks in a long continuous stream (Wolff, 1968a; 1968b). Wolff referred to the slow and the fast patterns as 'nutritive' and 'nonnutritive' modes of sucking. This terminology can lead to some confusion. Wolff used it to refer to different patterns of sucking, but it is sometimes also used to refer to distinctions between hunger-motivated sucking and sucking motivated in other ways (e.g. comfort motivated), or to different consequences of sucking, for example whether it does or does not result in milk intake. Although Wolff demonstrated these different sucking patterns using infants sucking on bottles, comparable patterns are found during breast-feeding when milk flow rates are fast and slow (Drewett & Woolridge, 1979), for example at the beginning and end of feeds. Sucking patterns can therefore be a useful indicator of breast-feeding problems. A slow, continual pattern of sucking by the infant is a useful clinical sign that breast milk is readily available to the infant, while rapid sucking with pauses suggests that it is not.

2.2 Taste and flavour sensitivity

Substances that are sweet, salty, sour or bitter stimulate taste receptors in adults, and there is evidence that these taste systems function very early in life, though it is more difficult to investigate their properties in infants than it is in older children or adults.

One way of examining taste sensitivity in infants is to examine the facial expressions they make in response to small quantities of fluids (Steiner, 1973). Rosenstein and Oster (1988) carried out studies of this kind two hours after the infant's birth using the Baby Facial Action Coding System. This system codes changes in facial expression using the smallest distinguishable actions of the muscles of the face; it does not depend on any interpretation of the different faces made. Rosenstein and Oster examined the responses of eight newborn human infants to four taste stimuli, 25% sucrose, 4.3% sodium chloride, 2.5% citric acid and 0.25% quinine hydrochloride, which in adults taste sweet, salty, sour and bitter respectively. The facial responses of the infants showed that they distinguished sweet stimuli from the others, and also sour from bitter stimuli. There was no distinctive response to the salty taste.

How does the taste of a fluid affect its consumption? Immediately after birth, human infants consume larger quantities of water if the water is sweetened (Desor, Maller & Turner, 1973; Nisbett & Gurwitz, 1970). This has been shown for sweetening with glucose, and with lactose, the sugar which is naturally present in milk, though the effect is larger with sucrose, which tastes sweeter to adults. They also consume larger amounts of milk if the milk is sweetened (Beauchamp & Cowart, 1985). These responses reflect a rather general liking for sweet tastes in omnivorous species, which has probably evolved because sweet tasting substances tend to be high in energy. Sweet tastes also affect infants in a number of other ways that are not obviously related to their nutritional needs. They have, for example, a striking analgesic effect. This has been examined in relation to pain stimuli to which infants are subjected for other reasons during the course of their medical care. For example, Blass and Hoffmeyer (1991) randomly assigned infants to a group given a sucrose solution or water before blood was withdrawn with a heel lance to test for phenylketonuria, an inherited metabolic disorder characterised by high blood phenylalanine levels. The sucrose group were given 2 ml of a 12% sucrose solution in water, and the control group just the water, and crying in response to the heel lance was recorded. The amount of crying was halved by the prior consumption of sucrose. In a second study they examined responses to circumcision, a considerably more painful (and less easily justifiable) procedure. In this trial infants were given a pacifier dipped in a 24% sucrose solution before being 'gently strapped down' on the circumcision board. One group of control infants were given nothing, and another group a pacifier dipped in water. The infants given the sucrose cried significantly less than the infants in either of the other two groups. Such analgesic effects of sucrose have been reliably shown in both term (Haouari et al., 1995) and preterm infants (Ramenghi et al., 1996). They are attributable to the sweetness of the sucrose, as they are also found with other sweet tasting substances (Ramenghi et al., 1996), but not with a soluble carbohydrate (polycose) that is not sweet (Barr et al., 1999); and sucrose itself has no analgesic effect if it is given directly into the stomach rather than by mouth (Ramenghi, Evans & Levene, 1999).

The effect of salty tastes on the consumption of milk and water by infants is less simple, and seems to differ with the age of the child. The consumption of water by infants is not affected by the addition of small concentrations of salt up to 4 months of age (Beauchamp, Cowart & Moran, 1986; Desor, Maller & Andrews, 1975). This insensitivity to the taste of salt may have been responsible for a tragic episode of salt poisoning in newborn infants in an American hospital in 1962 (Finberg, Kiley & Luttrell, 1963). Formula milk made up in the hospital for newborn infants was accidentally prepared with salt rather than sugar, leading to the deaths of six infants and the illness of five others. Evidently the infants took the salty milk in the usual way. From 4 to 24 months infants consume more of a salty than an unsalty solution, but from 31–60 they consume less (Beauchamp, Cowart & Moran, 1986). These authors attributed the first change to the maturation of neural mechanisms underlying salt perception and the second to an effect of experience, perhaps a result of the relative unfamiliarity of salty water.

Flavours in our normal foods are partly taste-based, but also involve extensive contributions from odours. Infants fed on milk are not usually faced with a *choice* between alternative flavours, in the way that older children are, but there is nonetheless evidence that their feeding behaviour is influenced by flavours in the milk they consume. Flavours consumed by the mothers of breast-fed infants, for example, appear in their breast milk, and affect the feeding of the breast-fed infant. Mennella and Beauchamp (1991a; 1993b) compared the nursing behaviour of infants on a control day and a day on which their mothers had consumed garlic extract capsules. The odour of garlic was detectable on the mother's milk about 2 hours later. The infants spent longer feeding, as measured by time attached to the nipple, on the day on which the mother had taken the garlic. There was no difference in their milk intake, though milk intake, of course, depends on the mother's milk supply as well as on the behaviour of the infant. This effect on the infants' feeding behaviour was a transient one which was lost after repeated exposure to the garlic. A rather similar result was found with vanilla (Mennella & Beauchamp, 1996), which also flavours breast milk when consumed by the mother. Infants fed when the mother had consumed a vanilla extract spent more time feeding and consumed more milk. The same effect was found if the vanilla was added to formula milk, showing that it was a response to the flavour of the milk and not, for example, to breath or skin odours in the nursing mother. Again, this effect was lost with repeated exposure to the flavour. Alcohol in breast milk has a different effect, leading to reduced breast milk consumption by the infant (Mennella & Beauchamp, 1991b; 1993a). The interpretation of this effect is not so simple as alcohol can block the milk ejection reflex, which would lead both to reduced milk intake and to changes in sucking behaviour associated with a lower milk flow rate. Subsequent work has indeed shown that milk transfer is somewhat reduced even when a breast pump is substituted for the infant (Menella, 1998), suggesting that it is milk synthesis or milk ejection that is affected by the alcohol; and when infants were fed formula milk flavoured with alcohol their milk consumption at the meal went up rather than down (Menella, 1997). A naturally occurring change to the flavour of breast milk occurs when lactating mothers take vigorous exercise, which increases the lactic acid concentration of their milk and makes it less acceptable to their infants (Wallace, Inbar & Ernsthausen, 1992).

A question which has attracted some interest is whether early experience with flavours might shape later preferences for different foods. This is an interesting possibility, and might lead to differences in later eating behaviour between breast-fed and bottle-fed infants, since the flavours associated with breast milk are likely to be much more variable. Mennella and Beauchamp (2002) examined it in an ingenious study which capitalised on the different flavours of different types of infant formula. Compared with traditional milk-based formulas, formulas based on soy proteins are described as sweeter, more sour and bitter, and as having a 'hay/beany' odour, and hydrolysed protein formulas have an unpalatable and offensive sour and bitter taste. These formulas are used in efforts to avoid allergic reactions, and in the dietary treatment of phenylketonuria. Tested when they were 4–5 years old, children who had earlier been fed the soy formula were more likely to prefer a bitter apple juice than children earlier fed the milk formula. Children who had earlier been fed the hydrolysed protein formula were more likely to prefer a sour apple juice, and less likely to display negative facial expressions when tasting it than were children fed the usual milk formula. These results do suggest that early experience with different flavours influences flavour preferences some years later, and this effect may well be important in determining the acceptability of different foods over the weaning period.

It is also possible that similar effects might result from experience before birth (Ganchrow & Mennella, 2003). Three studies have found an interesting correlation between a mother's sickness during pregnancy and salt appetite in the offspring of the pregnancy (Crystal, 1995; Crystal & Bernstein, 1998; Leshem, 1998). The possibility of an effect of this kind was initially raised by Nicolaïdis and colleagues (Nicolaïdis, Galaverna & Metzler, 1990). They treated pregnant rats with polyethylene glycol, which leads to a reduction of extracellular fluid and to 'extracellular thirst' stimulated by reduced plasma volume rather than increased osmolality. This treatment of their mothers led to a significantly greater salt intake in the offspring rats when they were adults. A similar reduction in plasma volume can result from the loss of fluids and electrolytes as a result of vomiting, and Crystal and Bernstein (1998) showed that in

16-week-old infants salt preference, measured both by facial expressions and by fluid intake, was related to a history of sickness in pregnancy in their mothers. Even more remarkably they showed a long-term effect of the same kind. They asked college students to find out from their biological mothers whether they had been affected by pregnancy sickness while pregnant with them. They investigated the students' salt usage and the extent to which salt was important to their enjoyment of their food. More than half the mothers were sick during pregnancy, and vomiting during pregnancy was associated with increased salt use in these mothers' children (Crystal, 1995). Lesham (1998) reported a similar association, and showed that a similar long-term preference for salty tastes also resulted from diarrhoea and vomiting in the child.

2.3   The control of energy intake in infancy

Because infants cannot feed themselves, a readiness to feed must be signalled to their mother, and the mother must respond to the signal by feeding the infant. The most insistent signal available to the infant is crying. Crying indicates distress of some kind, but distress can also follow if the infant is in pain or discomfort, or is startled or tired, as well as if the infant is hungry. It has been suggested that infants have a number of discrete cry types, one of which is a 'hunger cry' (Wasz-Höckert et al., 1968), but there is little convincing evidence that there is a specific hunger cry, that is, a cry that specifically signals a readiness to feed. Infant cries are graded signals that differ in intensity with the degree of discomfort, and in speed of onset, and they mean different things to observers in different contexts (Gustafson, Woods & Green, 2000). Pain, for example, can have a sudden onset leading to a sudden cry, but there is no similar situation in which hunger has a sudden onset. Sudden pain cries and hunger cries are distinguishable, therefore, in most contexts, by their onset characteristics. But hunger, fatigue and discomfort all have slow onsets, and crying stimulated by each of these does not have differing characteristics that make its causes easily distinguishable (Gustafson, Woods & Green, 2000). Subtler signs of a readiness to feed are the 'directed head turning response' or 'rooting reflex' (Prechtl, 1958), and, of course, the taking of the nipple into the mouth and sucking itself.

Since milk is the infant's source of energy and of other nutrients, including water, we would expect the infant's internal physiology to control their milk intake, at least to some extent, in response to their nutritional needs. This would imply that infants actively control their own milk intake, rather than simply taking passively what milk they are offered. There is, indeed, good evidence that breast-fed infants do actively control their milk intake. They do not, for example, normally take all the milk that is available to them. This has been established experimentally by randomly selecting the breast that breast-fed infants first fed from, and then measuring the milk taken from the first and second breast (Drewett & Woolridge, 1981). The infants took about half as much milk from the second breast as from the first; since the order of the breasts was randomised this shows they were satiating before the supply of milk from the second breast ran out. Further evidence comes from the lactations of women nursing twins (Rattigan, Ghisalberti & Hartmann, 1981; Saint, Maggiore & Hartmann, 1986). They produce about double the milk of women nursing singletons, so the milk intake of a singleton is unlikely to be limited by limitations in the milk supply of the mother. Infants, then, are generally able to control their own milk intake – they are not simply passive recipients of what is provided by the mother. How is this control achieved?

We tend to assume that the motivational systems controlling ingestive behaviour in infants are similar to those controlling it in adults, but as mentioned at the end of Chapter 1 a little thought will show that this assumption is not necessarily justified. Adults can control food and water intake separately, and the hunger and thirst systems are responsible for the separate regulation of each. But breast-feeding does not allow the separate intake of food and water, so the separate regulation of each is not possible. Is milk intake controlled by hunger, then, or thirst, or both, or neither? One suggestion has been that milk intake is controlled by its own distinct motivational system, separate from the hunger and thirst systems, and that the hunger system of adults only takes over the control of intake when the infant starts to feed on solid food (Drewett, 1978; Hall & Williams, 1983). A second possibility is that milk intake is controlled by a hunger system, but in a somewhat different way from the way hunger controls food intake in adults. Himms-Hagen, for example, has suggested that milk intake in infants is controlled by hunger stimulated by a thermo-regulatory system (Himms-Hagen, 1995a; 1995b). Briefly, the theory proposes that a periodic drop in body temperature in infants leads to activation of the sympathetic nervous system and increased heat production from brown adipose tissue. This leads to increased glucose utilisation, and so to a decline in blood glucose levels, and this decline in turn provides a signal for increased milk intake. The increased body temperature as a result of brown adipose tissue activation then leads to the termination of feeding. Because of the high ratio of their surface area to mass, infants lose heat readily, and a theory relating energy intake to thermoregulation in infants is an attractive one. But at the moment there is very little direct evidence that a decline in body temperature normally precedes the onset of feeds in human infants.

Whatever the underlying mechanism, infants do show some motivational characteristics that suggest that they are sensitive to the energy content of their feeds. This was demonstrated by Fomon and his colleagues in meticulously conducted studies using formula feeds. They compared the energy intake of infants fed formulas in which 29% of the energy was present as fat and 62% as carbohydrate with infants fed formulas in which 57% of the energy was present as fat and 34% as carbohydrate (Fomon et al., 1976). The energy intake of the infants was the same, which suggests that they were regulating energy intake in some way. In a second series of studies they (Fomon et al., 1969) compared feeding on a formula with approximately the energy density of breast milk (2.8 kJ/ml) and a formula with twice the energy density (5.6 kJ/ml). The infants who were fed the more energy dense formula took in less, as one would anticipate if they were regulating their energy intake, though they still ended up taking in more energy. When the energy contents of the formulas were lower (2.2 and 4.2 kJ/ml), compensation was partial up to 41 days of age; thereafter it was exact, with energy intake equal in the two groups (Fomon et al., 1975). So there is evidence that infants can regulate their energy intake, at least in the limited sense of adjusting their intake when the energy content of the milk varies. There is, however, little evidence that water intake is actively regulated in infancy. Adults increase their water intake in response to osmotic stimuli (Baylis & Thompson, 1988), but infants do not, as far as we know, respond to osmotic stimuli of the kind that increase thirst in adults by increasing their milk intake (Janovský, Martínek & Stanincová, 1967; Simpson & Stephenson, 1993). Janovský et al. actually loaded infants with salt via a stomach tube. The quantity used was sufficient to reduce their urine excretion, but the infants did not increase their milk intake at all. Normally breast-fed infants obtain an ample water supply from breast milk, and do not need any supplementary water even in warm climates (Almroth, 1978; Ashraf et al., 1993; Sachdev et al., 1991). So an infant taking in enough milk to satisfy their energy requirements would automatically satisfy their water requirements.

It will be clear that our knowledge of the control mechanisms underlying milk intake in human infants is really quite limited. It is, however, important to appreciate that infants do actively regulate their intake, and through their sucking, regulate the milk production of their mothers. When we consider infants whose milk intake (or food intake) is insufficient to maintain the normal rate of growth, a key issue is the extent to which this results from regulatory problems in the infant and the extent to which it results from problems of adequate care or of the food they are provided with.

2.4   Feeding problems in milk-fed infants

Anxieties about the feeding of infants and young children can have various sources. They can derive from the child's growth, or from their behaviour. It is probably true to say that professionals are more likely to be concerned about their growth, and parents about their behaviour. Behavioural problems can cause havoc in the child's family, but without necessarily having any adverse effect on the child's own growth or their development. Sleeping and crying problems, for example, are generally problems not so much for the infants themselves as for their exhausted parents.

In the UK we have an excellent source of data on early infant feeding from the Infant Feeding Surveys that have been carried out by the Office of National Statistics every five years from 1975. The early surveys in this series were models of what research of this kind should be. They involved nationally representative samples, with extensive efforts to ensure as comprehensive a response as possible. The latest of these surveys was conducted in 2000 (Hamlyn et al., 2002). According to this source, the commonest initial problem reported by breast-feeding mothers was with the infant's initial sucking or attaching to the breast. This was reported by over half the mothers as a problem while they were in hospital, and by about a quarter after they left hospital.

A detailed study of the initial stages of lactation recruited 280 newly delivered mothers and followed the course of the lactation through the first two weeks (Dewey et al., 2003). The initiation of milk production (lactogenesis) is a response to declining progesterone levels in the mother's blood after the birth. Milk production is initially very low (mean values 50–60 ml a day), and increases about tenfold (to mean values of 500–600 ml a day) by the fifth day (Neville et al., 1988). The infant's milk intake is correspondingly low in the early days after delivery, and weight is lost over this period, though linear growth is maintained (Bishop, King & Lucas, 1990). The initiation of milk production can be detected by the mothers by a feeling of fullness in the breast, which correlates both with the volume of milk produced and with the first appearance of casein in the milk (Dewey et al., 2003). The Infant Breast-feeding Assessment Tool, which uses ratings of arousal, rooting, time taken to latch onto the breast and feed well and sucking effectiveness, was used on the day of birth and on the third and seventh day. Relatively low scores on this scale were significantly associated with delayed lactogenesis and with excess weight loss by the infant. They were much more likely in the infants of women with flat or inverted nipples. Attaching to the breast is harder if nipples are flat or inverted, so this again indicates the importance of attaching problems in early lactation.

We saw at the beginning of this chapter that the control of milk synthesis and milk ejection involves reflex pathways in the central nervous system. A consequence of this is that milk flow in humans is easily disturbed by pain and anxiety, which inhibit the milk ejection reflex (Newton & Newton, 1948). In a randomised controlled trial, Feher *et al.* (1989) showed that the expression of milk by the mothers of infants born preterm was considerably facilitated by the use of a taped relaxation/imagery exercise, which is designed to reduce anxiety. An earlier pioneer in research on breast-feeding, Mavis Gunther, provided evidence that a delayed milk ejection led to a maintained high negative pressure on the nipple and areola, and suggested that this led to petechial lesions and the 'sore nipples' that are a common problem of breast-feeding mothers (Gunther, 1945). 'Sore' is too kind a word, since they can be intensely painful and very distressing, and are one of the commonest reasons given for terminating breast-feeding in the first two weeks (Hamlyn, Brooker, Oleinikova & Wands, 2002).

Another common problem is the infant being unsatisfied or having insufficient milk, which was reported in the UK survey by 32% of mothers after leaving hospital (Hamlyn *et al.*, 2002). This is the problem of 'perceived breast milk insufficiency'. It is of major importance internationally (Hillervik-Lindquist, 1991; Hillervik-Lindquist, Hofvander & Sjölin, 1991) since it leads to the generally undesirable use of formula feeding as a supplement to or substitute for breast-feeding. Lactation in humans can occasionally fail due to a primary failure of milk production (Neifert, Seacat & Jobe, 1985). This, however, is very rare, while the problem of perceived breast milk insufficiency is very common. In the study of Hillervik-Lindquist a cohort of 51 well-educated Swedish women were followed longitudinally through the first 18 months after birth. The aim of the study was to investigate the incidence, causes and consequences of perceived breast milk insufficiency (which the author also referred to as 'transient lactational crises'). The mothers were well fed and well educated, keen to breast-feed and mostly intending to do so for at least six months. Yet even in this group of mothers perceived breast milk insufficiency was reported by just over half (55%). The study involved serial measurements of breast milk intake by the infant and measurements of their growth, and there was clear evidence that milk production was lower in the mothers with transient lactational crises, and that their infants gained weight less rapidly. This finding shows that the mothers' perception of breast milk production did have some relationship with their actual milk production, but since the weights of the infants in this group were in fact about average for infants of their age, it does not show that their intake was insufficient, and the milk production of these mothers is more appropriately referred to as relatively low rather than as insufficient.

Because milk production in breast-feeding mothers is stimulated by the sucking of the infant, one possible response to a perceived breast milk insufficiency is to increase the stimulus to milk production by increasing the frequency or duration of nursing (Dewey et al., 1991; Dewey & Lönnerdal, 1986). Dewey and Lönnerdal (1986) showed that most of a (quite small) group of mothers they studied were able to increase their milk production in response to an additional expression of breast milk with a breast pump, and concluded that it was generally a lack of demand from the infant rather than fundamental limitations on the mother's milk supply that led to lower levels of milk intake by some infants.

A further big class of feeding-related problems in infancy concerns their sleeping patterns. Infants in the period immediately after birth feed throughout the night, and this inevitably takes its toll on the sleep of their parents. There is evidence from a number of studies that breast-fed infants are more likely to wake for a feed in the night than bottle-fed infants. This was found in independent studies by Wright and colleagues (Wright, Fawcett & Crow, 1980; Wright, Macleod & Cooper, 1983), by Eaton-Evans and Dugdale (1988) and by Wailoo, Peterson and Whitaker (1990). A study by Pinilla and Birch (1993), however, has shown that the sleeping patterns of breast-fed infants are actually quite malleable. They randomly assigned 26 mothers and infants to treatment and control groups. Starting in the first few days after birth, parents in the treatment group followed a protocol in which they offered a scheduled 'focal feed' between 10 and 12 at night, and accentuated the differences in the cues they offered the infant between the day and night periods. From three weeks they gradually increased the interval between the focal feed and the next night-time feed, mainly by delaying feeding in response to the infant's night waking, and responding to the infant in other ways. The parents in the control group were not asked to follow any particular procedures for feeding their infants. Both groups of parents kept diaries of the infant's feeding and sleeping and measured their milk intake by test-weighing. This intervention led to striking differences in the over-night sleeping of the infants. By 8 weeks the average time sleeping over the period midnight to 5 a.m. was 4 hours 50 minutes in the intervention group, while it was only 3 hours 42 minutes in the controls. The inter-vention had no adverse effect on overall milk intake, which was the same in the two groups. This reflects the capacity of infants to regulate their milk intake: they took less in the night-time period, but compensated by increasing their milk intake at the early morning feed.

Another common problem is colic. Colic is a term used of a particular pattern of crying in infancy; the classic criteria formulated by Wessel and colleagues (Wessel *et al.*, 1954) involve crying for more than three hours a day for at least three days a week for at least three weeks (the 'rule of threes'). While this clearly identifies a pattern of crying that is above average, there isn't any very good reason at the moment to think that colic identified by this criterion is qualitatively different from normal crying. It certainly tends to have the same temporal organisation as normal crying, with peaks in the evening and a rising prevalence to the second or third month of life followed by a spontaneous decline (Barr, 1990). There is some evidence that colicky crying at 6 weeks of age is more prevalent in breast-fed than in bottle-fed infants (Lucas & St James-Roberts, 1998). Lucas and St James-Roberts found a prevalence of 31% in infants fed on the breast, but only 12% in those fed on bottles – an interesting finding in view of the tendency to attribute colic at about six weeks to reactions to infant formula. The evidence on this is not, however, entirely consistent (Lucassen *et al.*, 2005). Nor is it clear that the 'normal crying' of infants in Western societies is normally found in other cultures (Lee, 1994).

As its name suggests, colic is often thought of as a feeding problem. Although it is not clear at the moment to what extent it is one, recent evidence suggests that in clinically referred children, at any rate, colic is to some extent associated with other feeding problems, with more disorganised feeding and more gastrointestinal reflux in children referred with colic (Miller-Loncar *et al.*, 2004). A number of attempts have been made to provide specific gastrointestinal explanations of colicky crying. One possibility that has been explored is that colic is related to the levels of a hormone, motilin, that is involved in the movements of the gut. Lothe and colleagues (Lothe *et al.*, 1990) showed that infants who had higher levels of motilin as measured in the umbilical cord at birth and in venous plasma on the first day of life were *subsequently* more likely to develop colic. This does suggest a gastrointestinal element in the causation of colic, though the exact way in which high motilin levels are linked to later crying has not yet been determined.

A second possibility is that colic is an adverse reaction to milk, caused, for example, by an allergic reaction to cows' milk proteins or by incomplete absorption of the milk sugar lactose. Adverse reactions to cows' milk proteins can be examined by changing the composition of the milk fed to the infant, though this needs to be done in a way that does not confuse an improvement resulting from a change in the milk with the normal improvement in colicky crying as infants get older. It is also important to control properly for placebo effects. In a study of colicky infants involving multiple blind switching between cows' milk and a casein hydrolysate-based formula, Forsyth (1989) showed increased crying when the infants were switched to cows' milk, though the first switch had a much bigger effect than the second. Lothe and Lindberg (1989) have examined reactions to bovine whey protein and a placebo, given double-blind to infants maintained on a cows' milk free diet for the duration of the challenges. Significantly more of the infants responded with increased crying to the whey protein than to the placebo. This provides further evidence that some infants cry in response to cows' milk proteins. To what extent it provides a general explanation for colic is harder to determine, as the infants in this study were selected because their colic had not been improved by other treatments, and they were all formula fed, as any infant reacting adversely to cows' milk must be. It has been suggested that colic in breast-fed infants may be associated with cows' milk consumption by their mothers, but the evidence for this is inconsistent (Miller & Barr, 1991).

Lactose, the sugar in milk, is split by a lactase into its two constituent simpler sugars, glucose and galactose, before absorption from the small intestine. If this hydrolysis is incomplete the remaining lactose ferments in the gut. This fermentation can be detected because it is the only known source of hydrogen in the breath (Ostrander et al., 1983). A study of breath hydrogen in infants found that incomplete lactose absorption was common in the early months, reached a peak in the second month and declined in the third, and day by day there was some evidence that it had a peak in the afternoon, which corresponds at least approximately to the pattern shown by colicky crying (Barr et al., 1984). Infants with colic did indeed have significantly higher maximum levels of breath hydrogen (Miller et al., 1989). Additional evidence concerning lactose malabsorption comes from studies which have added a lactase to formula milk. Kearney et al. (1998) examined the effects of this in 13 infants with colic, using a cross-over design in which each infant was fed formula after it had been treated with lactase over two periods and a placebo over another two periods, the order being randomised. Treatment with the lactase reduced crying time by 44% (just over an hour a day).

A related possibility is that colic in breast-fed infants may be exacerbated by breast-feeding practices in which infants are fed to an equal extent from both breasts at each feed, rather than by alternating breasts from feed to feed (Woolridge & Fisher, 1988). The fat content of breast milk rises over the course of a feed (Hytten, 1954) and as lactose is in the aqueous component of the milk the lactose content goes down over the course of the feed. The suggestion is that feeding from both breasts leads to an excessive consumption of the lactose rich foremilk rather than the fat rich hindmilk, and so leads to colicky crying in infants who have a limited capacity to hydrolyse lactose. An attempt to examine this experimentally was reported by Evans, Evans and Simmer (1995). They allocated breast-feeding mothers and their newborn infants to two groups. One group was encouraged to nurse equally on both breasts at each feed, while the other was encouraged to nurse on one side only, alternating the sides at each feed. The reported prevalence of colic was 23% in the group nursed on both sides at each feed, and 12% in the group nursed on one side only. The women were not allocated at random, but allocated to one group over five months and the other over the next five months. Nonetheless this result does offer some support for this interesting hypothesis.

2.5 Breast-feeding, health and cognitive development

In the opening pages of this book I said that it was concerned with two types of problem – with the development of eating behaviour in children, and with the later consequences of malnutrition, or more generally of different types of nutrition. So far we have been dealing with problems of the first type. Now we turn to a problem of the second type. Because of their major importance to health in infancy, extensive research has investigated the way different types of infant feeding affect physical health; and there is now also a large body of work dealing with their effects on psychological development. This research is principally epidemiological in nature, and provides a useful introduction to the particular problems of research of this kind.

It is reasonably simple to record whether infants are breast- or bottle-fed, though knowing whether a child has ever been breast-fed is less informative than knowing for how long they have been breast-fed. It is possible to follow the children up over time and to assess their health and their psychological development, though this is harder than it sounds. Keeping track of the extent to which a child has suffered from respiratory or diarrhoeal diseases over a five-year period, for example, is no easy task. The central problem here, however, is that a simple comparison between infants who are breast- and bottle-fed is of limited value, because the way an infant is fed is related to other characteristics of their family, which may independently affect both their health and their psychological development. In principle this can be dealt with in two ways. The first, the simplest in theory, is to randomly allocate infants to different groups (say a breast- and a bottle-fed group) and then follow them up. The random

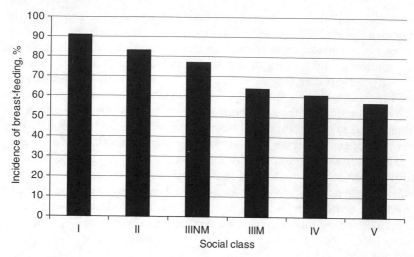

Figure 2.2 Incidence of breast-feeding by social class, United Kingdom, 2000. Data from Hamlyn *et al.*, 2002, Table 2.5. The 'incidence' of breast-feeding in this survey is the proportion of infants who were breast-fed at least once. Social class is based on the current or last occupation of the husband or partner.

allocation, provided it is properly conducted with sufficiently large groups, ensures that all other relevant characteristics (covariates) are equated across the groups. If this kind of approach is not feasible, as it is not here, the second possibility is to decide what the relevant covariates are, to measure them and to take them into account statistically. Studies using the first approach are generally referred to as experimental studies, or in a medical context as randomised controlled trials (RTCs). Studies using the second approach are generally referred to as observational or correlational studies.

The problems in respect of breast-feeding are clearly illustrated in the UK 2000 Infant Feeding Survey. The *incidence* of breast-feeding as defined in this study is the number of infants put to the breast at least once, and the *prevalence* is the number breast-fed at different times after the infant's birth. The incidence in 2000 was 71% in England and Wales, 63% in Scotland and 54% in Northern Ireland. But it also varied strikingly with the social class of the infant's family. Figure 2.2 shows the incidence of breast-feeding in the UK subdivided by the family's social class, as it has traditionally been defined by the occupation of the father, and there is clearly a strong association between the two. Given this strong association, it is unsurprising that the incidence of breast-feeding was also associated with other maternal characteristics that tend to vary with social class. It was associated with the mothers' education: in women who completed their full-time education by the age of 16 the incidence was 54%, rising to 70% in those who completed it at 17 or 18 and to 88% in those who completed it later. It was also associated with the mother's age, rising from 46% in mothers under 20 to 78% in those 30 or older. The *prevalence* of breast-feeding steadily declined after the infant's birth, and on average women from higher occupations and women who had a longer full-time education breast-fed for longer. Although differences in their socio-economic position tend to have large and pervasive effects on the development of children, there are other differences between families that also need to be taken into account. Within each social class, for example, women who smoke are less likely to breast-feed (White, Freeth & O'Brien, 1992), and they tend to breast-feed for shorter periods (Scott & Binns, 1999). Smoking in pregnancy and in the years after the birth is itself associated with poorer health and with lower subsequent intelligence in the child of the pregnancy (Mortensen et al., 2005). Clearly, then, any examination of the effects of infant feeding on health and development has to take these associated differences into account. The associated differences are not necessarily the same in different cultures. The relationship between social class and breast-feeding is similar in the UK and the USA, for example, but no relationship was found in a Mexican population and the opposite relationship was found in Peru (Rogers, Emmett & Golding, 1997). Nor are they necessarily the same in the same culture at different times. Children born in the 1920s in Hertfordshire in the UK were *more* likely to be breast-fed if their fathers were employed in manual than in non-manual occupations (Gale & Martyn, 1996).

Internationally the best documented of all the benefits of breast-feeding is protection against diarrhoeal diseases, which are among the commonest illnesses of young children. Motarjemi et al. (1993) review studies which indicate that about 1400 million episodes of diarrhoea occur annually in young children. In 1990 this led to the death of over 3 million children, which gives an indication of the scale of the health problems involved. Many different organisms are involved, including bacteria such as *Escherichia coli*, protozoa such as *Giardia lamblia* and enteric viruses (Motarjemi et al., 1993). The relationship between type of infant feeding and diarrhoeal disease was reviewed by Feachem and Koblinsky (1984), who estimated relative risks for diarrhoeal disease by comparing risks in infants receiving no breast milk and infants who were exclusively or partially breast-fed. The relative risk was 3.0 for infants 0–3 months old, 2.4 for infants 3–5 months old and 1.3 to 1.5 for infants 6–11 months old. A later review found protective effect of similar magnitude (Golding, Emmett & Rogers, 1997). Although the benefits of breast-feeding are particularly important in poorer countries, they are not restricted to them. A recent study in Scotland, for example (Howie *et al.*, 1990), showed that breast-fed infants there were significantly less likely to develop a gastrointestinal illness throughout the first year of life. This effect was independent of social class, maternal age and parental smoking. In many parts of the world diarrhoeal diseases have a high mortality, and where they do the benefits of breast-feeding extend to the actual survival of the child. Habicht, DeVanzo and Butz (1988), for example, examined infant mortality in Malaysian infants. They examined both the effects of breast-feeding and their interaction with the domestic sanitation available in the child's home. Adjusted for a range of confounding factors, the infant mortality rate was two and a half times as high for infants who were not breast-fed in households with a toilet and piped water supply. It was five times as high in families without them. A pooled analysis from six of the less developed countries (WHO Collaborative Study Team on the Role of Breast-feeding on the Prevention of Infant Mortality, 2000) has estimated the odds ratio of death (i.e. the odds of death in infants who were not breast-fed, compared with those who were) as 5.8 in the first two months, 4.1 in months 2–4, and 2.6 in months 5–6.

   All this work was observational in nature, like almost all research on the benefits of breast-feeding. Further evidence for the benefits of breast-feeding to the health of infants can be gained, however, through studies of the health outcomes of breast-feeding promotion, which can be introduced in the form of a randomised controlled trial. Health promotion can be carried out at an individual level, or in whole communities or organisations. A major recent study (Kramer *et al.*, 2001) was carried out in hospitals in Belarus in the former Soviet Union. Similar hospitals and their corresponding polyclinics were paired. One of each pair, chosen at random, became an intervention hospital and the other a control hospital. In the intervention hospitals in addition to normal clinical care a breast-feeding promotion programme based on the Baby Friendly Hospital Initiative was implemented. The designation of hospitals as 'Baby Friendly' is used if they do not accept free or low-cost substitutes for breast milk, or feeding bottles or teats, and if they implement the 'Ten Steps' (ACC/SCN, 2000). The Ten Steps were developed by the World Health Organisation (WHO) and the United Nations Children's Fund (UNICEF) and combine interventions shown in controlled trials to increase the duration and exclusivity of breast-feeding. The ten steps are:

1. Have a written breast-feeding policy that is routinely communicated to all health care staff.
2. Train all health care staff in the skills necessary to implement the breast-feeding policy.

3. Inform all pregnant women about the benefits and management of breast-feeding.
4. Help mothers initiate breast-feeding soon after birth.
5. Show mothers how to breast-feed and how to maintain lactation even if they are separated from their babies.
6. Give newborn infants no food and drink other than breast milk, unless medically indicated.
7. Practise rooming-in, allowing mothers and infants to remain together 24 hours a day.
8. Encourage breast-feeding on demand.
9. Give no artificial teats or dummies to breast-feeding infants.
10. Foster the establishment of breast-feeding support groups and refer mothers to them on discharge from the hospital or clinic.

In the control hospitals the women were just provided with normal clinical care. As part of normal clinical care, all infants in both groups were seen monthly, and information about infant feeding, growth and illnesses was collected. This was a very large study, involving a total of 17,046 mother–infant pairs. The intervention was clearly effective; the infants in the intervention group were seven times as likely to be exclusively breast-fed at 3 months and thirteen times as likely at 6 months, and they were more than twice as likely to be breast-fed at 12 months. In the intervention groups there was a significant reduction in gastrointestinal tract infections in the first year (from 13.2% to 9.1%). There were also significant reductions in atopic eczema, though not in respiratory tract infections. The infants gained significantly more weight over the first 9 months, though by 12 months there was no difference (Kramer et al., 2002). A similar outcome has been reported from another study examining the efficacy of home-based peer counselling to promote breast-feeding in Mexico City (Morrow et al., 1999). In this study families were randomly allocated in clusters to a control group or groups receiving peer counselling to promote and support breast-feeding. The counselled groups were much more likely to be exclusively breast-feeding when their infants were 3 months old, and their infants were less than half as likely to have had an episode of diarrhoeal disease. These experimental studies therefore confirm the protective effects of breast-feeding against diarrhoeal diseases.

These health benefits of breast-feeding are of major importance to child health internationally, but they are not its only benefits. A series of studies have documented relatively higher intellectual abilities in children who were breast-fed when they are compared with children who were bottle-fed (Anderson, Johnstone & Remley, 1999; Golding, Rogers & Emmett, 1997). At the time of the later of these reviews, there were

20 published reports of studies of this issue. These were all observational studies, and the conclusions that can be drawn from them therefore depend critically on appropriate control for other variables that are related both to breast-feeding and to the child's intellectual development. Intelligence in children is associated with a large number of other variables: 73 were documented in the study of 4-year-old white American children by Broman, Nichols and Kennedy (1975). The two that best explained IQ scores were the education of the mother and a socio-economic index. The distribution of IQ also has a substantial heritable component (Devlin, Daniels & Roeder, 1997), so the IQ of parents is another important variable that needs to be taken into account. This is particularly true of studies using IQ as the outcome measure in older children; the IQ of parents is less highly correlated with scores on the developmental tests in younger children (Defries, Plomin & LaBuda, 1987). Ideally the IQ of both parents should be measured, though the intelligence of children is more strongly associated with the IQ of their mother than that of their father (Scarr, Weinberg & Waldman, 1993). IQ is also related to the size of the family (Rodgers et al., 2000).

The fact of breast-feeding, and its duration, can be accurately established by questionnaires to the mother (Launer et al., 1992; Vobecky, Vobecky & Froda, 1988), and cognitive outcomes can be measured by direct testing of the child. Most published studies in this area have used Bayley Scales or other developmental tests in young children and IQ tests in older children, and have controlled for a variety of relevant covariates, including maternal IQ and education, the socio-economic status of the family and the birthweight and birth order of the child. A summary of results from 11 of the best controlled studies, taken from the meta-analysis of Anderson et al. (Anderson, Johnstone & Remley, 1999), is shown in Figure 2.3. Averaged over these studies, and adjusted for other variables, the IQ of breast-fed children was 3.16 points higher. The largest difference, however, was found in low birthweight infants (which would include infants born before term); the difference in normal birthweight infants was 2.66 IQ points. The effect was found throughout childhood, both in developmental tests in infancy and in IQ tests in older children, with no obvious difference in magnitude between studies with the earliest testing (in the first 2 years) and those with the latest (at 10–15 years). So the advantage associated with breast-feeding does not 'wash out' with time. The benefit was greater with a greater duration of breast-feeding, up to 28 weeks. A similar effect of the duration of breast-feeding was found in a later study by Angelsen et al. (2001). This study was carried out in Norway and Sweden, in a population in which virtually all mothers breast-fed their infants. The focus of the study, therefore, was on the

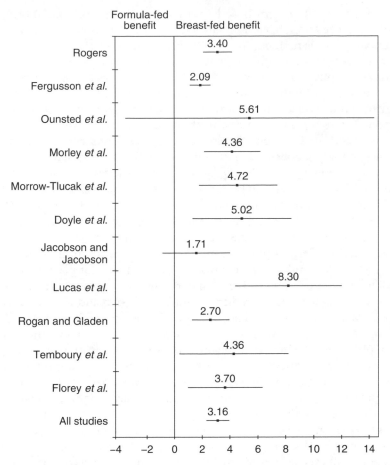

Figure 2.3 Relationship between IQ and breast-feeding in 11 studies (Anderson *et al.*, 1999). The figures show the mean IQ benefit in breast-fed children in each study, with 95% confidence intervals. If the confidence interval does not include zero the difference is statistically significant. The overall weighted mean difference and its confidence interval is shown at the bottom ('all studies'). Studies referred to are referenced in the original paper. Reproduced with permission from the *American Journal of Clinical Nutrition*. © American Journal of Clinical Nutrition, American Society for Nutrition.

relationship between the *duration* of breast-feeding and the outcome measures, which were developmental scores at 13 months and IQ scores at 5 years. Both scores were progressively higher in infants breast-fed for longer; for example mean IQ was 103.6 in children breast-fed for less than 3 months, 107.9 in those breast-fed for 3–6 months and 111.0 in those breast-fed for longer. This effect was reduced, but not eliminated, by controlling for the mother's age, smoking, education and her own IQ score. Another recent study (Oddy *et al.*, 2003) was carried out on a large Australian cohort, and as well as replicating the basic effect of breast-feeding contains interesting data on the interaction between infant feeding and maternal education. Contrary, perhaps, to what one might have expected, the benefits of breast-feeding were greater in the children of the more educated women. Within the limitations of observational studies, studies of the relationship between breast-feeding and IQ have generally been well conducted, and the IQ advantage associated with breast-feeding, though it is quite small, can be considered reasonably well established.

There are a number of possible explanations for the relationship between breast-feeding and later intellectual abilities. The first possibility is that, although each of the studies has controlled for a number of relevant covariates, all the relevant covariates have not been identified, or satisfactory simultaneous control for them all has not been achieved, and the difference in IQ is due to uncontrolled covariates (variables that are associated both with whether a child is breast-fed and with their later intellectual ability). This is a possibility of the kind that it is always hard to entirely eliminate in observational studies. We need to know more, for example, about the fathers of the infants. Although assortative mating is likely to mean that they share some characteristics with their mothers, it is still possible that controlling separately and simultaneously for maternal and paternal IQ, education and occupational class might eliminate the small differences that are still found between breast- and bottle-fed infants. A second possibility would be that the difference is a consequence of the greater incidence of gastroenteritis and other infections in the bottle-fed infants, which might have an effect on the developing brain (Golding, Rogers & Emmett, 1997). A third possibility might be that the mother–infant interactions differ in breast- and bottle-feeding in such a way as to benefit the development of breast-fed infants (Wright & Deary, 1992). A fourth possibility is that breast milk contains nutritional components that have been absent from formula milks and that benefit neurological development, such as fatty acids. This is the possibility that has been most extensively investigated.

The long-chain polyunsaturated (LCP) fatty acids arachidonic acid (AHA) and docosahexaenoic (DHA) acid are formed in adults from the 'essential' fatty acids linoleic acid and α-linolenic acid, which are taken in as components of the diet. Infants, however, lack enough of the enzyme activity necessary for this transformation, and rely more on dietary sources of AHA and DHA. Fatty acids can be utilised as a general source of energy, but they have a more specific role in the cell membranes in the brain and in some other tissues (Cockburn, 1994). The membranes of retinal photoreceptors (rods and cones) and of the synaptosomes of neurones in the grey matter of the cerebral cortex contain high concentrations of LCP fatty acids. The fatty acids are taken in via the mother in the third three months of pregnancy, and their incorporation into retinal and brain tissue of the infant is at its highest at that time (Kurlak & Stephenson, 1999). This maternal supply is no longer available to an infant delivered before term. After birth, LCP fatty acids are contained in breast milk, but are not present in substantial amounts in formula milk as traditionally manufactured, and there is direct evidence that breast-fed infants have significantly greater concentrations of DHA in cerebral cortical tissues (Farquarson et al., 1992).

Because the accumulation of DHA in the brain and retina mostly occurs in the last three months of pregnancy, preterm infants fed formula milk might be particularly vulnerable to a lack of DHA, and Carlson and her colleagues (Carlson et al., 1994) examined the effect of adding it as fish oil to the formula fed to preterm infants in two randomised controlled trials. Visual acuity was tested at birth and at 2, 4, 6.5, 9 and 12 months. Acuity was better at 2 and 4 months in one of the trials, and at 2 months in the other; but later in infancy there was no difference between the groups, a finding which has since been replicated in a third study (Carlson, Werkman & Tolley, 1996). This suggests that the benefit gained is a transient one, which may be because the fatty acids in cell membranes are constantly being turned over, so when the diets of infants fed in different ways become more similar after weaning the initial benefits to the earlier supplemented infants are lost (Kurlak & Stephenson, 1999). Although these studies were carried out on infants born preterm, results of one similar study in term infants shows similar effects, with an effect at 2 months but not later (Carlson, Werkman & Tolley, 1996). A second study with term infants showed no effect at all of supplementation in formula fed infants using either behavioural or electrophysiological procedures to determine visual acuity (Auestad et al., 1997). A third study did show such an effect, both at 16 and 30 weeks of age, using an electrophysiological procedure (Makrides et al., 1995).

A number of studies have also examined effects of LCP fatty acids on behavioural and cognitive development. These studies have produced rather mixed results. Carlson et al. (1994) examined effects of supplementation with DHA on later Bayley Scale scores in two randomised controlled trials. DHA improved scores significantly in one of the trials but not the other; both were quite small, with under 30 infants per group. In a recent large study (Lucas et al., 1999) 309 term infants were randomly assigned to a traditional formula or one supplemented with AA and DHA from egg, and the two groups of infants were tested at 18 months using the Bayley Scales. There were no significant differences in their development. Nor were there in another large study of preterm infants, also tested at 18 months (Fewtrell *et al.*, 2002). There were in a third (Clandinin *et al.*, 2005). Developmental tests in infancy such as the Bayley Scales are only partly cognitive in nature, and provide rather global measures of psychological development. A more specific cognitive skill, means-end problem solving, was tested by Willats *et al.* (1998). This involved 10-month-old infants in the planning and executing of a series of actions to achieve a goal, retrieving a toy from underneath a cover. Abilities of this kind develop rapidly in the second half of the first year, and are correlated with later intellectual abilities as measures in IQ tests (Slater, 1995). Willats *et al.* randomly assigned bottle-fed infants to a group fed conventional formula and a group supplement with AA and DHA, and showed that means-end problem solving was significantly better in the supplemented group. This was a relatively small study (44 infants). A much larger study of 239 term infants (Auestad *et al.*, 2005) again used the Bayley Scales, but also used two more specific measures, the Fagan Test of Infant Intelligence (at 6 and 9 months) and the MacArthur Communicative Development Inventory (at 9 and 14 months). No significant differences between the supplemented and unsupplemented groups were found for any of these measures.

We can conclude from this body of work that breast-feeding has clear benefits to the physical health of infants, which are found everywhere but are particularly important in countries where water supplies and sanitation are unsatisfactory. There is also consistent evidence that breast-fed infants score slightly higher on IQ and related measures. This advantage is found in spite of extensive control for other correlated variables that might account for the association. Fatty acids of the kind that are found in breast milk improve visual acuity in the early months of life, but the evidence that they promote general development or increase IQ in infants and young children is too inconsistent to be regarded as entirely convincing at the moment.

3 The development of feeding behaviour: weaning onwards

3.1 Weaning and the development of independent eating skills

Because of their early dependence on the mother's lactation, the development of feeding behaviour in mammals involves a striking discontinuity at the time of weaning. Weaning involves three separate changes, though they are linked in time. Firstly, there is a change in the kind of food taken, from milk to a range of solid foods. Secondly, there is a change in the mechanics of feeding behaviour, from the sucking characteristic of an infant feeding on milk to the biting and chewing characteristic of older children and adults feeding on solid foods. This change in the mechanics of feeding behaviour is only partly linked to changes in the kind of food taken. Adults, for example, also drink milk, but they do not drink it in the way infants do. Thirdly, there is a change from an obligatory dependence on the mother or another carer to more independent feeding. Because the diet of adults involves a wide range of foods, weaning calls for an extensive learning process, in which a child comes to distinguish foods from things that are not foods, and to choose between different foods.

As we saw in Chapter 1, the average energy expenditure of infants increases steadily over the course of the first year, from about 1 MJ per day at 1 month to about 2.5 MJ a day at 8 months, an increase of 150%. The milk production of exclusively breast-feeding women increases by only 30% over the same period (Neville et al., 1988). So weaning eventually becomes obligatory, because the milk production of the mother cannot keep pace with the growing energy needs of the child. The foods typically eaten by adults have a much higher energy content than the milk that forms the diet of infants. Boiled rice, for example, has about twice the energy density of milk, white bread and chips about three times and biscuits about seven times the energy density (Holland et al., 1991). Exact figures are not appropriate because of the variability within food types.

In breast-fed infants one might expect the timing of weaning to be partly a response to the growing mismatch between the infant's growing

43

energy needs and the mother's milk supply, but in fact the timing of weaning is very variable across cultures, and this variability across cultures cannot be accounted for by variability in milk supply. In a longitudinal study in Northern Thailand, for example, 15% of a group of 60 infants were given some solid foods (mostly rice) by 2 weeks of age, and 68% were given them by 6 weeks (Drewett *et al.*, 1993). In the UK, according to the latest infant feeding survey, only 3% were given solid foods by 6 weeks (Hamlyn *et al.*, 2002). In the Indian populations studied in the World Health Organisation (WHO) Collaborative Study of Breast-feeding (WHO, 1981), on the other hand, only 60% of the urban poor and 64% of the rural children were given solid foods by 1 year of age. In most of the cultures that have been studied, however, most infants are complemented by 6 months, and although cultural factors operating through the mother undoubtedly have a major influence on the timing of weaning, there is some evidence that within a culture it can partly be a response to changes in aspects of the infant's own behaviour which may reflect unsatisfied energy needs. Larger infants have larger energy requirements, and in the UK infants larger at birth are weaned earlier (Hamlyn *et al.*, 2002). In a more intensive longitudinal study which also showed the same relationship, three quarters of the mothers studied themselves said that solid food was introduced in response to an observed change in the behaviour of their infants (Harris, 1988). The change was generally either more frequent feeding or the return of night waking, both of which suggest an unsatisfied appetite.

Because of the benefits of breast milk, and the hazards associated with the early introduction of solids, especially in countries where it is difficult to prepare and store them in hygienic ways, attempts have been made to calculate the age at which breast milk would no longer be adequate on its own to support growth (Waterlow, 1981; Waterlow & Thomson, 1979). These calculations are difficult, and although they provide some guidance concerning the age at which complementary foods become necessary, more direct evidence is available from experimental studies, which suggest that exclusive breast-feeding up to 6 months of age provides enough energy and other nutrients for satisfactory growth (Kramer & Kakuma, 2002). This evidence comes principally from two controlled trials in Honduras. In the first (Cohen *et al.*, 1994) three groups of breast-fed infants were compared. These were a group exclusively breast-fed to 6 months of age; a group offered complementary foods from 4 months with *ad libitum* nursing; and a group offered complementary foods from 4 months with the maintenance of the baseline frequency of nursing. Allocation to groups was by week of birth, so it was not strictly random. Growth was the same in all three groups. Introducing complementary foods at 4 months, however, significantly reduced the infant's breast milk intake (though their total energy intake was not reduced because of the energy they were obtaining from the solids). The second study (Dewey *et al.*, 1999) concentrated on low birthweight, term infants, i.e., infants born 'small for gestational age' (SGA), and this study found broadly similar results. An additional study examined the timing of the introduction of solid food for formula-fed infants (Mehta *et al.*, 1998). Four groups were compared. Two groups were given commercially prepared solid foods, one group from 3 months and the other from 6 months; the other two were given the parent's choice of solid foods, again either from 3 months or from 6 months. The groups fed solids earlier consumed significantly less formula. Again, there was no overall difference in energy intake or in growth. These findings show the extent to which the infants regulate their own energy intake, so as to compensate for energy from one source by reducing energy intake from another. In general they also show that a milk diet is adequate to maintain satisfactory growth up to 6 months.

Changes in the infant's diet that take place over the weaning period call for changes in their feeding behaviour. They require new oral-motor skills, such as biting and chewing, and the development of other mealtime skills, such as hand-mouth coordination. An intensive longitudinal study of the feeding of seven Japanese infants over the weaning period is summarised in Figure 3.1 (Negayama, 1993). Initially, over the period 4–9 months, the infants were fed by the mother. Then the infants started to acquire self-feeding skills, first using their hands, from about 10 months, and later using tools (spoons, forks or chopsticks), from about 13 months. These skills are learned in collaboration with adults, often the child's mother, and over the weaning period being fed by the mother is combined with the progressive development of independent eating. At the end of the first year these are combined in the same meal, in proportions that vary from child to child and also from meal to meal in the same child. This makes the analysis of eating behaviour over this period, which can be important in a number of clinical contexts, more complex than at any other time in life, since both being fed by the mother and self-feeding need to be considered (Parkinson & Drewett, 2001).

There is some evidence that an element of hand-mouth coordination is present in infants at or soon after birth, and this may be an early precursor of the more functionally skilled actions that develop when the child is weaned. Butterworth and Hopkins (1988) examined in detail the contacts between the hand and the face in this early period. Contacts between the hand and the face in which the infant's hand landed on the mouth were preceded by an opening of the mouth significantly more often than

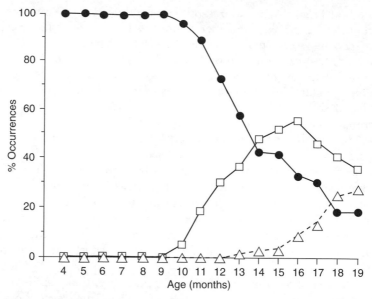

Figure 3.1 Development of eating in seven Japanese infants (Negayama, 1993). Passively fed by mother: ● Self-feeding with hand/mouth: □ Self-feeding with tools: △. Reproduced with permission from *Early Development and Parenting*, *2*, 29–37, copyright 1993, John Wiley and Sons Ltd.

contacts in which they landed on other parts of the face, implying that the infant was preparing the mouth for the hand to come to it. Lew and Butterworth (1995) subsequently showed that this preparatory opening of the mouth was hunger dependent, as the probability of the mouth opening before the arrival of the hand was higher before a feed than after a feed. The development of a related set of skills involved in the use of a spoon has been examined by Connolly and Dalgleish (1989), whose work gives a useful appreciation of the complexity of the learning involved in one of the earliest and most systematic uses of tools by a child. They describe the development of spoon-using skills over the first half of the second year of life (Figure 3.2). In the initial stages of its development the child engages in repetitive actions, pushing the spoon into the dish of food and removing it, and into the mouth and removing it. These separate actions then come to be combined, with the child first putting the spoon in the dish and removing it, and then putting it to the mouth. Then the sequence becomes functional, with the spoon actually being filled with food in the dish, and the food removed from the spoon in the mouth.

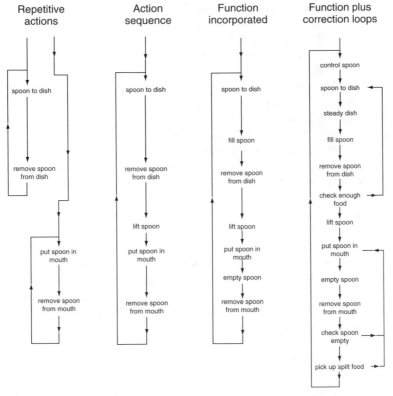

Repetitive actions	Action sequence	Function incorporated	Function plus correction loops

Figure 3.2 Development of the control of spoon use in 1-year-old children (Connolly & Dagleish, 1989). In the first stage the spoon is put in the dish, or in the mouth, as two unconnected actions. Then the two are joined into a single sequence. Function is incorporated next by filling the spoon in the dish, and emptying it in the mouth. Then error correction loops are incorporated, in which the child checks, for example, that the spoon has enough food in it when it is removed from the dish. Reproduced from *Developmental Psychology*, 25, 894–912, copyright 1989, with permission from the American Psychological Association.

Finally, error correction loops are incorporated, involving visual checks that the spoon contains food on leaving the bowl, and has been emptied in the mouth, with appropriate remedial actions if necessary. Eating in other cultures, of course, will call for the learning of other types of manual skills, peeling fruit in Thailand, for example, or picking up food with chopsticks in China (Lansdown *et al.*, 1996).

Once food is in the child's mouth, chewing, the preparation of the food bolus for swallowing and swallowing itself come into play. In most children we can take the steady development of these oral-motor skills for granted, like the development of speech, but like speech these skills are, nonetheless, highly complex (and indeed, speech therapists have an important professional role in the analysis and treatment of eating problems). Swallowing involves the synchronized activity of 31 muscle pairs (Stevenson & Allaire, 1991), and oral-motor skills are not only important in the swallowing of food but also critically important in the protection of the airway against the accidental ingestion of food or fluids into the lungs. Gisel (1991) has carefully examined the development of the chewing of foods of different textures in children 6 months to 2 years old. She used bites of food that were either solid in texture, viscous or puréed. Children were video-taped while they were offered ten trials of foods of each of these textures. A chewing cycle was defined as one down-and-up movement of the lower jaw, and chewing duration as the time in seconds from placing the food in the mouth to its final swallowing. Solids took substantially longer to chew and swallow than viscous or puréed foods, essentially because they required more chewing cycles. The time per cycle was very similar for the three types of food. As children got older and more experienced with solid foods there was no change in the time per cycle, but older children took fewer cycles to chew the foods before swallowing them. Overall feeding time was reduced as a result, most markedly for solid foods. In these 'typically developing' children there was no relationship between the chewing efficiency of the children and their growth. But in children with neurological disorders such as cerebral palsy problems in the acquisition of these independent eating skills can have major adverse effects on their food intake and growth, which will be examined in Chapter 6.

Because of the difficulties associated with the early development of eating skills, the energy density of the weaning foods offered can be important in ensuring adequate nutrition over the weaning period: if food is denser, less has to be successfully eaten. This is of practical importance in countries in which malnutrition is common, where the diets of weaning children can be very low in energy. Many of the weaning foods comprise gruels prepared from flours made from starchy staples, which on heating with water form thick and bulky pastes of low energy content as a result of the gelatinisation of the starch (Walker, 1990). Two studies have examined the effects of varying the energy density of the diet on energy intake in young children (Sanchez-Grinan, Peerson & Brown, 1991; Stephenson et al., 1994). In the first of these studies (Sanchez-Grinan, Peerson & Brown, 1991) the responses of nine young children

7–16 months old were examined. Semi-solid mixed diets with a low or high energy density were offered five times a day for seven consecutive days, with the order of the two diets alternated in different children. The amount of food eaten by the children was significantly lower when they were fed the high energy diet, but their energy intake was significantly higher and they gained significantly more weight. Similar results were found in the second study (Stephenson *et al.*, 1994). In this study a low density and a high density porridge were compared. Two versions of the high density porridge were compared; one was treated with amylase to reduce its viscosity. Each porridge was fed four times a day for four consecutive days. Again, the amount of food eaten was higher with the low energy porridge, but energy intake was higher with the high energy porridge. Thinning of the porridge with amylase had no significant effect on intake. These studies show that the energy compensating capacities of children in the weaning period are not always sufficient to compensate for very low energy diets; sometimes, presumably, the volume that would need to be eaten exceeds the child's capacity to eat it at this stage of development.

3.2   Food choice and neophobia

An infant suckled at the breast can choose how much to consume, but it is only from weaning that a child can choose to eat one food rather than another. How much children eat has important effects on their physical development, and almost certainly on their psychological development. What they choose to eat is also important, since after weaning the choice of foods determines the nature of the nutrients consumed. This makes the development of food choice a central topic in nutritional psychology. A useful framework for considering its development in infants over the weaning period relates the problems involved to the general dietary problems of omnivores (Birch & Fisher, 1995; Rozin, 1976).

Some animals are specialist feeders, relying on a single type of food. Examples among the mammals include the koala bear, which eats only eucalyptus leaves, and the giant panda, which eats only bamboo. The benefit of this strategy is that it makes food identification easy. What is a food and what is not a food is simple and clear-cut. So it avoids the risks involved in consuming new foods – especially the risk of poisoning. The cost of the strategy is that the food may cease to be available. There are currently only about 1600 giant pandas in the wild population, and they are suffering now from a shortage of bamboo forests in Western China as a result of increased farming and industrial development. The shortage of bamboo forest means that when bamboo is not available to eat, the pandas cannot easily move into adjacent areas where different bamboo species are available. Bamboo can cease to be available to eat because about every 60 years or so bamboo species flower en masse and then die back, taking 10 years to recover (Barkham, 2005). This happened on a large scale in the 1970s, causing the death from malnutrition of about 250 giant pandas, and it has happened again recently in the north-western province of Gansu in the Baishuijiang state nature reserve (and in my garden, where I evidently have a bamboo clone from the same population).

Other animals are generalist feeders (omnivores), and rats, for example, successfully pursue this strategy, utilising a wide variety of different foods. Human beings are also omnivores, so a major task of infants over the weaning period is to learn to distinguish things that are foods from things that are not foods, and in an omnivorous diet there is no simple way in which to do so. The importance of the task can be seen in the developmental course of accidents and injuries (Agran et al., 2005). In a fine grained study of over 20,000 injuries to young children sufficient to lead to hospitalisation in California in the late 1990s, Agran et al. found that poisoning was the second commonest cause of injury (after falls). The incidence of poisoning showed a striking rise in children over the period from 6 to 24 months (i.e. over the weaning period), when it increased by a factor of four. A similar pattern was shown with the ingestion of foreign bodies. Over the weaning period a child has to learn not only what to eat but also what not to eat.

Adults accept or reject 'potentially eatable substances' for a complex range of reasons (Rozin et al., 1986). One involves the sensory and affective qualities of the food, and there is an inborn element to this, seen from birth in the infant's preference for sweet tasting substances and their aversion to those that are bitter. A second involves the anticipated consequences of a food, for example that it might be poisonous. A third involves culturally transmitted ideas about the acceptability of different substances. Some substances are not considered to be foods (paper, for example). Others are considered offensive, and elicit disgust, such as faeces or cockroaches. Infants do not need to make these discriminations about different foods while fed on milk, or in the early stages of weaning while foods are selected for them by adults; but they become important as independent feeding develops.

Rozin et al. (1986) examined the development of food rejection in children over the period from 16 months to 5 years. They prepared examples from five categories distinguished by adults. The first comprised foods that were accepted by adults (for example, sugar pops). The second comprised acceptable foods in unacceptable combinations (such as a hot dog with chocolate syrup poured on it). Other categories comprised items rejected by adults as disgusting (faeces, grasshoppers), dangerous (liquid soap) or inappropriate for some other reason (dog biscuits). They examined food rejection by the children using behavioural tests in which the child was actually offered each substance (using either real or safe simulated examples) and invited to consume it. A much higher range of items was put into the mouth by the younger (16–29-month-old) children. Children 30–60 months old accepted foods that adults accepted, and continued to accept foods that adults rejected as unsuitable combinations; but they progressively came to reject those substances that adults rejected as disgusting, dangerous or inappropriate.

A plausible case can be made that disgust as an emotion initially evolved to provide protection from the risk of infectious disease (Curtis & Biran, 2001). Curtis, Aunger and Rabie (2004) examined responses to paired visual stimuli constructed so that although the items were generally similar, one of the pair implied a greater disease risk than the other. Examples are a louse and a wasp, or an underground railway carriage with people in it or without. They found that the stimuli implying a greater disease risk were systematically rated as the more disgusting in all parts of the world. An important risk for infection comes from eating contaminated foods, and adults reject food that is contaminated. In an initial study of the development of contamination sensitivity in 3–12-year-old children (Fallon, Rozin & Pliner, 1984) a series of scenarios was presented in which a glass of a drink that a child liked was first contaminated with a grasshopper or the faeces of a dog. A number of manipulations followed, with the contaminating substance being removed, the glass emptied of the drink and refilled, or the glass emptied, washed and refilled. All the children disliked the drink that contained the foreign bodies. But children under 7 years old liked the drinks again after the foreign bodies had been removed. These children did not, therefore, show a contamination response of the kind shown by older children or adults, who wanted the glass washed; half the adults were not even happy to drink from the glass however much it was washed. This study was based on stories, but a subsequent study used more direct behavioural tests (Rozin, Fallon & Augustoni-Ziskind, 1985). Three types of actual (closely simulated) contamination were employed in relation to a drink of apple juice or the eating of a cookie. In the case of the apple juice, the contamination involved stirring the apple juice with a comb, apparently one that the child had just seen used to comb the experimenter's hair, or contamination with a grasshopper (which was in fact sterile). In the case of the cookie, contamination was with 'ground up grasshopper'. The child was asked 'Will you drink some juice?' Children in the youngest age group (3–6) clearly showed the least contamination sensitivity, with 77% willing to drink apple juice stirred with the comb. Older children showed much greater contamination sensitivity, with less than 9% prepared to drink the juice. A difficulty raised by the authors themselves and considered in more detail by Siegal (1997) concerns the extent to which the different responses of the younger and older children might reflect differences in their responsiveness to the demand characteristics of the experimental situations used, rather than differences in their understanding of contamination. Is it simply that younger children are more willing to go along with what adults suggest (such as to drink contaminated juice)? Siegal varied the test, again using real objects to illustrate contamination (a glass of milk containing a cockroach, a comb or a spoon) but asking whether another child would get sick if they drank the milk (Siegal, 1988), and found evidence for contamination sensitivity even in 4–5-year-old children.

Because omnivores eat a very varied diet, identifying a food that is actually toxic is a key problem for them, and one which has led to the evolution of specialised feeding habits and associated specialised learning abilities. These were first documented in rats (Rozin, 1976). Wild rats do not initially eat newly provided foods in any quantity, which makes it difficult to control them with poisons (they are 'bait shy'). They sample only small amounts of a newly offered food, and increase their intake of it only if it does not lead to adverse gastrointestinal consequences. They can selectively associate the tastes of newly eaten foods with illness symptoms even if the symptoms follow after many hours, and only in the absence of such symptoms do they gradually come to accept new foods after some experience with them. Given the generally important role of this 'neophobic' behaviour in omnivores, it is perhaps not surprising that young children are also neophobic, and tend not to accept new foods at all readily. Birch *et al.* (1987) showed that faced with their first exposure to novel foods 69% of 2 year olds refused to taste them. The neophobia weakened with age, with 29% of 3 year olds refusing novel foods but none (0%) of the 5 year olds.

Is this neophobia in relation to food in children really a phobia, or is the term being used in a figurative sense? In a relatively early study on children (Pelchat & Pliner, 1986) measures of food neophobia were not related to shyness or fearfulness. These were measured in a rather *ad hoc* way, however – the fearfulness scale comprised only two questions, for example, one of them about nightmares. A later study (Pliner & Loewen, 1997) examined the relationship of food neophobia to temperament dimensions in 5–11-year-old children. One of the dimensions was shyness, which is related to behavioural inhibition in infancy, and to anxiety disorders developing later (Kagan, Reznick & Snidman, 1988). Pliner and Loewen found that there was a correlation between neophobia and shyness, which was statistically significant though quite small. Galloway, Lee and Birch (2003) found that neophobia was significantly related to anxiety in 7-year-old girls, and there is evidence in adults that neophobia is related to state and trait anxiety (Pliner & Hobden, 1992; Pliner, Pelchat & Grabski, 1993) and that it is increased by induced fear (Pliner, Eng & Krishnan, 1995). All these findings suggest that there is a literally phobic response at work. On the other hand, most anxiety-related disorders are more prevalent in females (Kessler et al., 1994). Gender differences in food neophobia are absent in some studies (Cooke, Wardle & Gibson, 2003; Pliner & Hobden, 1992), but where they have been found neophobia is commoner in males (Hursti & Sjödén, 1997). Most phobias are reduced or eliminated by exposure to the feared stimulus (Linden, 1981). Food neophobia is not reduced *simply* by exposure to a new food: the food must actually be tasted, as noted above (Birch et al., 1998).

Whatever its exact relationship with other types of anxiety, a certain amount of evidence suggests that neophobia as assessed in research is related to naturally occurring patterns of food intake. Hursti and Sjödén (1997) found that more neophobic children were less likely to have sampled a range of different foods, and Cooke et al. (2003) found that they consumed vegetables (and, to some extent, fruit, meat and eggs) less frequently. Similar findings are reported by Falciglia et al. (2000), though the only nutrient that the neophobic children in this study did not consume in adequate amounts was vitamin E. The corresponding benefits of neophobia have not been studied; we do not know, for example, whether children who are more neophobic are less likely to be poisoned.

The familiarity of a food can be changed, and children come to accept a wide range of foods as a result of continual exposure to them. This has been experimentally demonstrated, for example, for cheeses (Danish Esrom, Philadelphia cream cheese, Norwegian gjetost, Nauvoo blue and Wisconsin cheddar), for fruits (lychees, dried apricots, kadota figs, Queen Anne cherries and dried bananas) and for vegetables (Birch & Marlin, 1982; Sullivan & Birch, 1994; Wardle et al., 2003). Adults also come to prefer novel food tastes more with exposure to them (Pliner, 1982). Actual consumption of the food is necessary: simply looking at or smelling the food does not make it more acceptable (Birch et al., 1987). In early childhood quite prolonged exposure is necessary, and preferences continue to change over 10–20 samplings of a novel food (Birch & Marlin, 1982), but there is some evidence that over the early weaning period, when infants are first learning to accept solids, exposure learning is much more rapid, and preferences are increased by a single exposure to a novel food (Birch *et al.*, 1998). This provides the possibility of promoting desirable food preferences by exposing children to appropriate food over the weaning period; but also, of course, of promoting undesirable food preferences.

3.3   Food preferences

By the time they are 3 or 4 years old children can be asked directly about their food preferences, and there is evidence that they do indeed choose more of foods that they say they prefer (Birch, 1979b). In children of this age there are two characteristics of preferred foods – they tend to be more familiar and they tend to be sweeter. This has been demonstrated, for example, for sandwiches (Birch, 1979b) and for fruits (Birch, 1979a). The preference for familiar foods is the converse of the neophobia discussed in Section 3.2. The preference for sweet foods has almost certainly evolved because of the high energy content of foods that contain sugars. There isn't much evidence that person to person variations in food preferences are genetically based (Rozin & Millman, 1987). They are a product of experience, as the great variability in preferred foods in different culture attests. Food preferences are important because they are likely to be related to the child's energy intake, since a preference for sweet and, particularly, fatty food is likely to lead to the consumption of food with a relatively high energy density. The consumption of other specific foods or food types can also have other specific benefits, or, in some cases, disadvantages.

Salt intake, for example, is a risk factor for hypertension. There is some evidence that even in infancy higher salt intakes are associated with a higher blood pressure later in life. This evidence comes from a Dutch study in which infants were randomly assigned to a normal or a low sodium diet for the first six months of life (Geleijnse *et al.*, 1996). The infants assigned to the low sodium diet had lower blood pressures at the time, and also when they were later followed up as adolescents. We saw earlier that after about two and a half years of age children come to reject saltier water. They do not, however, reject saltier foods; when soup or cereal is salted, children of this age prefer it (Beauchamp & Moran, 1984). This preference may be partly a consequence of experience with salty foods. Harris and Booth showed in an observational study that preference for salted cereal in 6-month-old infants was higher the higher their salt intake was over the previous week (Harris & Booth, 1987; Harris, Thomas & Booth, 1990). However, in another, controlled, study in which salt was added to a vegetable over a 10 day period no clear preference for the salted vegetable emerged (Sullivan & Birch, 1994). Older (4–5-year-old) children did come to prefer the salted version of a food if they were exposed to it, but the preference was restricted to the food that the salt was added to: there was no evidence the children came to prefer saltier versions of other foods (Sullivan & Birch, 1990). Even if the preference is not generalised it is obviously undesirable that children should be given foods that have an unnecessarily high salt content, as many processed foods still do.

Preferences can be altered in other ways than by simple exposure. Feeding in infants and young children is inherently social, and the eating of a novel food is facilitated if an adult eats the same food at the same time (Addessi et al., 2005). In older children with developed language abilities their capacity to generalise from particular examples to wider classes of foods using verbal labels clearly makes the development of food preferences a more conceptually based process. Horne and colleagues (Horne et al., 1995; Horne et al., 1998) have designed a programme to change food preferences in children that specifically seeks to employ generalisations of this kind. Preferences for foods can also be altered by their nutritional consequences, either to make the food more acceptable or to make it less acceptable, by processes of associative conditioning. This has been demonstrated by pairing a novel flavour in an arbitrary way with foods that have different post-ingestional consequences; for example, the energy yield of foods can be varied by altering their carbohydrate or fat content. When this is done flavours paired with a higher energy food come to be preferred over those paired with a low energy food (Birch et al., 1990; Johnson, McPhee & Birch, 1991). There is some evidence that an association of this kind underlies some everyday food preferences in children. Gibson & Wardle (2003) have shown that there is a strong correlation between the energy density of fruits and vegetables and the preferences of 4–5-year-old children for them, as reported by their mothers. Since the energy density of fruits is determined by their sugar content this might simply be an effect of their sweetness. In vegetables, however, starch or protein also contributes to total energy content and the association is independent of the sugar content of the foods.

The opposite of a food preference is a food aversion. Bitter tasting foods are often rejected, and food aversions can also be learnt. In other species of mammals, when a particular taste is associated with gastrointestinal illness as a result of poisoning a specific taste aversion develops to the flavour in question. This kind of learning has also been demonstrated in children receiving drugs that led to adverse gastrointestinal consequences as chemotherapy for cancers (Bernstein, 1978). If the children were offered a novel flavoured ice-cream before the chemotherapy their liking for the ice-cream was strongly reduced, when they were compared with children given the ice-cream without the chemotherapy, or the chemotherapy without the ice-cream. As a practical problem in the care of children needing chemotherapy this effect can be ameliorated by the use of 'scapegoat' foods (Andreson, Birch & Johnson, 1990; Broberg & Bernstein, 1987). Novel foods (for example, coconut or halva) given before chemotherapy come to be aversive, but can to some extent protect foods that are a familiar part of the diet from themselves becoming aversive.

An important food aversion is seen in children who avoid drinking cows' milk. Cows' milk provides a wide range of nutrients, but one that is particularly important is calcium. Calcium is essential for the formation of bone, which is necessary for linear growth, and also for peak bone mass, which is important for preventing osteoporosis in the later years of life. Black et al. (2002) compared 50 New Zealand children 3–10 years old with a history of cows' milk avoidance and 200 control children from the same town. Mean dietary calcium intakes in the cows' milk avoiders was 400–500 mg/day, while in the controls it was between 11,000 and 13,000 mg/day. The avoiders were significantly shorter, and their total body bone area and bone mineral content was significantly lower. The reasons for the milk avoidance fell into three classes. One group (40%) were milk intolerant, as a result of an inability to break down lactose (the sugar contained in milk) or as a result of an allergy to cows' milk. A second group (42%) said they thought milk had a 'bad taste', though most of them did not report any adverse symptoms from drinking it. A third group (18%) were described as avoiding cows' milk as a lifestyle choice – their families chose soy or goats' milk instead. A high proportion of these milk avoiders had already had broken bones. Ten, for example, had had fractures of the distal forearm, an annual incidence three or four times greater than expected. The higher incidence of fractures was confirmed at a follow-up two years later (Goulding et al., 2004). In this example there was a clear continuity in the child's food avoidance over time – most of the children were breast-fed, started avoiding cows' milk in the second year of life and continued to avoid it subsequently.

A related but much more widespread problem is that calcium intake tends to be too low in adolescents, partly because milk tends to be displaced from the diet by fizzy drinks (Wyshak, 2000; Wyshak & Frish, 2000). High consumption of such drinks is associated with a substantially increased risk of bone fractures in teenage girls, which is partly due to reduced milk intake and probably partly also to an increased intake of phosphorus from the fizzy drinks. In younger (5-year-old) girls the relative intakes of milk and soft drinks have been shown to be associated with similar relative intakes in the girls' mothers (Fisher et al., 2000). It does not seem to be particularly difficult to increase milk intake in adolescent girls if they do not have a specific milk avoidance. Cadogan et al. (1997) randomised 82 12-year-old girls to two groups. A pint of whole or reduced fat milk was delivered daily to the home of all the girls. One group was asked to consume as much of it as possible; the other to continue with their usual diets: 80 of the 82 girls completed the trial. Bone mineral acquisition over 18 months was significantly greater in the group who were asked to consume extra milk. To maximize bone density in children both high levels of calcium intake and periodic vigorous activity are needed, since the two have a synergistic effect (Rowlands et al., 2004).

In other cases, such as fruit and vegetable intake, it is less clear to what extent we are dealing with characteristics of the child's behaviour that are stable over time or can easily be modified. Fruit and vegetables have an important role in a healthy diet for a number of reasons. They provide a range of important vitamins and minerals. They tend to be low in fat and relatively low in energy, so they help protect against obesity. And epidemiological evidence shows that high fruit and vegetable consumption is associated with a lower risk of cancer and of heart disease (Key et al., 1996). There is evidence now that adult heart disease has roots in childhood, and is associated with the same kind of cardiovascular risk factors in childhood (Berenson et al., 1989). In the Framlingham Children's Study higher levels of fruit and vegetable consumption were associated with a lower rise in blood pressure over an eight-year period (Moore et al., 2005).

There is some evidence that childhood habits also influence the eating of fruit and vegetables later on when the children are adults. In a national survey of fruit and vegetable consumption in the USA (Krebs-Smith et al., 1995), the belief of nutritional epidemiologists that health is benefited by five or more portions of fruit or vegetables a day was shared by remarkably few members of the adult population – only 8%. The proportion was higher in women (11%) than in men (4%). After taking demographic variables into account, a habit of eating fruit and vegetables since childhood, as reported by the respondents, was a significant predictor of adult fruit and vegetable consumption. Rather disconcertingly, the proportion of respondents reporting such a childhood habit fell steadily with their age, from about 50% in those who were 65 or older to 25% in those 18–34 years old at the time of the survey, suggesting that in this respect the nutrition of children has been getting steadily worse. The habit was also less common in wealthier and better educated members of the population. Dietary intake of fruit and vegetables partly reflects nutritional knowledge, and the relationship between fruit and vegetable consumption and social class in the UK is partly attributable to differences in nutritional knowledge (Wardle, Parmenter & Waller, 2000). Children begin to acquire this knowledge very early; Anliker *et al.*, for example, found significant levels of nutritional knowledge in children at 3 years of age (Anliker *et al.*, 1990).

A number of other studies have examined continuities in the dietary habits in children as they grow up (Resnicow *et al.*, 1998; Singer *et al.*, 1995). In the first of these studies (Singer *et al.*, 1995) the tracking of nutrients was examined from 3–4 to 7–8 years of age. Ten different nutrients were examined, including energy from different sources (protein, carbohydrate and fat, and from saturated and unsaturated fats), calcium and sodium. Over this five-year period, the rank order correlations ranged from .35 to .62. The median correlation was less than .5. These are not particularly high correlations; of the children in the top 20% for calcium intake at 3–4, for example, only 40% were in the top 20% at 7–8. The second study (Resnicow *et al.*, 1998) investigated fruit and vegetable intake, and the tracking examined was for foods (servings of fruit and vegetables) rather than for nutrients. The children were followed over the two years from 8 to 10. Again, the correlations were not particularly high, ranging from .35 (vegetables in boys) to .50 (fruits in boys). These studies involved following children over a relatively short period: the correlations for longer periods, particularly through the teenage years into adult life, are likely to be substantially smaller. An optimist might take encouragement from this, since it shows that nutritional habits can change. A pessimist might think that the scope for useful nutritional interventions in the school years is going to be limited, since even if the interventions are effective at the time the children's dietary habits are not likely to be very stable over the years.

Because of the evidence for its benefits to health, the National Cancer Institute in the USA has sought to promote the eating of five portions of fruit or vegetables a day (Foerster *et al.*, 1995). Similar recommendations have been made in the UK by the Department of Health and more generally by the World Health Organisation. However, daily intakes of fruit and, particularly, vegetables are much lower than this both in the USA and the UK (Basch, Zybert & Shea, 1994; Gibson, Wardle & Watts, 1998; Krebs-Smith *et al.*, 1996). The study of Krebs-Smith *et al.* was based on a nationwide sample of US households and provided the first nationwide estimates of fruit and vegetable consumption of children in the USA. Only 16.4% of males and 17.5% of females 6–11 years old ate five or more portions (of fruit and/or vegetables) a day. The proportion meeting this target was substantially lower in poorer families. Gibson *et al.* (1998) found in a sample of 10-year-old children in London that their average intake was one portion of fruit and one of vegetables a day, together with some fruit juice. Fruit intake, but not the intake of fruit juice or of vegetables, was related to economic deprivation in the family, with fruit intake about 30% lower in the more deprived families. Both fruit and fruit juice consumption were higher if the child's mother was better educated, though vegetable consumption was not. A similar finding has been reported in 9–15-year-old Finnish children (Laitinen *et al.*, 1995).

Clearly to change dietary habits to the extent that is needed to optimise later health requires population-based interventions, and as all children go to school attempts have been made to increase fruit and vegetable consumption through school-based interventions. An example is the '5-a-day power plus program' in Minnesota (Perry *et al.*, 1998). In this study 20 elementary schools in the St Paul district were matched in pairs. The matching took into account school size, ethnic composition and the proportion of children receiving subsidised meals. Ten schools were allocated at random to receive the intervention. The other ten acted as control schools (though they subsequently received the intervention at a later stage). The intervention took place in the fourth and fifth grades, when the children would have been 9–10 years old. It involved four components: behavioural curricula, parental involvement and education, changes to the school food service and the involvement and support of the local food industry. The behavioural curricula included skill building and problem solving activities, and snack preparation and taste testing. Parental involvement included information and activity packs brought home by the child, and 'snack packs' prepared by the school food service containing food and vegetable food items for the child to take home and prepare snacks for their family. The school food service intervention sought to encourage the selection and consumption of fruits and vegetables at school lunch, by increasing the variety and choice of fruits and vegetables available, by enhancing their attractiveness and by direct promotion at the point of sale. The industry component involved support from industry for the activities involved in the intervention. This was, then, an impressively comprehensive intervention. The outcome measures included both direct observation of food choices during school lunch and data from 24-hour food recall (by the child) and telephone interviews (with their parents). Significant increases were found in fruit consumption in all children. Some increases were also found in vegetable consumption, but these were limited to girls at lunchtime. The authors suggest that the greater readiness of girls to increase their vegetable consumption might be related to their being generally more diet conscious, as they have also been shown to be more receptive to other dietary health education programmes (Perry, Kelder & Klepp, 1994). These changes were all measured soon after the end of the intervention. While the results are encouraging, this does not necessarily mean that the children's diet will be altered in the long term. Impressive short-term effects have been found in a similar school-based programme dealing with the prevention of smoking, for example (Best *et al.*, 1984; Flay *et al.*, 1985), but a longer-term follow-up showed a discouraging lack of long-term benefits (Flay *et al.*, 1989).

3.4   Feeding problems from weaning

As feeding behaviour changes over the weaning period into the eating behaviour characteristic of older children and adults, so a range of new problems can arise. Learning to eat solid foods can lead to a series of problems with the handling of foods of different textures, and the range of possible foods available to older children can lead to problems associated with food choice. A valuable study of early feeding and eating problems was carried out by a group of clinical psychologists at the University of Uppsala (Lindberg, Bohlin & Hagekull, 1991). It was population based (the study samples comprised the parents of all the infants born in Uppsala over specified periods) and two independent samples of parents and children were studied about a year apart. A population-based study provides a better basis for generalisations than a clinic-based study, and a replicated sample is valuable because an association found in two independent samples is much less likely to be due to chance than one found only in a single sample. The infants in the study were 30–71 weeks old in the first sample and 30–60 weeks old in the second, and both earlier feeding problems and problems still current at the time were investigated. As we might expect from the problems dealt with in Chapter 2 the most commonly reported earlier feeding problem was colic, affecting 7.9% and 11.3% in the first and second sample respectively. Vomiting was reported in 3.4% and 6.2%. Refusal of solids was reported for 4.7% of the children in the first and 3.9% in the second sample. In the weaning period, after the first six months, refusal of solids and a related cluster of behaviour including poor appetite, refusal to eat and difficulty swallowing were the more common problems. As reported by the parents of both samples, the siblings of index children with feeding problems also had significantly more feeding problems than the siblings of controls, and both parents of the 'refusal to eat' children also had significantly more feeding problems themselves.

Feeding problems are problems for parents, but as with sleeping problems this does not necessarily mean that they are problems for the children. To examine this we have to consider what adverse effects, if any, are associated with the behaviour that the parents see as a problem. One outcome that is always important in children is their growth. Dahl and Kristiansson (1987) examined growth up to 2 years of age in 42 children with feeding problems. The criteria for a feeding problem in this study were rather strict, and involved both the parents and a Child Health Care Organisation nurse concurring that the child had a feeding problem. The problem had to exist continuously for at least one month, and to be resistant to primary care help given at the Child Health Care Organisation. These, then, were likely to be feeding problems of the more severe and persistent kind. The main problems identified in this sample were colic (9 infants), vomiting (8 infants), and a refusal to eat (28 infants). Colic did not affect growth, measured either as gain in weight or in length. Vomiting did affect it at the time, but growth had recovered by the time the children were 2 years old. Refusal to eat, however, was associated with poor growth as reflected in both weight and length, and the effect persisted to 2 years of age. These children were followed up in subsequent studies at 4 and 9 years of age (Dahl, Rydell & Sundelin, 1994; Dahl & Sundelin, 1992). At 4 years old they were still significantly lighter and shorter than controls and were still three times as likely to have feeding problems. They were also more likely to be described by the parents as 'hyperactive'. By 9 years of age, however, they were no different from the controls in height or weight, general behaviour or health. They still presented more eating problems at home though, and at school as reported by their class teachers. There is some evidence that this refusal to eat is transgenerational. Again the mothers were more likely to have had early feeding problems themselves, a finding reported by the mothers themselves but also scrupulously checked by interviews with the mothers' parents and examination of their own growth records (Dahl, Eklund & Sundelin, 1986).

Another source of difficulty for parents is the inconsistency in children's food intake from meal to meal. This has been formally documented in a study in which energy intake was measured accurately in 15 children 2–5 years old over a six-day period (Birch et al., 1991). The children were offered ample amounts of food in standardised meals, and the quantities taken were weighed and the child's energy intake calculated. Viewed meal by meal, the food intake of the children was very variable. An individual child could take, for example, a breakfast of 420 kJ on one day and of 1470 kJ on another. Variability of this kind can be summarised as a coefficient of variation (CV), the standard deviation expressed as a proportion of the mean. The average CV for different meals was 31% for breakfast, 30% for the morning snack, 44% for the afternoon snack,

39% for dinner and 35% for the evening snack. This variability in a child's intake can make it difficult for parents to plan for meals, but over more extended periods energy intake tends to be more stable. Over the whole day the CV was only 10.4%. The same characteristics of food intake are found if the normal intake of children in their natural environment is analysed (Shea *et al.*, 1992).

If meal times are fixed then children can only compensate for the variability of energy intake at one meal by varying their energy intake at subsequent meals, and this compensation for earlier meals may partly underlie the variability in energy intake at meals in young children. That they do compensate has been shown formally in studies in which the effect of an energy load on a child's subsequent food intake is examined. Birch and Deysher (1986) first investigated this. The children were 2–5 years old, and in the study their food intake at a lunchtime meal was compared after high and low energy preloads. The preload was a pudding-like snack; the high energy snack contained four times as much energy as the low energy snack. Adults were studied at the same time. The results are shown in Figure 3.3. On average this compensation was very accurate in the young children; indeed, it was much more accurate than in the adults. In what may be a related finding, Rolls, Engel and Birch (2000) found that 3-year-old children ate the same amount of macaroni cheese regardless of the size of the portion they were offered. Older (5-year-old) children, on the other hand, ate more when they were offered a larger portion. In their ordinary lives Mrdjenovic and Levitsky (2005) showed that in 5–6-year-old children the amount served to the child was by far the strongest predictor of energy intake at a meal.

In studying energy intake we are usually concerned with the quantities of foods eaten. They may be too low, leading to poor growth and other sequelae of malnutrition, or too high, leading to the storage of fat and potentially to the development of obesity. There is some evidence that the capacity to regulate energy intake precisely varies from child to child, and that it is related to these body weight problems. This evidence will be considered in Chapters 7 and 8. Other problems concern the intake of specific nutrients, such as vitamins and minerals, and problems of this kind are often viewed more generally as problems of the variety rather than the amount of food taken. The working assumption of most parents (and professionals) is that if a sufficiently varied diet is consumed it will include adequate quantities of all the essential nutrients. Problem children are those who eat only a restricted range of foods. These children are described as 'choosy', 'faddy', 'finicky' or 'picky' eaters.

Terminology dealing with the eating behaviour of children is not used very consistently. *Appetite* is a desire for food, or hunger. To talk of a child

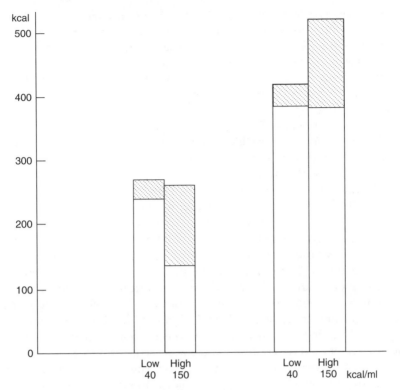

Figure 3.3 Energy compensation in young children. Adapted by permission from Birch and Deysher, 1986, using the original scale in kcal (40 kcal = 167 kJ; 150 kcal = 628 kJ). 'Low' and 'high' show the average intakes with a low- and a high-energy preload in children (left) and adults (right). The children have compensated for the preload, with no overall increase in energy intake (unlike the adults). Reproduced from *Appetite*, 7, 323–31, copyright 1986, with permission from Elsevier.

with a *good* or *poor* appetite refers to their overall willingness to eat. *Anorexia* is a lack of appetite (though the diagnostic term *anorexia nervosa* confusingly refers to a condition characterised by a fear of fatness, and not by a lack of appetite). *Choosy, faddy, finicky* or *picky* eaters are characterised by selective eating of foods, limiting the variety that is eaten rather than the quantity, although it is sometimes not clear, either in lay or professional usage, to what extent these concepts of selective eating are differentiated from concepts relating to the child's overall willingness to eat, nor is it clear to what extent a poor appetite might lead to finickiness.

Rydell, Dahl and Sundelin (1995), for example, studied primary school children (6–11 years old) described as *choosy* eaters, but the criteria used to identify them (eats small portions, refuses food, 'disinterested' in food) do not clearly relate to the variety rather than the amount of food eaten. *Neophobia* more specifically involves an unwillingness to eat novel foods, though again some authors treat neophobia and finickiness as equivalent (Carruth & Skinner, 2000).

How do children described by their parents as 'finicky', 'picky', 'faddy' or 'choosy' eaters actually differ from other children? As we have seen, there is no simple natural division between foods and non-foods, and all children must be choosy eaters – they must choose to eat what is nutritionally valuable, non-toxic and microbiologically safe. The term is a relative one. Choosy eaters are slightly more choosy than their parents would like them to be. Carruth *et al.* (1998) studied picky eaters as toddlers, using criteria that did identify children who ate a lower diversity of foods, but whose overall energy intake was almost identical to that of another group of children who were used as controls. Intakes were reported for a range of different nutrients. Compared with Recommended Dietary Allowances (RDAs) the picky eaters consumed less than recommended levels of calcium, zinc, vitamin D and vitamin E; but this was also true of the control children, and there was no significant difference in this between the picky eaters and the controls. There was also no evidence that height or weight were adversely affected in the picky eaters. From the mothers' descriptors, neophobia was clearly a major component, at least, of picky eating, the mothers saying, for example, that '(he) is unwilling to try new things, anything new at all' and 'wants to eat the same thing – won't try anything new' (p. 183). These children were followed up until they were 7 years old. The behaviour persisted, but no differences from the control children in either dietary intakes or growth emerged. There was no clear evidence in this study, then, that picky eating defined in this way was actually associated with poorer nutrition for the child. Galloway, Lee and Birch (2003), however, did find a relationship with vegetable consumption in 7-year-old girls. Picky eaters ate fewer servings of vegetables, as recorded in 24 hour recall over three days, though the level of vegetable consumption was undesirably low in all the girls, whether they were picky eaters or not. A much larger study of a more representative population of children from 4 to 24 months followed (Carruth *et al.*, 2004). The proportion of children deemed by their carers to be picky eaters increased systematically with age, from 19% at 4–6 months of age to 50% at 19 to 24 months. Although in this large sample intakes of some nutrients were significantly lower in the picky eater group, especially over the second half of the first year, mean intakes were well above the Recommended Dietary

Allowances in both groups. There was an association with weight: picky eaters were more likely to be below the 25th centile of weight for age. But in a culture in which the principal nutritional problem is overweight and obesity, this should not be necessarily be seen as an adverse effect.

In a study that involved direct behavioural observation as well as parental reports Jacobi et al. (2003) examined picky eating during the feeding of standardised meals to 3–5-year-old children. The children were observed in a laboratory, eating lunch from a standard buffet, and food was also provided from two standardised coolers for the assessment of food intake at home over 24 hour periods. The picky eaters were identified by means of the parent's response on a five point Likert scale to the question 'Is your child a picky eater?' Of the 135 children, 29 (21%) were identified as picky eaters. Boys and girls were equally likely to be picky eaters, and there was a quite strong consistency between the children identified as picky eaters at 4 years and at 5 years (the correlation was .68). The parents reported that the picky eaters ate a limited variety of foods, requested that food be prepared in specific ways, and were less likely to accept new foods readily. They were more likely both to have strong likes and strong dislikes, and were less likely to be reported as fast eaters. Data from food intake at home showed that the 'picky eaters' identified in this way did eat a lesser variety of foods, though the difference was small (on average one food less than the controls, who ate 12 or 13 different foods). They were significantly more likely to avoid eating vegetables (especially the boys). The energy intake of the picky eaters was not substantially lower, but there was an interesting gender specific effect: the picky girls actually reduced their energy intake from 3 to 5 years of age, while the non-picky girls and all the groups of boys increased it. There were no differences between the two groups in the measured meal durations or in the rate of eating (bites per minute). The children were involved in a longitudinal study from birth, so interesting comparisons concerning their early feeding history and their parents' eating styles were possible. The picky eaters made on average over 100 fewer sucks in feeds observed during the first month of life, and took in significantly less milk. Indeed 17% of the picky children had refused to suck at all, twice as many as in the non-picky group (8%). There were, therefore, clear precursors of picky eating in the early feeding behaviour of the children, of a kind that might suggest a lower appetite generally. The eating style of their parents was assessed at the child's birth using measures of dietary restraint and disinhibition from the Three-factor Eating Questionnaire (Stunkard & Messick, 1985), their body dissatisfaction using a subscale for the Eating Disorder Inventory (Garner, Olmsted & Polivy, 1983) and their body mass. There were no significant differences in any of these.

Although picky eating can be worrying to parents, and it is quite common in young children, internationally the single most important problem associated with weaning is its association with diarrhoeal disease. Infants of any age can suffer from diarrhoea, but exclusively breast-fed infants are largely protected against it, so its prevalence in predominantly breast-fed populations is generally highest in the second half of the first year (Waterlow, 1981). One major source of diarrhoea is weaning food itself. For example, in rural areas of the Gambia infant foods are prepared in sufficient quantities to last all day (Rowland, Barrell & Whitehead, 1978). The extent to which the foods are contaminated varies with storage time and the time of year, being higher in the wet than the dry season. In the dry season 6.8% of foods sampled contained unacceptable levels of pathogenic bacteria soon after preparation, and 70.7% did after 8 hours; in the rainy season 34.9% contained unacceptable levels soon after preparation, and virtually all did after 8 hours (96.2%). In rural Bangladesh 41% of samples of food fed to children 5–18 months old contained *Escherichia coli*, an indicator of faecal contamination (Black et al., 1982). Another source of infection leading to diarrhoeal disease is environmental contamination. The weaning period is also a period in which children learn to crawl and then to walk, and this greater mobility in the second half of the first year may expose them more readily to environmental sources of contamination. The extent of diarrhoeal disease shows that disgust-based aversion to source of contamination in the child can only protect them to a very limited extent, if at all. It may have important benefits via the mother, however, for example in stimulating hand washing (Curtis, 2003). Hand washing is very important in protecting against diarrhoeal diseases, and disgust sensitivity is stronger throughout the lifespan in women than in men (Curtis, Aunger & Rabie, 2004).

Diarrhoeal disease reduces growth rates in children (Black, Brown & Becker, 1984; Bohler & Bergstrom, 1996; Cole, 1989). This is to some extent attributable to effects on the absorption of nutrients, but these illnesses also directly affect food intake itself. Although the withdrawal of food by parents during episodes of diarrhoea is a tradition in some cultures (Khan & Ahmad, 1986; Kumar et al., 1985), the reduction in the child's food intake is also a result of a direct anorexic effect of the illness (Brown, 1991; Brown et al., 1995). Brown et al. (1990), for example, measured the energy intake of children in the first year of life in Huascar (Lima) in Peru, and also recorded fever, diarrhoea, and respiratory and other illnesses. Diarrhoea and fever reduced energy intake by 5–6%. Intake of breast milk was unaffected, as was the frequency of breast-feeding and the total time the infant was suckled; intake of food from other sources was reduced by 20–30%. The infants' mothers reported episodes of anorexia associated with illness with reasonable accuracy, as shown by the correlations with food intake made on the same day; the child's appetite was also suppressed on the day before the illnesses became apparent to the mothers (Brown *et al.*, 1995).

It is easy to attribute malnutrition to a lack of food, or, if there is no lack of food, to a lack of parental care. Of course it can be due to either. But the problem of malnutrition is more complex than this. Golden points out that even in countries in which malnutrition is common, when one visits the home of a malnourished child food is almost always available (Golden, 1991). But the diet offered to young children is often very monotonous. In Jamaica they may be fed tea and a maize-based porridge at every meal (Golden, 1991). 'Sensory specific satiety' has been demonstrated both in adults and in children – the palatability of a particular food is specifically reduced in the short term when the particular food is eaten (Birch & Deysher, 1986). Correspondingly, food intake at a meal increases if a variety of food is offered. So one would expect a very monotonous diet to be associated with a lesser intake of food. In addition, as we saw above, learned food aversions can result if the intake of a food is followed by symptoms of gastrointestinal illness. In countries in which diarrhoeal disease is common, which are generally the same as those in which malnutrition in infancy is common, it seems plausible that learned food aversion to the commonly offered staples is also likely to be common, though at the moment this is not something on which we have direct evidence. A further problem is that many nutrient deficiencies themselves lead to anorexia (Golden, 1991). This has been shown experimentally, for example, in relation to zinc deficiency (Hambidge, 1986; Krebs, Hambridge & Walravens, 1984). Thus there is a whole series of reasons for expecting malnourished children to have poor appetites: the anorexic effects of diarrhoeal diseases, conditioned food aversions, sensory specific satiety and the effects of micronutrient deficiencies may all have a role.

Although research on this topic is limited, there is direct evidence that malnourished children frequently do not eat food which they are offered. This has been shown, for example, by the careful systematic observation of children in Mexico (Garcia, Kaiser & Dewey, 1990b). In this study 45 two- to five-year-old children were tracked throughout a single day using the method of 'child following'. The child was kept in sight by an observer from when they woke up in the morning until they went to bed, a period of 11–15 hours. All the food prepared in the home and eaten by the child was weighed, and all feeding and food-related behaviour, including verbal behaviour, was recorded. Growth stunting was common in the villages the children came from, and was recorded in 10 of the 45 children in the study (most of the other children were more mildly malnourished).

However, both in the less malnourished and in the more malnourished children substantially more food was made available to the children than they actually consumed, and most requests of the children for food (which were common) were granted. Higher food intake was associated with more frequent eating (especially snacking) and with more frequent requests for food from the child (Garcia, Kaiser & Dewey, 1990a). The same has been shown in children in Peru (Brown, 1991). There is also good evidence from a number of different countries (including Peru, Nicaragua, India and Nigeria) that the mothers of young children detect the anorexia associated with infectious diseases, are concerned about it and respond to it appropriately by trying to encourage their children to eat more (Bentley *et al.*, 1991; Engle & Zeitlen, 1996).

4   Born too small or born too soon

4.1   Growth before birth

Nutritional deficiencies in childhood tend to be most prevalent in the first three years. This is partly because young children have relatively high nutritional needs. They are growing rapidly in the years immediately after birth, and their small body mass gives them a relatively higher requirement for energy, as they lose heat more readily. In addition, as noted at the end of Chapter 3, in many countries there is a high prevalence of infectious disease in the early years, with diarrhoeal disease, particularly, leading both to anorexia and reduced food intake, and to poorer absorption of the food that is eaten. And the weaning of infants in the first year calls upon them to learn a whole new range of feeding skills which are initially not well developed.

Up to the time of birth, of course, an infant's nutrition is derived entirely from the mother, via the placental circulation. But this does not mean that all children receive the optimal nutrition before birth, or that malnutrition cannot occur before birth. It can and does. In considering the effects of malnutrition on psychological development, therefore, we need to begin at the earliest stages of development and consider first effects that might result from malnutrition occurring in the first nine months from conception, when the child is usually still *in utero*.

Partly because of the difficulties involved in measuring food intake, nutritional monitoring in childhood is mainly carried out by measuring growth, and malnutrition is usually identified by poor growth. Although linear growth is continuous from the beginning of fetal life through to adolescence, the measurement procedures used to monitor it are different at different stages of development. At birth and after birth the child's *length* can be measured, and from 2 years of age their *height*. The difference is that length is measured lying down while height is measured standing: the two measurements are nearly but not exactly equivalent. Length is a difficult measurement to make at birth, and in older infants, as infants tend to lie curled up, so two people (and special apparatus) are

69

needed to make the measurement accurately. Routine measurements of length made at birth with a tape measure tend to be very inaccurate. This is one reason why the key measurement made at birth is birthweight, which is routinely measured in most countries immediately after the infant is delivered. Modern electronic balances are very accurate provided they are properly calibrated. Partly for the same reason, growth in the first year is routinely monitored by weighing infants, rather than by measuring their length. Before birth neither weight nor length can be measured, but using ultrasound the dimensions of skeletal components of the body can be, for example the width of the skull. These provide measures of linear growth before birth, though of a slightly different kind than are available after birth.

An infant's birthweight can be unusually low because they have grown poorly during a pregnancy of normal length (born too small), or because they have been born after a shorter pregnancy than usual (born too soon), or both. In this chapter we consider the later development of children born too small or born too soon. In the case of infants born too small a key psychological question is whether prenatal malnutrition has enduring effects on cognitive or other abilities, or on other aspects of psychological development. In the case of infants born too soon, complex questions concerning the development of feeding behaviour arise, since these infants are born at a developmental stage at which they would naturally be fed in utero via the maternal circulation, rather than by feeding orally in the way a term baby does. Questions concerning the long-term effect of early nutrition are also important in connection with infants born too soon, and there is now a substantial body of work dealing with these questions.

Birthweight is a key indicator of the health and welfare of human populations. It is used, for example, in international comparisons of child health. A *low* birthweight is defined for these purposes by the World Health Organisation as a birthweight below 2500 g. The definition used to be a birthweight less than or equal to 2500 g, but it was changed in 1976. The difference is only important if weight is recorded in large units, say 100 g. A low birthweight can be due either to a shorter than usual pregnancy or to slower than usual growth before birth, or both, and although measuring a child's birthweight is simple, distinguishing the causes of a low birthweight is not. It depends critically on knowing the date of conception, and the date of conception is not always easily determined. The average duration of pregnancy is actually just over 38 weeks (Berg & Bracken, 1992), but a pregnancy is normally dated from the last known menstrual period, which is about two weeks earlier than the ovulation that results in the pregnancy, so the average duration of pregnancy is usually deemed to be 40 weeks. Using this scale of *gestational* age, infants born too soon, or *preterm*, are those born before 37 completed weeks of gestation, and comprise 6–8% of infants born in Britain (Wolke, 1998). Infants whose growth is markedly below average during pregnancy, whether they are born preterm or not, are referred to as *small for gestational age* (SGA) or as having *intrauterine growth retardation* (IUGR). The terms do not mean exactly the same thing, as the second term explicitly implies that growth has been abnormally slow, while the first does not, though the terms are often used as if they are interchangeable. At birth a weight below the 10th centile of an appropriate standard of birthweight for the child's gestational age is often used as a criterion. A preterm infant's *chronological* age is their age from birth, but clearly term and preterm infants of the same chronological age may be at quite different stages of development, and this needs to be taken into account in comparing their development. The term *corrected* age is used of the age of preterm infants in the first three years of life, and is their age as dated from the expected date of delivery – i.e. the age they would be had they been born at term.

Errors in the identification of preterm births can arise in a number of ways – for example if non-menstrual bleeding in the first trimester of the pregnancy is mistaken for menstrual bleeding, or if a missed early miscarriage leads to two pregnancies being confused. Dating of gestational age can be confirmed by an ultrasound scan early in the second trimester (when the infant is 16–18 weeks old), from which the width of the skull can be determined. This is a measure related to head circumference, and so to linear growth. Comparisons of gestational age determinations from menstrual dating and from such scans over a large sample (11,045 births) have shown that of infants assumed to be born preterm from the timing of the last known menstrual period, about 23% were in fact born at or after term, and of infants assumed to be born at or after term, about 3% were in fact born preterm (Kramer *et al.*, 1988). To add to these complexities, slow growth before birth is one reason for inducing a preterm birth, and so about one third of infants born preterm in the UK are also small for gestational age (Tanner, 1989). Poor growth before birth is also the strongest predictor of a spontaneous preterm birth in women having their first child (Gardosi, 2005).

There are, then, obvious problems in identifying the developmental effects associated with a low birthweight, or with being born preterm, as each is associated with the other. Ideally for research purposes birthweight and the duration of pregnancy should both be recorded for each child and the two variables considered together, a procedure that was followed in one of the earliest major studies of their intellectual sequelae (Goldstein & Peckham, 1976). This study involved a follow-up (the National Child Development Study) of the survivors of 17,000 children born in one week of March 1958, who were initially studied in the Perinatal Mortality Survey. Both birthweight and gestational age were recorded for each child, so the effect of each could be examined taking the other into account. In an alternative research procedure, effects of birth-weight can be determined independently of the duration of pregnancy by keeping gestational age constant: in practice, this has generally meant restricting the analysis to infants born at term, as in the study of Grantham-McGregor and colleagues (Grantham-McGregor *et al.*, 1998). A second requirement for studies in this area (and for studies of malnutrition of other kinds) is a properly selected control group. This may seem obvious, but substantial numbers of studies have been pub-lished without one. In a meta-analysis of outcome studies of low birth-weight which reviewed studies published in the decade up to 1989, for example, a control group was only used in 25 of the 80 studies (Aylward *et al.*, 1989). In studies that have not used control groups, reliance has usually been placed on the assumption that the average IQ in a normal population is known to be 100. But there is a strong secular trend (change over time) in IQ, which has been rising systematically since IQ tests were first developed (Flynn, 1999), so the assumption that the average IQ is 100 is only reasonable if an IQ test is used which has been recently standardised on the same population as the sample of children being studied. And infants with low birthweights, or infants born preterm, may come from families which differ from those of other children in social or other characteristics. They need, therefore, to be compared with children from families who are comparable in other respects, rather than with the whole remaining population. A third important require-ment concerns the follow-up of the children. All prospective longitudinal studies suffer from attrition, the loss of participants to follow up. Unfortunately, attrition is not random: in a follow-up of infants born preterm, for example, loss to follow-up was more likely if the mother was less well educated, and if the child was seriously developmentally delayed or disabled (Wolke *et al.*, 1995). Fourthly, when children are tested it is very desirable that the testers of the children should not be a party to information concerning their birth history. This is commonly referred to as the requirement that the testing should be blind; it avoids bias resulting from expectations on the part of the tester based on the child's history.

4.2   The development of children born too small

In developing countries the major determinants of intra-uterine growth retardation include poor maternal nutrition during pregnancy, as mea-sured either by weight gain during pregnancy or by measured energy intake during pregnancy, and a low maternal weight before pregnancy (Kramer, 1987). Conversely, birthweight can be increased by nutritional supplementation of the mother. Although the effect is not large in most populations (Kramer, 1993), it is in circumstances in which women are obviously malnourished (Rasmussen, 2001), for example in Gambian women during the 'hungry' season (Ceesay et al., 1997). This evidence for effects of poor nutrition during pregnancy on birthweight is one reason for believing that children born small for gestational age may be affected by malnutrition before birth. But there are, of course, other causes of a low birthweight in infants born at term. In developed countries its most important cause is cigarette smoking. Poor nutrition during pregnancy and a low maternal weight before pregnancy are also important; other causes include primiparity, preeclampsia and alcohol and drug use during pregnancy (Kramer et al., 1999). Some of these, however, can also interfere with the nutrition of the infant during pregnancy by interfering with nutrient flows from the mother to the fetus (Warshaw, 1985). Recent evidence also suggests that maternal depression is an independent predictor of low birthweight (Patel & Prince, 2006), so in some circumstances psychological sequelae of low birthweight might be related to depression in the child's mother.

The later development of children born small for their gestational age has attracted a great deal of interest in recent years, partly as a result of epidemiological interest in the fetal origins of adult disease (Barker, 1992). Children born small for gestational age are more likely to be short as adults (Karlberg & Albertsson-Wikland, 1995), and their physical health as adults is also adversely affected. They are more likely to develop 'syndrome X' (Barker et al., 1993), and to die of ischaemic heart disease (Barker et al., 1989). Syndrome X is a combination of Type 2 diabetes, hyperlipidaemia and hypertension, and is now more often known as the metabolic syndrome. The associations are strong; the proportion of men with syndrome X in studies in separate samples in Hertfordshire and Preston was over ten times as high in the adults in the lightest compared with the heaviest birthweight category, and was independent of the duration of gestation, and of the body mass index, smoking and drinking habits and the social class of the men when adult. Our concern here is principally with the possibility that low birthweight might be related to psychological development, but it is important to keep the wider health effects of low birthweight in mind, since these could provide a mechanism by which birthweight could affect psychological development indirectly, at any rate in later life.

Being born preterm and being born small for gestational age are both relatively more common in developing countries. According to Villar and

Belizan (1982) preterm births are about twice as common, but being born SGA is six to seven times as common. This much higher incidence of SGA births in developing countries has meant that they have provided the setting for some of the most important research in this area. An example is the study of Grantham-McGregor *et al.* (1998) in Northeast Brazil. In this study a group of infants with birthweights of 1500–2499 g and born at term were recruited, along with control infants with birthweights of 3000–3499 g. They were assessed at six and twelve months using the Bayley Scales of Infant Development, and development was clearly delayed in the children in the SGA group. At six months there was a difference of about 4 points in the MDI, which increased to 7 points at 12 months. There was a difference of 7 points in the PDI, which increased to nearly 10 points at 12 months. Efforts were made to control for the social and economic characteristics of the infants' homes and for the literacy of the parents. An interesting feature of the results was that the child's birthweight interacted with other variables that were related to the child's developmental scores. The literacy of the mothers, for example, was related to the development of the low birthweight infants but not to that of the controls.

Because birthweights are routinely recorded in child health records there has also been considerable scope in Western countries for examining the relationship between birthweight and later development in large samples of children in which psychological assessments have been carried out later in life, in the course of educational testing or at conscription into the armed forces. In studies of this kind the relationship between birthweight and later intellectual ability or educational attainment has generally been examined across the whole range of birthweights, rather than in a comparison of low birthweight infants and controls. This is a valuable approach, since there is an arbitrary element in the definition of a low birthweight. The usual cut-off for low birthweight is related to the risk of mortality in infants, but the range of birthweights associated with a higher risk of death may not correspond to the range of birthweights associated with poorer intellectual outcomes. If information is available on the outcomes associated with the whole range of birthweights the appropriateness of the traditional definition can be examined. In fact the evidence strongly suggests that there is no disadvantage specifically associated with a low birthweight (say, a birthweight below the traditional cut-off of 2500 g) but rather a general relationship between birthweight and later development across the whole range of birthweights.

The first major study of this general relationship between birthweight and later psychological outcomes was reported by Record, McKeown and Edwards (1969). This study was based on records for all infants born alive in Birmingham over a period of about five years from 1950, nearly 87,000 children in all. Data on birthweight and the duration of gestation were available for just over 40,000, and a verbal reasoning score for just over 50,000. This is an IQ related score with a mean of 100 and a standard deviation of 15, and it was used in the eleven plus examination in placing children into what were deemed to be appropriate schools. In infants born at 40 weeks of gestation or later, verbal reasoning scores increased steadily from those born below 2.5 kg to those born at 4.5 kg or over: the difference over this range was about 10 points. Other variables that were also related to the verbal reasoning scores were sex, the duration of gestation and the number of previous siblings born to the mother. Control for these was principally by graphical examination. There was no control for other variables, apart from length of gestation, but a small difference in favour of the heavier child at birth was found when siblings were compared within families, a comparison which controls for many family-related variables.

In a second large study the relationships between birthweight and an actual measure of educational attainment were examined. Goldstein and Peckham (1976) analysed data from the National Child Development Study, a longitudinal study conducted in the UK by the National Children's Bureau, which followed up children from 17,000 births in one week in March 1958. They examined scores on a reading comprehension test when the children were 11 years of age. As mentioned above, Goldstein and Peckham classified the children both by their birthweight, in bands of 500 g, and by their gestational age at birth, in weeks. The relationships between these and the child's reading comprehension were very clear: reading improved with every 500 g birthweight band, over the whole birthweight range, and with every week of gestational age from 34 to 41 (infants born after 42 weeks or *postterm* did less well). There was no interaction between the two variables, i.e. the differences between birthweight bands was the same for each gestational age at birth and the differences between gestational age at birth the same for each birthweight band. A substantial proportion of the difference between the very early preterm and the term infants (about a half) was eliminated when birthweight was controlled for. The relationships were not eliminated by controlling for social class, family composition or the age of the child's mother. Jefferis, Power and Hertzman (2002) used data on the same children and found graded effects of birthweight in relation to all childhood cognitive and educational tests, including tests of mathematics and reading and of verbal and non-verbal ability. It was striking how little the associations found were influenced by the quite extensive control for covariates used in the study: for example, controlling for gestational age, maternal age, parity, breast-feeding, social class at birth and parental education did not reduce at all the association between mathematics scores at age 7 and birthweight in girls, and reduced it only slightly in boys. The differences with different birthweights were stable over childhood, and were still present on tests conducted at 16 years of age, and similar differences were found in respect of adult educational qualifications.

A major recent study of the relationship between cognitive ability in adults and birthweight was published by Sørenson et al. (1997). Nearly all Danish men have to register with the draft board and are given a physical and mental examination. The main exceptions are men with chronic illnesses. The mental examination involved a test developed for the purpose, the Boerge Prien test; scores on this test correlate highly (.82) with IQ scores on the Wechsler Adult Intelligence Scale (WAIS). Danish citizens are given a personal number at birth, which allowed the cognitive scores to be linked accurately to birth registration data, collected by midwives attending the birth. (Making links of this kind is much more difficult in England and Wales.) The linkage allowed examination of the relationship between birthweight and adult cognitive abilities, which were systematically related to birthweight, with higher birthweights associated with higher cognitive scores (Figure 4.1). Again the effect was not restricted to infants of low birthweight using conventional criteria. It extended over the whole range of birthweight up to 4.2 kg. The analysis controlled for gestational age, length at birth, the mother's age, parity and employment status, and whether they were married or unmarried. There was no additional control of social factors, though social class is much more homogeneous in Denmark than in the UK. There was also no control for smoking (or drinking) during pregnancy or for the IQ of the parents.

Another recent study of the same relationship has been reported by Shenkin et al. (2001). This study used birth records kept in Edinburgh for children born in 1921, a cohort whose intellectual abilities were assessed using the Moray House Test when they were 11 years old in 1932. Shenkin et al. matched the birth records and the Moray House Test records successfully for just under half the children. Birthweight was significantly associated with the test scores over the whole range. The test scores were also associated with social class, as one would expect, but the two effects were independent; the effect of birthweight was not attributable to a confounding with social class, nor was the effect of social class attributable to social class differences in birthweight. Shenkin et al. (2004) subsequently systematically reviewed studies on this relationship. The six studies that met their inclusion criteria each independently

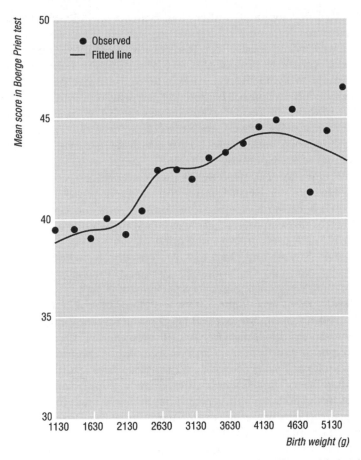

Figure 4.1 Cognitive ability in children of different birthweights (Sørenson *et al.*, 1997). The scores come from the Boerge Prien test. The sample size was 4300. Reprinted from *British Medical Journal*, *315*, 401–13 and reproduced with permission from the BMJ Publishing Group.

showed a significant relationship between higher birthweight and higher cognitive abilities. The relationship is found across the whole range of birthweights, except possibly at the very highest (Shenkin, Starr & Deary, 2004). The difference between the highest and lowest birthweight category was about 10 IQ points, though this was somewhat reduced when adjusted for covariates. This quite substantial body of evidence therefore suggests that effects on intellectual ability associated with being born SGA reflect a more general association between birthweight and intellectual development, rather than being a specific effect associated with particularly poor intra-uterine growth. It is possible we are still dealing with a nutritional effect. It may be important for optimal intellectual development to provide the very best nutrition before birth rather than simply to avoid the worst. But there are other possibilities. It is always difficult to control completely for other confounding variables. In none of these studies, for example, was the IQ of the mother or father taken into account – for very good reasons, since data on adult IQ are not usually available, and would be prohibitively expensive to collect in studies on the scale of many of these.

A different way of controlling for such variables is to compare children within families, as Record *et al.* did in their initial study (Record, McKeown & Edwards, 1969). This controls for a substantial number of variables that are common to all children within a family even though they cannot be measured or even identified. A later study of this kind was reported by Strauss and Dietz (1998). This was based on data from the American 'National Collaborative Perinatal Project', a major study examining the relationship between perinatal risk factors and later growth and development in a cohort of 55,760 children. Using only data from children born at term, Strauss and Dietz made two comparisons. The first was between children born after IUGR (identified in this study simply by birthweight of 2500 g or less) and the remaining children in the cohort. The mean IQ at 7 years of age of children born after IUGR was 6.2 points lower than that of the remaining children in the population. The comparison was based on large numbers and the difference was highly significant statistically. There were, however, many other differences between the groups. The infants born IUGR were more likely to be female, which reflects the use of a criterion for low birthweight ($\leq$2500 g) that does not take the sex of the infant into account. They were also more likely to be firstborn and to have Apgar scores $\leq$6, reflecting a less satisfactory physical state at birth. The mothers of the IUGR children were significantly shorter; significantly more likely to have especially low incomes and to have suffered from hypertension or toxaemia of pregnancy; and less likely to be white. Any of these might be associated with a slightly lower IQ in the child. An additional comparison was therefore made between same-sex sibling pairs, in which one sibling was born after IUGR and the other was not. This eliminated most of the other differences between the pairs, and almost entirely eliminated the differences in IQ, which was reduced to 1.3 points and was not statistically significant. This comparison was based on 154 pairs. Although this suggests that intra-uterine growth retardation *per se* is not associated with a lower subsequent IQ, there are two points to note. Firstly, the sibling control children themselves were born substantially lighter than the control children in the population as a whole (by 300 g). Secondly, in the group born too small children with a head circumference 3 cm or more smaller than their sibling controls had significantly lower IQs (the difference was 6 IQ points). A more recent study has re-examined this question using the same data set but with further controls (Matte et al., 2001). This re-examination was based on over 3000 children. Only singleton infants born at term ($\geq$37 weeks) and with weights between 1500 g and 3999 g were included in the sample. IQ was assessed at 7 using the Wechsler Intelligence Scale for Children (WISC). Adjusted for ethnicity, mother's education, mother's age, a family socio-economic index and for birth order there was a systematic relationship between birthweight and IQ. The average difference was 4.6 IQ points per kg birthweight in boys, and 2.8 IQ points in girls. The study also examined differences between same sex sibling pairs within the same family. Within sibling pairs, the average difference per kg difference in birthweight was 5 IQ points in boys and 1 IQ point in girls. The difference was not statistically significant in the girls, but it was in the boys.

Even better control is possible if a comparison is made between monozygotic twins, who develop from a single fertilised ovum. They are less appropriately known as 'identical' twins, but there are many ways in which monozygotic twins are not identical (Gringras & Chen, 2001). One is that their birthweights can differ substantially, and if they do the heavier twin tends to have a higher IQ: the mean advantage for 73 pairs in three studies reported by James (1982) was 3.3 IQ points. Lynn (1990) has collated data from additional studies showing comparable effects. Even a study of Boomsma et al. (2001), which was reported as a negative result, showed a significant IQ advantage for the heavier of monozygotic twins at 5 years, though the difference was absent at later ages. Although there are other possibilities, the IQ advantage to the heavier twin of a monozygotic pair may also reflect a prenatal nutritional advantage, resulting from a more efficient placental supply of nutrients to the heavier twin.

While most of the data from these studies is at least consistent with an adverse prenatal effect of poor nutrition on intellectual development, evidence from an important study of the effects of the 1944–5 Dutch famine is not, or at least appears not to be. Details of the study, as summarised here, are given in Stein et al. (1972). The Dutch famine resulted from a transport embargo on Western Holland instituted by the occupying Nazis in 1944, as a reprisal for a strike of Dutch railway workers timed to coincide with an attempt by British paratroops to bridge the Rhine at Arnhem. The canals also froze in the winter, transport by barge was prevented, and food became very scarce in the large cities. The famine lasted about six months. At its worst, official food rations allowed only 450 calories (less than 2 MJ) per day. The death rates increased, with many deaths attributed to starvation; clinical reports during the famine and surveys immediately after liberation confirmed its severity. Later epidemiological examination of the effects of the famine was carried out by comparing cohorts of children born in cities in Western Holland before, during and after the famine, with cohorts of children born in control cities in the south, east and north over the same time period. At military induction at 18 years of age virtually all the men in these cohorts were examined medically, and assessed psychologically using the Dutch version of the Raven Progressive Matrices. Of the males who survived and still lived in the Netherlands 98% were included in the study. This gave very large numbers; data were available on more than 100,000. There was, however, no detectable reduction in Raven scores in the cohorts conceived or born during the famine. This is surprising, if malnutrition before birth does affect intellectual performance. One problem in the study considered by the authors is that more impaired fetuses may have died as a result of their mother's malnutrition, leaving only the less impaired to survive. Another is that birthweights were not available for individual men in the study. The data shown on birthweight (in their Figure 2) compare data from maternity hospitals in a famine and a control city (Rotterdam and Heerlen respectively). These figures suggest a decrease in birthweight of only about 300 g when it was at its lowest at the end of the famine period, presumably because the fetus was nutritionally protected in mothers with reasonably good nutritional status at the start of the famine. In addition, IQ was used grouped into six levels (1–6) with the mean level rather than the mean score used as the outcome variable. This is a course grouping, with about 20% of the population in each of bands 1, 2 and 3, for example, which would reduce the power of the study and may have made the detection of relatively small effects difficult.

Although birthweight has the great advantage of being a measure that is easy to make and is widely recorded as a part of routine clinical care, it provides only a summary of weight gain before birth, with no information on the time in pregnancy when weight gain was below average. Much more fine-grained information can be obtained using repeated ultrasound measurements during pregnancy, though obviously these are not available in large-scale studies of the kind described above. An example of what can be done can be found in the study of Harvey et al. (1982). The children studied had birthweights below the 10th percentile for gestational age after allowing for maternal height and weight and for the baby's sex (Tanner & Thompson, 1970). The growth of the infants was monitored prenatally using ultrasound, which allowed serial measurement of the width of the skull (biparietal diameter), a measure related to head circumference. Figure 4.2 shows examples of a child with intrauterine growth retardation from early in pregnancy (top) and a child who grew normally early in pregnancy, with growth retardation from week 34 (bottom). The children whose growth retardation began before the 26th week of pregnancy, 10 in number, had a mean birthweight of 1.80 kg. The children with later developing growth retardation, 41 in number, had a mean birthweight of 2.40 kg. The children were compared with control children with birthweights above the 10th percentile (mean 3.36 kg). The control children were matched individually on sex, social class, birth order and birth date. The children were tested at about 5 years of age by testers who did not know the obstetric history of the children, using the McCarthy Scales of Children's Abilities, an IQ-like test used in young children. The group of 10 with growth retardation before 26 weeks had significantly poorer abilities than their controls (the difference was 9.1 points). There was no significant difference between the children with later growth retardation and their controls.

Having considered the different source of evidence available, what conclusions can we draw concerning prenatal malnutrition and later cognitive development or educational attainment? Apart from the Dutch famine study, the evidence that birthweight is associated with later development is reasonably, though not completely, consistent. There is, however, good evidence that it is not only at the lower end of the birthweight range that the association is found; ability later in life increases with birthweight even at higher birthweights. This is not, perhaps, what one would expect if this is a nutritional effect, though it does not rule one out – it may be that for prenatal nutrition to be optimal for intellectual development it has to be better than average, rather than just average. A very large Swedish study has shown that infants born small for gestational age are virtually unaffected if their growth after birth is good, which suggests that good nutrition after birth can compensate for being born too small (Lundgren et al., 2001).

There is now some evidence emerging that birthweight is also associated with a number of other aspects of later psychological functioning. For example, low birthweight is associated with psychological distress in adult life (Cheung et al., 2002). This study was based on data from the National Child Development Study, in which 17,000 people born in one week in March 1958 were followed up into adult life. At 23, 33 and 42 years of age scores were obtained for the Malaise Inventory, which has scales of psychological and of somatic symptoms. Lower birthweight was associated with psychological distress but not with somatic

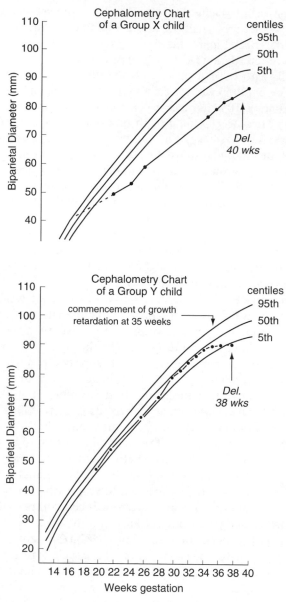

Figure 4.2 Fetal head growth in infants born small for gestational age (Harvey *et al.*, 1982). Group X (example above) grew slowly from early in pregnancy; group Y (example below) grew slowly only from late in pregnancy. Reproduced with permission from *Pediatrics*, *69*, 296–300. Copyright © 1982 by the American Academy of Pediatrics.

symptoms. It is also associated with depression late in life (Thompson *et al.*, 2001). One possible explanation is that this is an effect of the lower IQ associated with a lower birthweight, since some studies show that the risk of depression and of suicide is higher in men with lower intellectual abilities (Gunnell, Magnusson & Rasmussen, 2005; Van Os *et al.*, 1997). Another possible explanation is that men with lower birthweights are less likely to marry (Phillips *et al.*, 2001; Vågerö & Modin, 2002). Another is that the depression is associated with illness. As noted above, children born small for gestational age are more likely to develop diabetes and heart disease later in life. These are themselves associated with depressive symptoms in older adults, as shown in a large longitudinal study of a nationally representative sample of Americans (Schnittker, 2005). Evidence from the Dutch Famine Study has also been brought to bear in this area (Brown *et al.*, 1995; Brown *et al.*, 2000), in this case support- ing the possibility that we are dealing with an effect of prenatal malnu- trition. Brown *et al.* examined hospitalisation rates for major affective disorders in birth cohorts of children who were or were not exposed to the famine, and found good evidence that hospitalisation rates were signifi- cantly higher in those who were. This is consistent with a direct prenatal effect of malnutrition on the infant, though the authors raise the alter- native possibility that maternal stress resulting from the famine might have mediated the effect via effects of stress on the unborn child. There is growing evidence for prenatal effects of stress of this kind.

4.3   The development of children born too soon

The early care, health and survival of infants born preterm depends on how early they are born, and is improving all the time. Infants born just a few weeks early can breathe for themselves and usually need only normal care. Infants born very early (say before 28 weeks of gestation) are more likely to survive than not, but generally need special care. Those born at 25 weeks of gestation, who would not have been considered viable 20 years ago, now have a 10–40% survival rate. The mothers of preterm infants differ statistically from those of term infants in many ways, includ- ing maternal age, parity, ethnicity and social class, and they are more likely to smoke and to be obese (Gardosi, 2005).

An example of a study examining cognitive skills in preterm infants is reported by Rose and Feldman (2000); 63 preterm and 46 full-term infants were compared in a longitudinal study that lasted until they were 11 years old. The families were similar in other respects. Nearly 60% were unskilled or semi-skilled, and the mothers were comparable in age, ethnicity and educational attainments. The preterm children were all born below 1500 g, with an average gestational age of about 31 weeks. Compared using the Bayley Scales at 7 months, 1, 1.5 and 2 years, scores were about 10 points lower in the preterm group at each age. Compared using IQ tests at 3, 4, 5, 6 and 11 years of age, scores were again about 10 points lower in the preterm group at each age. In this study, a number of more specifically focussed tasks were also used both in infancy and in childhood. In infancy a test of visual recognition memory was used at 7 months, and tests of visual and tactile recognition memory, cross-modal transfer and object permanence at 12 months. At 11 years, picture recognition, name-face association tasks and learning and memory tasks were used. These allowed composite measures of processing speed and memory to be derived – two of the key types of ability that underlie successful performance on intelligence tests. The children born preterm were significantly poorer on all the infancy tasks except cross-modal transfer, and on all the childhood memory tasks. The composite speed and memory measures accounted for most of the difference between the groups in IQ, verbal ability and spatial ability, suggesting that it might have been these that were most fundamentally affected. A recent meta-analysis of psychological sequelae at school age of a preterm birth, restricted to controlled studies with a loss to follow up of less than 30% (Bhutta *et al.*, 2002), summarised results from 15 studies of cognitive outcomes. On average, the children born preterm scored 10.9 IQ points lower than their controls. Most of the studies that were summarised excluded children with major neurological disabilities; if the two that did not were omitted from the overall estimate, the deficit was only slightly reduced to 10.2 IQ points. Attention-deficit hyperactivity disorder (ADHD) was also substantially more common in the children born preterm. These differences came from studies in which cases were matched to controls on at least one demographic feature, though the children were not necessarily tested blind. Preterm births are also associated with motor disabilities, including cerebral palsy, the prevalence of which is 10–18% among children born before 26 weeks (Bracewell & Marlow, 2002).

There are many possible ways in which cognitive abilities later in life might be related to a preterm birth. They might be associated with the characteristics of mothers who deliver preterm, rather than with the preterm birth itself – for example, with their education or social class. Perinatal brain injury is also quite common in infants born preterm (Reynolds, 1996). The injury can be due to bleeding within the brain (cerebral haemorrhage) or to an inadequate oxygen supply to the brain (hypoxia-ischaemia). They might be associated with the intra-uterine growth retardation that is an important risk factor for a preterm birth. In the group of preterm infants studied by Rose and Feldman (2000), for example, 44% were also born small for gestational age. And, in addition, it is difficult to ensure optimal feeding of preterm infants after birth. They are born at a time of very rapid growth at a developmental stage at which they are not adapted to oral feeding, and even when they have passed the age at which infants are normally born motor disabilities associated with a preterm birth can make feeding difficult. So there is a distinct possibility that infants born preterm might also suffer from less than optimal nutrition, both before and after birth, which might also adversely affect their intellectual development.

Effects of early nutritional interventions on the cognitive development of infants born preterm have been investigated in a number of studies. Lucas *et al.* (1989), for example, studied infants lighter than 1850 g at birth and born about 7 weeks preterm in three neonatal units in Cambridge, Ipswich and King's Lynn. The study was a large one, with 502 infants randomly allocated to two groups and 400 examined developmentally at 9 months. One group was given banked breast milk and the other a preterm formula, in each case either as their sole food or as a supplement to breast milk provided by the mother. At 9 months of age the infants were assessed using a developmental screening inventory for infants (Knobloch, Pasamanick & Sherard, 1966) based on the Gesell developmental schedules. Overall, the developmental scores were significantly higher in the group given the preterm formula (mean score 100.4 compared with 97.9). The difference was apparent in most of the subareas tested (adaptive behaviour, gross motor skills, language and personal-social skills).

In a second study, infants born lighter than 1850 g and about 7 weeks preterm and admitted to Special Care Baby Units in Norwich and Sheffield were randomly allocated to standard term or a special preterm formula, again either as their sole food or as a supplement to milk provided by the mother (Lucas *et al.*, 1990). Compared with the standard term formula, the special preterm formula contained higher levels of protein and more energy and was enriched with minerals and vitamins, carnitine and taurine. Initially 424 infants were enrolled; 334 of the 377 survivors were followed up to 18 months, when the infants were tested using the Bayley Scales. A statistically significant difference was found on the motor scale (PDI) in favour of the group provided with the special preterm formula (the difference was 6.1 points). A much smaller and non-significant difference (1.7 points) was found on the mental scale (MDI). For reasons given in Chapter 1 a difference of this kind found using developmental tests in infancy does not necessarily imply an adverse long-term effect, and these infants were also studied when they were 7–8 years old (Lucas, Morley & Cole, 1998). At that age, a simple comparison between the groups did not show significant differences in IQ between the groups; the means were 100.0 and 101.4 respectively in the groups fed standard formula and the special preterm formula. Nor were there significant differences when comparisons were restricted to verbal or performance scales, or to the infants receiving the highest intakes of the trial diets. There was some evidence for effects of diet in the boys in the study, particularly effects on verbal IQ in boys with the highest intakes. Some caution, however, is needed in interpreting effects found in comparisons that are restricted to particular subgroups. In a further development of this research two different supplements were added to human milk fed to infants born preterm, a control supplement and a 'fortifier' (Lucas et al., 1996). The control supplement contained phosphorus, sodium, potassium and a range of vitamins. The fortifier contained additional protein, fat, carbohydrate, phosphorus, calcium and magnesium. These two supplements were allocated at random to 275 preterm infants who were tested developmentally at 9 months (using Knobloch's developmental inventory) and at 18 months (using the Bayley Scales). In this study there were no significant differences in developmental scores at either 9 or 18 months; nor did significant differences emerge from examination of particular subgroups.

These studies provide some evidence for effects in infancy of the early postnatal diet in infants born preterm. The overall effects are not large. They may be larger in some subgroups, however, and it is important to note that the differences in diets were restricted to quite small periods (about a month) and for many of the infants they involved only a part of the diet. The evidence that there are enduring effects in not very strong at the moment; it is stronger for boys than girls. Nor is the mechanism of the effect clear. The term and preterm formulas used differed in many constituents, including protein, energy, fat, minerals and vitamins. The infants taking the preterm formula in the study of Lucas et al. (1989) grew faster (Lucas et al., 1986) and so were discharged home earlier, which might have affected their development in other ways. It is also possible that better earlier growth might have facilitated later feeding and so improved later nutrition.

Feeding is a complex process involving the coordination of sucking, swallowing and breathing. In infants sucking is possible from about 24 weeks of gestational age, but it is not then fully coordinated with swallowing and breathing, so infants born preterm are often initially fed parenterally or by intragastric tube, and subsequently switched to feeding by mouth. Traditionally this switch has been made at 33 or 34 weeks, but there is some evidence that full oral feeding is possible earlier than this. Casaer et al. (1982) followed the feeding behaviour of 100 bottle-fed preterm infants born at 25 to 37 weeks of gestation age, and weighing from 780 g to 1990 g, evaluating feeding efficiency principally by recording the rate of milk intake (in ml per minute). Feeding efficiency increased progressively with gestational age, and also with the duration of feeding experience. Simpson, Schanler and Lau (2002) showed that early introduction of oral feeding (from about 30 weeks gestational age) was associated with earlier progression to full oral feeding, which was attained by 32 or 33 weeks in over half the infants. It has sometimes been assumed that for a preterm infant bottle-feeding must be easier, and perhaps safer, than breast-feeding, but there is no real evidence to support this (McCoy *et al.*, 1988). Meier compared the two types of feeding in a group of five preterm infants who were fed both from the breast and from the bottle, and found evidence that breathing was less disrupted during breast-feeding (Meier, 1988). A subsequent study using a similar design showed a lower average oxygen saturation during bottle-feeds, and a significantly lower saturation in the infants with lung problems, which again suggests that breathing is less disrupted by breast than by bottle-feeding. The infants in this study took significantly less milk during breast-feeds than bottle-feeds. Some advantages have also been demonstrated in allowing infants who are fed by tube to suck non-nutritively on dummies. There is evidence that this reduces the time until the infant can switch to oral feeding, and reduces the time in hospital, although there is no clear evidence that it improves weight gain (Pinelli & Symington, 2005).

In the study of Casaer *et al.* (1982) feeding scores recorded in the first week of feeding in infants born preterm were significantly associated with developmental assessment made using the Bayley Scales at 7 months of corrected age, and poorer feeding soon after birth in these infants is also associated with later feeding problems (Hawdon *et al.*, 2000). A group of 35 infants provided with neonatal intensive care over a three-month period, of whom 28 were born preterm, were assessed at around 36 weeks gestational age using the Neonatal Oral Motor Assessment Scale (NOMAS), which differentiates between normal, immature and aberrant feeding patterns in infancy. The 14 infants with abnormal feeding patterns at 36 weeks were born earlier (more preterm) and were fed by tube for longer. They were more likely to cough when fed at 6 and 12 months, were more likely to be unable to take lumps at 12 months and their parents were more concerned and less likely to enjoy feeding them. In another study persistant feeding problems over the first 15 months were three to four times as common in infants born preterm (Motion, Northstone, Emond & the ALSPAC study team, 2001), and even after they have passed their normal time of delivery, the growth of infants born preterm is generally slower than that of infants born at term (Casey *et al.*, 1991). We shall consider some of these later problems in Chapters 6 and 7.

5   Nutritional deficiencies

5.1   Iron deficiency

There are potentially many types of nutritional deficiency, because food contains many different nutrients. Golden (1995) classifies them into two types. Type 1 nutrients are needed for specific metabolic functions, and deficiencies in these nutrients lead to specific clinical signs that are characteristic of deficiency diseases, such as beri-beri (a result of vitamin B_1 or thiamine deficiency), scurvy (vitamin C or ascorbic acid deficiency), xerophthalmia (vitamin A or retinol deficiency). There are body stores of most of the nutrients in this class. When consumption of the nutrients is inadequate, growth continues but the body stores of the nutrient are used up, leading to the specific clinical signs. These deficiencies can be measured biochemically (for example, by measuring thyroxine in iodine deficiency disorders). Type 2 nutrients, on the other hand, are needed for metabolism in general in all the tissues and organs of the body. These include the components of protein, but also, for example, zinc, potassium, sodium and magnesium. There are no body stores of most of these nutrients except the normal tissues of the body. So rather than leading to specific nutritional deficiencies with specific clinical signs, an inadequate intake of any of these nutrients leads to a generalised growth failure. There are no specific biochemical tests for these deficiencies. They are normally detected by the associated growth failure, measured anthropometrically.

Iron is a Type 1 nutrient, and iron is of key importance physiologically as it is essential for the production of haemoglobin, which transports oxygen from the lungs to the other tissues of the body. Two thirds or more of the iron in the body is functional (i.e. is a component of haemoglobin, myoglobin in muscle cells or of enzymes). But there is also a store of iron, held in reserve, mainly in the liver, in the form of ferritin and haemosiderin. Iron is transferred between cells bound to a protein, transferrin. Some relevant aspects of the physiology of iron in infancy are summarised by Pearson (1990). Infants are born with about 75 mg of iron per kg body weight, about three-quarters of which is contained in haemoglobin in circulating red blood cells. The relatively low partial pressure of oxygen in the arterial blood of infants before birth leads to the production of red cells, so at the end of the pregnancy infants have large numbers of them. At birth there is a rapid rise in arterial oxygen, and red cell synthesis stops. Over the next two months haemoglobin levels fall from an average of 16.5 g/dl to an average of 11.0 g/dl, in what is termed the *physiological anaemia* of infancy, and iron released from the haemoglobin is stored elsewhere in the body, leading to an increase in serum ferritin levels. From about 2 months of age, the synthesis of red cells starts again, and iron moves back out of the iron stores into the newly synthesised haemoglobin. The iron stores last until the infant is about 6 months old, when requirements for further iron must be met from dietary sources. Because infants are growing very rapidly iron requirements are high. Nearly a milligram of iron a day is needed over the second half of the first year.

Human breast milk contains 0.2–0.4 mg/l of iron (Pearson, 1990). Only half of this iron is absorbed, and few infants will take in as much as a litre of breast milk a day. So infants are at risk of iron deficiency from about 6 months of age unless their iron requirements are met from other sources. Unfortified cows' milk has about the same iron content as human milk, but the iron is less well absorbed, and the consumption of cows' milk can lead to blood loss from the gut. Loss of blood from the gut can also result from parasitic infestations, especially with hookworm, though this is more of a problem in older children (Stoltzfus *et al.*, 2001; Watkins and Pollitt, 1997). The absorption of iron in other foods is relatively good if it comes from animal sources (haem iron), but its absorption from most plant sources is poor, though it is enhanced by the simultaneous consumption of ascorbic acid (vitamin C). The second half of the first year is therefore a period over which infants are particularly at risk of iron deficiency.

Iron deficiency leads firstly to a reduction in iron stores, then to an impairment of haemoglobin synthesis and falling haemoglobin levels. When the haemoglobin levels fall below a threshold, *iron deficiency anaemia* is diagnosed. The threshold is defined statistically, in general terms as a value more than two standard deviations below its average value in a healthy population of children of the same age and sex (Yip, 1990), and is different in different age groups. Values for the threshold recommended by the World Health Organisation and others are 110 g/l in children 6–59 months old; 115 g/l from 5 to 11 years; and 120 g/l from 12 to 14 years (ACC/SCN, 2000). In a slightly different approach, used for example by Walter *et al.* (1989), the response to a therapeutic trial of iron supplementation can be used as a criterion for iron deficiency anaemia, on the assumption that if a child's haemoglobin levels increase as a result of iron supplementation iron deficiency must have contributed to their initial low levels. Iron deficiency can be found without anaemia, i.e. without any associated impairment of haemoglobin synthesis or haemoglobin levels. Iron deficiency without anaemia would arise if iron intake was low, leading to a reduction of iron stores, but not sufficiently low to have affected haemoglobin production. Biochemical indicators of such iron deficiency include a decreased ferritin level, decreased transferrin saturation, raised erythrocyte protoporphyrin and a decreased mean red cell volume. Because iron is used in the central nervous system as well as in red blood cells (Pollitt, 1993), adverse psychological effects could in theory be found in iron deficiency without anaemia. And anaemia can also be found without iron deficiency, as a consequence of a range of disorders affecting red blood cells which may result either in a reduced number of cells or in a reduction of their haemoglobin content, in both cases reducing the oxygen carrying capacity of the blood. An example of anaemia without iron deficiency is found in the genetic abnormalities of red blood cells found in sickle cell disease. In theory, anaemia without iron deficiency could also affect a child's psychological development.

The world–wide epidemiology of anaemia has been reviewed by De Maeyer and Adiels-Tegman (1985). The estimated prevalence of anaemia in children, based on a large number of local surveys, was 49% up to 5 years and 36% from 6 to 12 years. In less-developed regions of the world the corresponding figures were 51% and 38% respectively; in more developed regions they were 10% and 12%. The commonest causes of iron deficiency in infancy and early childhood are a poor dietary intake of iron, and loss of blood from the gastrointestinal tract as a result of cows' milk intolerance or gut parasites. In the United States, surveys of large nationally representative samples are conducted by the National Center for Health Statistics Center for Disease Control and Prevention (CDC) in order to assess the health and nutritional status of the American population. The second and third National Health and Nutrition Examination Survey (NHANES II and NHANES III) provide very good data on the prevalence of anaemia in the USA (Looker et al., 1997; Yip, 1990). In NHANES III (carried out 1988–94) in addition to the WHO criteria for anaemia, three indicators of iron deficiency were also examined, transferrin saturation, serum ferritin and erythrocyte protoporphyrin, and to be counted as iron deficient a child had to have abnormal levels in at least two (Looker et al., 1997). By this criterion 9% of children under 2 were iron deficient, and 3% were anaemic. Among 3–11-year-old children 2–3% were iron deficient, and less than 1% anaemic. There is considerable evidence for a progressive reduction in iron deficiency and anaemia in young children in the USA from the early 1970s, as a result of increased breast-feeding, delaying the introduction of cows' milk, the fortification of infant formulas and cereals with iron, and the Special Supplemental Food Program for Women, Infants and Children (WIC).

In the UK, a study by Emond *et al.* (1996) examined the epidemiology of iron deficiency in 8-month-old infants. This study was based on a sample who were part of the Avon Longitudinal Study of Pregnancy and Childhood (ALSPAC), which aimed to enrol all children born in the Bristol and District Health Authority area between 1 April 1991 and 31 December 1992. It successfully enrolled 14,185 infants (over 80% of those born) from which a random sample of 1560 were selected from those born in the previous six months. A heal prick blood sample was taken and haemoglobin and ferritin were measured in the blood. A striking result was that using the WHO recommended criterion for anaemia (a haemoglobin level less than 110 g/l) 23% of the surveyed children were classified as anaemic. Almost equally striking was the complete lack of association between haemoglobin levels in the children and the educational attainments of the mother. It is easy to assume that nutritional problems will be especially widespread in poorer or less-well-educated families. The assumption is often true, but not always.

5.2   The development of iron deficient children

The studies cited above show that even now and even in industrialised countries iron deficiency is remarkably common in infants, and there is evidence from a large number of studies that children with iron deficiency anaemia in the first two years are developmentally delayed when compared with control children (Pollitt, 1993). An example is the study of Walter (1989). This was carried out in Chile, in a geographically defined, predominantly lower-middle-class urban community with stable housing, running water, sewerage and electricity. Previous work demonstrated that anaemia in the area was due to a nutritional iron deficiency, and was not associated with high blood lead levels, which can complicate the interpretation of iron deficiency in some areas because lead can also have adverse effects on development (Walter *et al.*, 1989). The infants in the study were assessed using the Bayley Scales at 1 year of age, blind to their iron status. The average Bayley Scale MDI scores of the anaemic infants were 7 points lower than those of the controls, and the average PDI scores just over 11 points lower. Both differences were highly significant. There were no significant differences between the groups in their weight, length or head circumference at the time of the test, which suggests that the iron deficiency was not associated with a more general state of malnutrition. Nor did they differ in a socio-economic index, in the mother's age or number of pregnancies, in the child's birthweight, in the duration of breast-feeding or in morbidity (illnesses). In a regression analysis examining all these variables simultaneously only the child's height and haemoglobin levels were significantly related to their Bayley Scale scores. Items that the children failed on the Mental Scale related predominantly to the use of language; on the Motor Scale they related predominantly to body control and balance. A comprehensive recent review confirms this association between iron deficiency anaemia and developmental delay in infancy (Grantham-McGregor & Ani, 2001). The effect is quite large, from a half to one standard deviation in size.

Some studies have suggested that iron deficiency *without* anaemia may also affect behavioural development. But in the study of Walter *et al.* (1989), although the anaemic children were developmentally delayed, there was no indication that iron deficient children who were not anaemic were delayed. In a more recent study of Lozoff *et al.* (1987) infants were recruited with graded degrees of iron deficiency and anaemia as assessed from haemoglobin levels and measures of other iron deficiency indicators (ferritin, transferrin saturation and free erythrocyte protoporphyrin levels). An anaemic iron deficient group had haemoglobin levels <105 g/l, low ferritin and transferrin saturation levels and high free erythrocyte protoporphyrin levels. An intermediate iron deficient group had haemoglobin levels between 106 and 119 g/l and the same levels of the other iron deficiency indicators. A non-anaemic group had haemoglobin >120 g/l. Within this non-anaemic group an iron deficient group had abnormally low levels of all three iron status indicators; an iron depleted group had only low ferritin levels; and an iron sufficient group had normal levels of all three (and of haemoglobin). The groups were comparable in other respects. There were no significant differences in birthweight or in length, head circumference, weight for length or arm circumference at enrolment. As assessed using the Bayley Scales in the second year of life, it was only the anaemic, iron deficient group who were developmentally delayed. Their average score was 96.6, compared with 104.6 in all the other groups combined. There was no evidence for any delay in any of the non-anaemic groups, or, indeed, in children in the anaemic group who were only mildly anaemic (haemoglobin >100 g/l).

A similar finding has been reported by Sherriff *et al.* in the ALSPAC study in the UK (Sherriff *et al.*, 2001). Haemoglobin levels were measured in a representative sample of children in the Avon population at 8, 12 and 18 months, and behavioural development assessed at 18 months using the Griffiths Scales. Potential confounders taken into account were maternal parity, gender, ethnicity, whether the child was breast-fed, smoking during pregnancy and the educational attainments of the mother. Haemoglobin levels at 8 months were significantly associated with Griffiths Scale scores, but there were only associations of borderline statistical significance at 12 months and none at 18 months. At 8 months the only clear effect was on the locomotor scale; there was no association with the overall development quotient. On the locomotor scale scores increased systematically up to haemoglobin levels in the 96–100 g/l range, after which there was no further improvement, with mean scores no higher in the 101–05, 106–10 or 110–49 ranges. As noted above, using the WHO cut-off point for anaemia (Hb < 110 g/l), 23% of the infants in this population were classified as anaemic at 8 months. But examining these behavioural outcomes, only about 4% of the children had haemoglobin levels sufficiently low to affect their locomotor scores.

These studies concerned behavioural development in the first two years of life, but there is some evidence that adverse effects of iron deficiency anaemia early in life are still found in later childhood. Lozoff and colleagues followed up the children first studied in infancy (Lozoff *et al.*, 1987) after 5 and then 10 years (Lozoff *et al.*, 2000; Lozoff, Jimenez & Wolf, 1991). At these follow-ups the growth and iron status of the children was excellent, but the children still showed cognitive deficits associated with iron deficiency measured in infancy when they were 5 years old. At 10 years, after adjustment for background variables, including the mother's IQ, there were (non-significant) differences of about two IQ points compared with controls, and significant differences in attainment in arithmetic and reading, and on a perceptual and a spatial memory task.

A number of different mechanisms might underlie the effect of iron deficiency on development. Lack of iron could affect neurotransmitter metabolism in the CNS. One suggestion (Pollitt, 1993) is that a reduction in dopamine D2 receptors in the cortex that depend on iron alters dopamine dependent neurotransmission and so impairs cognitive function. Alternatively, iron deficiency might interfere with myelination in the developing brain. Roncagliolo *et al.* (1998) review the evidence for this effect of iron deficiency. Much of it is based on studies in rats. The localisation of iron in the brain is similar in rats and humans, with particular concentration in the basal ganglia, and in both species the period of myelination is primarily postnatal (Felt & Lozoff, 1996). In rats transferrin and iron move into the brain immediately after birth. The iron concentrates in oligodendrocytes, which need iron for myelin production. There are lasting deficiencies in both brain iron and myelination in rats that are made iron deficient early in development. Roncagliolo *et al.* ingeniously sought direct evidence of altered myelination in iron deficient human infants by examining auditory brainstem evoked potentials (electrophysiologically recorded brainstem responses to auditory stimuli). They did indeed find that the central conduction time for auditory stimuli was longer in infants anaemic at 6 months of age, indicating a slower nerve conduction velocity of the kind one would expect with delayed myelination. A similar effect was subsequently shown in visual system pathways (Algarin *et al.*, 2003). However, anaemia could also have indirect effects, as suggested in the 'functional isolation' hypothesis. According to this hypothesis, which was originally put forward in relation to protein-energy malnutrition (Chavéz & Martinez, 1975; Levitsky & Barnes, 1972), malnutrition leads to changes in the child's emotional state, attention or activity levels which results in their seeking less stimulation from the environment, and this in its turn leads to their eliciting less stimulation from their parents or other people caring for them. In relation to iron deficiency, there is direct evidence from two different studies that children who are anaemic stay closer to their mothers than children who are not (Lozoff *et al.*, 1998; Lozoff, Klein & Prabucki, 1986).

All the studies dealt with above are concerned with naturally occurring associations between iron deficiency and behavioural development. They necessarily rely on statistical control for other variables that might be related both to iron deficiency and also to delayed development (for example, lead intake or a poorer family environment). But, in addition, a considerable number of therapeutic trials in which children have been treated with iron have been reported, and are incisively reviewed by Grantham-McGregor and Ani (2001). Trials in children under 2 years old with a short intervention period (less than 15 days) have generally not shown a beneficial effect of treatment. Haemoglobin levels in infants with iron deficiency anaemia are only restored to normal after about 8 weeks of treatment, so these short periods of therapy would not reverse the infants' anaemia, though they would make additional iron available to central nervous system cells (Pollitt, 1993). Longer-term trials that would reverse iron deficiency anaemia, with treatment for periods of 2–6 months, show a more mixed pattern of results. Double blind placebo controlled RCTs provide the best kind of data, and two studies of children under 2 were of this kind (Auckett *et al.*, 1986; Idjradinata & Pollitt, 1993).

Auckett *et al.* (1986) screened 470 children 17–19 months old through child health clinics in Birmingham. Using the WHO criterion, 26% of the children were anaemic. Eight (2%) were severely anaemic, with a haemoglobin concentration below 80 g/l, and these were treated immediately. The other less-severely anaemic children were divided randomly into two groups. One group was treated with an iron supplement and vitamin C, which improves the absorption of iron, and the other with vitamin C alone. Testing was carried out blind to the child's group, using items from the Denver Developmental Screening Test (Frankenburg & Dodds, 1967), before and after treatment. The iron treatment increased haemoglobin levels and improved weight gain when compared with the placebo treatment. Overall, the rate of behavioural development was no greater in the iron treated than in the control group, though some evidence was found that children in the treated group were more likely to show the fastest rates of development, especially if their initially low haemoglobin levels increased by at least 20 g/l.

The Idjradinata and Pollitt (1993) study was carried out in Bandung in Indonesia. Infants attending a child health clinic at 12–18 months of age were classified into one of three iron status groups. The iron deficiency anaemia (IDA) group had haemoglobin ≤105 g/l, transferrin saturation ≤10% and serum ferritin ≤12 µg/l. The non-anaemic iron deficiency group had the same transferrin saturation and ferritin levels but normal haemoglobin levels (≥120 g/l). The iron sufficiency group had normal levels of all these indicators. Before any treatment, the children were all tested and the Bayley Scale scores of the IDA group were significantly lower than those of infants in the other two groups. Infants in all three categories were divided at random into a group treated with iron (ferrous sulphate syrup) and a group treated with a placebo syrup. Iron treatment significantly increased haemoglobin levels in the IDA group, and also, to a smaller extent, in the non-anaemic iron deficiency group. The Bayley Scale Scores of the IDA group were significantly improved by the iron treatment, which entirely eliminated the adverse effect of iron deficiency. The iron treatment did not improve scores in either of the non-anaemic groups.

In older children and adults there are more controlled trials of this kind. Grantham-McGregor and Ani (2001) summarise results from nine, in which significantly beneficial treatment effects were found in four, and suggestive effects in three others. There was no effect of iron treatment in the remaining two. Two of the studies (Groner *et al.*, 1986; Lynn & Harland, 1998) examined effects of iron treatment in adolescents. Lynn and Harland (1998) sampled about 400 12–16-year-old children attending seven comprehensive schools in a single city in north-east England. Their IQs were determined using Raven's Standard Progressive Matrices, and their iron status measured using assays for haemoglobin and serum ferritin. They were then divided into two groups matched for age, sex and IQ. One group was supplemented with iron over a 16 week period, using tablets of iron combined with vitamin C. The other group was given a placebo which looked the same. After the period of supplementation, the children were tested again with the Progressive Matrices. The study was conducted double blind, with the contents of the tablets known only to the manufacturer until the end of the trial. Overall, the iron supplementation had no significant effect on IQ as assessed using the Progressive Matrices. When the children were divided into three groups, however, based on their initial ferritin levels, there was a significantly greater rise in IQ in the iron supplemented group, who improved by about 3 IQ points, while the low ferritin controls lost about 3 IQ points. As Grantham-McGregor (2001) points out, it is theoretically possible that this could have been a beneficial effect of the vitamin C rather than the iron. Groner et al. (1986) recruited 38 young women in the early stage of pregnancy, and determined their iron status. They were randomised into two groups. Both groups were treated with prenatal vitamins, in one of the groups with an added iron supplement, over a period of one month. A number of psychometric tests were used; significant differences in favour of the iron treated group were found in one memory test and one subsection of a test of attention deficits. There was, unfortunately, a substantial loss of participants before the psychological testing (13, 10 of whom were in the control group).

One approach to iron deficiency in children would be to routinely supplement the children in a community with iron over the period in which iron deficiency would be most likely to occur. A number of studies have examined the effects of supplementation of this kind; examples are Moffatt et al. (1994) and Lozoff et al. (1997). In the first of these studies (Moffatt et al., 1994) 283 healthy bottle-fed infants from low-income families were randomly assigned to two groups, one of which was fed with a standard infant formula and the other with an iron-fortified formula. Testing used the Bayley Scales at 6, 9, 12 and 15 months. As one would expect, given the proper randomisation of groups of this size, they were closely similar on such background variables as the mother's age and education, parity and gestational age, and also on the HOME scores. (The HOME inventory was used to assess aspects of the child's home environment related to their intellectual development.) The iron-treated group were significantly improved on all the measures of iron status used. They were also significantly more advanced on the PDI scale of the Bayley Scales, but not on the MDI scale. Even on the PDI, the difference was transient, and was no longer statistically significant at 15 months of age. In the second study (Lozoff et al., 1997) 944 Chilean infants were randomly assigned to a supplemented and a non-supplemented group over the period 6–12 months. Anaemia at 12 months was reduced by the supplementation from 24% to 4%, and iron deficiency from 49% to 15%, but there were no significant differences in the MDI or PDI scores, which were virtually identical in the two groups.

General programmes of supplementation could not be justified on the basis of these results, though they might be justified on other grounds.

But the evidence for adverse developmental effects of iron deficiency is certainly strong enough to justify efforts to reduce its prevalence by improving the diets of young children, though it has proved frustratingly difficult to establish unambiguous effects of iron deficiency on psychological development, especially in the long term, in spite of the high quality of much of the research in this area.

5.3   Protein-energy malnutrition

Iron deficiency is a single nutrient deficiency. The term *malnutrition* as it is more generally understood usually refers primarily to protein-energy malnutrition (PEM) which reflects a generally low food intake. But as we saw in Chapter 1, food intake itself is extremely difficult to measure accurately, so in practice protein-energy malnutrition is usually detected in children by measuring one of the most obvious effects of low food intake, poor growth. Height (or length) and weight are measures of growth which have been widely used in the assessment of the nutritional status of children and are relatively easy to make. So in practice protein-energy malnutrition is identified by reference to a child's height or weight. But it needs to be borne in mind that children who are malnourished by this criterion may be short of micronutrients (iron or zinc, for example) as well as of sources of protein or energy (Pollitt, 1995).

   How does one decide from these anthropometric measures whether a child is malnourished? To do so one has to compare the height or weight of a child with the heights and weights of well-nourished children of the same age, and this involves comparison with children in a reference population. In recent years the reference population most commonly used internationally has been the one described by the US National Center for Health Statistics (Hamill *et al.*, 1979). Although it was based on American children, it has been recommended for international use by the World Health Organisation (WHO, 1986). The international use of a single reference population presupposes that well-nourished children will grow in comparable ways in all or most populations, and that the wide differences in growth rate in different populations are mainly environmental in origin. While this is to some extent an open question (Cole, 1993) it is probably generally at least approximately true (Habicht *et al.*, 1974). It is important not to confuse differences in growth rates between different populations with differences in final attained heights. Final attained heights are also determined by the timing of puberty. Children whose growth rate is poor, in any population, are usually malnourished.

   Heights and weights differ with the child's age, so the comparisons used are specific to each age and are referred to as height-for-age and weight-for-age. Separate references are used for males and females. Taller children weigh more, so a measure of weight adjusted for height (weight-for-height) is also in common use. Weight-for-age is largely accounted for by height-for-age and weight-for-height (WHO, 1986), so the measures of nutritional status that are usually used are height-for-age and weight-for-height. Children below an agreed threshold for these have been called 'stunted' and 'wasted' respectively (Waterlow *et al.*, 1977). Alternative and more everyday terms are 'short' and 'thin', though these do not carry the same evaluative implications (a stunted child is not just short, but shorter than they should be). Stunting (assessed by height-for-age) tends to reflect long-term chronic malnutrition, while wasting (assessed by weight-for-height) tends to reflect short-term malnutrition, as in famine conditions.

At any age an anthropometric measurement has an average and a spread of values around the average. The average is generally specified as the median or the mean, and the spread as a set of centiles or as a standard deviation. Height has a distribution close to the Gaussian (normal) so if we are dealing with height the median and the mean are the same and the standard deviation can be used to generate the centiles. A child's weight or height can be related to the reference population by expressing it as a centile ('weight on the 5th centile') or, equivalently, in standard deviation (SD or z score) units ('weight SD or z score − 1.65'). An advantage of centiles is that they are more readily comprehensible to most people, and for this reason they are commonly used in clinical practice; a disadvantage is that they become difficult to use in the extremes of the distribution (where centiles are below 1 or greater than 99) and are less easy to handle statistically. A standard deviation or z score is the 'distance' a child is from the average in SD units (−1 SD, −2 SD etc.), and 1 SD identifies the same proportion above and below the average if the distribution is normal. Not all anthropometric characteristics have a normal distribution. Weight generally doesn't, for example, because there tend to be small number of very heavy people with no corresponding very light people. But SD scores can still be used for these characteristics, though the procedures involved have to take into account the exact shape of the distributions (Cole, 1990). Contemporary studies that classify children into groups based on anthropometric indicators tend to use standard deviation scores to do so, following the recommendations of Waterlow *et al.* (1977). A height more than 2 SD below the mean of the reference population (i.e. < -2 SD) is commonly used as a criterion for 'stunting', and a weight-for-height more than 2 SD below the mean as a criterion for 'wasting' (Waterlow *et al.*, 1977).

The relatively uniform use of these criteria across different studies allows the examination of trends in malnutrition over time. A recent analysis of 241 nationally representative surveys of stunting in children, for example, examined its current prevalence and trends in its prevalence over the period since 1980, with projections to 2005 (De Onis, Frongillo & Blössner, 2000). The standard definition of stunting was used, a length for age more than 2 SD below the average of the NCHS/WHO reference population (WHO, 1995). Overall, the estimated prevalence of stunting in all developing countries for the year 2000 was 32.5%. This has dropped steadily from 47.1% in 1980, showing a considerable improvement in the nutrition of children. All regions of the world were improving over this period, with the exception of East Africa, which showed an increase in stunting (from 46.5% to 48.5%). This area includes Djibouti, Ethiopia, Madagascar, Rwanda and Zambia. In spite of the general improvement, overall, the estimated number of stunted children in the year 2000 was still 182 million.

Protein-energy malnutrition, then, is still a major health problem in children. Longitudinal studies show that malnutrition as assessed anthropometrically is clearly associated with later mortality. Figure 5.1, for example, shows the relationship between a child's weight-for-age and their subsequent risk of death in six longitudinal studies in the first five years (Pelletier, Frongillo & Habicht, 1993). Even mild malnutrition is associated with a greater subsequent mortality. Epidemiological evidence from 53 developing countries suggests that over half the deaths of children under 5 in these countries are due to malnutrition, acting synergistically with infectious diseases (Pelletier et al., 1995). Although the risk associated with severe malnutrition is obviously greater, mild to moderate malnutrition is much more widespread so most of this increased mortality (over 80%) is attributable to mild to moderate malnutrition.

There is also evidence that malnutrition has adverse effects on intellectual development. As with iron deficiency, the evidence is mostly observational. An important early study examined the intellectual outcomes of early malnutrition in a group of Korean infants adopted by 3 years of age by American parents (Winick, Meyer & Harris, 1975). The children in the study were adopted through the Holt Adoption Service in Korea, and were all female and born at term, with no physical defect or chronic illness at the time of adoption. A malnourished group, below the 3rd centile for weight and height at the time they came into the care of the adoption agency, was contrasted with a well nourished group, who were at or above the 25th centile, and a moderately nourished group intermediate between the two; 110 children (equal numbers from each group) had their IQ recorded at school. The average IQ of the malnourished group was 102,

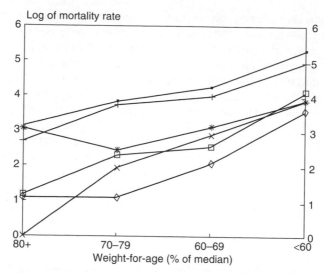

Figure 5.1 Malnutrition and subsequent mortality in infants and young children (Pelletier *et al.*, 1993). The data are the (natural) logarithms of mortality (deaths per 1000 children per year) and come from six different studies in Tanzania, Papua New Guinea, Bangladesh and India. Reproduced from the *American Journal of Public Health*, *83*, 1130–3. Copyright 1993, with permission from the American Public Health Association.

in the intermediate group it was 106 and in the well-nourished group it was 112. Similar differences were found in school achievement scores. Inevitably a study of this kind has some limitations, and follow-up was restricted to about 70% of the children. The adoptive homes were primarily middle class, but other details of their characteristics are not available, though the authors indicate that the distribution of the children into their adoptive homes was 'entirely at random'. The most interesting feature of the results is that the effects of early malnutrition apparently persisted even though the children had all been brought up in relatively prosperous homes from an early age, and even though the mean IQ for all the children was actually above average.

A more recent example of an observational study examining the relationship between nutrition and early intellectual development is an investigation of the functional effects of mild to moderate malnutrition in rural Kenya (Sigman *et al.*, 1991; Sigman *et al.*, 1989; Sigman *et al.*, 1988). The study population were Kiembu-speaking Embu families. They hold land and farm on a small scale, producing food for the household and cash crops. Their homes are small mud huts with two rooms and thatch or tin roofs. Data were reported on 110 children, who were observed and tested between 18 and 30 months of age. Each month throughout this period food intake was measured for two days principally by direct weighing, combined with some maternal recall of foods eaten overnight. In addition, performance abilities were assessed in both parents using Raven's Progressive Matrices, and their reading and writing skills were tested. A locally developed questionnaire to assess socio-economic status was administered (it correlated quite well with the local Embu subchief's assessment of the ranking of the households). The length and weight of the children were measured at 30 months, and their development assessed using a locally modified version of the Bayley Scales. In addition, interactions between the child and other members of the household were recorded by direct observation, as was the child's functional and symbolic play. The final report from this series examined the children when they were 5 years old. The children were assessed with a verbal meaning test that used pictures previously used in East Africa, and with a non-verbal test (Raven's Matrices). Evidence that scores of these tests were stable over time and related to school examination success was provided by a previous study in older Embu children. As one would expect, the five-year cognitive scores were significantly related to a wide range of variables. Significant associations with nutritional variables were found with animal protein and fat intake over the 24–30 month period and with length and weight at 30 months. Significant associations with non-nutritional variables were found with SES, parental IQ and literacy and with early schooling. In simultaneous analyses using regression methods both SES and animal protein intake remained significantly related to five-year cognitive scores.

A study examining the relationship between malnutrition in the first two years of life and subsequent intellectual development over a longer period comes from the Cebu Longitudinal Health and Nutrition Survey (Mendez & Adair, 1999), a community-based prospective study of a 1-year birth cohort in the area surrounding the second largest and fastest growing city in the Philippines. Data on the nutrition and growth of the children were collected every two months for the first two years, and the children were followed up when they were 8 and 11 years old. This was a large-scale study, with data available on more than 2000 children. A locally developed non-verbal intelligence test (the Philippines Non-Verbal Intelligence Test) was administered at both ages, and an English and Mathematics Achievement Test at 11. An extensive set of covariates was taken into account, including household income, the education of the mother and father, parity, the number of younger siblings, and the schooling history of the child. A number of different measures related to the child's linear growth were used. Children with an early height-for-age more than 2 SD below the WHO/NCHS median were identified as stunted. Severe stunting was an SD score below -3. To examine the timing of stunting, the six-month interval in which the child first met the criterion for stunting was identified (0–6 months, 6–12 months, 12–18 months or 18–24 months). Significant intellectual deficits at 8 years were found with both moderate and severe stunting early in life; deficits were also found at 11 years, but restricted to children with severe early stunting.

In a second recent longitudinal study with a long follow-up (Liu *et al.*, 2003; Liu *et al.*, 2004) malnutrition of a number of kinds was assessed by means of clinical signs rather than by measures of weight and height. The signs were angular stomatitis, kwashiorkor, sparse, thin hair and anaemia. The first of these is principally a reflection of riboflavin (vitamin B_2) deficiency with some contribution from other vitamin deficiencies. The second is principally due to protein deficiency, and the third to protein-energy malnutrition. Anaemia of course is a reflection of iron deficiency: the criterion in this study was a haemoglobin level below 85 g/l. The study involved following up a birth cohort of 1795 children born in two towns on Mauritius in 1969–70. At 3 years of age about a quarter of the children (22.6%) had at least one indicator of malnutrition. Cognitive abilities were measured at 3 and 11 years of age, and indices of psychosocial adversity were also collected at both ages. The results showed significantly lower IQ at both 3 years and 11 years of age in the malnourished children; the difference was about 5 IQ points at 11. All four indicators of malnutrition were related to cognitive outcomes, but the most consistent effects were with anaemia. Deficits in reading and school performance and on tests involving visuomotor tracking, motor speed, attention and working memory were also apparent. These deficits were systematically related to the number of indicators of malnutrition, with more indicators predicting greater deficits, and remained significant after adjustment for 9 indicators of social adversity at age 3 and 14 indicators at age 11 (though no information is given on the size of the effect of malnutrition after adjustment for these indicators). The children in this study were recruited at 3 years of age, and its main limitation is the lack of information on prenatal variables. Externalising behaviour (hyperactivity, aggression and related behaviour) was also assessed in this study and was also found to be related to malnutrition, being more prevalent at 8, 11 and 17 years of age in children with more indicators of malnutrition (Liu *et al.*, 2004). This effect, however, was mediated principally via the effects of malnutrition on intellectual ability.

A wide variety of candidate explanations is available to explain the cognitive effects associated with childhood malnutrition. The first possibility must be that the adverse effects are not in fact a result of malnutrition itself, but of other characteristics of the children's family backgrounds that are associated with malnutrition. Malnutrition is often associated with poverty and other forms of adversity, and it is extremely hard to control statistically for all the relevant covariates (it is hard to know what they all are, let alone to measure them all reliably). The second possibility is that malnutrition may have a direct (perhaps structural) effect on the CNS of the growing child, of such a kind as to adversely affect their later intellectual performance. Effects of malnutrition on brain growth and development are reviewed by Dickerson, Merat and Yusuf (1982). There certainly are such effects, though Simeon and Grantham-McGregor point out that 'although biochemical and structural changes have been found in the brains of severely malnourished children who die, it is not clear if they persist in children who survive' (Simeon & Grantham-McGregor, 1990). A third possibility is that parents may respond more to a child's size than to their age, treating growth delayed children as if they are younger than they are (Pollitt et al., 1993), and so fail to provide in an age-appropriate way for their intellectual development. A fourth possibility, as with iron deficiency, is 'functional isolation'. Malnutrition may reduce activity levels, for example (Pollitt et al., 1993; Simeon & Grantham-McGregor, 1990), and reduced activity may reduce learning by reducing interactions with the environment (Pollitt et al., 1993; Strupp & Levitsky, 1995).

There is some direct evidence that malnutrition is associated with reduced activity levels (Grantham-McGregor, Stewart & Powell, 1991). In this study a group of children hospitalised with severe malnutrition in the first two years was compared with a group hospitalised for other reasons. Data were collected by direct observation of the child's behaviour, although the actual observation time was quite limited (5 minutes). The malnourished children were only about half as active as the control children on admission to hospital during unstructured observation when the children were alone in their cribs. During structured observations, in which they were provided with toys, they handled fewer toys, played less and were less exploratory. In a study of this relationship in the Gambia, Lawrence et al. (1991) used time-sampled activity diaries over the period from early in the morning until the child fell asleep for the night. Every two and a half minutes an electronically generated signal alerted the observer to note down the child's activity at the time. The children were divided into three groups by age (6, 12 and 18 months) and into two by nutritional status. At 6 months the less-well-nourished children were significantly less active than the better nourished children; differences at later ages, though in the same direction, were not statistically significant.

The best test of the functional isolation hypothesis to date is by Gardner *et al.* (1995). These authors used direct observation over extended periods in the child's home to compare activity levels in different groups of children up to 2 years old. They examined a stunted and a non-stunted group. Children in the stunted group were randomly assigned to one of four treatment groups, provided with psychosocial stimulation or nutritional supplementation alone, or the two combined or neither. The group that were not stunted were significantly more active at enrolment (about 19 months of age). But they were not more active six months later, and changes in the child's activity did not predict changes in scores on the Griffiths Mental Development Scales. Control children who were not supplemented were just as active as the supplemented children (and the non-stunted children) after the six-month intervention period.

Studies using nutritional supplementation of this kind have thrown further light on the general associations between malnutrition and later intellectual development. In a house to house survey in most of the poor neighbourhoods of Kingston, Jamaica, Grantham-McGregor and her colleagues (1991) identified children 9–24 months old whose lengths were more than 2 SD below the mean of the NCHS reference population. The 129 children were stratified by age and sex, and allocated using a quasi-random procedure to one of four groups, a supplemented group, a group given developmental stimulation, a group who were both supplemented and given developmental stimulation, and a control group. The supplemented group were allocated 1 kg of a milk-based formula, sufficient to provide 3.15MJ of energy and 20 g of protein per day. Cornmeal and skimmed milk were also provided for the rest of the family, to try to avoid the sharing of the child's supplement with the other family members, which is a commonly encountered problem in studies of this kind. The group given developmental stimulation were visited for one hour a week by community health aides, who taught the mothers how to play with their children in ways that would promote their development, using homemade toys.

The nutritional supplementation significantly improved the growth of the children over the course of the study, as measured by greater increases in length, weight and head circumference than were found in the control group or in the group given developmental stimulation (Walker *et al.*, 1991). The development of the children was assessed using the Griffiths Mental Development Scales, modified for use in Jamaica (Grantham-McGregor *et al.*, 1991). At enrolment, each of the stunted groups had significantly lower Griffiths scores than the non-stunted group. The results of the intervention are shown in Figure 5.2. Both nutritional supplementation and psychosocial stimulation improved development.

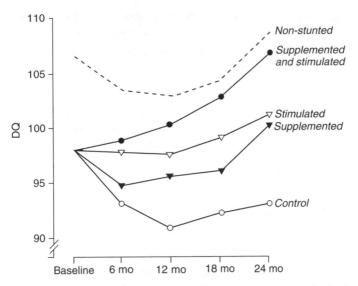

Figure 5.2 Effects of nutritional supplementation and psychosocial stimulation in 'stunted' children (Grantham-McGregor *et al.*, 1991). The development quotient (DQ) is adjusted for initial age, and for initial score in the four stunted groups. Reproduced from *The Lancet*, *338*, 1–5. Copyright 1991, with permission from Elsevier.

The two together had an additive effect leading to the greatest improvement of all. The growth of the children was investigated a further four years after the intervention, when the children were 7–8 years old (Walker *et al.*, 1996). At this age 122 of the original 129 children (95%) were located, a remarkably complete follow-up given that the study was conducted in a poor neighbourhood in Jamaica. At this age there were no significant differences between the four groups on any measure of growth (height, head circumference, weight, arm circumference or triceps or subscapular skinfold thickness). The cognitive attainments of the children were examined at the same age (Grantham-McGregor *et al.*, 1997), using a wide range of tests, including IQ tests and a number of other verbal and performance tests, several tests of learning and memory, achievement tests assessing reading, spelling and arithmetic and a test of fine motor coordination. Factor analysis of the tests led to analysis based on three factors, a factor reflecting general cognitive function, a perceptual-motor factor and a factor reflecting long-term semantic memory. There was no significant effect of supplementation in early childhood on any of the factors. The children were studied yet again when they were 11–12 years old (Walker *et al.*, 2000), using a range of different measures including an IQ test (the WISC-R), measures of visual reasoning ability, language comprehension and other verbal abilities and a range of other neuropsychological measures. Although growth restriction was associated with lower scores on almost all the measures, again no significant beneficial effect of nutritional supplementation was found.

As with iron deficiency, studies on protein-energy malnutrition provide reasonably consistent evidence for adverse developmental effects that endure at least into later childhood. And as with iron deficiency, the evidence is not entirely beyond question, as this very carefully conducted study shows. An excellent specialist review deals with these issues in more detail (Simeon & Grantham-McGregor, 1990).

5.4   Secular trends in intelligence

Over the last half century there have been very striking gains in measured intelligence in many industrialised countries. This fact has been hidden from view by the regular restandardisation of intelligence tests, so that their mean has remained approximately 100. It was first brought to light by Flynn (1987), who has recently provided an updated review of the topic in a book published under the auspices of the American Psychological Association (Flynn, 1998). Data from 20 different nations each show large gains in IQ over time. They include most European and other English-speaking nations, Israel and urban Brazil, Japan and urban China. Research published since this review shows a comparable effect in a rural area of Kenya (Daley et al., 2003). Indirect evidence suggests that these improvements probably date from the early period of industrialisation. The best direct evidence comes more recently from comprehensive assessment of nationally representative samples, either of school children or of military personnel. The data are strongest in respect of tests of 'fluid' intelligence, such as the Raven Progressive Matrices. Examples of the change using matrices tests are shown in Figure 5.3. The median rise per generation (30 years) is about 18 IQ points. Similar results have been found with data from Wechsler performance tests. Tests of verbal IQ have generally shown a trend in the same direction, but averaging about 9 IQ points (Flynn, 1998).

It is not easy to be certain exactly what a secular trend of this kind means. Flynn has emphasised the importance of identifying the 'package of enhanced cognitive skills' that have improved over time as IQ scores have risen (Flynn, 1998). There is, unfortunately, very little evidence concerning secular trends in other measures of intellectual skills. A good case has been made that the quality of high-level chess players has improved over the same period (Howard, 2005). A recent study has

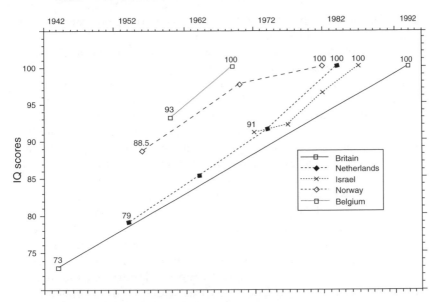

Figure 5.3 Secular trends in intelligence in five countries (Flynn, 1998). The data for Britain come from the standardisation and restandardisation of the Raven Progressive Matrices, and for other countries from comparable military samples of persons of the same age taking equivalent tests (derivatives of the Raven). Reproduced from *The Rising Curve: Long-term Gains in IQ and Related Measures*, ed. U. Neisser, American Psychological Association, Washington DC. Copyright 1998, with permission.

investigated a possibility that there may be a similar secular trend in inspection time (Nettelbeck & Wilson, 2004). In inspection time studies two vertical lines of slightly different length are presented simultaneously, and the task is to detect whether the shorter is on the right or the left hand side within a very short time restricted by a backward masking stimulus. Inspection time provides a measure of central nervous system processing speed that is reliably correlated with psychometric intelligence (Grudnik & Kranzler, 2001; Nettelbeck, 2001). In 2001 Nettelback and Wilson re-examined inspection time in children in a school in which it had initially been examined in 1981 (i.e. after an interval of 20 years). Children of the same age were used, and the same apparatus and procedure were used as in the original 1981 study. The children's IQ was measured using the Peabody Picture Vocabulary test, in the same form as initially used in 1981. Comparing the two cohorts there was an increase in the estimated IQ scores (of almost 5 points) over the 20-year period, but there was no significant decrease in average inspection time.

Although the secular trend in IQ is usually and reasonably attributed to changes in the environment, Mingroni (2004) has suggested that a purely genetic mechanism, heterosis, might have led to the change. Heterosis or 'hybrid vigour' increases when the local genetic variability between small human populations (towns and villages) is reduced as a result of demographic changes that reduce reproductive isolation. Reduced reproductive isolation increases heterozygocity, and there is some direct evidence that outbreeding is associated with higher IQ (Mingroni, 2004). Although this hypothesis has not been tested systematically, it makes reasonably precise predictions that should be testable in principle. Lynn (1990) has argued, however, that the most likely explanation of this secular trend is environmental, and that it derives from improved nutrition. The first line of evidence for this is that the secular trend in intelligence has generally accompanied a secular trend in height. The increase in height is most plausibly attributed to improved nutrition, and there is, indeed, evidence that poor nutrition was widespread in economically developed countries in the 1920s and 1930s (Lynn, 1990). Secondly, comparable trends have been found for head circumference. Head size has been shown to be correlated with measured intelligence in a large number of studies; results from 54 samples are collated in Vernon et al. and show a pooled correlation between the two of about .2 (Vernon et al., 2000). Lynn notes that there has been a larger increase in visual-spatial (performance) IQ than in verbal IQ, and also suggests that visual-spatial abilities are more sensitive to nutrition.

Another possibility is that it is changes in schooling, rather than in nutrition, that underlie the secular trend in IQ. Data on the trend in young children before they reach school age would be of particular value here, but the data available on young children are very limited. There is some evidence for a secular trend similar to the trend in IQ in motor development (Capute et al., 1985), and in head circumference, which is strongly related to brain weight (Cooke et al., 1977; Ounstead, Moar & Scott, 1985). A similar improving trend has also been found in data collected during the course of a revision of the Griffiths scales in children under 2 years of age (Hanson, Smith & Hume, 1985). Over the period between the first standardisation in 1947–51 and data collection for the revision in 1978–82, the mean score increased from 99.7 to 110.2. Differences in the samples were carefully considered but did not provide an explanation of this increase. It is interesting to note that the average difference was quite consistent across infants of different ages and was clearly present in the first month of life. This might suggest a prenatal rather than a postnatal nutritional effect – it certainly does not suggest an effect of changed educational practices. Also consistent with a nutritional cause is evidence suggesting that the secular trend has particularly affected the lower part of the IQ distribution (Colom, Lluis-Font & Andrés-Pueyo, 2004; Lynn & Hampson, 1986; Teasdale & Owen, 1989). The Kenyan study (Daley *et al.*, 2003) referred to above was carried out over a 14-year period from 1984, and in addition to scores on Raven's Progressive Matrices extensive data on other changes in the community were collected, including nutritional data, though different methods of collection were used in 1984 and 1998; at the first time point the nutritional data were collected by direct observation and weighing of the ingredients and the food intake, and at the second by 24-hr recall and food frequency measures. Overall intake of energy and protein was reported to increase over the period of the study, but iron deficiency and anaemia also increased. Competing non-nutritional explanations were also evaluated. Family size decreased, but whether a child was first-born was unrelated to test scores in either cohort. Parental education and literacy increased over the period of the study. Testing was carried out four months after the children started school, so school-based educational experiences were unlikely to have accounted for the rise in test scores in this population.

In good quality data the trends over time are remarkably similar over different decades and in different countries, as illustrated in Figure 5.3. This makes the trend over time particularly difficult to explain, as variation in the trend is necessary before associations between differences in the trend and differences in environmental variables over time or place can be established. If the effect is (purely) nutritional in origin, it is, perhaps, surprising that IQ has increased at such a similar rate over such a long period: one might have expected at least some levelling out of the trend in recent years, at least in affluent countries (Martorell, 1998; Teasdale & Owen, 1989).

6   Nutritional aspects of some physical conditions

6.1   Phenylketonuria

At the end of Chapter 3 we considered the effects of diarrhoeal diseases on food intake and growth. Diarrhoeal diseases are usually temporary, and can affect any child. In this chapter we will consider nutritional problems associated with some long-term illnesses or disabilities. Almost all long-term illnesses and disabilities have nutritional aspects to them and the examples considered here are just examples. I have chosen these examples because they illustrate important general principles (PKU), because nutritional aspects are central to the disorder (cystic fibrosis), because there can be a tendency to overlook disorders that are found only in minority ethnic groups (sickle cell disease) or because they relate to other problems dealt with in other chapters (cerebral palsy). But mainly I have chosen them because interesting and important research is available on them.

Phenylketonuria (PKU) has been described as a classic example of a genetic disorder (Scriver & Clow, 1980a; 1980b). It is inherited as an autosomal recessive trait. As a recessive trait, PKU develops in the child only if they have two copies of a gene for the condition. If both parents are heterozygotes (i.e. if they each have a single copy of the gene) one in four of their children, on average, will have two copies and so will develop the disorder. Children with a single copy are carriers, and they are only slightly different from children without any PKU genes. However, these slight differences may be enough to provide some reproductive advantage to the individuals concerned in some environments (Woolf, 1986). The incidence of PKU is high in the Irish and in Western Scotland, and quite high in other Northern European populations and in white Americans. It is rare in populations in the Mediterranean and outside Europe, and relatively rare in African Americans. This distribution of PKU in different populations and its apparently Celtic origins have led to one plausible suggestion for a reproductive advantage to PKU heterozygotes. Heterozygous women in Ireland and Western Scotland have a lower

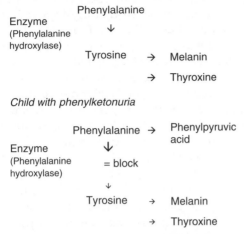

Figure 6.1 Metabolic pathways in phenylketonuria. Phenylalanine is taken in as a component of food, and converted to tyrosine by phenylalanine hydroxylase. In children with phenylketonuria, who lack this enzyme, phenylalanine intake leads to high blood levels of phenylpyruvic acid.

spontaneous abortion rate, perhaps because the heterozygous condition protects them against the effects of ochratoxin A, a toxin of fungal origin (Woolf, 1986). Ochratoxin A is most commonly found as a contaminant of barley and wheat in Northern Europe, unlike the aflatoxins, which need higher temperatures and are more commonly found as contaminants of maize, peanuts and oilseeds in tropical countries (Spooner & Roberts, 2005).

In its classical form, phenylketonuria is caused by a deficiency in the enzyme phenylalanine hydroxylase, resulting from an abnormal form of the phenylalanine hydroxylase gene on chromosome 12 (Figure 6.1). There are many variant forms of the gene that have this effect, and they reduce the enzyme's activity to varying extents. Phenylalanine hydroxylase catalyses the conversion of phenylalanine, an amino acid contained in many foods, to tyrosine. If the phenylalanine is not converted to tyrosine it builds up in the blood and damages the developing central nervous system, leading to severe intellectual disabilities. This suggests a possible dietary treatment for PKU – if intake of phenylalanine is reduced, then it might not build up in the blood to the same toxic extent.

The first attempt at dietary treatment of PKU has been documented by Bickel (1996). Bickel was working at the University Children's Hospital in Birmingham in 1949 when he suggested that children with learning disabilities should be tested routinely with the ferric chloride test for PKU. The third child tested was a little girl called Sheila, 2 years old and of Irish descent, who was severely disabled, could not sit or stand and took no interest in her surroundings. Sheila tested positive with the ferric chloride test. But in Bickel's own words (p. S2) 'Her mother was not at all impressed when I showed her my beautiful paper chromatogram with the very strong phenylalanine (Phe) spot in the urine of her daughter proving the diagnosis. She awaited me every morning in front of the laboratory asking me impatiently when I would at last find a way to help Sheila.' Responding to this mother's pressure, Bickel and his colleagues wondered whether the excess phenylalanine in the body fluids might have been responsible for the girl's intellectual limitations, and whether she might improve if her phenylalanine intake was reduced. A protein substitute was prepared, a casein hydrolysate that was low in phenylalanine, and begun as the main protein source in her diet when Sheila was just over 2 years old. Over the next few months she clearly improved, starting to sit and stand and to walk with assistance, and to develop better interaction with her carers. Phenylalanine was then added again to the diet ('unknown to the mother'). Within 24 hours her condition deteriorated and she reverted to her earlier state in a few days. The low phenylalanine diet was then reintroduced, and she improved again. Her mother, unfortunately, was unable to keep her on the diet that was necessary, and Sheila's own subsequent history was not a happy one.

More recently, though, the treatment of children with phenylketonuria by means of a low phenylalanine diet has been spectacularly successful – indeed it was so obviously successful so soon that randomised controlled trials that would make its success easy to demonstrate were never carried out (Birch & Tizard, 1967). There are, however, observational studies comparing children who have grown up with differing degrees of dietary control. There are three relevant variables – the child's age when the diet was initiated, the degree of dietary control, and their age when the diet was discontinued (Burgard, 2000). Statistical analysis in relatively large groups of children has allowed investigation of the effects of these variables. Smith, Beasley and Ades (1990b) studied 1031 children with PKU born in the UK between 1964 and 1990. As we saw in Chapter 5, over this extended period the average measured intelligence of children has increased in the UK, as it has in many other countries (Flynn, 1987), so an effort was made to adjust the IQ scores to take this into account, along with the social class of the child. IQ was lower by about 4 points for

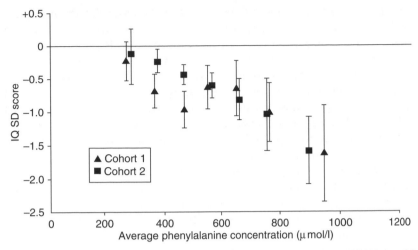

Figure 6.2 Intelligence and average phenylalanine levels in children with phenylketonuria (Smith, Beasley & Ades, 1990b). An IQ SD score of 0 corresponds to an IQ of 100, and an SD score of −1 corresponds to an IQ of 85. Reproduced from *Archives of Disease in Childhood*, 1990, *65*, 472–8 with permission from the BMJ Publishing Group.

each four-week delay in starting treatment. The same adverse effect was associated with each 300 μmol/l increase in mean phenylalanine concentration during treatment as shown in Figure 6.2.

There is currently some uncertainty as to how long the diet must be continued to fully protect the child. A number of studies suggest that the discontinuation of dietary control after 10 years does not generally have adverse effects (Burgard, 2000). Earlier dietary discontinuation was studied by Smith *et al.* in their group of children (Smith, Beasley & Ades, 1990a). This study showed that detectable adverse effects on IQ can be found at 8–10 years if phenylalanine levels are allowed to rise. There is some evidence that dietary relaxation affects persons with phenylketonuria due to different variant forms of the gene to different extents (Greeves *et al.*, 2000). In this study a group of 125 persons whose diet was relaxed after 8 years of age was examined. In all there were 46 different genotypes represented in the groups, with 27 different variant forms of the gene. Because of the number of variants, most of them occurring in small numbers of affected people, it was not possible to compare the effects of dietary relaxation directly in people with different forms of the genes. Instead the genotype was expressed as the predicted residual activity of the mutant enzymes (PRA), a measure of the extent to which normal enzyme function is still present. The PRA associated with different variants ranged from 0 to 55% of normal. Participants with a high PRA ($\geq$25%) were more likely to maintain or gain IQ points after the relaxation of the diet than those with a lower residual activity.

Does the dietary control of phenylalanine completely normalise intellectual development? The most illuminating studies of the normalisation of intelligence in treated children involve comparisons with unaffected siblings (Dobson et al., 1976; Koch et al., 1984). In the study of Dobson et al. (1976) a group of 36 children with confirmed PKU were identified through a collaborative study in 15 medical centres. The children were identified by routine screening at birth. Affected children were placed on a low PKU diet, all within 4 months and most within 1 month. Each of the children had one or more unaffected siblings, and they were compared with the sibling nearest to them in age. Intelligence was assessed with the same test in all the children when they were 4 years old. The mean IQ of the unaffected siblings was 99. In the affected children it was 94, significantly lower by 5 IQ points. Eight previously unidentified cases were also studied. These were children who were not known to have the condition until it was identified in a younger sibling by routine screening, and so were not treated early in life. The average IQ of these children was 77. This is a higher IQ than one might expect for children with untreated PKU. Two of the children may have had variant forms of PKU with less severe effects, and the authors also point out an obvious selection bias, since more severely disabled children would be less likely to remain unidentified. The later study of Koch et al. (1984) was based on the same collaboration and presumably involved some of the same children. In this study WISC scores were compared at 8 years of age in 55 affected children and their sibling controls. The mean IQ in the affected children was 100, while in the siblings it was 107. These data suggest that even with early treatment there is some remaining adverse effect of phenylketonuria on the intellectual development of the affected children in practice, though better dietary control might reduce it or even eliminate it entirely.

A different effect, and one that is also important, is the effect of PKU in a pregnant woman on the intellectual development of the child of the pregnancy. To safeguard the unborn child, the mother's PKU must be brought back under control by reinstating the kind of diet used in children with PKU. If this control is successfully re-established, PKU in the mother is compatible with normal intellectual levels in her offspring (Waisbren & Azen, 2005). If the PKU is poorly controlled quite severe adverse effects are found, with average IQ in the child in the low 70s, though this is not necessarily an effect solely of phenylalanine before birth. In this study the poorly controlled mother differed in a number of other ways – their social class was lower, for example, and they were much more likely to be in single-parent families.

Other data on cognitive outcomes in phenylketonuria come from more specific tests of neuropsychological function in relation to the 'executive dysfunction hypothesis' (Griffiths, 2000; Pennington *et al.*, 1985). Because phenylalanine hydroxylase catalyses the conversion of phenylalanine to tyrosine, phenylketonuria leads to reduced tyrosine levels as well as to increased phenylpyruvic acid levels, and tyrosine is a precursor of dopamine, a neurotransmitter in the central nervous system. Treatment of PKU therefore usually involves the replacement of tyrosine, as well as a reduction in phenylalanine intake. There is currently no convincing evidence that these tyrosine supplements improve psychological abilities (Poustie & Rutherford, 2003; Smith *et al.*, 1998). But phenylalanine and tyrosine are carried into the brain by the same transporter proteins, so higher than usual levels of phenylalanine could reduce the availability of tyrosine even when it is provided as a supplement in the diet. Neurones in the retina and neurones in the brain that project to the prefrontal cortex have a particularly heavy dependence on dopamine. Contrast sensitivity depends on the retina, and Diamond and Herzberg have shown that contrast sensitivity is significantly reduced in 5–10-year-old children with PKU (Diamond & Herzberg, 1996). This reduction was found in children treated early and continuously for PKU. Their overall average IQ was 99, and their visual acuity was unrelated to their IQ. Executive functions, which are involved in the initiation and control of actions, attention, planning and decision-making, depend on the prefrontal cortex. Welsh *et al.* (Welsh *et al.*, 1990) directly compared performance on a battery of executive function measures in preschool children with PKU and controls. The affected children were all treated early, and their average IQ (105) was similar to that of the control groups (108). Executive function measures in this study were derived from a visual search task, a verbal fluency task, a motor planning task and the 'Tower of Hanoi', which tests the ability to plan and carry out a series of moves to achieve a goal. The measures were examined individually, and also combined into an overall executive function composite measure. In addition, a picture recognition memory task was used as a control task not designed to reflect frontal functioning. Although the groups were small (11 children in each) there was a clearly significant difference in the composite executive function measure and in three of the six measures of which it was composed. There was no significant difference in the picture recognition task. The executive function composite measure was significantly and negatively correlated with mean lifetime phenylalanine levels and with phenylalanine levels at the time of the test. Diamond *et al.* (1997)

also showed deficits in young children consistent with the adversely affected development of executive function. Luciana *et al.* (2001) carried out a similar study but in adolescents about 18 years old, who were compared with peer controls nominated by the adolescents with PKU, and with a second control group of children of about the same age with a chronic illness of another kind (cystic fibrosis or juvenile onset diabetes). Again, a number of tasks were used to reflect executive functions, and three additional tasks to reflect cognitive functions of other kinds (psychomotor speed and accuracy, sequencing ability and recognition memory). There were no significant differences between the groups on any of the executive function measures, or on a composite measure, or of any of the control tasks. Although other explanations are possible, this might suggest that the effects reported in the Welsh *et al.* (1990) study are effects during development that do not endure into the adolescent period.

The diet used to control blood phenylalanine levels is based on a protein substitute, with measured quantities of phenylalanine, supplements of vitamins and minerals and a supply of energy-yielding foods (MacDonald, 2000). It is one of the most restrictive of all diets, and not surprisingly it is difficult to keep children on the diet. Parents of children with PKU differ in the extent of their knowledge of the condition, but these differences do not appear to be related to the extent to which the diet is successfully maintained (Bekhof *et al.*, 2003). One of the main problems is the acceptability to the child of the protein substitute, which supplies most of their protein requirements (MacDonald, 2000). The protein substitute is based on L-amino acids, which are bitter-tasting, and children do not generally like bitter foods. It has traditionally been taken in the form of a drink, and many parents have difficulty persuading their children to take it in this form (MacDonald, 2000). In a study of 13 1–5-year-old children with PKU half the mothers said they had difficulty with this (MacDonald *et al.*, 1997). One in five children took over an hour a day to drink the supplement; one child took seven hours. There is some evidence that if the amino acids are presented as flavoured powders, bars and capsules they are more acceptable and the level of control as assessed from blood phenylalanine concentrations is improved (MacDonald, 2000). Other problems that children on this diet have (as reported by their mothers), are poor appetites, eating a limited variety of foods, slow feeding and a variety of gastrointestinal symptoms (vomiting, constipation, diarrhoea and abdominal pain). They are more likely to dislike sweets and chocolates, puddings and cakes, dislikes which are almost never found in other children. This may be a familiarity effect, associated with the prolonged intake of the bitter-tasting protein supplement. There is evidence that other psychological problems are also more common in children with PKU compared with those without; for example, they are more prone to depression, anxiety and phobic tendencies, though not to antisocial or aggressive behaviour (Smith & Knowles, 2000; Weglage *et al.*, 2000). Whether these are effects specific to PKU or more general effects associated with chronic illness and its management is not entirely clear. Childhood diabetes is another chronic illness that requires a strictly disciplined management (including regular metabolic monitoring and dietary restrictions). In a study comparing children with these two conditions with healthy controls internalising (emotional) problems were found to be more common in both groups with a chronic illness, but they were no more common in the children with PKU than in children with diabetes (Weglage *et al.*, 2000). Nor were they related to how good the control of blood phenylalanine was.

6.2   Other genetic disorders

Cystic fibrosis is another recessively inherited genetic disorder, and is relatively common (about one in 2000 live births). It is normally diagnosed in the first year of life. In children with cystic fibrosis abnormal mucous secretions in exocrine glands interfere with the functioning of the pancreas and of the lungs. Energy intake is reduced as a result of the poor absorption of protein and fats from the gut, and energy needs are increased as a result of chronic lung disease and recurrent lung infections. Malnutrition can result, and poor weight gain is one of the earliest signs of the disease (Giglio *et al.*, 1997). Even today, children with cystic fibrosis tend to grow less well than other children, with average heights about half a standard deviation below the average for children of their age (Morison *et al.*, 1997). Poor nutrition is associated with poor lung function in cystic fibrosis, and with poor survival (Stark, 2003), and ensuring adequate nutrition is therefore a key aspect of its management. Until the 1970s low fat diets were provided for children with cystic fibrosis, but the exceptionally good survival of children given high fat diets in Toronto led to revised dietary advice, which now aims to increase energy intake from 120% to 150% of the normally recommended daily intake for the child's age, with 40% of the energy coming from fat. Beneficial though this high level of food intake may be, it is rarely achieved in practice (MacDonald, Holden & Harris, 1991), and problems inevitably arise from attempts to increase the child's intake beyond levels that they would naturally consume of their own volition.

Stark and colleagues have examined mealtime behaviour in a series of studies of children with cystic fibrosis of different ages, ranging from infancy to school age (Powers *et al.*, 2002; Stark *et al.*, 2000; 1997). Dietary intake was assessed using three-day diet diaries. Energy intake of children with cystic fibrosis was not significantly higher than that of control children at 18 months or at 2–5 years, but it was significantly higher at 6–12 years, though even then only about half the children reached an energy intake of 120% of the recommended intake for normal children. There were no obvious differences in mechanical aspects of eating (for example, in energy taken per bite), but in all three age groups meals took significantly longer to complete. In the youngest group children who took longer to eat tended to weigh less. Parents tended to characterise the older children as dawdling or refusing food more.

Life expectancy in people with cystic fibrosis is lower in young females than in young males (Rosenfeld *et al.*, 1997). Up to the age of 20 the death rates are about 20% higher in girls. The reasons for this are not known; the difference is not explained by any identified medical risk factor. One possibility that has been considered is that a desire to be thin in girls with cystic fibrosis might conflict with their need to consume a high energy and high fat diet (Truby & Paxton, 2001). In a study of children 7–12 years old with cystic fibrosis these authors found that both boys and girls were underweight compared with control children, and that lung function was worse in the more underweight children. But there was no evidence that the girls were relatively more underweight than the boys. An interesting finding was that the children with cystic fibrosis were generally more satisfied with their body weights than control children were. They also had lower average scores on the Dutch Eating Behaviour Questionnaire, indicating that they were less likely to engage in weight control and dieting, and were less likely to have high scores on the Children's Eating Attitudes Test (ChEAT), which assesses disordered attitudes to eating. Similar findings have been reported in adults with cystic fibrosis (Abbott *et al.*, 2000). In general, the Truby and Paxton study did not find any evidence that a desire for thinness was associated with a poorer nutritional level in girls with cystic fibrosis, and the largest study to date of survival in cystic fibrosis did not find that differences in nutritional status explained the different survival of young men and women with cystic fibrosis (Rosenfeld *et al.*, 1997).

Sickle cell disease is another inherited disorder, and again inheritance is recessive. It comprises a group of blood disorders that are characterised by a deformation of haemoglobin cells in the blood. It is found particularly in populations from sub-Saharan Africa and in African-Caribbeans. It is the most common major inherited recessive condition in the world (Helps *et al.*, 2003) and in this case the disorder is maintained in the population because in its heterozygous form it protects the affected person against the malarial parasite. The heterozygous form is known as the sickle cell trait. In its homozygous form (HbSS, or sickle cell anaemia) it is a very serious disorder, with a high mortality in childhood if appropriate medical care is not available. Two other common forms of sickle cell disease are HbSC and HbS-thalassemia, which are somewhat milder conditions.

Swift *et al.* (1989) examined the IQ of children with sickle cell anaemia and their siblings, who had either normal haemoglobin or the sickle cell trait. The average IQ in the affected children was 78, over 15 points lower than that of their siblings (94). The use of siblings in the comparison provides good control for many associated demographic and family variables. More recent studies have also found significantly low IQs, though the difference has been about 5 IQ points (Knight *et al.*, 1995; Midence *et al.*, 1996). Deficits more specific to particular neuropsychological functions have been found on measures of memory (Swift *et al.*, 1989), attention, executive function and the decoding of emotions (Helps *et al.*, 2003). There are a number of possible explanations for these deficits in sickle cell disease, which are not necessarily mutually exclusive. The deficits could be a result of direct central nervous system damage resulting from the cerebral vascular accidents (strokes) that often result from sickle cell disease. Or they could be related to absence from school or other educational problems associated with chronic illness. But it is also possible that they could be partly nutritional in origin, and result from protein-energy malnutrition or anaemia associated with the illness.

There is certainly evidence for direct central nervous system damage. Brown *et al.* (2000) examined a range of intellectual functions in children with sickle cell disease, and related these outcomes to overt cerebral vascular accidents in the child's clinical history and also to 'silent infarcts', which were detected by magnetic resonance imaging (MRI) scans. Children with MRI evidence of silent infarcts had significantly lower scores on most of the measures used than children who did not. There was, however, no control group of a kind that would make it possible to say that children without this kind of direct central nervous system damage were unaffected intellectually by the condition, so this study does not rule out the possibility of there also being deficits caused in other ways. White and DeBaun (1998) found only two studies of cognitive function in which children with sickle cell disease but without cerebral infarcts were compared with siblings without sickle cell disease (Craft *et al.*, 1993; 1994). In both studies the children were comparable to controls. Effects of a chronic illness operating through absence from school were examined by Fowler, Johnson and Atkinson (1985). They related school achievement to absence from school due to chronic ill health in 270 children in North Carolina. The children in the study were absent on average for 16 days, and there was a wide range in this, from 0 to 164 days. Even so, although there was a clear relationship between absence from school and poor school achievement in the population in general at the time, there was no correlation between the two in the children with chronic health conditions (the conditions included sickle cell disease).

Direct evidence for nutritional effects in sickle cell disease comes from studies linking lower IQ in sickle cell disease with poorer growth. Prenatal growth is normal in infants with sickle cell disease (Knight *et al.*, 1995), and for the first half of the first year newborn infants are protected against the effects of sickle cell disease by fetal haemoglobin. So anaemia in the first six months is unlikely to be a problem, though data on the early development of children with sickle cell disease are not yet available. Linear growth is affected over the first year, and children with sickle cell disease are significantly shorter than controls by 2 years of age (Knight *et al.*, 1995). Appropriate specialised nutritional support improves their growth (Heyman *et al.*, 1985). In the children in the study of Knight *et al.* the 5 point difference in IQ could not be accounted for by the affected children being absent from school or by dropping out from school, or by the occupational status of their parents. Differences in the children's growth, as reflected in their heights, did, however, account for the IQ differences between the groups. This does suggest some nutritional contribution to the poorer intellectual performance of children with this condition.

6.3   Cerebral palsy

Cerebral palsy is a neurological disorder which leads to problems with muscular coordination and motor control. It is a congenital but not an inherited condition, and as we saw in Chapter 4 it is quite common among children born preterm. In the ALSPAC study 37 children with cerebral palsy were identified at 4 years in a birth cohort of 13,971, a prevalence of 2.6 per 1000 (Motion, Northstone, Emond, Stucke & Golding, 2002). Of these about half (49%) were born preterm.

Infants with cerebral palsy are often found to be small for their age. An 11-year-old boy with spastic quadriplegia described by Cass *et al.* (1999), for example, weighed less than an average 2 year old, though this is an extreme case. The underlying causes of this poorer growth are varied. Children with hemiplegia (paralysis on one side of the body) are significantly smaller on the affected than on the unaffected size (Stevenson, Roberts & Vogle, 1995), which cannot be a nutritional effect. But inadequate nutrition undoubtedly does make a contribution to the poor growth of children with cerebral palsy. Factors that might contribute to this include a lack of the motor skills needed for self-feeding, and oral motor dysfunction, which leads to swallowing difficulties and choking, and also to problems in communicating hunger and requests for food. In an important early study Gisel and Patrick (1988) compared the feeding skills of children with severe cerebral palsy with those of control children of the same weight. The consumption of purées and solids was examined separately. Ten bites of each were given, and the average time taken to swallow the food compared. The children with cerebral palsy took on average about twice as long to swallow the solids, and three or four times as long to swallow the purées. In their population-based birth cohort study Motion et al. (2002) examined the early feeding history of children who were diagnosed with cerebral palsy at 4–5 years of age; 13% were described as extremely difficult to feed when they were infants, compared with 1% in the remainder of the population.

Reilly and Skuse (1992) studied a group of 12 children with cerebral palsy when they were 2–3 years old, comparing them with 12 control children of the same age, sex and ethnic group. Only three of these children were born preterm. Meal-time observations were made in both groups. The duration of the meals did not differ significantly, but the children with cerebral palsy were offered about 40% less food and consumed about 45% less. Eight of their 12 mothers said that meal times were not enjoyable, and six that they were having great difficulty feeding their children; and the mothers had significantly higher depression scores on the General Health Questionnaire. The birthweights of the children with cerebral palsy were average, but over the period to 3 months of age their weight gain was very poor, and it continued to be poor to 15 months, by which time their average weight was nearly two standard deviations below the mean. They were also shorter than average, and lighter for their lengths. In a subsequent population-based survey by the same authors, more than 90% of preschool children with cerebral palsy had a clinically significant impairment of oral motor functions, which was severe in one third (Reilly, Skuse & Poblete, 1996). Half these children had been born preterm. In 60% of this sample severe feeding problems had been evident before the diagnosis of cerebral palsy was made, and almost half the mothers said that feeding problems were one of the first indicators that something was wrong. Comparable findings in cerebral palsy have since been found in a bigger random sample in another area (Sullivan et al., 2002), and Thommessen et al. (1991) assessed both feeding problems and growth and energy intake in a group of children with cerebral palsy of around 5 years of age, and showed that height, weight for height, triceps skinfold thickness and upper arm circumference were all significantly lower in the children with oral-motor impairments.

Malnutrition has a series of adverse effects in children with cerebral palsy (Sullivan *et al.*, 2000). It decreases muscle strength, reduces the effectiveness of the immune system and delays the healing of pressure sores. If it has the same effects as in other children, it may also delay their development and adversely affect their cognitive abilities (Simeon & Grantham-McGregor, 1990), though these effects would be difficult to disentangle from the effects of the underlying neurological impairment on intellectual abilities. Although it is now well established that malnutrition is common in children with cerebral palsy, there is good reason to think that this problem is not routinely dealt with in an appropriate way. In the Oxford Feeding Study, which investigated feeding and nutritional problems in children with neurological impairments (93% of the children had cerebral palsy), feeding problems were very common (Sullivan *et al.*, 2000); 89% needed help with feeding and 56% choked on food. Prolonged feeding times of more than 3 hours per day were reported by 28%, and 38% of parents considered their children underweight. Yet the majority of the children (64%) had never had their feeding and nutrition assessed.

I have considered in this chapter four clearly identifiable medical problems that have important nutritional components, but many other illnesses and physical and other disabilities have adverse nutritional effects, and many are associated with feeding problems. Although different organic conditions may affect feeding in different ways there are clearly also common elements in the aetiology of feeding problems across conditions, and in the ways in which they may be successfully managed. Clinical aspects of these more general problems are considered by Harris, Blisset and Johnson (2000) and by Kerwin (1999).

7   Failure to thrive

7.1   Criteria for failure to thrive and its epidemiology

In the UK and many other countries infants are weighed at intervals through the first year of life. Figure 7.1 shows the weights of an infant recorded in the first year and plotted on a chart. The lines on the chart are intended to represent the distribution of weights of infants in the UK as a whole over the first year of life. Because the distribution differs in boys and girls, boys and girls have different charts. This was a boy. At birth his weight lay almost exactly on the 50th centile, i.e. it was very close to the average for British boys. But his weight gain over the first year was very slow. By 6 weeks he was below the 2nd centile. Only one or two boys in 100 would weigh less. By a year he was on the 0.4th centile. Only three or four in 1000 would weigh less.

If this were your child, you would probably be worried. Certainly your health visitor would be. But what is there, exactly, to be worried about? One possibility is that the child is ill. Poor weight gain in infancy can be a sign of a previously undetected physical illness – of cystic fibrosis, for example. Often, however, it is not, at least in societies in which health and health care are generally good. But if the child is not ill, poor weight gain is usually due to inadequate food intake. So one important set of questions concerns the reasons that underlie the child's inadequate food intake. Does it reflect poverty, or neglect, or even abuse? Is it a sign that the family cannot cope with the proper care of the child for other reasons – for example, because the mother is depressed? Or is there a problem with the child – a subtle motor disorder present at birth that interferes with feeding, for example, or a feeding problem of another kind? A second important set of questions concerns the *consequences* of this inadequate food intake in infancy. Does it have adverse effects on a child's early development, for example, or even an enduring effect on their later intelligence, in the way that malnutrition in other contexts can, as we saw in Chapter 5? Does it have developmental sequelae of other kinds?

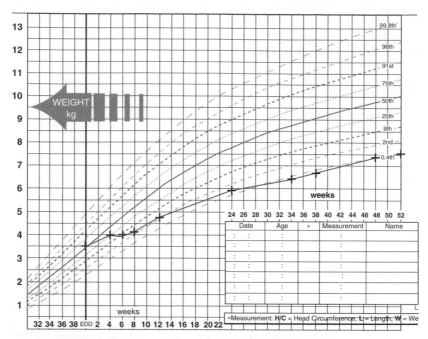

Figure 7.1 Weight of an infant male over the first year (Parkinson, 1998). The centile lines are from the UK 1995 growth reference chart. Published with permission of the author.

Infants whose weight gain is particularly slow are traditionally referred to as 'failing to thrive'. The term is not a very happy one, as it conveys a sense of failure while lacking any precise reference to the key sign, slow weight gain. *Growth faltering* and *weight faltering* have been suggested as more appropriate alternatives. The rather more general term 'failure to thrive' does however imply that there is more of a problem than simply a failure to gain weight, and indeed, there is. Failure to gain weight in infancy is certainly associated with developmental delay, and perhaps also with more enduring intellectual deficits.

The growth chart used in Figure 7.1 is based on the 1995 British growth standard (Freeman *et al.*, 1995; Preece, Freeman & Cole, 1996). The lines of the chart show the median weights of children at different ages, and the distribution around them. The median is the 50th centile, and the other lines on the chart show the 25th, 9th, 2nd and 0.4th centile. This apparently rather odd spacing is a result of these centile lines being chosen to be two thirds of a standard deviation apart (Cole, 1994) so that they can also be read as SD or z score lines. The chart thus neatly combines the two different ways of referring to the spread of weights in a population. If an infant's weight is plotted on the growth chart it is possible to see at once whether their weight is low for their age. A traditional criterion for failure to thrive based on the child's weight would be an attained weight that puts the child below the 3rd or 5th centile for weight, taking into account their age and sex. The exact centile used tends simply to depend on which growth chart was in use at the time of the study: most earlier charts have shown the 3rd or the 5th centile, rather than the 2nd.

A criterion for failure to thrive of this kind is analogous to those used to identify malnutrition internationally that we dealt with in Chapter 5, except that it is a weight-for-age rather than a height-for-age criterion. This kind of criterion is generally acceptable if its only purpose is to distinguish better nourished from less well nourished infants, but it is important to appreciate it does not distinguish slow weight gain before birth from slow weight gain after birth. A low weight for the child's age could result either from a low birthweight or from a slow weight gain after birth, or from a combination of the two. Immediately after birth, for example, an attained weight below the 3rd centile almost entirely reflects a poor prenatal weight gain. At 9 months it reflects equal periods of prenatal and postnatal weight gain. The distinction between poor prenatal and poor postnatal weight gain, however, is a very important one. Firstly, quite different explanations are needed for poor growth before birth and poor growth after birth, as the causes of the two are quite different. In particular, a child's own feeding behaviour, or the way they are fed by their mother, can only affect their growth after birth. Secondly, we already have good evidence that low birthweight is associated with poorer intellectual development, so to examine specifically the relationship between slow weight gain after birth and later development requires careful attention to the distinction between slow weight gain before and after birth. Traditionally these problems have not been dealt with well, and groups of infants identified as failing to thrive have generally also had lower than average birthweights (Sherry, 1999), confusing two different causes of a low weight for age.

To identify infants whose growth *after birth* has been poor requires a criterion based on weight gain rather than on attained weight at a particular age. This has led to criteria based on a declining relative position on growth charts, generally referred to as 'crossing down over centiles'. The boy whose weight is plotted in Figure 7.1 has an average birthweight, but his weight 'crosses down' over the centiles illustrated on the chart. This approach is correct in spirit, but children whose birthweight is low gain weight faster than children whose birthweight is high (Fergusson, Horwood & Shannon, 1980). So infants born relatively light tend to increase their centile position over time, moving upwards across centiles, while infants born relatively heavy tend to decrease it, moving downwards over centiles (Cole, 1998; 1993; 1995). This means that the child's birthweight needs to be taken into account in assessing their weight gain, as well as their age and sex. There is no simple way in which this can be done using a traditional growth chart. Procedures for doing so were first outlined in principle by Healy (1978), and they were developed into a workable method for identifying children who fail to thrive by Wright and her colleagues (Wright *et al.*, 1994) and by Cole (1995; 1996). The usual growth charts allow one to compare the weight or length of a child with that of other children of the same age and sex. To assess weight gain in the period after birth we need to compare the child's weight gain with that of other children of the same age, sex and birthweight. Essentially this would require different growth charts for children of different birthweights; in practice, computer-based methods have generally been used in research instead.

As we saw in Chapter 6, children may grow poorly because they are ill. Cystic fibrosis can lead to poor weight gain because infants with cystic fibrosis cannot absorb fats and proteins effectively, and cerebral palsy can lead to poor weight gain because it adversely affects oral-motor skills and food intake. Failure to thrive in infancy can be one of the earliest signs of both conditions. There are many other medical conditions that result in poor growth (Kessler & Dawson, 1999) and one of the reasons for the routine monitoring of an infant's weight is to detect previously undetected medical conditions of this kind. But in many infants poor weight gain is not due to any known medical condition. Wright and colleagues identified every child born in Newcastle-upon-Tyne over a one year period who met rigorous criteria for failure to thrive in the first year (Wright, Waterston & Aynsley-Greene, 1994; Wright *et al.*, 1994). The children were subsequently followed up and their medical histories examined when they were 7–9 years old (Drewett, Corbett & Wright, 1999). Less than 10% had had medical conditions that accounted for their poor weight gain. The diagnostic yield of laboratory tests in the investigation of children who fail to thrive is also typically very small (Berwick, Levy & Kleinerman, 1982; Rider & Bithoney, 1999). Berwick *et al.* reviewed hospital records of 122 infants admitted to a teaching hospital in the USA with a 'diagnosis' of failure to thrive with no obvious cause at the time of admission. In all, 4827 diagnostic tests were carried out on this group of infants, averaging 40 tests per child. Of these, 39 (0.8%) made a positive contribution to the eventual diagnosis. Clearly identified medical conditions were found in about a third of the infants (31%). The commonest were gastroesophageal reflux (13%) and chronic diarrhoea (8%), both of which are 'functional' disorders rather than specific medical diagnoses. Only 10% of the cases had abnormalities that were more specifically identifiable. While exact figures are not available, there are clearly quite large numbers of children with poor weight gain that is not due to an identifiable illness or other medical condition. The term 'organic' has traditionally been used of failure to thrive in which there is clear evidence of an underlying medical cause, and 'non-organic' in cases in which there is not. We will concern ourselves principally here with children in the latter group, though the distinction is not always an easy one to make.

What sort of family is likely to have a child who fails to thrive? The common assumption is that they are likely to be poor families (Frank & Zeisel, 1988; Kessler, 1999). Frank and Zeisel (1988), for example, say that 'poverty is the most important single social risk factor for failure to thrive, because of the close association between poverty and childhood malnutrition' (p. 1194). Lachenmeyer and Davidovicz (1987) state that 'Studies report that FTT families often come from low socio-economic background...' (p. 345). But these authors go on to note, correctly, that in fact 'Most of these studies ... studied only a low SES group.' To establish the relationship between failure to thrive in infancy and socio-economic conditions requires an epidemiological study, in which all infants from all socio-economic groups who meet an appropriate criterion for failure to thrive are identified and the characteristics of their families examined. Children identified as failing to thrive in clinics or hospitals do not provide a satisfactory sample for this purpose, as there is good evidence that the identification of children as failing to thrive in routine clinical care is not an unbiased procedure; even when they have a similar pattern of slow weight gain, the term is more likely to be used of children living in poorer circumstances (Batchelor & Kerslake, 1990), reflecting, no doubt, the widespread belief that failure to thrive is associated with poverty. The belief is not unreasonable, as internationally malnutrition in young children is associated with poverty. But this is not a safe basis for an assumption that failure to thrive in industrialised countries is also associated with poverty.

The first published epidemiological study that really threw light on the relationship between failure to thrive and material deprivation was by Wright, Waterston and Aynsley-Green (1994). They examined weight *gain* over the first year in a one-year birth cohort of infants born in Newcastle-upon-Tyne and still living there in their second year in November 1989. The child's local area of residence was classified as

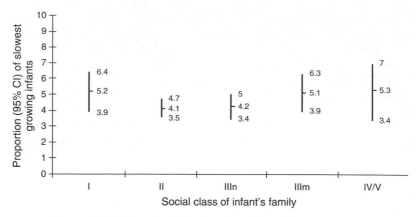

Figure 7.2 Failure to thrive in infants from families of different social class (Blair *et al.*, 2004). The sample size in this study was 11,718. Reproduced from *International Journal of Epidemiology*, 2004, *33*, 839–47 by permission of Oxford University Press.

affluent, intermediate or deprived; the classification was based on Townsend scores, which summarise census data on home ownership, overcrowding, car ownership and unemployment rates. Children were identified as failing to thrive if their weight gain was relatively poor over the first year of life (weight gain below the 5th centile nationally, from about 6 weeks to about 12 months). Compared with the intermediate areas, there were twice as many such children in the most deprived areas. But, unexpectedly, failure to thrive was also more common in the most affluent areas. In this study it was the child's area of residence that was classified, rather than their family itself. A subsequent study of the same relationship (Blair *et al.*, 2004) reported results from a large population cohort of 11,718 infants, and again examined the infants below the 5th centile for weight gain allowing for birthweight. In this study the families were classified individually, and the results are shown in Figure 7.2. The rates of failure to thrive identified using this criterion were 5.2% in social class I, 4.1% and 4.2% in social class II and IIIN, 5.1% in social class IIIM, and 5.3% in social class IV and V combined. There was no statistically significant difference between social classes. Nor were there any relationships with the educational attainments of the child's parents. The available epidemiological data agree, then, that in the UK at any rate failure to thrive is not more common in materially disadvantaged families than in better-off families. Other explanations must be sought for the poor weight gain of the infants.

7.2   Explanations of failure to thrive

The obvious explanation for poor weight gain in an infant who is not ill is inadequate food intake, so an obvious approach to take is to examine food intake in children who fail to thrive and control children, and try to identify a food deficit. But as we saw in Chapter 1, this is much harder in practice than it might seem in theory, because of the difficulty involved in making precise measurements of food intake over extended periods of time in ordinary living conditions. Pollitt (1975), and Pollitt and Eichler (1976) examined dietary intake in a group of 19 children who failed to thrive and 19 controls, when the children were on average about 3 years old. They recorded an estimated intake of 1700 calories (7113 kJ) in the cases and 1400 calories (5858 kJ) in the controls. The difference was statistically significant, but the determinations were not made blind to the child's group and were based on a method (24-hour dietary recall) that can be seriously inaccurate (Bingham, 1987). Heptinstall *et al.* (1987) reported no differences in mean food intake between 4-year-old cases and controls, comparing both daily energy intake reported by mothers and energy intake recorded by observers at a test meal. But in younger children who fail to thrive there is clear evidence of lower energy intake at test meals (Drewett, Kasese-Hara & Wright, 2002). In this study food intake was measured by the weighing of foods of known energy density, which gives very accurate measurements of intake at individual meals. Mean energy intake from foods was 30% lower in the cases than the controls. This result has subsequently been replicated in a second independent sample (Parkinson, Wright & Drewett, 2004).

The other relevant source of evidence comes from nutritional interventions. If failure to thrive is attributable to low food intake interventions to increase food intake should improve the infant's weight gain. An historically very important study of this kind was by Whitten and colleagues (Whitten, Pettit & Fischhoff, 1969). They set out to examine the then prevalent notion that growth failure in infants sometimes resulted from 'maternal deprivation', even when food intake was adequate. There are two general problems with this suggestion. One is that if growth is poor while energy intake is normal the excess energy has to go somewhere. It is always possible to make suggestions, for example, that the energy might be lost from the gut through a failure of absorption, or it might be lost as heat through inefficient utilisation, but no convincing evidence has ever been provided in support of any of these. The second general problem is showing that food intake is, in fact, adequate, given the difficulties in measuring food intake reliably. In an imaginative attempt to circumvent these problems Whitten, Pettit and Fischhoff examined the response of infants hospitalised with growth failure to increased energy intake. One group was adequately fed in hospital, but kept in very deprived conditions. Over a two-week period they were confined in a windowless room, 'were not talked to, smiled at or held for feeding, and with the exception of infrequent brief visits by parents, were only handled for basic physical care'. In spite of this treatment, most of the children gained weight rapidly, which strongly suggests that their poor growth was indeed a result of inadequate food intake.

Another intervention study took the form of a cluster-randomised controlled trial (Wright *et al.*, 1998). Children in Newcastle-upon-Tyne who failed to thrive were identified by a population screening programme over the two-year period from October 1991; 20 of the 38 primary care teams in the area (the 'clusters') were randomly allocated to take part in a programme which comprised specialist health visitor and dietetic intervention with an emphasis on dietary problems. Infants under the remaining primary care teams were used as controls. Weight gain was significantly better in the intervention than the control group. There is, therefore, reasonable evidence suggesting that slow weight gain in infants who fail to thrive for no identifiable medical reasons is due to low food intake, and there is, at the moment, no other plausible explanation for it in the majority of children.

If we assume that failure to thrive is generally attributable to low food intake, the question then arises: why is the infant's food intake so low? As we saw in Chapter 6, the weight gain of children with cerebral palsy can be very poor as a result of motor disorders which interfere with their eating. An analogous though less obvious motor disorder has been attributed to some children who fail to thrive (Mathisen *et al.*, 1989). Reilly *et al.* (1999) subsequently themselves commented that only tentative conclusions can be drawn from this study, as the sample size was small and the children had been identified for the study by health visitors; this can lead to a preferential selection of children with feeding problems as feeding problems tend to be very troublesome for parents (Batchelor & Kerslake, 1990). In the later study by the same authors (Reilly *et al.*, 1999), however, 47 children who failed to thrive were identified by screening all infants born in 1986 in participating practices and clinics in an inner-city health district in London. Their feeding skills were investigated using a screening version of the Schedule for Oral-Motor Assessment (SOMA) described by Skuse *et al.* (1995). The SOMA was developed to allow objective assessment of the oral-motor skills involved in feeding behaviour in children 8–24 months old. This is the weaning period, in which children gradually progress from a milk-based diet to one based on the kinds of solid foods characteristically taken by older children and adults. Reflecting this progress, the SOMA uses a series of 'oral-motor challenges' using liquids, purées, semi-solids and solids given with a spoon, and other solids requiring biting and chewing such as crackers and apples. Oral-motor responses to the foods are rated in detail using video-tapes of the feed. Normal responses to a purée, for example, would involve the lower lip drawing inwards around the spoon; the upper lip removing food from the spoon; and either lip being used to clean food off the spoon. In this group of 47 children who failed to thrive 17 were said to show significant oral-motor disorder. Interesting though this finding is, it is hard to interpret these figures in the absence of a control group of children whose weight gain was normal. The same comment applies to a subsequent study of a similar kind (Ramsay, Gisel & Boutry, 1993).

One of the known causes of failure to thrive in infancy when it is associated with an underlying medical condition is gastro-oesophageal reflux; in the study of Berwick et al. (1982) discussed above it was the commonest identifiable medical condition associated with failure to thrive in a group of infants admitted to hospital. In gastro-oesophageal reflux the sphincter at the bottom of the oesophagus allows regurgitation of the acid contents of the stomach back up the oesophagus, leading in severe cases to the painful condition of oesophagitis (inflammation of the oesophagus). It is a common condition of infancy, which in most children resolves by 2 years of age. Mathisen et al. (1999) compared 20 6-month-old infants with oesophagitis and 20 control infants using the same observation procedures as she used in her earlier studies of failure to thrive (Mathisen, Skuse, Wolke & Reilly, 1989). The children with reflux were quite severely affected. All 20 vomited during the test meal, more than half had respiratory symptoms and most cried and were miserable during feeds. Energy intake measured at meals was significantly lower than in the controls; 16 of the 20 children had moderate or severe oral-motor dysfunction as assessed from the videotaped feeding assessment schedule, while none of the controls did. The dysfunction affected all the (49) components of the child's oral-motor function that were assessed. Gastro-oesophageal reflux involves no central nervous system abnormalities, so clearly high scores on this kind of oral-motor feeding assessment do not necessarily indicate a central nervous system or neurophysiological abnormality, although they certainly show abnormalities in feeding behaviour. The distinction between abnormalities of feeding behaviour attributable to defective motor skills, as in cerebral palsy, and abnormalities of feeding behaviour of other kinds, is an important one, and it is not always made as clearly as is desirable. The title of the paper by Ramsay et al. (1993) refers to 'growth failure secondary to feeding skills disorder' and the summary proposes that this disorder 'is neurophysiological in origin'. However, the criterion used in this paper 'to make a diagnosis of feeding skills disorder' required the persistent presence from birth or soon after of two or more symptoms from a list of four. The first symptom is an abnormal duration of feeding time. The second is 'poor appetite'. The third is 'delayed texture tolerance' and the fourth 'deviant feeding behaviour', which include 'refusing breast, bottle or solids, falling asleep, being easily distracted' and 'fussy eating'. All four were very common in children who failed to thrive. None of these symptoms, however, unambiguously reflect a deficit in feeding *skills*, so we need to consider feeding problems of a much more general kind. And to judge by reports from their mothers, children who fail to thrive often do have feeding problems of other kinds. They were reported in about twice as many cases as controls in the study of Drewett, Corbett and Wright (1999) and have been reported in many other studies (Altemeier *et al.*, 1985; Iwaniec & Herbert, 1982; Kotelchuck & Newberger, 1983; Mathisen *et al.*, 1989; Pollitt & Eichler, 1976; Tolia, 1995; Wilensky *et al.*, 1996; Wright & Birks, 2000).

The study of Wilensky *et al.* (1996) was based on a whole population birth cohort in Israel and describes in some detail the nature of the feeding problems involved. The children who failed to thrive were described as less likely to show hunger, less likely to eat a variety of foods, less likely to show pleasure and more likely to be nervous at mealtimes, and to close their mouth, turn their head and spit out food. These sound like indications of a low appetite, rather than problems with feeding skills, but to further examine their nature objectively requires more detailed investigation. A study of mealtime behaviour in 1-year-old children who failed to thrive was carried out by Drewett, Kasese-Hara and Wright (2002) and involved direct observation of the children's behaviour during their meals. The children were studied over the weaning period, when feeding behaviour is in transition between infant and childhood modes, so procedures for coding two types of mealtime behaviour were required. Firstly, the child can be fed by his/her mother, and the child can accept or refuse the foods offered. Second, the child can feed him or herself, with the mother assisting their feeding, perhaps, by handing the child food to eat. A coding scheme developed by Young and Drewett (2000) and Parkinson and Drewett (2001) was designed to code for both types of feeding. In the study of Drewett, Kasese-Hara and Wright (2002), 28 children who failed to thrive were identified by a weight gain below the 5th centile over the first year of life, and 28 controls selected from the same local geographical area. A meal was given in the usual way by the child's mother in their own home, but made up of foods of known energy density to allow accurate determinations of food intake to be

made. As noted above, the children who failed to thrive did take significantly less food in at the meal. Analysis of the behaviour of the mother and
infant during the meal showed, however, that this was not because the
mothers did not offer as much food; indeed they offered food more often
than the control mothers. The children who failed to thrive refused the
food that was offered more, and they also fed themselves less.

A further investigation of the same children examined their energy
regulation, using the same kind of procedure as in Birch (1986), but
adapted for use in younger children who were still being fed by their
mothers (Kasese-Hara, Wright & Drewett, 2002). In this study the effect
of a high energy drink given before the meal on food intake during the
meal was examined. The children were fed by their mothers in the usual
way on two days, but using foods of known energy content. The food
intake of the children was carefully measured, and any spilt food taken
into account. On one of the two days a high energy drink (402 kJ) and on
the other day a low energy drink (1 kJ) was provided half an hour before
the meal. These were made up by an independent pharmacist, and given
double blind (their energy content unknown either to the mother or to the
experimenter). The control children in this study showed exactly the
same energy compensation as older children did in the study of Birch
(1986). Their food intake at the test meal was reduced on average by
1.18 kJ for every 1 kJ taken in the drink before the meal. The children who
failed to thrive, on the other hand, showed no compensation at all –
indeed their energy intake at the meal was somewhat greater following
the high energy drink. While this result does not in itself show why
these children were gaining weight so slowly, it does suggest that they
have abnormal appetite characteristics, and a number of other studies
have suggested that children who fail to thrive have low appetites. This
may be the problem in the 'contented' underfed breast-fed babies who fail
to thrive (Davies, 1979; Habbick & Gerrard, 1984). These are infants
that look undernourished but appear satisfied after feeds, and go for long
intervals between feeds, sleeping well at night. Another recent study has
shown that cytokine (interleukin 6) levels are raised in children who fail to
thrive, and cytokines have been shown to suppress appetite (Shaoul et al.,
2003). Children with a history of failure to thrive as infants also rate their
own appetites as low compared with their friends' when they are 12 years
old (Drewett, Corbett & Wright, 2006).

Appetite problems in the infant may make some contribution to their
slow weight gain, but traditionally it has generally been assumed that the
child's mother also has a role in the development of the condition. It has
even been assumed to be related to child abuse or neglect (Kotelchuck,
1980), though the evidence for this has never been very clear, perhaps

partly because the association is a difficult one to investigate. Again it requires a population-based study, preferably of all infants who meet the criterion for failure to thrive in a specified community. A recent study of this kind is reported by Skuse et al. (1995). This study was based on a further investigation of the 47 children in the 1986 London cohort referred to above (Reilly et al., 1999). Four years later (in 1990) information was gathered on all children born in 1986 living in the Southwark and North Lewisham Health District who had been subjects of a case conference, been placed on a Child Protection ('at risk') register, taken into care, on a place of safety order or subject to wardship proceedings, all of which are suggestive of child abuse or neglect. Over this four-year period 96 children from the original birth cohort of 2609 (4%) fell into one of these categories, and these included 6 of the 47 children who failed to thrive (13%). An entry onto the Child Protection Register was about four times as likely if the child failed to thrive. While this does suggest an association with child abuse or neglect it was in only one in eight (13%) of the children who failed to thrive that this independent evidence of child abuse or neglect was found, and even this may be an overestimate, because failure to thrive was explicitly mentioned as one of the indicators of neglect in the local multidisciplinary guidelines used in the District at the time, and neglect was specified as a ground for concern in five of the six cases (the sixth was a case of physical and suspected sexual abuse). The authors do state that non-organic failure to thrive was never the *only* reason for concern, but it may nonetheless have been an important reason for the child's registration. If failure to thrive was a sign that led to the child being registered in the first place it is not surprising that failure to thrive is associated with being on the register. I am not, of course, implying that slow weight gain in infancy is never to be found as a result of child abuse or neglect. It is the extent of the association between the two that we are concerned with.

Another possibility is that failure to thrive is associated not with child abuse or neglect *per se* but rather with subtler differences in the interaction between the infant and their carer (generally, at this age, their mother). Theories of this kind became dominant in the 1960s, when the work of Ainsworth and Bowlby focussed particular attention on the importance of mother–infant attachment. Attachment to the primary caregiver develops over the period from 8 to 12 months, and is now usually measured in the second year of life using the 'strange situation' (Ainsworth et al., 1978; Ainsworth & Wittig, 1969). In the strange situation the mother and infant are left together in a room, the mother sitting quietly while the infant plays. A stranger enters and talks to the mother. Then the mother leaves. The mother returns and the stranger leaves. Then the mother leaves again. The stranger re-enters the room, and finally the mother re-enters. The strange situation involves both stranger anxiety and separation anxiety and is moderately stressful for the infant. Based on the child's responses their attachment can be classified as *secure* or *insecure*. In a more detailed classification insecure attachment is subdivided into *avoidant*, *resistant* and *disorganised* attachment. It has been suggested that failure in the development of attachment may result in failure to thrive (Casey, 1999), and a substantial body of work has investigated attachment in children who fail to thrive. This is a valuable body of work because attachment has been systematically assessed using the same objective and well-validated procedures in a number of different studies. The first was by Gordon and Jameson (1979; Kotelchuck, 1980), and there have been five subsequent studies (Chatoor *et al.*, 1998; Coolber & Benoit, 1999; Skuse, Wolke & Reilly, 1992; Ward, Kessler & Altman, 1993; Ward, Lee & Lipper, 2000).

With a single exception (Skuse, Wolke & Reilly, 1992), these studies do show a higher level of insecure attachment in the infants who failed to thrive. But it seems unlikely that insecure attachment itself can be a cause of the failure to gain weight satisfactorily in children who fail to thrive. Studies that have examined failure to thrive in whole populations have generally found that the child's weight gain is poor from birth (Altemeier *et al.*, 1985; Drewett, Corbett & Wright, 1999; Skuse, Wolke & Reilly, 1992). Since attachment does not develop until late in the first year, the child's poor weight gain cannot simply be a result of insecure attachment, and some other explanation of the association found between the two in the studies cited above is needed.

One possibility is that the relationship is artifactual, and results from the way in which the cases are selected. Failure to thrive is often undetected (Batchelor & Kerslake, 1990; Batchelor, 1996; Wright *et al.*, 1998), and when it is detected not all children with the condition are referred for specialist care. Both the initial detection and later referral involve decisions that go beyond a simple assessment of the child's weight gain, and might include, for example, informal assessment of the child's developmental progress, social circumstances and responsiveness to management (Batchelor & Kerslake, 1990; Drotar, 1990). There is, therefore, a possibility that the greater prevalence of insecure attachment in the children who fail to thrive who took part in these studies is a consequence of the use of clinically referred samples, which may have included more children from families with additional problems. This possibility is made more plausible by the fact that in the only study that screened a whole population for children who failed to thrive (Skuse, Wolke & Reilly, 1992) there was no difference at all between the cases and controls in attachment patterns. It should be noted, however, that this study did not use the strange situation to assess attachment patterns, but a modified and less stressful procedure which has not been clearly validated (Melhuish, 1987; 1993).

A second possibility is that it is a precursor of insecure attachment, already present at or soon after birth, that underlies failure to thrive. The obvious possibility is to be found in maternal sensitivity, which has been shown in a range of studies to be associated with insecure attachment on the part of the infant (De Wolff & van IJzendoorn, 1997). There is, indeed, evidence that in clinic-based samples of children who fail to thrive traditional measures of maternal sensitivity do show less sensitivity than controls (Drotar et al., 1990). A rather similar relationship has been found in a population-based study in a poor area of Chile with a high prevalence of undernutrition in childhood, where Valenzuela (1990) has examined the relationship between attachment and nutritional status in detail. Children whose weight was below 90% of that expected for their age were identified by screening via data routinely collected in well baby clinics, avoiding any problems associated with clinically referred samples. Control children were selected from families within the same socio-economic categories, and were not significantly different on any meas-ured family characteristic. Of the 41 underweight children, only 7% were securely attached, while of the 40 control children, 50% were securely attached, a highly significant difference. Valenzuela subsequently pub-lished data on maternal sensitivity in the same sample (Valenzuela, 1997). This part of the study used a maternal sensitivity scale of Ainsworth, Bell and Stayton (1974). There were striking differences in maternal sensitivity rating between the mothers of the adequately nour-ished children, with a mean rating of 5.6 (between 'inconsistently sensi-tive' and 'sensitive') and the mothers of the chronically undernourished children, with a mean rating of 2.0 (between 'insensitive' and 'highly insensitive'). These ratings were made when the children were 18 months old, so it is theoretically possible that the differences they reflect could result from the child's malnutrition rather than causing it. If the rated insensitivity did precede the child's malnutrition, it might account for it, since a lack of sensitive and appropriate responding to the child's hunger cues would obviously not help their feeding. This might be especially important in children with poor appetites.

Another possibility that has received a good deal of attention is that failure to thrive might result from mental health problems in the child's mother. Early studies in this area were carried out before research proce-dures were very sophisticated, and did not use validated assessment instruments. For example, Fischhoff, Whitten and Pettit (1971) carried out a psychiatric study of the mothers of infants 3–24 months old with growth failure attributed to the 'maternal deprivation syndrome'; 12 mothers were examined. Of the 12, two were described as 'psychoneurotic' and each of the other 10 as having a 'character disorder'. The criteria used to identify these character disorders were not clearly explained (one mother was said to wear 'very tight-fitting clothes' and 'an excessive amount of make-up'). No control mothers from similar backgrounds were examined, and assessment was obviously not blind to the child's clinical condition. An early study using a reasonable methodology (Polan et al., 1991) did find more psychopathology in the mothers of children who failed to thrive, but other studies did not (Benoit, Zeanah & Barton, 1989; Iwaniec, Herbert & McNeish, 1985; Kotelchuck & Newberger, 1983; Pollitt, Eichler & Chan, 1975; Skuse, Wolke & Reilly, 1992; Wolke, Skuse & Mathisen, 1989). Many of these were based on rather small samples.

A large-scale study of the relationship between failure to thrive and maternal depression was carried out by Drewett et al. (2004), as part of the ALSPAC study, which sought to enrol all infants born to women living in what was then the Avon Health Authority area with an expected date of delivery between 1 April 1991 and 31 December 1992. Children from over 80% of the known births were successfully recruited into the study, a total cohort of nearly 14,000. Weights were recorded for most of these children at birth, about 6 weeks and about 9 months. Symptoms of depression in the mothers were also recorded using the Edinburgh Postnatal Depression Scale (EPDS), both at about 18 and 32 weeks of pregnancy and after the birth, when the child was 8 weeks and 8 months old. Infants were identified as failing to thrive if their weight gain put them in the slowest gaining 5%. Any with congenital illnesses or abnormalities were excluded.

Standard psychiatric diagnostic instruments, such as those designed to reflect the criteria used in the Diagnostic and Statistical Manual of the American Psychiatric Association, generally dichotomise people into two classes, for example those who are diagnosed as having a major depression and those who are not. But the Edinburgh Postnatal Depression Questionnaire does not dichotomise women into two classes; rather it provides a scaled score of depression symptoms with a possible minimum of 0 and a possible maximum of 30. If women score high on the scale it is probable that they have a clinically diagnosable depression. The probability (the positive predictive value) is greater than 65% if their score is 12 or more, and greater than 85% if it is 15 or more (Murray & Carothers, 1990). In the ALSPAC cohort, the prevalence of depression (scores greater than 12) among the mothers was 10.2% eight weeks after the birth and 8.8% eight months after the birth. The rates of failure to thrive in the infants of the depressed mothers were 5.0% in mothers depressed at eight weeks and 4.3% in controls. In the infants of mothers depressed at eight months the rate was 4.3% in both groups. At neither age was the difference statistically significant. Nor did significant differences emerge if the more stringent criterion for depression was used (an EPDS score of 15 or more). This result was based on large numbers. Over 1000 women met the criterion for depression at eight weeks, and over 500 infants met the criterion for failure to thrive over the first year.

Infants born preterm are particularly difficult to care for, and one might expect an association between maternal depression and failure to thrive to be particularly likely in infants born preterm. An interaction of this kind has been found for insecure attachment, for example. Poelmann and Fiese (2001) found that maternal depression is associated with insecure attachment in infants if they are born preterm, but not if they are born at term. The infants born preterm in the ALSPAC study (Drewett *et al.*, 2004) were substantially more likely to meet the criterion for failure to thrive than infants born at term. Their mothers were also more likely to be depressed. But again there was no significant association between failure to thrive in the infants and depression in their mothers. A similar result was reported by Kelleher *et al.* (1993). They followed up about 900 infants born preterm at eight large university medical centres in the USA over a nine month period. The mental health of their mothers was assessed at three time points, one, two and three years after the birth, using the General Health Questionnaire, which in spite of its title assesses mental rather than general health. Nearly 20% of the infants were identified as failing to thrive, but there was no association between failure to thrive in the infants and poor mental health in their mothers.

O'Brien *et al.* (2004), however, did find a relationship between failure to thrive and maternal depression in another study. This study involved the identification by health visitors of all children of up to 2 years of age in North Staffordshire whose weights 'fell across 2 centile channels' or fell below the 2nd centile. They were compared with control children identified from the district child health computer system who were matched on age, sex, ordinal position and postcode location. The groups were large (196 case children and 567 controls). The mothers of the children were compared initially with the EPDS and with the Hospital Anxiety and Depression Scale (HADS) and then, if they met a screening criterion, with a clinical diagnostic interview for depression (CIS-R). Significantly higher levels of depression were found in the mothers of the children who failed to thrive. This was reflected both in higher numbers of mothers with scores above the threshold on the EPDS (and the HADS anxiety scales) and in higher numbers of mothers with a diagnosed 'depressive episode' on the diagnostic interview. The proportion with a depressive episode was 11.1% in the control mothers and 21.4% in the case mothers. The study was carefully designed and carried out, and it is hard to explain why its results differ from those of the other large studies of this association (Drewett et al., 2004; Kelleher et al., 1993). Although a screening instrument, such as the EPDS, tends to detect more potential cases of depression than are confirmed using a diagnostic instrument such as the CIS-R, the difference is not attributable to the way depression was assessed. The association in this study was found with the EPDS as well as with the CIS-R, and the EPDS was the instrument used in Drewett et al. (2004). One problem may be the extent to which the health visitors actually identified all the children meeting the specified criteria for failure to thrive. In fact, in the *control* group 9% of the children met these criteria. This is a very high proportion, and might suggest that large numbers of cases were not identified by the health visitors. If so, it would be consistent with what is known from studies in other areas (Batchelor & Kerslake, 1990) if those who were identified differed in other ways from those who were not – they might, for instance, have mothers who were more likely to be depressed.

There are, however, now three studies in developing countries which also show a relationship between maternal mental health and malnutrition in infants (Anoop et al., 2004; Patel, DeSouza & Rodrigues, 2003; Rahman et al., 2004). In the first of these studies, in Goa in India, 171 mother–infant pairs were studied. Infants were weighed and 'lengthed' at 6 months, and the mental state of the mothers assessed using the EPDS translated into Konkani, the most widely spoken language of Goa. Of the mothers, 22% met the criteria for postnatal depression. The weights and lengths of the infants of these mothers were significantly lower at 6 months, after taking into account their birthweights and a range of other variables. The second study was carried out in Vellore, also in India (Anoop et al., 2004). Here infants were monitored with monthly weighings in 85 villages as part of a community development programme. From the central register, 72 infants malnourished in the second half of the first year and 72 matched controls were identified. Postpartum depression was identified using the Structured Clinical Interview for DSM-III-R depression, and was about five times more common in the mothers of the malnourished infants. Malnutrition was also associated with low maternal intelligence. In the third study, in Pakistan (Rahman et al., 2004), 172 consecutive infants and their mothers attending for immunisation against measles were recruited over a three-month period. The infants were weighed, and maternal mental health was assessed using the WHO SRQ-20, a self-report questionnaire designed to identify mental distress in the community. Comparisons were then made between infants with weights below the 3rd centile of the NCHS/WHO growth reference (there were 82) and those with weights above the 10th centile (there were 90). Depression is very prevalent in rural Pakistan, affecting about half the women in two earlier studies. In this study the prevalence of mental distress was 40%, although a high cut-off was used, meaning that a high proportion of the women would have been suffering from clinically significant symptoms. Undernutrition was also common; 48% of the infants were below the 3rd centile for weight of the reference population. Here the infants of mothers with poor mental health were two to three times more likely to have weights below the 3rd centile. This effect remained even after adjusting for relevant confounders, including the child's birthweight, the number of children in the family and their socio-economic status.

It is a striking possibility that in countries in which malnutrition is widespread, maternal mental health may be an important determinant of the nutritional status of young children. But there is little evidence at the moment for a similar important role for maternal mental health problems in the UK or other industrialised countries. Indeed, we have no clear explanation for the slow weight gain of infants who 'fail to thrive' in these countries. Although it is unlikely that a single explanation will suffice for all children, even when identifiable medical illnesses have been excluded, there is evidence from various sources that as a group children who fail to thrive have lower appetites and resist normal feeding more. It is possible that this interacts with the way the child is cared for – for example, that it needs a particularly sensitive kind of maternal care if the child's weight gain is not to be adversely affected.

7.3   Developmental delay and later cognitive outcomes

Failure to thrive in infants in industrialised countries is clearly related to the protein-energy malnutrition found in children in less developed countries. It tends not to be so severe, and its causes are not necessarily the same: poverty and infectious diseases (and perhaps depression too) have a much bigger role in malnutrition in infancy in poorer countries. But whatever the underlying causes of slow weight gain in infants who fail to thrive in industrialised countries, the possibility that it might also be associated with sufficiently poor nutrition to adversely affect the child's intellectual development is a serious one. It was first raised in 1968 (Glaser et al., 1968) and has been the subject of considerable research since.

To be convincing, research into this possibility must meet a number of requirements. The first concerns the criteria for identifying failure to thrive. In clinical practice the criteria often involve not only slow weight gain but also a more general developmental delay. Clearly if children are recruited into a study because they are developmentally delayed, they will be found to be developmentally delayed, so for research purposes it is important that purely anthropometric criteria are used to identify the children. The second concerns the population from whom the cases are sampled. In most early work they were identified via clinical services, and therefore comprised children who failed to thrive and who had been identified and referred to the clinical services concerned. But there is good evidence that this identification and referral process tends to be focussed on children from poorer circumstances, and it may well be biased in other ways: for example, children who are developmentally delayed may be identified or referred more readily. Substantial advances in this area came with attempts to study all the children in a population who met anthropometric criteria for failure to thrive, rather than only those already identified through clinical services (Mitchell, Gorrell & Greenberg, 1980; Skuse, 1993). The third requirement concerns appropriate control groups. Because low birthweight is itself associated with lower intellectual abilities, appropriate control for birthweight is necessary, as well as control for other relevant variables such as parental and family characteristics.

These requirements have been met reasonably satisfactorily in a number of recent studies, and the evidence that slow weight gain in infancy is associated with developmental delay is now quite convincing. This has been shown in three well-controlled studies of children born at term (Black *et al.*, 1994; Skuse *et al.*, 1994; Wilensky *et al.*, 1996) and in one of children born preterm (Kelleher *et al.*, 1993). In each of these studies cases were identified by a reasonable approximation to the screening of a whole population and solely on anthropometric criteria, so it is very unlikely that selection biases account for the association with developmental delay.

As we have seen, developmental delay in infancy is not necessarily associated with later intellectual impairments, and although there may be tests in infancy that correlate better with later intelligence than the developmental tests used in these studies, no test in infancy satisfactorily predicts later abilities. So the only way to determine whether failure to thrive in infancy is associated with later intellectual deficits is to follow the children up as they get older and investigate their later abilities. An important early study with a reasonably appropriate control group and a standardised test of intelligence was reported by Oates *et al.* (1985).

At about 14 years of age they found a 10 point reduction in IQ when comparing children who failed to thrive with controls; the difference was not actually statistically significant, but the group sizes were small (14 children in each). A later study by Mitchell *et al.* (1980) is notable as the first study to screen children for failure to thrive in primary care, though intellectual ability was only assessed in a limited number of the children. They too found an effect that was moderately large (5 points) but not statistically significant (again the group sizes were small).

The first study to convincingly show a clear association between failure to thrive and lower IQ in childhood was by Dowdney *et al.* (1987; Skuse, 1993). This study screened a birth cohort of 2145 children within a single health district in London, and identified all children who failed to thrive in infancy and had persisting growth retardation to the age of 4. At 4 their McCarthy Scale General Cognitive Index Scores were about 20 points lower than those of a control group (the mean was 97.7 in the control and 77.1 in the children who failed to thrive). This is a very large difference (more than a standard deviation). The controls were carefully matched to the cases on length of gestation, birthweight, ethnic origin and ordinal position in the family, and they were generally chosen from the same health clinic or nursery. But although there are no obvious flaws in this study, such a large deficit has never been found elsewhere.

Two subsequent studies were reported by Drewett, Corbett and Wright (1999) and by Boddy, Skuse and Andrews (2000). In the first of these a one-year birth cohort of all children born in Newcastle-upon-Tyne in 1987–8 was investigated. Their weights over the first 18 months were retrieved from case records in child health clinics, and cases were the slowest growing 5%, as identified by their weight gain. Along with these 136 cases, 136 controls were chosen who were born within one month of the cases in the same local area. They were not otherwise matched to the cases, but the similarities in their families were striking. There was no significant difference, for example, in any economic characteristics of the families, or in their mother's educational attainments. Although the cases were identified solely on the basis of their weight gain over the first 18 months, they were significantly shorter at 8 years of age, and had significantly smaller head circumferences. But in spite of these substantial and enduring differences in their growth there was only a small difference in their IQ at 8 (3 IQ points), and no difference in their reading skills. The second study (Boddy, Skuse & Andrews, 2000) was a follow-up of children studies by Skuse *et al.* (1994). The cases were selected by screening a one-year birth cohort born in an inner London health authority. Their weights were below the 3rd centile for at least three months in the first year, and they were matched to controls on birthweight and a number of other

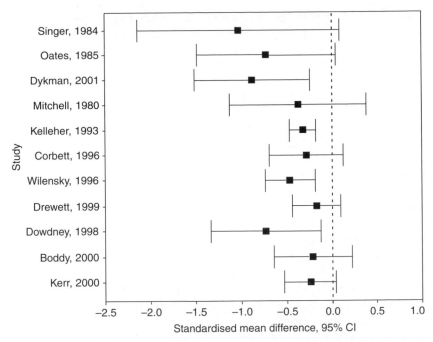

Figure 7.3 Cognitive outcomes in children who failed to thrive (Corbett & Drewett, 2004). Results are shown for 11 controlled studies (using IQ tests, except for Wilensky *et al.*, 1996, who used the Bayley Scales). The top three are from studies of cases from hospital or other specialist clinics. The remainder are from studies of cases recruited in primary care clinics or by whole population screening. The overall weighted mean difference for the seven studies using IQ tests in primary care or whole population samples corresponds to 4.2 IQ points (95% CI 2 to 6). Studies referred to are referenced in the original paper. Reproduced from *Journal of Child Psychology and Psychiatry*, 45, 641–54. Copyright 2004, with permission from Blackwell Publishing.

variables. Although they were significantly delayed on the Bayley Scales in their second year, there were only small differences between the groups on the general cognitive index of the McCarthy Scales at 6 years of age.

The results of these studies taken together are not very clear and suggest that rather large group sizes would be needed to determine with precision the size of the intellectual deficit associated with failure to thrive, if there is one. Corbett and Drewett (2004) reviewed all the relevant published studies, and provide quantitative summaries of the association between failure to thrive and later cognitive outcomes. Results are shown in Figure 7.3. Data based on seven controlled studies with 502 cases and 523 controls provide a statistically significant overall average difference of 4.2 IQ points. These seven studies all identified their cases by screening whole populations, and therefore provide the most unbiased estimate of the effect. Three studies that used cases referred to hospitals or specialist clinics found much larger effects, with an average mean difference of about 13 IQ points. This clearly shows how important case identification procedures are: the IQ deficit found in cases identified via hospitals or specialist clinics was over three times as great as the deficit found when all the children with the condition were identified in whole populations.

All these data come from observational studies, and as in all other observational studies there is a possibility that uncontrolled variables associated with slow weight gain might account for its relationship between failure to thrive and later intellectual abilities. The controlled studies providing the estimate in Corbett and Drewett (2004) controlled for a range of other variables, including birthweight, ordinal position in the family, and the IQ of the child's mother. Where slow growth in infancy is strongly associated with poverty, poor maternal education and low social status these can be difficult to control for in a sufficiently comprehensive way. But, as we saw above, slow weight gain in infancy in the UK is not strongly associated with these; indeed in the largest study of the epidemiology of failure to thrive to date it was not associated with them at all (Blair *et al.*, 2004). In one of the studies relating failure to thrive to later abilities, in infants born preterm in the USA, mothers with more advanced education were actually *more* likely to have infants who failed to thrive (Kelleher *et al.*, 1993); yet the adverse effect of failure to thrive on their infants' IQ was still found. The evidence does, therefore, suggest that failure to thrive in Western countries, whatever its causes, is associated with developmental delay and with a somewhat lower IQ at school age.

7.4   Other outcomes

Weight gain patterns in infancy are associated with a range of other outcomes, which have attracted attention in recent years principally as a result of developments in lifespan epidemiology (Barker, 1991). Important work on physical health originated in the observation that heart disease was strongly related to the place of birth, suggesting that the environment early in life was an important determinant of later health (Barker & Osmond, 1986). A subsequent study (Barker *et al.*, 1989) examined the relationship between weight gain in infancy and later cardio-vascular health using records carefully kept by midwives and

Table 7.1. *Standardised mortality ratios for ischaemic heart disease according to birthweight and weight at 1 year*

Weight (lb) at 1 year	Weight at birth (lb)			
	Below average ($\leq$7)	Average 7.5–8.5	Above average ($\geq$9)	Total
Below average ($\leq$21)	100 (80)	100 (77)	58 (17)	93 (174)
Average (22–23)	86 (34)	87 (67)	80 (29)	85 (130)
Above average ($\geq$24)	53 (14)	65 (42)	59 (32)	60 (88)
Total	88 (128)	85 (186)	65 (78)	81 (392)

Note:
All the men were breast-fed. The data are given in the units in which the records were originally made (1 lb is about 0.454 kg). Reproduced from *The Lancet, II,* 578–80. Copyright 1989, with permission from Elsevier.
Source: Barker *et al.*, 1989.

health visitors in Hertfordshire under the supervision of the formidable Miss Burnside, the 'Chief Health Visitor and Lady Inspector of Midwives' (Barker, 1994). From 1911, attending midwives had to notify every birth to the county Medical Officer of Health, and as well as the mother's name and address, the date of birth and birthweight of the infants were recorded. Throughout the first year the infants were visited by health visitors, and further information was recorded, including whether the infant was breast- or bottle-fed and their weight at 1 year of age. In all about 8000 male children born in the period from 1911 to 1930 had birthweights and weights at 1 year recorded, and 7613 had identification data sufficient to allow an attempt to trace them through the NHS Central Register at Southport. Of these children, 74% were successfully traced, and if they had died their causes of death were determined. Of the 1186 who had died, 434 had died due to ischaemic heart disease (heart attack). Table 7.1 shows the relationship between the standardised mortality ratio for ischae- mic heart disease, weight at birth and weight at 1 year. A higher birth- weight is association with a reduced mortality; this is an effect related to prenatal growth. But within each birthweight category, a higher weight at 1 year is associated with a reduced mortality, an effect associated with weight gain in the first year. This study was subsequently replicated in women (Osmond *et al.*, 1993). A further replication by Ericksson *et al.* (2001) was carried out on a quite different cohort, of men born in Helsinki in Finland in the decade 1934–44. Of the sample 4630 had measurements of height and weight over the first year, and 357 subsequently developed coronary heart disease. Lower birthweight was associated with higher levels of heart disease, and so too was slower growth over the first year, as measured by weight or length at 1 year, adjusted for birthweight. A particularly worrying possibility is that especially adverse effects might be associated with a low birthweight or early infant weight gain combined with an excessive adiposity later in life, a combination that would be found especially in societies in transitional stages of development in which poor nutrition early in life is followed by a relatively more abundant food intake later (Prentice & Moore, 2005).

A number of studies have also examined relationships between weight gain in infancy and later emotional development. The children who failed to thrive in infancy studied by Drewett, Corbett and Wright (1999) were examined again when they were 12 years old (Drewett, Corbett & Wright, 2006). At 12 the children had lower BMIs and were significantly less likely to be overweight. They were also more satisfied with their own body weights, and were less likely to be restrained eaters. These are effects of their lower BMIs, and are comparable to the effects we saw in young women with cystic fibrosis (Abbott et al., 2000; Truby & Paxton, 2001). The children who failed to thrive were no more likely to have low self-esteem or symptoms of depression or anxiety. However, effects of this kind do appear to develop later in life. Using data from the National Child Development Study, a birth cohort study of about 17,000 people born in England, Wales and Scotland in one week in March 1958, Cheung, Khoo, Karlberg and Machin (2002) showed that psychological distress measured with the Malaise Inventory (Rutter, Tizard & Whitmore, 1970) was significantly higher at 23, 33 and 42 years of age in people whose weight gain was lower over the first seven years of life. This association remained statistically significant after controlling for sex, gestational age at birth and birthweight, and for a range of social variables including the social class of the father and the mother's marital status and parity. Even more remarkably, perhaps, Barker et al. (1995) found that the lifetime risk of suicide was also associated with low weight gain over the first year. The explanation of these links is unclear. They may be mediated via lower IQ (Gunnell, Magnusson & Rasmussen, 2005; Van Os et al., 1997) or via later physical illness (Schnittker, 2005).

Another important possibility is that failure to thrive might have cognitive effects that become apparent only in old age. This possibility underlies the concept of 'cognitive reserve'. A number of studies have shown that persons with greater brain size are to some extent protected against clinical effects of Alzheimer's disease. In a population-based study (Graves et al., 1996) global cognitive scores as measured with the Cognitive Abilities Screening Tests were strongly related to head circumference in participants with (probable) Alzheimer's disease, after taking into account age, sex and education. Gale *et al.* (2003) similarly found that cognitive decline as assessed over a three and a half year period using the Wechsler Logical Memory Test in men and women 66–75 years old was systematically related to their head circumference when adults, with smaller head circumference associated with a greater risk of cognitive decline. The children in the sample were born in the Jessup Hospital in Sheffield, and records were available of their head circumference at birth. Head circumference at birth was unrelated to cognitive decline, and adjusting for it did not reduce the association between adult head circumference and cognitive decline. The implication of this is that it must have been head growth (and by inference, brain growth) after birth that provided the protection. Children who fail to thrive have smaller head circumferences at school age (Drewett, Corbett & Wright, 1999), so they may suffer more from cognitive decline late in life, though there is at the moment no direct evidence that they do.

8 Adiposity and obesity

8.1 Adiposity and its correlates

In previous chapters we have dealt with adverse effects of undernutrition in children. This is a widespread problem of long standing, and in many countries it is one that has been improving in recent years. A more recent problem and one that is clearly getting worse is 'overnutrition' – the increased fat storage that results from a higher food intake than is necessary to provide for a child's energy expenditure.

The body of a child can be thought of as comprising different compartments, which may be identified in terms of the tissues involved (for example, bone, muscle, adipose tissue, blood) or in terms of their chemical composition (for example, mineral, protein, fat, water). The two do not correspond exactly. Fats have a wide range of different functions in the body (Pond, 1998). The brain, for example, is about 60% fat, mostly in the form of phospholipids and cholesterol in cell membranes. These are *structural* lipids. Adipose tissue, which is unique to vertebrates, differs from other fat containing tissues in the body because it has evolved as a specialised store of fat, available to provide energy as required. The fat is stored in the specialised fat storage cells of the body, the adipocytes, which contain *storage* lipids based on triacylglycerol molecules. It is these storage lipids that we are concerned with here, so measuring adiposity is simple in theory – we dissect out the adipose tissue, extract the storage lipids from it and weigh them. But again, what is simple in theory is not simple in practice. In practice the accurate measurement of adiposity in living children is rather difficult.

Many methods have been used, and are still in use. An old established method is the measurement of skinfold thicknesses with callipers, which provides a direct measurement of the fat mass, but only under the skin and only at a limited number of sites (the biceps, triceps, subscapular and suprailiac skinfolds are often chosen). Another old established method involves a combination of weighing in air and weighing under water. From the two weighings the proportion of the body that is fat can be

148

estimated. The method depends on the different densities of fat (about 0.9 g/ml) and the fat-free mass (about 1.1 g/ml in adults, though it is somewhat lower in children). Essentially this method divides the body into two components (fat and the fat-free mass) and measures the ratio between them. In an alternative method, the water content of the body can be measured using radioactive or stable isotopes of oxygen or hydrogen. These isotopes spread through the water in the body, which can be measured by the extent to which they are diluted. From this measurement of its water content the fat-free mass of the body can be estimated, and so, indirectly, its fat mass. Bioelectric impedance measurements also provide a means of estimating body fat, because electrical conduction depends on water and the electrolytes dissolved in it, which are virtually absent from fat. The electrical conductivity of the body therefore also varies with the ratio of fatty to fat-free tissues in the body. More recently, imaging methods have been used, such as magnetic resonance imaging (MRI) and dual energy X-ray absorptiometry (DXA) scanning, a method which relies on the attenuation of X-rays emitted at different energies by different tissues.

No method available for use in living humans produces a measurement of body fatness that is known to be correct. The measurement is made more precise if more of the different components of the body are separately determined. Adiposity measurements determined by underwater weighing can be made more precise, for example, if they are supplemented with direct assessments of the water content and mineral content of the body. Its water content can be measured using isotope dilution methods, and its mineral content estimated from bone measurements determined using DXA scanning. Using a procedure of this kind Wells et al. (1999) determined the body composition of a group of 8–10 year old children using a four-component model which partitioned the contributors to body weight into fat, mineral, protein and water. Estimates of adiposity using a variety of simpler methods were then related to body fat determined more precisely in this way. The most acceptable of the simpler methods involved the estimation of body water using deuterium dilution, or DXA based procedures, both of which were unbiased on average. Underwater weighing underestimated fatness, and methods based on the measurement of skinfold thickness or bioelectrical impedance showed poor agreement with fatness calculated in the four-component model.

In practice most research has measured weight rather than adiposity. We generally monitor changes in our own adiposity by weighing ourselves, and this works, to some extent, for comparison of the same adult person over time because their height is always the same. In comparisons of different people weight *per se* is not a useful measure, because although it is related to adiposity, it is also related to height. A measure of relative weight that takes height into account is therefore needed, and the Body Mass Index (BMI) is a measure of weight that is more or less independent of height in adults. The body mass index is normally calculated as weight in kilograms divided by the square of height in metres, i.e.

$$BMI = Weight\ (kg)/Height\ (m)^2$$

The BMI has been widely used in research, for good reasons (Kraemer, Berkowitz & Hammer, 1990). It is non-invasive and the measurements involved, height and weight, can be made reliably and can also be self-reported. Although this is useful for large-scale studies, self-reported weights are biased (Bowman & DeLucia, 1992). They are generally lower than measured weights, and the bias is greater in people trying to lose weight.

Traditional criteria for identifying excess weight in adults are a BMI greater than 25 or greater than 30 (WHO, 1997), sometimes referred to as criteria for *overweight* and *obesity* respectively. These criteria can be used at all ages in adults, and in both men and women. The assumption underlying them is that increased health risks are found if the BMI increases beyond the criterion values. In order to establish this large studies are needed in which health outcomes are measured over long periods of time in persons of known BMI. Studies of this kind using mortality as the outcome, for example, were collated by Troiano *et al.* (1996) who provide quantitative estimates of the relationship between body weight and subsequent mortality derived from 23 studies which together followed up over half a million people. Using a 30 year follow-up, the BMI in men associated with the minimum risk of mortality was 24. The risk steadily increased with higher BMI, and was twice as high at a BMI of 30. It also steadily increased with BMIs below 24, and was twice as high when the BMI was below 20. There were fewer studies of women, and data could only be summarised for a 10 year follow-up. A similar relationship was found in women who smoked, though there was little relationship between BMI and mortality in women who did not smoke.

In older children the BMI correlates quite strongly (>0.7 at each age from 9 to 15 years) with adiposity as measured more directly by four skinfold thicknesses (Lazarus *et al.*, 1996). But it is not entirely independent of height, and it varies markedly with age. BMI decreases steadily from 1 to 5 years of age, then increases again. Because the average BMI in children changes with age, a single criterion for overweight or obesity in children at all ages of the kind that can be used in adults is not available. Many published studies have simply treated the fattest children in their

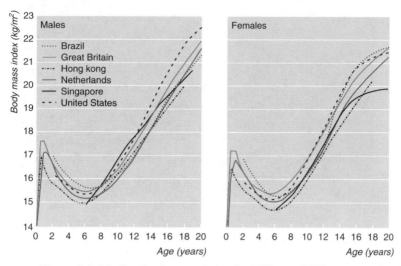

Figure 8.1 Median body mass index in children of different ages in six countries (Cole *et al.*, 2000). Reproduced from *British Medical Journal*, *32*, 1240–3. Copyright 2000 with permission from the BMJ Publishing Group.

age groups as overweight or obese (say those above the 85th or 95th centile for the BMI). However, standard BMI-based criteria for overweight and obesity in children of different ages have recently been proposed (Cole *et al.*, 2000). Centile curves for the BMI were established for six large nationally representative growth surveys, each providing information on the BMI from over 10,000 children aged 6–18. The surveys came from Brazil, Great Britain, Hong Kong, the Netherlands, Singapore and the United States. Figure 8.1 shows the average BMI at different ages for these countries. This illustrates clearly the change in BMI in children as they grow up. A new centile curve was interpolated for each data set, which corresponded to the centiles for BMIs of 25 and 30 at age 18, so as to give the same prevalence of overweight and obesity at younger ages (2–18) as was identified in the country in question at 18 years of age. These interpolated centile curves were then averaged. This procedure has provided a table of BMIs that can act as international criteria for overweight and obesity in childhood (the International Task Force on Obesity or ITFO criteria). The criterion for overweight in males, for example, is 18.41 kg/m^2 at 2 years, drops to 17.42 at 5 years and then rises steadily through 19.84 at 10 and 22.62 at 14 to reach the adult value of 25 kg/m^2 at 18.

Whatever the exact criterion used to identify it, studies have regularly found that the prevalence of obesity has increased steadily in recent years.

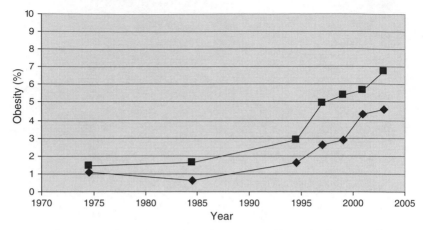

Figure 8.2 Prevalence of obesity in 5–10-year-old children in England, 1974–2003. Data from Stamatakis *et al.*, 2005, Table 2. Males: ♦ Females: ■.

For the period 1972 to 1994 data were collected via the National Study of Health and Growth, which surveyed state primary-school children in England and Scotland. Over this period weight adjusted for height increased in Scotland in all the age groups studied (from 5 to 10 years), and increased in England in the 8–10-year-old children (Hughes, Li, Chinn & Rona, 1997). Triceps skinfold thicknesses, which provide a more direct measure of fatness, increased in both age groups in both countries. For the period 1995 to 2003 data were collected via the Health Survey for England, which surveyed nationally representative samples of children from 2 to 10 years old (Jotangia, Moody, Stamatakis & Wardle, 2005). Data from both these sources were collated by Stamatakis *et al.* (2005), and trends in overweight and obesity examined using the ITFO criteria referred to above (Cole *et al.*, 2000). The trends are shown in Figure 8.2. There are other data sets from the UK which confirm these trends in younger (Bundred, Kitchener & Buchan, 2001) and in older children (Adamson *et al.*, 1992). Data for nationally representative samples in the USA are available from the National Health Examination Survey (NHES) cycles II and III, from 1963 to 1970, and from the National Health and Nutrition Examination Surveys (NHNES) I, II and III from 1971 to 1994 and are reviewed by Troiano and Flegal (1998). Over this period the mean BMI increased in every age group (6 to 17) in both males and females. The prevalence of overweight increased from 3.9% to 11.4% for children aged 6–11, and from 4.6% to 11.4% for children aged 12–17. Similar secular trends have been found in other studies (Freedman *et al.*, 1997).

Obesity in adults is related to socio-economic class, with higher rates in more deprived populations. The relationship is typically stronger and more consistent in women than in men (Guillaume & Lissau, 2002). The relationship between the two in children, however, is much less clear (Guillaume & Lissau, 2002; Saxena *et al.*, 2004; Sobal & Stunkard, 1989; Troiano & Flegal, 1998). In the study of Saxena *et al.*, in England, for example, there was no social class difference in obesity in either boys or girls from 2–20 years of age, though there were marked differences between ethnic groups, with the highest rates among boys in samples of Indian and Pakistani origin and in girls of Afro-Caribbean origin. However, more recent data from the same population suggest that the increase in rates of obesity in recent years in children has been greater among more disadvantaged families (Stamatakis *et al.*, 2005). There is no social class gradient in obesity in the USA in younger children (<10 years old), though there is in older children, with a higher prevalence in children from lower-income families (Wang, 2001).

Associations with more specific adverse early circumstances have been suggested by a prospective longitudinal study of Danish children in the Copenhagen area (Lissa-Lund-Sørensen & Sørensen, 1992). The children were initially sampled when 9–10 years old in 1974, when their heights and weights were measured. Their mothers responded to a questionnaire dealing with the school education. The occupational status of the family and an area-based measure of housing standards were also recorded. The children were recontacted when they were 20–21 years old, when they reported their adult weights and heights. The usual positive correlation was found between the participants' BMI when they were children and their BMI when they were adults. There was no significant association between their BMI when they were children and any of their parents' educational or occupational variables, or their housing standards as reflected in the area-based measure. This reflects the more general lack of association between adiposity and social class in young children. But children brought up in the areas with poor housing standards were more likely to be overweight as adults, though becoming overweight was not related to their parents' education or occupational status. This result is not entirely easy to interpret, but it suggests that area of residence in childhood is a more important determinant of later obesity than traditional family-based educational or socio-economic measures. More recent research has shown that objectively assessed adverse features of the local neighbourhood are associated with overweight in adults, independently of socio-economic status, probably because they are associated with lower activity levels (Ellaway, Macintyre & Bonnefoy, 2005).

The very clear evidence for increased adiposity in children in Western countries is paralleled to some extent by rising trends in overweight in some developing countries. Data on this come from the World Health Organisation Global Database on Child Growth and Malnutrition, which was developed in 1986 to make available the results from nutritional surveys worldwide (De Onis & Blössner, 2000). As expected, the commonest problem has been wasting (low weight for height), and countries with high rates of wasting tended to have low rates of overweight. But the global prevalence of overweight in preschool children reported in this study was 3.3%, and over the period from 1985 to 1998 it increased in 16 of the 38 countries for which more than one survey was available. Some countries (Uzbekistan, Kiribati and Algeria) managed to have high prevalences of both wasting and overweight at the same time.

Recent increases in adiposity and obesity in Western countries might actually be greater than is implied by these changes in the BMI, because the BMI is a measure of weight adjusted for height, rather than of adiposity *per se*, and it is possible that the relationship between the BMI and adiposity might have changed over time. Lesser physical activity, for example, would tend to increase adiposity, which would increase the BMI, but might also reduce the bulk of muscles, which would reduce it. There is a lack of reliable data on changes in the body composition of children, but a number of lines of evidence do suggest that the relationship between BMI and fatness might have changed in this way in recent years. Wells *et al.* (2002) compared the average adiposity of children in Cambridge with that of the 'reference child' of Fomon (Fomon *et al.*, 1982). The reference child was constructed to represent the average body composition of children of different ages at the time, though there is no way of being certain how accurately it did so. A group of children up to 11 years of age who were studied in Cambridge from 1989 to 1999 were compared with the reference child, and although their average BMI was not greater, they were significantly fatter than the reference child. In a further study, McCarthy *et al.* (2003) compared measurements of waist circumference in British children from a survey conducted in 1997 with measurements from earlier surveys in 1977 and 1987 for girls and boys respectively. Both BMI and waist circumference increased over this period, but waist circumference increased more.

The steady rise in adiposity and obesity in children is likely to be of environmental origin, and must have involved an increase in energy intake or a decrease in energy expenditure or both. That much is obvious. But to pin down its causes more precisely is difficult. In adults the change over time seems to have correlated with changes in energy expenditure, as assessed through a surrogate measure, television viewing, rather than with changes in energy (or fat) intake (Prentice & Jebb, 1995). The best data we have in children do not suggest any substantial increases in energy intake over the 30 year period from 1965, and the proportion of energy derived from fatty foods actually went down (Cavadini, Siega-Riz & Popkin, 2000; Troiano et al., 2000). By inference it is also likely to have been changes in energy expenditure that were responsible in children, though we do not have any direct measures of energy expenditure in children over this period.

Adiposity in childhood is of concern partly because adiposity tends to correlate ('track') over the lifespan (Power, Lake & Cole, 1997). The evidence consistently indicates that children with higher BMIs are more likely to have higher BMIs later in life. For example, in the 1958 British Birth Cohort children with a BMI above the 98th centile at 7 were over four times as likely to meet the BMI criterion for obesity in their early thirties, and those with a BMI above the 98th centile at 16 were over five times as likely to. Although this clearly indicates correlation between childhood and adult BMIs, there is some controversy over whether it represents correlations in adiposity *per se*. The BMI reflects muscle mass and bone mass as well as adiposity, and in a longitudinal study in which children initially measured at 9 were followed up at 50, although BMI at 9 was significantly correlated with BMI at 50, it was not correlated with body fatness at 50 as assessed using bioelectric impedance (Wright et al., 2001). However, significant correlations of around .5 have been found between childhood BMI and adult skinfold thicknesses in another study (Freedman et al., 2005) and similar findings have been reported elsewhere (Power, Lake & Cole, 1997). Weight in infancy (Charney et al., 1976; Poskitt & Cole, 1977) and weight *gain* in infancy (Cameron et al., 2003; Gunnarsdottir & Thorsdottir, 2003) are also associated with later measures of overweight. One reason for concern about the growing adiposity of children, then, is that it is likely to be associated with later obesity when the children are adults, and so with the health problems that follow from it.

In children themselves health problems arising directly from obesity are not common, but they are beginning to be seen as a result of the rising prevalence of obesity in childhood (Dietz, 1998; Must & Strauss, 1999). Major problems tend to be found in the most severely obese. Because children are still growing, their bones are softer, with unfused growth plates, and they are not well adapted to carry the body weight associated with severe obesity, which can give rise to a bowing of the legs and other orthopaedic problems. Respiratory problems can lead to obstructive sleep apnoea, and raised blood pressure in the brain to headaches, vomiting, blurred vision and other symptoms. More commonly found are hyperlipidaemia (increased blood lipids), a risk factor for heart disease, and glucose intolerance and non-insulin-dependent diabetes (Berenson *et al.*, 1989).

Psychological problems are another possibility. These have been investigated in a number of studies. Particular interest has been shown in self-esteem. There is good reason for this. Self-esteem is based on our appraisal of ourselves in respect of qualities that are important to us, but this is at least partly based on the judgements that we believe others will make. Differences in physical characteristics such as adiposity are highly conspicuous, and correlations between self-esteem and perceptions of physical appearance in general are high (Emler, 2001). They are especially high in adolescence, so effects of adiposity on self-esteem are likely to be related to the age of the child.

Most substantial studies of young children have not found that self-esteem is lower if they are fatter. In 3–5-year-old children Klesges *et al.* (1992) examined the relationship between scores on the Harter Pictorial Scale of Perceived Competence and Social Acceptance and their adiposity as assessed using triceps skinfold thicknesses, and found no relationship between the two. There was some evidence that children with lower physical perceived competence were fatter one or two years later, even after taking into account their initial fatness. Although the effect was quite weak (and was lost by the third year) it does draw attention to the possibility that low physical self-esteem might be a risk factor for obesity, as well as a consequence of it. Children with low physical self-esteem might, for example, be less willing to engage in physically demanding activities.

Mendelson and White (1982) in a small study of children 7–12 years old showed that 'body esteem' was related to obesity, but self-esteem more generally was not. Hill, Draper and Stack (1994) replicated both these findings in a large sample of 9-year-old children in the UK (213 girls and 166 boys). Self-esteem can be measured either globally or in relation to particular domains (academic, social, athletic etc.), and Phillips and Hill (1998) examined this issue further in a large school-based sample of preadolescent (9-year-old) girls using a more discriminating measure, the Harter Self-Perception Profile for Children (Harter, 1982). This assesses self-esteem in five areas, scholastic competence, social appearance, athletic competence, physical appearance and behavioural conduct, and takes into account the importance the child attributes to each domain. In addition, peer nominations of popularity were obtained. The self-esteem measures showed that girls with a BMI in the top 5% ('obese') and in the next 10% ('overweight') did have lower self-esteem, but only in the restricted domains of athletic competence and physical appearance. Their global self-worth was not significantly lower. They were less likely to be seen by their peers as attractive, but were not less popular. The study of Strauss (2000) of 1377 9–10-year-old children confirms that global self-esteem is not related to obesity in children of this age.

As regards older children, in an early study of self-esteem in 8–16-year-old children Sallade (1973) compared 120 who were obese and an equal number of controls, chosen from a single school. The obese children were identified by a recently collected weight taking into account their age and sex, and adiposity was checked using triceps skinfold thicknesses, to exclude those who were heavy but not obese. There was evidence that self-concept was poorer in the obese children. A subsequent replication of this study in 9–14-year-old children, however, did not find any relationship between the two (Wadden *et al.*, 1984) although this also involved a reasonably large number (210). In 9–18-year-old black children Kaplan and Wadden (1986) found statistically significant correlations between the two, but they were small and were restricted to children 9–11 years old. In a study of older (14- and 16-year-old) girls Martin *et al.* (1988) found that self-esteem was significantly lower in the girls with the highest BMIs. Two other large studies (Kostanski & Gullone, 1998; O'Brien *et al.*, 1990) found no association. All of these studies used the Rosenberg self-esteem scale, which evaluates a single dimension of global self-esteem. In a study of over 1000 adolescents aged 12–15 years, French *et al.* (1996) related BMI to scores on the Harter Self-Perception Profile for Adolescents, which assesses self-esteem in eight subdomains as well as globally. BMI was related to physical appearance self-esteem in both males and females (higher BMI associated with lower self-esteem). It was also related to global self-esteem in females, though not in males. The relationship was not very strong, however: the significant correlation in females in the French *et al.* study was only –.14. The evidence for a substantial correlation between self-esteem and body weight then, even in adolescents, is not very strong. One reason for this may be that poor body image is very widely prevalent, especially in females, even in those who are not objectively overweight.

Low self-esteem is related to depression; indeed they are related so strongly that mild depression and low self-esteem might even be considered the same thing (Emler, 2001). Using a measure of depression rather than self-esteem, Wadden *et al.* (1989) found no relationship between BMI and depression in a community (school-based) sample of adolescent girls about 15 years old, though there was strong evidence that the heavier girls were more dissatisfied with their weight. Similarly there was no relationship between obesity and depression in girls in a large longitudinal study of just under 1000 rural American children (Mustillo *et al.*, 2003). There was, however, in boys, though only if the obesity was chronic. It was not possible to establish in this study whether obesity led to the depression or vice versa.

8.2   The genetics of obesity

The body mass index tends to be somewhat similar in members of the same family. The correlation between spouses, for example, is about .1, between parents and children it is about .2 and between siblings it is between .2 and .3 (Bouchard & Pérusse, 1993). These familial correlations involve genetic and environmental components, which are traditionally disentangled in studies of monozygotic twins. A direct estimate of the heritability of the BMI can be obtained by examining the correlation between BMI in monozygotic twins reared in separate families. There are three recent studies of this kind (Allison *et al.*, 1996; Price & Gottesman, 1991; Stunkard, Sørenson & Schulsinger, 1983). Stunkard *et al.* (1990) studied 93 monozygotic twins reared apart and identified through the Swedish Twin Register. In adult life (at an average age of about 60) the correlation between the BMIs of the twins was .70 in men and .66 in women. Ideally for studies of this kind separation would be at birth, but in practice it tends to occur later, so the children share a common environment for a period after birth. In this study, however, age at separation was not related to the similarity between the twins later in life, in either height or weight. Price and Gottesman (1991) examined the BMI in 34 twins reared apart and 38 reared together, from a cohort originally investigated in a study of personality and intelligence by Shields (1962). The BMI correlation for the twins reared apart was .61, and it was not significantly different in those rated as having been raised in more or less similar environments. Allison *et al.* (1996) pooled three sets of twins, a Finnish, a Japanese and a predominantly American set, giving 53 twins reared apart in all. The correlations between the twins for the BMI were .63, .73 and .85 for the three sets, and .79 for all the twins pooled. Adjusting for relevant covariates (sex, age, source of data) reduced the estimates somewhat. Pooling their own data and the data previously collated by Stunkard *et al.* and by Price and Gottesman, the overall estimate of the heritability of the BMI calculated by Allison *et al.* was .675. This suggests that more than half the variability in the BMI in the populations studied was of genetic origin. All these studies used data from adults, but Koeppen-Schomerus, Wardle and Plomin (2001) subsequently examined genetic contributions to weight in 4-year-old children. This study was based on 3636 twin pairs born in the UK in 1994. The heritability estimates for weight adjusted for height (a measure similar to the BMI) was .64 for boys and .61 for girls. Twin studies are not the only source of heritability estimates, and other studies report estimates of parent–offspring and sibling correlations and from adoption studies. The estimates of heritability from these studies tend to be slightly lower than those from twin studies, explaining 20% to 80% of the variance in BMI in family studies reporting parent–offspring and sibling correlations and 20% to 60% in adoption studies (Maes, Neale & Eaves, 1997).

Given the evidence that there is a genetic contribution to relative body weight, what are the pathways involved? This is not, unfortunately, an easy question to answer. The genetic data come largely from studies of the BMI. BMI is something that can be measured easily and reliably in large numbers of people, and for that reason it is a preferred measure of adiposity in epidemiological work, including work in epidemiological genetics. But the BMI is only an indirect measure of adiposity, and it is theoretically possible that the heritability of the BMI could be at least partly the result of genetic influence on other components of the BMI (muscle mass or skeletal mass for example) rather than of adiposity per se. There are very few studies of the heritability of adiposity using other methods of assessing it (Börjeson, 1976; Bouchard et al., 1988; Brook, Huntley & Slack, 1975). Assuming that the heritability studies are principally assessing the heritability of body fat, genetic effects could involve physiological mechanisms relating to fat storage, or behavioural mechanisms involving either side of the energy balance equation, i.e. energy intake or energy expenditure. There is, for example, evidence that physical activity levels 'run in families' (Moore et al., 1991), though not necessarily for genetic reasons. Energy expenditure can be measured reliably using tracer methods, but there is no reliable way of measuring food intake that does not interfere with normal eating patterns that can be used on a large scale. Even if there were, there would still be multiple pathways to investigate. Increased food intake might result, for example, from a higher set point for body fat, a greater hedonic response to food, a greater appetite or less effective satiating mechanisms. There are likely to be many different genes involved in the control of adiposity, and they may operate in many different ways.

In summary, studies of twins show a very substantial genetic contribution to variability in body weight. They show too, of course, a substantial environmental contribution. The exact estimates vary from study to study, but exact estimates are of limited interest. Firstly, as they are based on the BMI they are estimates of the heritability of weight rather than of adiposity per se. Secondly, they are specific to populations studied at particular times and places: changes in the nutritional environment, or in other aspects of the environment that affect weight gain, would change the heritability estimates. Thirdly, general estimates of heritability do not provide any basis for intervention. It is only information about specific genetic effects (or specific environmental effects) that might suggest possibilities for change. To examine specific genetic effects means examining the effects of specific genes, and a number of single genes that have major effects on adiposity have now been identified.

The most striking of these involve the hormone, leptin, which we met in Chapter 1. Leptin was first identified through its absence in a strain of abnormally fat mice, the *ob* strain (Friedman, 1997). Leptin is normally produced in adipocytes and reduces appetite. In mice which are homozygous for a mutant recessive form of the *ob* gene, leptin is not produced. The mice eat excessively and become grossly obese. The first study to show related effects in humans was by Montague *et al.* (1997). These authors studied two children of families of Pakistani origin in which there was extensive intermarriage. The children were cousins, and they each developed severe and intractable obesity. The birthweights of both children were about average (3.46 kg and 3.53 kg respectively), but both gained weight rapidly early in life. The weight of the older child is shown in Figure 1.3 (Chapter 1). By the time she was 8 years old, she weighed 86 kg, and her body was 57% fat. The male cousin was 2 years old at the time of the report and weighed 29 kg, with 54% body fat. This obesity was a consequence of a single recessive gene for which the two affected children were homozygous. As expected, all four parents were heterozygous for the same gene. The parents were essentially unaffected, but the two homozygous children had extremely low plasma levels of leptin, and both children were said to be persistently hungry and to have eaten considerably more than their siblings from early in infancy. A subsequent report described the effects of treatment with leptin in the older of these children, when she was 9 years old and weighed 94.4 kg (Farooqi *et al.*, 1999). She lost weight within two weeks of the treatment starting, and continued to do so over the year for which she was treated, losing 16.4 kg in all. Evidence from test meals and food diaries showed that this weight loss was accompanied by a considerable reduction in food intake. Detailed laboratory-based study of leptin deficient adults (Williamson *et al.*, 2005) has also shown that treatment with leptin reduces hunger and the rate and duration of eating, and so reduces overall food intake. A similar genetically based leptin deficiency that also resulted in obesity has been found in a second family of Turkish origin (Strobel *et al.*, 1998). In a third family, of Kabilian origin, a gene variant affected leptin receptors rather than the production of leptin (Clément *et al.*,

1998). Again the family was consanguineous, but in this family leptin levels were not reduced: it was the receptors that respond to leptin that were abnormal, rather than the production of leptin. Three affected sisters were studied. Each gained weight very rapidly from early in life, and weighed more than 100 kg by the time of the study, when they were in their teens.

Another important genetic condition leading to obesity in childhood is melanocortin-4 receptor (*MC4R*) deficiency, first identified in 1998 (Vaisse, Clement, Guy-Grand & Froguel, 1998; Yeo *et al.*, 1998). *MC4R* deficiency is inherited dominantly, or more precisely codominantly. Obesity is found in people who are homozygous for the condition, but also those who are heterozygous, though their obesity is less severe (Farooqi & O'Rahilly, 2005). Again it is associated with overeating: affected children ate three times as much as their unaffected siblings at a test meal (Farooqi *et al.*, 2003). There is evidence that the melanocortin pathway is involved in the appetite suppressing effect of leptin, and a homozygous child who completely lacked melanocortin-4 receptor activity gained weight in infancy and early childhood in a way that precisely paralleled that of children lacking normal leptin receptor functioning (Clément *et al.*, 1998; Lubrano-Berthelier *et al.*, 2004). Probably because the associated obesity is found in heterozygotes as well as homozygotes, and because it does not interfere with fertility, this is a relatively common condition, found in 6% of severely obese children (Farooqi *et al.*, 2003).

Another cause of obesity in humans is the Prader-Willi syndrome, which is characterised by obesity, delayed sexual development and intellectual disabilities. It has a prevalence at birth of about 1 in 25,000. The Prader-Willi syndrome may involve one or a number of genes, and is the consequence of an absence of the normal paternal contribution to the long arm of chromosome 15. This absence can have various causes. The most common is simply a missing piece of the chromosome, and the next most common is maternal disomy, in which both strands of the chromosome have come from the mother. Infants with Prader-Willi syndrome are hypotonic (floppy) at birth and are slow in reaching motor milestones. They gain weight very poorly over the first year (Ehara, Ohno & Takeshita, 1993), often meeting criteria for failure to thrive, and also have feeding problems (Gilmour, Skuse & Pembrey, 2001). But after the first year or so affected children develop a striking pattern of excessive food intake (hyperphagia) which is a cardinal symptom of the disorder and which underlies the development of their obesity. Holland *et al.* (1993) have documented this hyperphagia carefully in a study in which adults with Prader-Willi syndrome (and controls without the syndrome) were offered a meal made up of a free supply of relatively unpalatable

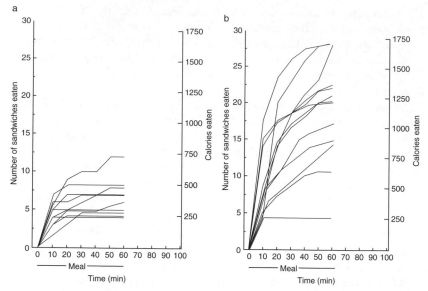

Figure 8.3 Eating patterns during a test meal in people with and without Prader-Willi syndrome (Holland *et al.*, 1993). The cumulative number of sandwiches eaten is plotted against time from the start of the meal, for a group of 13 people with Prader-Willi syndrome (right) and 10 people without (left). Energy is shown in the units used in the original publication. Reproduced by permission from Macmillan Publishers Ltd. *International Journal of Obesity*, *17*, 527–32. Copyright 1993.

sandwich quarters over an hour-long period. The food intakes of the two groups is shown in Figure 8.3. The people with Prader-Willi syndrome ate three and a half times as much as the controls. Recent research has shown that the Prader-Willi syndrome is associated with high levels of the stomach hormone ghrelin, which enhances appetite and increases food intake in humans (Delparigi *et al.*, 2002), and this may contribute to the hyperphagia. The hyperphagia in Prader-Willi syndrome is associated with a range of behavioural problems, which might include taking food from others, hoarding food and stealing money to buy food (Russell & Oliver, 2003). The study of Holland *et al.* cited above compared people with Prader-Willi syndrome and normal weight controls of the same age and sex. Gilmour and Skuse, however, compared food-related behaviour in children with Prader-Willi syndrome and children who were equally fat for other reasons, using a questionnaire given to their parents, and they found no obvious difference between these groups (Gilmour & Skuse, 2003). The questionnaire dealt with hyperphagia (overeating), pica (eating items that are not normally eaten) and foraging behaviour (such as eating from dustbins). Although no significant differences were reported between the two groups in this study, Prader-Willi syndrome is undoubtedly difficult to deal with, and requires constant supervision of access to food if excessive weight gain is to be avoided (Holland *et al.*, 1995). The study of Gilmour and Skuse suggests that the feeding-related problems associated with the syndrome might also be found in other children obese for other reasons.

A large number of other genes are likely to be involved in the control of adiposity (Chagnon, Pérusse & Bouchard, 1998), but although there are clearly important genetic causes underlying some of the variability in adiposity between different people, it is important not to assume that this means that differences in adiposity are 'inborn'. It is the gene that is inborn, not the adiposity, and to argue that 'body weight is primarily genetic and metabolic' and that 'it is normal for some children to be fat' (Satter, 1996) is to oversimplify complex issues. The examples of genetic pathways that we have considered above all involve behavioural mechanisms, and all genes operate in interaction with the environment, so the most that should be said is that it is normal for some children to be fat in some environments. The rising prevalence of obesity shows that genetically similar populations of children become obese to different extents in different environments, and the environments characteristic of industrialised societies are clearly changing so that it is normal for more children to be fat. It would be quite possible, and would be desirable, to reverse some of these changes so as to make it less normal.

8.3   The development of adiposity

To recapitulate, family and twin studies of obesity have provided estimates of the relative importance of environmental and genetic factors to the variability in adiposity in contemporary Western populations, but this information has limited practical utility unless more specific information about the particular genes or the particular environmental variables involved and their effects can be obtained. In Section 8.2 progress in respect of a small number of specific genes was examined. In this section we shall consider the development of adiposity in children more generally, examining some environmental variables and the role of the child's own behaviour in its development.

Overnutrition, like malnutrition, can begin before birth. Indeed, Dietz has suggested that the prenatal period may be one of a number of *critical periods* for the development of obesity in childhood (Dietz, 1997). This term can be a rather confusing one, as it can mean different things in different contexts. Its origins are in embryology. During the early period of development different organ systems develop at different times, and pathological agents can have seriously adverse effects on their development which are restricted to clearly defined developmental stages. The classic example is the rubella virus. This virus causes serious abnormalities in the fetus, but only if the fetus is exposed to it in the first trimester of pregnancy. From its origins in embryology the idea of a critical period was taken into ethology, when Konrad Lorenz used it in relation to the imprinting of young birds (Bateson, 1979). The concept has been useful in other areas in which environmental stimuli have effects that are limited to particular periods, or particularly strong in particular periods, such as are found in the visual system and in second language learning. It has also been used with reference to sexual differentiation.

Dietz suggests that the prenatal period may be a critical period in the development of obesity, during which under- or overnutrition might have enduring effects on adiposity, perhaps as a result of influences on the development of the hypothalamic systems involved in appetite, or on adipocyte numbers. He provides two examples suggesting prenatal effects of this kind. The first example comes from the Dutch famine study, which we first dealt with in Chapter 4 in connection with cognitive effects of prenatal malnutrition. Men whose mothers were exposed to the Dutch famine of 1944–45 were examined when they were 17 years old (Ravelli, Stein & Susser, 1976). Those whose mothers were in the first two trimesters of pregnancy during the famine were substantially more likely to be obese at 17 than controls born at different times or in different areas, and the effect was specific to the first two trimesters, and was not found if the famine coincided with the last trimester and the early months of postnatal life; indeed, in such cases infants were less likely to be obese. This study therefore provides evidence that undernutrition in the first two trimesters of pregnancy is associated with a higher prevalence of later obesity, and there is some evidence here for temporal specificity of a kind that makes reference to a critical period appropriate. But the famine was severe, resulting in fetal growth retardation and perinatal deaths, and in the deaths of 10,000 adults, so an effect of this kind is unlikely to indicate a very general risk factor for obesity in affluent countries. The second example comes from a study of diabetes during pregnancy (Pettitt *et al.*, 1983). It was conducted among the Pima American Indians of Arizona, a population particularly prone to diabetes and obesity. The study examined whether women who were diabetic when pregnant gave birth to children who were more likely to be obese. Mothers were divided into three groups: a group who were diabetic while pregnant, a group who were prediabetic (and only developed diabetes after the pregnancy) and a non-diabetic group. Diabetes in pregnancy leads to an abnormally high availability of nutrients, and the offspring of the diabetic mothers had significantly heavier birthweights. This difference was maintained for at least 15 years, with three times as many becoming obese later in life.

This example comes from a specific medical condition on a specific population, but there is a more general correlation between birthweight and later adiposity. Braddon et al. (1986) found an association between heavier birthweight and 36-year-overweight in men, though not in women. Seidman et al. (1991) followed up over 30,000 infants born in Jerusalem between 1964 and 1971. Birthweights were recorded at the time of delivery and weights and heights at 17 years of age, in the Israel Defence Forces draft medical examination records. Birthweights were allocated to 500 g categories. The adolescents were defined as overweight or severely overweight if they were above the 90th centile (BMI 24.6 kg/m^2) or 97th centile (BMI 27.8 kg/m^2) for the sample. There was a clear increase in the proportion overweight and obese at 17 in each birthweight category above 3.5 kg; it was over twice as high in the highest birthweight category in both males and females.

This correlation between birthweight and later adiposity may reflect the working of a critical period, but Allison et al. (1995) have raised the alternative possibility that it might simply be a genetic correlation (as, indeed, had Dietz himself). Allison et al. investigated this by examining the association in monozygotic twins between differences in their birthweight and differences in their adult BMI. Since monozygotic twins are genetically identical, differences in their birthweight must be of environmental origin. In this study there was, as expected, a statistically significant correlation between birthweight and adult BMI. But there was no significant correlation between differences in birthweight and differences in adult BMI in the twin pairs, so there is no clear evidence here for any effect of the prenatal nutritional environment on later BMI. Another problem, of course, is that correlations between birthweight and later BMI do not necessarily reflect correlations between adiposity at birth and at later ages, because neither birthweight nor BMI are direct measures of adiposity. They also reflect lean body mass, and studies that have sought to measure lean body mass and fat mass separately have generally found that there is a positive correlation between birthweight and later lean body mass, rather than between birthweight and later fat mass (Rogers, 2003).

Another early environmental variable that may be associated with later adiposity is breast-feeding. Although earlier research gave rather equivocal results (Butte, 2001), a number of recent studies have shown that infants who were breast-fed are less likely to be fat later in childhood (Dewey, 2003). A large Scottish study of over 30,000 3-year-old children

(Armstrong, Reilly & the Child Health Information Team, 2003) showed a substantially lower risk of obesity (BMI on or above the 95th centile) and severe obesity (98th centile) in those exclusively breast-fed at 6–8 weeks, compared with those exclusively bottle-fed. Some control for the other characteristics of the families was included, using a geographically based deprivation index. In a study in Bavaria, von Kries *et al.* (1999) recorded heights and weights of 5–6-year-old children, and examined their early feeding history via questionnaires given to the parents. In just over 9000 children information on breast-feeding and its duration was available. Of the children who were bottle-fed, 12.6% were overweight and 4.5% obese; of those who were breast-fed, 9.2% were overweight and 2.8% obese. As in other European countries, there was a strong association between breast-feeding and the social characteristics of the child's family, and parental education was also associated with overweight and obesity in the child. The association between breast-feeding and obesity, however, was not eliminated by controlling for the education of the parents, though the use of this variable in two categories (parental education for less than 10 years, or 10 or more years) is unlikely to have fully controlled for social characteristics of the family. A very large study in the Czech Republic (Toschke *et al.*, 2002) examined the relationship in a group of 33,768 children aged 6–14. Breast-fed children were about 20% less likely to be overweight or obese. This was after adjustment for parental obesity, parental education, maternal smoking, birthweight and other variables, and the effect showed no obvious decline with age over the ages studied. Gilman *et al.* (2001) studied a large (>15,000) group of 9–14-year-old children in the 'Growing up Today' study in the USA. The children in this study were the offspring of registered nurses. The children who were mostly or only fed breast milk in the first six months had a risk of being overweight about 22% lower than those mostly or only fed infant formula. Controlling for the mother's own BMI, household income and a range of other variables did not eliminate this association.

In general, then, these studies do show a lesser tendency to overweight and obesity in breast-fed infants. Given that an infant is breast-fed, a number of these studies have also examined whether there is a relationship between the *duration* of breast-feeding and obesity, with varying results. In the study of von Kries *et al.* (1999), for example, the overall adjusted odds ratio (for obesity in children who were ever being breast-fed) was 0.75. The adjusted odds ratios for being obese for children breast-fed for ≤2 months, 3–5 months, 6–12 months and ≥12 months were 0.90, 0.65, 0.57 and 0.28 respectively. Although this graded relationship is sometimes conceptualised as studying the 'exposure' or 'dose-response relationship' (Dewey, 2003), and was described as a dose-response effect in this study, it might be better to avoid this terminology as it ignores the possibility that the child's own behaviour may contribute to the duration of breast-feeding. As we saw in Chapter 3, infants with a bigger appetite who gain weight more rapidly may be moved on to solids earlier. To show that infants exclusively or predominantly breast-fed for a longer period (say 6 months) are less likely to be obese than infants exclusively or predominantly breast-fed for a shorter period (say 3 months) doesn't in itself show a protective effect of longer breast-feeding. The same effect might be found if one compared exclusive or predominant bottle-feeding for 3 and 6 months. Infants with a lower appetite may accept exclusive milk feeding (breast or formula) for longer, and also be less likely to be obese later. The appropriate comparison, therefore, is not with all bottle-fed infants but with infants exclusively bottle-fed for the same period.

This reservation does not, however, apply to the fundamental finding of an association between breast-feeding and a lower risk of obesity, which is now reasonably well established. What explanations might there be of this association? One possibility is that it could be due to associations with other variables that have not been completely controlled for, in spite of all the efforts that have been made. An indication that this may be so comes from a study of sibling pairs in which one sibling has been breast-fed but not the other (Nelson, Gordon-Larsen & Adair, 2005). This design controls for shared aspects of the family environment, since the siblings come from the same family. Contrary to what would be expected if breast-feeding protected against adiposity, there was no evidence that the breast-fed children were less likely to be overweight in later life than their bottle-fed siblings. If the association found in the other studies does reflect a real effect of breast-feeding, a second possibility could be that it is a metabolic effect resulting from differences in the composition of breast and formula milk (Dewey, 2003). A third possibility that has attracted some interest (Dewey, 2003) is that it reflects differences in the ability of breast and bottle-fed infants to regulate their own milk intake (Drewett, Wright & Young, 1998; Wright, 1987; Wright, Fawcett & Crow, 1980). Wright et al. (1980) provided evidence from an observational study that during bottle-feeds the termination of sucking episodes in a feed is more likely to be due to the mother than the infant, while during breast-feeds the decision is more equally shared between the two. As we shall see below, there is some evidence that children who regulate their own energy intake effectively are less likely to be overweight, and being breast-fed does appear to be associated with more opportunity to do so. Breast-feeding might also alter the behaviour of the mother, and a recent large-scale study (Taveras *et al.*, 2004) has shown that breast and bottle-feeding mothers do differ in their later child feeding behaviour.

In a direct study of the influence that mothers might have on the weight gain of their infants, Kramer *et al.* (1983) developed scales to measure a mother's preference for fatter or thinner infants (the Ideal Infant Body Habitus Scale, IBH), and to assess their tendency to 'push' food on their infants (the Maternal Feeding Attitudes Scale, MFA). Pushiness measured at birth using this scale was associated with pressure to eat by the mother at 7 years (Duke *et al.*, 2004). In a further study of Kramer *et al.* these scales were administered at birth, and the infants followed up to the end of the first year, with measurement of their weight, BMI and skinfold thicknesses (Kramer *et al.*, 1985). The scores measuring the pushing of food were not related to weight or BMI after taking birthweight into account. The only relationship was with skinfold thickness at 6 months, when the relationship, paradoxically, was negative (more pushy mothers had infants who were less fat).

There is a tendency, still, to treat infants as if they are just the passive recipients of feeding by the mother, but the evidence reviewed in Chapter 2 would suggest that infants should to some extent control their own energy intake, and the above study suggests that they can do so even when their mothers are trying to push food on them. There is in fact good evidence that the appetites of infants very early in life do influence early weight gain and adiposity. Agras *et al.* (1987) examined this directly by using a nipple that recorded sucking pressure and milk flow (Kron, Johannes & Goddard, 1968). They found that the infants who became fatter by 1 or 2 years of age sucked more rapidly and at a higher pressure in the first month of life. Their suck and burst durations were longer, and the intervals between bursts of sucking were shorter. As a result their energy intake was higher. Sucking is directly under the control of the infant, and is therefore a reasonable indicator of their appetite. It is important to note that these differences in sucking were not associated with adiposity at the time the measurements were made, but with the development of adiposity over the next year or two. The same sucking characteristics predicted adiposity at 3 years, though not at 6 years.

This is the period of the 'adiposity rebound' (Rolland-Cachera *et al.*, 1984), which has been considered as another candidate for a sensitive or critical period in the development of obesity (Dietz, 1997). As shown in Figure 8.1, a child's BMI tends to decrease from about a year of age to 3–7 years of age, and then steadily increase until the child becomes an adult. Except for a brief period around birth, the BMI is therefore at its lowest at some point over the 3–7 year age range. The exact point varies in different children, and the age of the adiposity rebound is the age at which the BMI is at its minimum (and so the age at which it starts to increase again). Rolland-Cachera *et al.* showed that an earlier adiposity rebound in childhood predicted a higher BMI later in life. This finding has been replicated in other studies (Whitaker *et al.*, 1998), and there is no reason to doubt it. Questions do, however, arise concerning its interpretation (Dietz, 2000). In a clear analysis of the determinants of the timing of the adiposity rebound, Cole (2004) shows that an early rebound is associated with a high BMI and with upward centile crossing (i.e. with an above-average increase in the BMI). The finding that an earlier adiposity rebound is associated with a higher BMI later in life therefore may show nothing more than that children who are already relatively heavier or are getting relatively heavier at the time of the adiposity rebound are more likely to be relatively heavier as adults. This correlation does not in itself provide grounds for referring to a 'critical period'. That would need evidence that such correlations are not also found at other stages of development, or are not as strong. It is not even clear that differences in the timing of the adiposity rebound reflect differences in the environment. They may reflect inherent differences in the children. This interpretation is strengthened by evidence from a large-scale longitudinal study of the timing of the adiposity rebound in children (Dorosty *et al.*, 2000). The timing of the adiposity rebound was not associated with the dietary intake of energy or protein in the children or with their mother's education or the social class of their family. But the parents of children with an early adiposity rebound had higher BMIs and were more likely to be obese, characteristics which as we have seen show reasonably high heritability.

Energy intake is one component of energy balance; the other component is energy expenditure. Several studies have used the doubly labelled water method to examine the importance of individual variation in energy expenditure to variation in weight gain in infancy, mostly in comparisons of the children of overweight or obese parents and of lean parents, who for genetic and other reasons have differing risks of developing obesity themselves. Davies *et al.* (1995) found no significant relationship between energy expenditure in 12-week-old infants and the adiposity of their mothers or fathers. Stunkard *et al.* (1999) examined both energy expenditure and energy intake simultaneously in 78 infants, half of them born to obese and half to lean mothers. When the infants were 3 months old nutritive sucking behaviour and milk intake were measured, and at 1 year of age body composition was measured using anthropometric and electrical conductivity methods. As one would expect, weight and sex at

3 months strongly predicted weight at 1 year. The other significant predictors at 3 months were the total number of sucks measured during a test meal, and energy intake over a three-day period. As in the earlier study of Davies *et al.* (1995), total energy expenditure measured using the doubly labelled water method was not associated with weight at 1 year. These studies suggest, then, that in infancy variability in energy intake is a better predictor of the development of adiposity than variability in energy expenditure.

Goran *et al.* (1995) examined these relationships in 5-year-old children, and also found that there was no relationship between parental obesity and the energy expenditure of their children. An attempt to relate the energy expenditure of the children to their own adiposity also led to negative results (Goran *et al.*, 1998). In this study a range of methods was used to determine changes in relative fat mass in the children over a four-year period, from about 5 to about 9 years of age. Over this period the children were growing, and their body fat also increased, from 16.4% to 20.4% on average. The three variables that predicted fat mass accumulation were the child's sex (girls accumulated more than boys), their initial adiposity and the adiposity of their parents – the accumulation of fat was strikingly higher in the children with two obese parents. But there was no evidence that energy expenditure was lower in the children that accumulated more fat. Energy expenditure was measured using the doubly labelled water method over 14-day periods once a year. This is a very precise method, but the authors clearly spell out the great difficulties involved in measuring energy intake and expenditure with the accuracy that might be required to explain even the excessive accumulation of fat in children who have two obese parents. Although obesity involves the accumulation of large *amounts* of fat, the *rate* at which the fat is accumulated is low – in this study the children of two obese parents gained less than 1 kg a year more than expected. This is less than 3 g a day, equivalent to a daily energy imbalance of 113 kJ (27 kcal). The accumulation of fat is not simply a result of a relatively low energy intake, or of a relatively high energy expenditure, but of an excess of energy intake over expenditure. Measuring a difference between the two of this size is not an easy task.

More promising, perhaps, are studies involving the measurement of everyday lifestyle variables that are related to energy expenditure. One study which has successfully related activity levels in children to changes in body fat over childhood was reported by Moore *et al.* (2003). They measured changes in fat mass over an eight-year period, from 4 to 11 years of age, using the BMI and the sum of five skinfolds. Activity was measured using electronic motion sensors (accelerometers), worn for three to

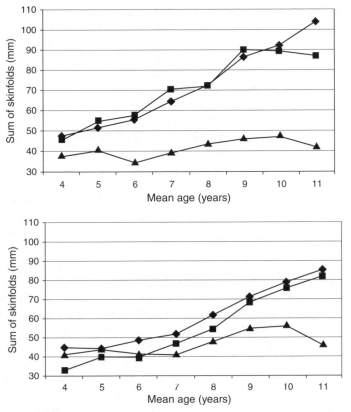

Figure 8.4 Changes in skinfold thicknesses, from 4 to 11 years of age in children with different activity levels (lowest tercile ♦; middle tercile ■; highest tercile ▲). Adjusted for baseline age and BMI. Top: girls. Bottom: boys. From Moore *et al.* (2003). Reproduced from *Preventive Medicine*, *37*, 10–17. Copyright 2003, with permission from Elsevier.

five consecutive days and usually twice a year, every year. Figure 8.4 shows the change in skinfold thicknesses, separately for boys and girls, in three groups (the most active third, the middle third and the least active third). The success of this study in relating the two may have come from the use of an automated rather than a self-reported measure of activity, from the measurement of activity over a number of days per year and over eight years, and from the direct measurement of fatness in the sum of skinfolds. The accumulation of fat is a slow process that takes place over extended periods of time, and the variables that underlie it need also to be measured over extended periods of time if the two are to be successfully related. Again, not an easy task.

Other studies have involved less direct measures related to activity, such as time spent watching television. Although measures of this kind are not simply measures of energy expenditure, they can be used in large-scale studies, and may provide guides to possible interventions in a way that physiological measures of total energy expenditure do not. Television watching is of particular importance because of the sheer time children spend on it. Estimates reviewed by Tinsley (2003) suggest that from 2 to 18 years of age the average time spent watching television is from 15,000 to 18,000 hours and exceeds the time spent in class (12,000 hours) and on any other activity except sleeping.

Dietz and Gortmaker (1985) first investigated the relationship between television watching and obesity in children. Their data came from the second and third cycles of the National Health Examination Survey (NHES), which investigated a representative sample of children in the USA in the 1960s. Children were studied at 6–11 years of age in the second cycle, and at 12–17 in the third cycle, with some children studied in both. Measures of adiposity were based on triceps skinfold thickness. Children with a triceps skinfold thickness at or above the 85th centile for their age were identified as obese, and those above the 95th as 'super-obese'. The prevalence of obesity in 12–17-year-olds watching different amounts of television (according to their own reports) is shown in Figure 8.5. On average, the more obese children watched more television. A similar though slightly less clear relationship was shown in the 6 to 11 year old children between obesity and television watching as reported by their parents. A wide range of control variables was examined, including the education of the mothers and fathers, their age, income and race, the birth order of the child and the number of their siblings, but none of them altered the relationship between television watching and adiposity to any major extent. Obesity could lead to more television watching, but in this study longitudinal analyses showed that the relationship between television watching and obesity in the third cycle remained statistically significant when adjusted for earlier obesity as measured in the second cycle. This suggests that it was not the obesity leading to greater television watching, but vice versa.

In a subsequent study, however, a significant relationship between television viewing and adiposity was not found (Robinson et al., 1993); 671 children participated in a cross-sectional study when they were about 12 years old. Body mass index and triceps skinfold thickness were both measured, and hours spent watching television assessed by self-report. There was a moderate correlation between television watching at the time and when the assessment was repeated two years later. The correlation between hours spent watching television and the BMI in these children,

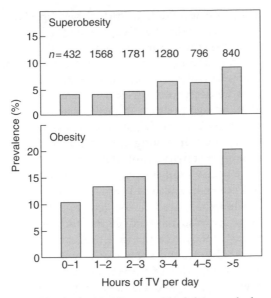

Figure 8.5 Obesity in 12–17-year-old adolescents by hours of television watched (Dietz & Gortmaker, 1985). Reproduced with permission from *Pediatrics*, *75*, 807–12. Copyright © 1985 by the American Academy of Pediatrics.

however, was very low (.053) and was not statistically significant. On the face of it this study contradicts the earlier study of Dietz and Gortmaker, which did show a statistically significant relationship between the two variables. But statistical significance depends on the numbers involved as well as the strength of a relationship, and in the Dietz and Gortmaker study the numbers were about ten times as big. The actual correlation between the two variables was not given for their study, but Robinson *et al.* estimate the correlation from the p values and number of children in the study; the estimated correlation was .03 to .05, so in fact the associations found in the two studies are very similar. The conclusion consistent with both studies is that there is probably a very small association between hours spent watching television and adiposity.

Andersen *et al.* (1998) re-examined these relationships in children investigated in the third National Health and Nutrition Examination Survey (NHANES III) in the United States between 1988 and 1994. Data were available for over 4000 children aged 8–16. Television watching and rates of vigorous exercise ('enough to make them sweat or breathe hard') were examined in relation to the BMI and to an index of trunk fat (the sum of subscapular and suprailiac skinfolds). The BMI increased with hours of television watched. In girls it was unrelated to vigorous exercise. In boys it was actually slightly higher in the group who exercised more, perhaps reflecting muscular development rather than fatness. The index of trunk fat was unrelated to vigorous exercise but increased systematically with hours of television watched. Although the strength of the association cannot be determined from the analyses provided, the evidence from this study suggests that adiposity is more strongly related to time spent in sedentary activity (watching television) than it is to time spent in vigorous activity. In young children far more time is spent in sedentary than vigorous activity. Children who have a television in their own bedroom have been found to spend more time watching television, and are more likely to be overweight (Dennison, Erb & Jenkins, 2002).

Television watching is a sedentary activity which reduces energy expenditure, but it can also have effects on food intake, as it exposes children to extensive food advertising. Studies in this area have been reviewed by Tinsley (2003), and show that television watching is associated with a higher consumption of high fat and high sugar foods in a range of countries, including the USA, Canada, Puerto Rico, Mexico, Great Britain, Italy, Australia and New Zealand. Food advertisements tend to promote foods that are high in fat and sugar (Wilson, Quigley & Mansoor, 1999). Taras et al. (1989) showed that there was a significant association between weekly hours of television watching and the requests made by children for foods advertised on TV, and with the purchases of these foods by parents, at least according to the mothers' own reports. Television watching is also associated with lower levels of fruit and vegetable consumption in 11-year-old children (Boynton-Jarrett et al., 2003) and more generally with having unhealthy conceptions of food and bad eating habits (Signorelli & Lears, 1992). These are a few examples of the many studies that have been conducted in this area, which have been comprehensively reviewed on behalf of the UK Food Standards Agency (Hastings et al., 2003). They come from research in 'media studies', an academic area too important to be dismissed in the facile way it sometimes is.

Whatever the common characteristics of their nutritional environment, children (and adults) vary widely in their adiposity. Individual differences in energy intake and energy expenditure clearly contribute to this variation, but another interesting possibility that has been examined is that there may be individual differences in the capacity to regulate energy intake, that is, to adjust food intake in response to variations in its energy content. When children take in energy as a preload before meals, they compensate for the energy they take in by reducing the energy subsequently consumed at a test meal, as discussed in Chapter 3. The extent to which they compensate depends on their age – older children compensate less completely than younger children (Birch & Deysher, 1986). But even in children of the same age, the precision with which they compensate varies from child to child, and it is related to the child's adiposity (Johnson & Birch, 1994). Johnson and Birch examined the extent to which children of 3–5 years of age compensated for a high energy preload by reducing energy intake at a subsequent test meal. They summarised the compensation characteristics of each child as a compensation index – the ratio of energy reduction at the meal to the energy consumed in the preload. Perfect energy compensation gives a compensation index of 100%. For a given child, the index shows some stability over a one year period. The average compensation index was 46.2%. It was higher in boys (57.1%) than in girls (36.0%), and it was significantly correlated with the sum of skinfold thicknesses in the girls. The correlation was negative, showing that fatter girls compensated for their energy loads less effectively. There was no correlation between the two in the boys. Perhaps reflecting this poorer energy compensation, overweight 5–7-year-old girls are also more likely to eat when they are not hungry. This was shown in a later study (Fisher & Birch, 2002) in which children ate from a free access lunch until they were 'full' (their own description). They were then given an opportunity to snack on a range of palatable foods, including popcorn, chocolate chip cookies and ice cream. Again, the consumption of snack foods in the absence of hunger was a reasonably stable characteristic over the two year period (5–7 years of age). Children overweight at both ages or with a BMI above average at both ages were significantly more likely to eat larger amounts of snack food in the absence of hunger. These characteristics of the child's food intake may be effects or causes of their greater adiposity. This cannot be determined from the data available. Even if poorer energy compensation is an effect of greater adiposity, it is likely to make some contribution to the maintenance of obesity and its resistance to treatment.

There is also evidence that energy compensation in young children is related to the child feeding practices of their mothers. This was first shown in the energy compensation study (Johnson & Birch, 1994). In this study child feeding practices were assessed using six items from a Child Feeding Questionnaire, which records the extent to which mothers control their children's food intake. Children whose mothers were more controlling of their food intake showed poorer energy compensation, which may have been because maternal control interferes with the child's ability to learn to regulate their own energy intake by overriding internal signals relating to hunger and satiation. As poorer energy compensation is related to adiposity in girls, one might expect that mothers who are more controlling would be more likely to have overweight daughters, but the direct evidence for this is not very strong. Saelens, Ernst and Epstein did not find any relationship between maternal control and the obesity of children in a discordant sibling analysis (Saelens, Ernst & Epstein, 2000). In this study 18 families were identified in which one sibling was obese and another was not. The children were all 7–12 years old, and the average age of the obese and the non-obese siblings was the same. The 'control' scale of the early version of the Child Feeding Questionnaire (Johnson & Birch, 1994) was used to provide a measure of maternal control. There was no difference between the scores provided by the mothers in respect of the obese and the non-obese siblings. The sample was small, though, and included males as well as females. However, in a much larger population based study of 8–9-year-old children no positive correlation was found between the two across families – indeed there was a marginally significant negative correlation in girls, with greater parental control associated with a slightly lesser degree of overweight as assessed both by the BMI and by triceps skinfold thicknesses (Robinson *et al.*, 2001). This study involved over 700 children from 13 public elementary schools, and again used the control scale from the Child Feeding Questionnaire to measure parental control.

There is, however, evidence that one component of control, restriction, is more consistently related to the child's adiposity (Faith, Scanlon, Birch, Francis & Sherry, 2004). In another study a more comprehensive model of the relationships between mothers' feeding practices and the appetite control and relative weight of their daughters was developed, based on data from nearly 200 white families with 5-year-old daughters (Birch & Fisher, 2000). Mothers' control was measured with the eight questions from the restriction subscale of a later version of the Child Feeding Questionnaire (Birch *et al.*, 2001). The more comprehensive model is summarised in Figure 8.6, and fitted the data well by the usual statistical criteria. The model summarises a number of important findings. First, the restriction of the daughters' food intake by their mothers was associated with the mothers' perception of their daughters being overweight; and the mothers' perceptions of their daughters' weight was strongly influenced by their daughters' actual weight. Mothers who themselves had higher restrained eating scores tended also to restrict their daughters' food intake more. Second, the mothers' restriction of their daughters' food intake appeared to be effective – it was associated with an actual lower daily energy intake by the daughters. As in the earlier study, however, the mothers' controlling behaviour was also associated with poorer energy compensation in their daughters, and poorer compensation in the daughters was associated with a relatively higher energy

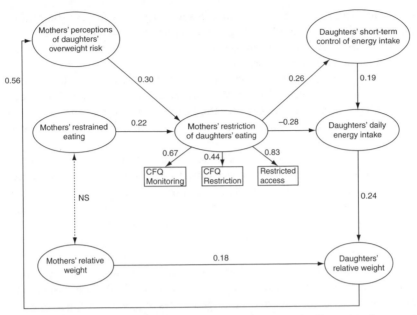

Figure 8.6 Relationships between mothers' feeding practices and adiposity in their daughters (Birch & Fisher, 2000). The path diagram summarises hypothetical influences on girls' eating and weight. Mothers' restriction reduces the daughters' daily energy intake directly, but increases it indirectly via effects on their control of energy intake (CFQ: Child Feeding Questionnaire). Reproduced with permission from the *American Journal of Clinical Nutrition*. © American Journal of Clinical Nutrition, American Society for Nutrition.

intake. We have, in other words, an indication of two effects of the mothers' restricting behaviour on their daughters' energy intake operating in opposite directions – it reduces their food intake by a direct effect, but increases it by leading to poorer energy compensation. The direct negative effect, however, was substantially bigger than the indirect positive effect.

In a further study of 120 children Spruijt-Metz et al. (2002) examined the relationship between mothers' child feeding practices and 11-year-old children's adiposity as measured using DXA scanning. This provides a more direct measure of fat mass than the BMI. Maternal restriction was significantly related to total fat mass in the children, as was concern about the child's weight. In multivariate studies a range of control variables was taken into account, including the child's sex and the ethnicity and social class of the family. The mother's pressure to eat and their concern about their child's weight were then both significantly related to the child's adiposity, the first negatively and the second positively. As the authors point out, this study can be interpreted as an indication that mothers tend to press their thinner children to eat, but are concerned about those who are heavier, with their child-feeding practices being a response to the children's adiposity rather than a cause of it. Mothers can be sensitive to the relative weights of their children from an early age (Baughcum et al., 2001) though this varies with the family – mothers from low-income families can be rather unworried about their children's weights (Jain et al., 2005).

In general, the evidence seems to me to show that mothers respond to their children's weight, often responding to overweight in their daughters by attempts to restrict their food intake. The evidence that these attempts to control food intake themselves lead to increased adiposity is not strong. But whatever its causes, approaches to the tackling of a tendency to obesity that attempt to target the child's regulation of energy intake, rather than their energy intake or energy expenditure per se would be worth pursuing since it is the relationship between the two that is critical. This approach has been investigated by Johnson (2000). She assessed the energy compensation of children of 3–4 years of age in response to a high energy drink, and then instituted an intensive programme of education designed to get the children to attend to internal cues of hunger and satiety. They were then assessed again for energy compensation. Over the two assessments, there was a significant improvement in energy compensation. Children who undercompensated at the first assessment and children who overcompensated both tended to compensate better at the second assessment. This suggests that the intervention was effective, though this would need to be confirmed with a control group who were given the two assessments but not the intervention.

8.4   Treatment and prevention

We saw earlier in this chapter that epidemiological evidence suggests that television watching is a risk factor for obesity. It occupies a large proportion of waking time in most children over most of the childhood years, and a simple and obvious possibility for the treatment of obese children is therefore to try to encourage them from television watching into less sedentary activities.

One attempt of this kind cleverly sought to capitalise on the rewards of TV watching for children in order to increase their physical activity. Faith et al. (2001) examined the effectiveness of an intervention in obese children which used a bicycle powered television. The study was a small one, with ten 8–12-year-old children studied over a 12-week period. The children were randomly assigned to two groups. Both groups were provided with a bicycle ergonometer, but in the experimental group cycling activated power to the TV set, with a minute's cycling earning one or two minutes' TV. This reinforcement contingency had dramatically large effects both on pedalling time and on TV viewing time. Over the 10-week period of the intervention the average time spent pedalling the bicycle by children in the control group was 8.3 minutes per week; in the intervention group it was 64.4 minutes. The control group watched 21.0 hours of TV a week; the intervention group watched 1.6 hours. Happily the intervention appears to have been well accepted by both the parents and their children. These authors were even able to show a significantly greater reduction in total percentage body fat over the period of the intervention in the children in the intervention group. This is a promising result, but if work in adults is any guide, the problem will be not so much in not bringing about a loss of weight in the short term, as in ensuring that it is maintained in the long term.

There is one set of studies in children that not only demonstrated weight loss in the short term, but also followed up the children involved over a long period (ten years). The treatment involved a comprehensive family-based behaviour modification programme (Epstein, Wing, Koeske, Andrasik & Ossip, 1981). The programme was available to families in which at least one 6–12-year-old child and one parent were overweight. The average BMI of the children was above $24 \, \text{kg/m}^2$. All the families were given dietary information, which took the form of the 'traffic light' diet which uses a colour coded food exchange system, in which foods are categorised as red, yellow or green according to their energy density. All three groups were given information on exercise and an aerobic exercise programme, and all three were given advice on social learning principles (modelling, the use of praise and contracting). The families were randomly assigned to three groups. In one group the intervention was targeted at both the parents and the child, and in a second at the child alone. The third group was a control group in which no specific target was set. The targeting took the concrete form of a contract in which a deposit paid when the treatment started was progressively returned at each treatment session, in the first group if both the parent and child lost weight, in the second group if the child lost weight, and in the third group simply in response to attendance at the session. The intervention also involved differences in self-monitoring, in social reinforcement and calls from the therapist between sessions, and in contingency management procedures (which are designed to ensure that participants know what they should do and do it). Although some differences were reported at the end of the intervention, there was no significant difference in the average weights of the children in the three groups; all three groups had lost substantial amounts of weight (Epstein *et al.*, 1981). Yet at a long-term follow-up five years (Epstein *et al.*, 1987) and ten years later (Epstein *et al.*, 1990) there were clear differences, with the weight loss much better maintained in the parent-child group than the child alone group, who in turn did better than the children in the families in which no specific target was set. The traditional problem with the treatment of obesity is the distressing tendency for weight that has been lost in treatment to be regained. This study shows that interventions that may seem equally effective at the time might have quite different levels of effectiveness in the long term. Ten-year follow-ups are not easy to conduct, not cheap and certainly not quick, so the development of evidence-based interventions for obesity in children is clearly going to involve a major investment of time and effort.

These studies do suggest that treatment for obesity in children can be effective, and the studies of Epstein *et al.* (1994) involving ten-year follow-up are the only published studies that demonstrate procedures for the treatment or prevention of obesity in children that are effective in the long term. But family-based treatments are labour intensive and expensive to implement. They also obviously depend on the child's parents recognising in the first place that they are in need of treatment, and there is evidence that parents are generally rather poor at recognising obesity in their children (Jeffrey *et al.*, 2005). This problem can be to some extent circumvented by school-based treatment programmes, and there is evidence that school-based treatment programmes for obesity are also effective, at least in the short term. But there has been less research involving these in recent years, perhaps because of the risk they carry of stigmatising obese children in their schools (Story, 1999).

In most areas of medicine preventing a condition and treating the condition involve quite different procedures. Skin cancer, for example, is prevented by reducing exposure to the sun, but treated by surgery. Obesity may also be treated surgically, using gastrointestinal operations designed to reduce the intake or absorption of food, but this is a last resort. Initial attempts at treatment always involve trying to reduce energy intake and increase energy expenditure – and these are the same interventions that would be used to prevent obesity developing in the first place. Considerable emphasis is now placed on efforts to prevent the development of obesity in children, rather than to treat it once it has developed. Because almost all children go to school, these efforts have often also involved school-based educational interventions. Because the same interventions can be used both to prevent and to treat obesity there is an obvious advantage in a school context in using universal prevention

(prevention aimed at the whole population) as it avoids stigmatising overweight or obese children, and the procedures used in prevention will also be appropriate treatments for children who are already obese. This assumes, of course, that the programmes are effective, and serious attempts are now being made to investigate the effectiveness of school-based obesity prevention programmes.

The best procedure available for this purpose is the randomised controlled trial, which uses the standard methodology of the comparative experiment in which, in its simplest form, some participants, chosen at random, are given an appropriate treatment while others are used as controls. Provided it is carried out properly and provided the groups are sufficiently large the effect of the randomisation is to balance all other variables across the groups. In dealing with an educational intervention, however, the simplest form of a randomised controlled trial is not appropriate. Educational interventions cannot easily be given to some members of a class and not others. It is confusing for teachers. Children talk to one another and may share what they learn. And social facilitation may mean that educational interventions given to whole groups are more effective than those given to some children in a group only. If additional components are added to the educational intervention, such as changes in school meals or sports facilities, these also obviously need to be provided for all the children. The general solution to this problem is the use of 'cluster randomisation' in which groups rather than individuals are randomised. In dealing with children schools form the obvious unit, though in some studies classes within schools have been randomised. Cluster randomisation leads to some tricky problems of research ethics (how can the individual children in the clusters give their informed consent?) and are generally difficult to conduct, but there are nonetheless some examples in this area of research of very high quality.

The Christchurch obesity prevention project in schools, which was directed at children 7–11 years old in junior schools in southwest England, was based on an effort to reduce the consumption of fizzy drinks in schools (James et al., 2004). Six schools took part, and the design involved cluster randomisation with 29 classes in the six schools as the clusters. Each class in each school was randomly allocated to an intervention or a control group, so both were represented in each school, with over 600 children taking part. The intervention consisted in a series of classes designed to discourage the consumption of 'fizzy' drinks, and some evidence was provided that it was effective in doing so. The proportion of children meeting the criterion used for overweight and obesity (BMI > 91st centile) increased substantially in the control group and decreased slightly in the intervention group, though there was no

significant difference in the change in mean BMI. Some appropriate res-
ervations have been expressed concerning the analyses used in this report
(French, Hannan & Story, 2004), but it does suggest that reducing the
availability of fizzy drinks might usefully be examined in future intervention
studies, especially as this might also improve bone health (Chapter 3).

In the light of the epidemiological evidence concerning the relationship
between television viewing and the development of adiposity the effect of
reducing television viewing has also been formally examined in a randomised controlled trial (Robinson, 1999). The reduction was effected by
incorporating 18 hours of classroom time into the standard curriculum,
in which the monitoring of television watching was taught, together with a
reduction of television watching and video game playing, initially to
nothing for 20 days and then to 7 hours per week. The household
received, free of charge, a TV time manager which budgeted the use of
TV viewing time for each household member by the use of personal
codes. The intervention was implemented in one of two comparable
schools in California, chosen at random. Intermediate outcome measures
included time spent watching television, assessed via reports from the
children and their parents and the number of meals eaten in front of the
television. The adiposity-related outcome measures were the BMI, triceps skinfold thickness, waist circumference, hip circumference and
waist-to-hip ratio. Hours watching television were substantially reduced
by the intervention, and relative to the controls the children in the
intervention group showed reduction on all the adiposity measures
(except hip circumference). Because only two schools were used in this
study it is possible that some other characteristic of the two schools gave
rise to the difference in their children's weight gain, and the follow-up was
immediately after the intervention, so long-term gains cannot be
assessed. But the study clearly justifies a more comprehensive study in
which a larger number of schools is randomised to each group with a
longer follow-up; and its results are consistent with the epidemiological
evidence implicating television watching in weight gain in childhood.

A more comprehensive primary-school-based intervention to reduce
risk factors for obesity in the UK has been reported by Sahota and
colleagues (Sahota et al., 2004a; 2004b). Ten schools were randomised
into two groups of five, and one of the groups received an intensive
intervention programme (the 'APPLES' programme). The programme
was designed to influence the children's diet and physical activity, and
involved teacher training, planning for healthy eating and physical activity
and the modification of school meals. There was some evidence that the
intervention increased vegetable consumption, though this was based on
the children's own self-reports. There was no evidence for an effect on

BMI; indeed there was no difference at all in BMI between children in the intervention and the control schools. One problem with school-based interventions is that changes appropriately made to diet and activity within the school can be undermined by compensatory changes in the opposite direction outside school. There is some evidence for effects of this kind in the study of Donnelly *et al.* (1996).

Another large and important study in this area is the Kiel Obesity Prevention Study (Müller *et al.*, 2001). Children from 5 to 7 years of age took part. They were recruited over a six-year period, and intervention carried out in three of the children's schools every year. The children were compared with children from control schools matched for socio-demographic characteristics, and in alternate years the intervention schools became control schools and vice versa. The design involved a four and an eight year follow-up. The intervention involved healthy life-style advice given to all parents and children (reduce the intake of high fat foods, keep active at least an hour a day, decrease TV viewing to less than an hour a day), combined with nutritional education for children, their parents and their teachers. This universal prevention was combined with selective and targeted prevention directed at families with overweight or obese parents or children. Analysis of results from a study of this kind is complex, and at the time of writing only provisional results are available. These show that as measured by triceps skinfold thickness adiposity was lower in the intervention than in the control children. This is a promising result, but the reliability of a single skinfold measurement is not high. Further long-term results from this study will be awaited with interest.

A major school-based study in the USA (Perry *et al.*, 1998) was the Child and Adolescent Trial for Cardiovascular Health (CATCH). This involved a substantially larger number of schools (56 intervention and 40 control schools) with more than 5,000 individual participants. School-based interventions comprised an intervention to modify the school food service, which was designed to lower the fat and saturated fat content of school meals and to reduce their sodium levels, an intervention in PE classes which was designed to increase the amount of moderate to vigo-rous physical activity, and an intensive health education programme delivered through 55 lessons. A randomly chosen subgroup of the inter-vention schools also had a home curriculum based on 19 activity packs. Behavioural outcomes, reported by the children, showed substantial reductions in energy intake from fat and increases in vigorous activity. But in spite of this very intensive intervention no differences were found in blood pressure, BMI or cholesterol measurements.

A second major school-based study evaluated the 'Planet Health' intervention (Gortmaker *et al.*, 1999). In this study 1,295 children of

11–12 years of age took part over two school years. The intervention focussed on reducing television viewing to less than 2 hours a day, increasing moderate and vigorous physical activity, decreasing consumption of high fat foods and increasing consumption of fruit and vegetables to five or more a day. It was designed to emphasise lifestyle changes and to improve the activity and diet related behaviour of all the children rather than just those especially at risk of obesity. The curriculum approach of Planet Health is interdisciplinary, using material in language, arts, maths, science and social studies lessons as well as lessons focussed on reducing television watching and on physical fitness. Ten schools took part, randomised five each to intervention and control groups. The results provided a good deal of evidence that behaviour did change as a result of the intervention. Average television watching was reduced by over half an hour per day in the girls, their fruit and vegetable consumption went up and their estimated energy intake increased less over the two years of the trial. The prevalence of obesity in the girls in the intervention group was significantly reduced, compared with the prevalence in the control group. The difference was principally due to changes in television watching. There was also some reduction in television watching in boys, but no significant change in other aspects of behaviour or in obesity in the boys.

A third major school-based study, Pathways, was designed to prevent the development of obesity in American Indian schoolchildren. This was another very large study, in which schools that taught American Indian children were randomised into two groups, an intervention group and a control group, and the children were followed up over three years (Davis et al., 1999). The principal outcome variable was percentage body fat, measured using height and weight, skinfold thickness and bioelectrical impedance. The intervention promoted activity and healthy eating, and involved school-based changes to the curriculum and to physical education, and to the school meal service, together with family education. Immense pains were taken to ensure that the intervention was culturally appropriate. For example, it emphasised learning modes that were valued within American Indian cultures, including learning through observation and practice, learning from story-telling and learning cooperatively. Because the study involved so many schools (41 schools, with results from more than 1,300 children) it had the statistical power to detect a small difference in fatness between the children in the two groups (2.8%). Sadly, after three years there was not even a difference of this size between the groups (Lohman et al., 2001). Per cent body fat was 41.9% for boys and 41.6% for girls in the intervention group, and 41.6% for boys and 41.5% for girls in the comparison group. Nor was there a significant difference in the BMI.

What are we to make of these studies? School-based intervention programmes are more likely to be generally effective than any other kind. They can reach virtually all children. Schools are used to delivering educational programmes in a systematic and disciplined way, and have the appropriate expertise to do so. Meals are eaten in schools, and physical activities taught there, providing a context for practical as well as classroom-based interventions. The child's family can be accessed through the school, and schools are familiar with the need to involve parents in supporting their child's education. There is some evidence from some of the studies that school-based interventions can be effective, but even in those that are we have only short-term follow-ups at the moment. Overall they seem to show quite how hard it is to bring about changes that are going to have any substantial effect on the prevalence of obesity in children.

9   Adolescence and the eating disorders

9.1   Eating disorders

In infancy and early childhood there are three 'feeding and eating disorders' that are formally recognised in DSM-IV, the Diagnostic and Statistical Manual of Mental Disorders of the American Psychiatric Association (APA, 1994). The first two are *pica* (the persistent eating of non-nutritive substances) and *rumination disorder* (the persistent regurgitation and rechewing of food). Both these are often associated with developmental disabilities. The third, *feeding disorder of infancy or early childhood*, essentially refers to failure to thrive when it is associated with failure to eat adequately.

The eating disorders that characteristically arise over the period around puberty, however, are much more obviously psychiatric disorders, related to depression and the other affective disorders of adults. In DSM-IV two eating disorders are given specific diagnoses, *anorexia nervosa* and *bulimia nervosa*. A third category, *eating disorder not otherwise specified*, is used when some of the criteria for the two specific diagnoses are met, but not others.

There are four diagnostic criteria for anorexia nervosa (APA, 1994). The first involves a refusal to maintain a body weight at or above a defined minimum, specified as 85% of the 'expected' weight given the person's age and height. This may result from a loss of weight, or in young people who are still growing, from a failure to gain weight. The second is an intense fear of gaining weight or becoming fat. The third involves disturbances in the way body weight or body shape are experienced, an excessive influence of body weight or shape on self-evaluation, or the denying of the seriousness of the low body weight. The fourth is an absence of at least three consecutive menstrual cycles (amenorrhoea), a criterion that can obviously apply only to women who have passed the menarche.

Anorexia nervosa was recognised as a psychiatric disorder by the end of the nineteenth century. Bulimia nervosa, on the other hand, came to

186

attention much later as a result of a key paper by Russell in 1979, though case histories comparable in many ways were also described in a 1976 paper by an American counselling psychologist (Boskind-Lodahl, 1976). Russell initially referred to the condition as an 'ominous variant' of anorexia nervosa, and the DSM-IV classification of mental disorders gives a 'binge-eating/purging type' as one type of anorexia nervosa (the other being the 'restricting type'). The 'binge-eating/purging type' of anorexia nervosa is identified if the person involved has 'regularly engaged in binge-eating or purging behaviour (i.e., self-induced vomiting or the misuse of laxatives, diuretics or enemas)' in the course of a current episode of anorexia nervosa. However, it became clear quite soon that similar patterns of behaviour were found in young women, especially, who maintained a normal or near-normal body weight, and therefore did not meet the first criterion for anorexia nervosa, and this led to the identification of a separate disorder, bulimia nervosa. Bulimia nervosa was introduced into the formal DSM-IV psychiatric classification in 1980 (APA, 1980).

Bulimia nervosa is characterised by recurrent episodes of binge eating, which involve eating an amount that is definitely larger than most people would eat over the same period of time and in the same circumstances, combined with a sense of a lack of control over the eating. The second criterion is the recurrent use of compensating behaviour of an inappropriate kind in order to prevent weight gain (for example, self-induced vomiting, the use of laxatives, diuretics or enemas, or fasting or excessive exercise). Both the binge eating and the compensatory behaviour should occur at least twice a week for three months. Again, there is an excessive influence of body weight or shape on self-evaluation. A final criterion is that the eating disturbance should not occur only during episodes of anorexia nervosa.

Although bulimia nervosa was identified initially as a variant form of anorexia nervosa, the independent disorder is in fact now considerably more common than anorexia nervosa itself (Rutter, Caspi & Moffitt, 2003). The binges can be elicited in controlled conditions in laboratories, and a summary of six studies which have done so (Mitchell et al., 1998) showed that in these conditions binges involved an average energy intake of 15.3 MJ (3,647 Kcal). The average daily intake of 18-year-old girls is about 10 MJ (see Figure 1.2).

The DSM-IV diagnostic category *eating disorder not otherwise specified* (EDNOS) also includes *binge eating disorder* as an additional specific diagnosis for provisional use (APA, 1994). Binge eating disorder is characterised by binge eating in people who do not meet the other criteria for anorexia or bulimia nervosa. In particular, they do not regularly use the other compensatory behaviours (purging, fasting or excessive exercise) that characterise bulimia nervosa. Although they both involve binge eating, and both improve spontaneously, bulimia nervosa and binge eating disorder tend to run a different course (Fairburn et al., 2000). After five years under 20% of women starting out with binge-eating disorder had any form of clinical eating disorder while the proportion in women starting out with bulimia nervosa was about 50%. The key distinction between binge eating disorder and bulimia nervosa is the absence in binge eating disorder of the behaviour engaged in to control body weight (vomiting, taking laxatives, fasting, and excessive exercise) that young women with bulimic disorders use to compensate for their binge-eating episodes. Understandably, then, binge-eating disorder is particularly common among obese people, reaching a prevalence of 30% in people enrolled in weight control programmes (Spitzer et al., 1992). But Spitzer et al. also found a prevalence of 2.5% among first-year students of about 20 years of age. Closely similar prevalences (29% and 2.6% respectively) were found in these two groups in a second large survey (Spitzer et al., 1993). In the community-based study of Striegel-Moore et al. (2000) half the respondents with binge eating disorder were obese, compared with 18% of controls.

As with psychiatric diagnosis more generally, two related questions arise concerning the eating disorders. One is the extent to which there is a genuine discontinuity between the disorders with different specific diagnoses in DSM-IV, and the other is the extent to which there is a genuine discontinuity between having an eating disorder at all and not having one. Issues of this kind are not usually easy to resolve, and it may be best to conceptualise the feeding disorders as discontinuous for some purposes and as continuous for others, an approach often taken in developmental psychopathology.

Some very useful points concerning these classification problems in the eating disorders are offered by Herzog and Delinsky (2001). As regards anorexia nervosa, a key feature is weight loss, but the threshold has been changed from a loss of 25% in DSM-III (APA, 1980) to 15% in DSM-IV. The reason for the change was partly to assist diagnosis in young women who are still growing before puberty (Garfinkel, Kennedy & Kaplan, 1995; Herzog & Delinsky, 2001). Amenorrhoea itself is a criterion that is clearly inapplicable in young women before the menarche (and to men of any age), and there is little evidence that amenorrhoea is related to the psychological characteristics of the condition. The cessation of menstrual cycles is principally an effect of low body fat levels and usually follows when the BMI drops below about $18 \, \text{kg/m}^2$ (Kraemer, Berkowitz & Hammer, 1990). This is the average BMI of a 12-year-old girl. In 100 patients admitted to a general hospital with anorexia nervosa the average

BMI on admission was 14.4 and a very similar figure (14.5) was found in 50 patients in a private hospital (Beumont, Al-Alami & Touyz, 1988). Cachelin and Maher (1998) compared 40 women who fully met the DSM-IV criteria for anorexia nervosa with 11 who were under treatment for the condition but did still have menstrual cycles. The two groups were very similar on almost all measures of psychopathology, including body image disturbance, eating disorder symptoms and depression; they differed principally in that the group with amenorrhoea had a lower body weight and were somewhat younger. Amenorrhoea for periods exceeding three months (i.e. three cycles) is not uncommon even in healthy adolescents in the first year or two after menarche (Fisher et al., 1995).

Even the key criterion concerning a fear of gaining weight or becoming fat has been called into question. Lee and colleagues (Lee, Chiu & Chen, 1989; Lee, Ho & Hsu, 1993) have reported that this symptom is frequently absent in Chinese patients with anorexia nervosa in Hong Kong. In a study of 70 such patients less than half gave any indicators of a fatness phobia. The patients with and without a fatness phobia were comparable in most other ways, except that the premorbid BMI was lower in those who were fat phobic. Although morbid self-starvation may currently be widely associated with fear of gaining weight or becoming fat in Western cultures, the authors suggest that it may be generated in other ways in other cultures. Indeed, it has been suggested by Russell (1995) that even in Western populations the dread of fatness may be a recent development in the symptomatology of anorexia nervosa, perhaps arising over the period from 1949 to 1981 in which thinness became a fashionable ideal in the media (Silverstein et al., 1986; Silverstein, Peterson & Perdue, 1986). Silverstein and colleagues documented this development by examining bust-to-waist ratios in women pictured in *Vogue* and in the *Ladies Home Journal*. There was in fact an earlier period in which a thin body ideal developed even more dramatically, from 1909 to 1925. Unfortunately statistical data on the eating disorders are not available over this earlier period, though there is evidence that the BMI of young women entering college also declined over these years. Drawing on the concepts of the psychoanalyst and anthropologist George Devereux, Gordon (2000) conceptualises the eating disorders more generally as 'ethnic disorders', analogous to *amok* in Malaysia, Indonesia and New Guinea and to *koro* in southern China (or to *hysteria* in Western Europe in the nineteenth century). A key characteristic of the ethnic disorders is that they reflect conflicts and sources of anxiety that are widespread in the culture, and involve in an exaggerated form behaviour that is normal, and highly valued, in the culture, as dieting and the pursuit of thinness by women is in ours.

Waller (1993) has argued that diagnostic classification *within* the eating disorders (i.e. classification into restrictive anorexia, bulimic anorexia, bulimia etc.) is of little significance psychologically. Essentially his argument is that persons with eating disorders have a core symptom in common, a general concern over food, weight and body shape. As in many other areas of psychopathology, the threshold at which this is considered to reflect a clinically diagnosable disorder depends on the extent to which it is disabling or distressing. Further classification of persons with a disorder of this kind into more specific diagnostic groups on the basis of more specific symptoms may not help in dealing with the underlying core symptom, though it may be necessary, of course, in the medical management of the specific symptoms.

In fact much of the developmental research in this area has used questionnaire or interview procedures designed to assess the symptoms characteristic of eating disorders instead of, or as well as, providing a diagnostic classification. These procedures include the use of a self-report questionnaire, the Eating Disorder Inventory (Garner, 1991; Garner, Olmsted & Polivy, 1983), and a semi-structured interview, the Eating Disorder Examination (Cooper & Fairburn, 1987), both of which assess symptoms of anorexia and bulimia nervosa and can also be used as diagnostic instruments. The Eating Attitudes Test (Garner & Garfinkel, 1979; Garner *et al.*, 1982) distinguishes groups with eating disorders from controls, but does not distinguish anorexia nervosa from bulimia nervosa (Williamson *et al.*, 1995). The ChEAT is a children's version of the Eating Attitudes Test, designed to be usable from 8 years of age (Maloney, McGuire & Daniels, 1988). A children's version of the Eating Disorder Inventory is also available. Other scales assess symptoms of more specifically defined disorders – for example the BITE scale assesses bulimic symptoms (Allison, 1995). Assessing symptoms, rather than using a diagnostic classification, is essential in developmental research in psychopathology, as the early precursors of a psychiatric disorder by definition will not meet the diagnostic criteria for the full-blown disorder.

One of the most striking and universal features of the eating disorders is that they are much more common in women than in men. Because these disorders are quite rare, with a prevalence of about 1.3 per 1000 for anorexia nervosa and 10 per 1000 for bulimia nervosa, exact figures for both males and females from general population surveys are not easily obtained, but studies based on case registers and general practice research databases suggest about ten female to every male case (Rutter, Caspi & Moffitt, 2003). A similar marked female preponderance is found for general population surveys of related but milder eating attitude problems (Patton *et al.*, 1997). Rare though the eating disorders may be, even the prevalence of anorexia nervosa of 0.48% reported by Lucas *et al.* (1991) in Rochester in the USA made it the third most common chronic condition among adolescent girls there, after asthma and obesity. (It is interesting to note that two of the three most common chronic conditions were nutritional in nature.) Contrary to a longstanding supposition, there is no good evidence that eating disorders are more common in upper-class girls (Gard & Freeman, 1996).

Like other psychiatric disorders in which there is a preponderance of female cases, eating disorders tend to develop around adolescence (Rutter, Caspi & Moffitt, 2003), and they are associated with other psychiatric disorders, and with the personality traits related to them (O'Brien & Vincent, 2003). Valuable data on psychiatric disorders associated with anorexia nervosa come from a study in Sweden by Råstam (1992). Great care was taken to identify all the cases in a one-year birth cohort in Göteborg in Sweden; 51 young people who met DSM criteria for anorexia nervosa were compared with an equal number of controls, comprising the children of the same sex closest to them in age in the same school. The most striking personality association was with obsessive-compulsive personality disorder, which was found in nearly a third of the cases, and was nine times as common as in the controls. Anorexia nervosa itself does not have one of the key characteristics of an obsessive-compulsive disorder, because the preoccupations and compulsions concerning food and bodyweight in anorexia nervosa are not seen by the affected person as 'ego-dystonic', that is, intrusive and inappropriate (Garfinkel, Kennedy & Kaplan, 1995). Nonetheless, 4 of the 18 cases in this study with an obsessive-compulsive personality did develop a clinical obsessive-compulsive disorder. A second trait strongly associated with anorexia nervosa, and a component of obsessive-compulsive personality disorder, is perfectionism. Among many studies of this association Halmi *et al.* (2000) measured perfectionism using the Multidimensional Perfectionism Scale (Frost *et al.*, 1990). This scale measures six aspects of perfectionism – concern over mistakes, personal standards, parental expectations, parental criticism, doubts about actions and organisation – and provides an overall perfectionism score. Compared with those from a control group, perfectionism scores were higher in all the groups with anorexia nervosa tested. Råstam also found a strong association between anorexia nervosa and depression (Råstam, 1992); 35% of the young people in the sample with anorexia nervosa met criteria for major depression at the time, and 94% had met them at the time or previously (the figures were 4% and 25% respectively in the controls). Deaths in people diagnosed with anorexia nervosa are often associated with depression, or with alcoholism (Korndörfer *et al.*, 2003), which is itself related to depression, rather than with malnutrition *per se*. Other studies have shown associations with anxiety (Bulik *et al.*, 1997; Deep *et al.*, 1995). Bulik *et al.* examined the prevalence and age of onset of adult and childhood anxiety disorders in women with anorexia or bulimia nervosa and in depressed and randomly selected controls. Because anxiety is very common the lifetime prevalence of anxiety disorders was high even in the random controls (32.7%) and even higher in the women who were depressed (48.2%). But it was higher still in the anorexic and bulimic women (60.3% and 56.9% respectively). Deep *et al.* found a lifetime diagnosis of one or more anxiety disorders in 75% of women recovered from anorexia nervosa. In both studies there was evidence that in most of the women the anxiety disorders preceded the eating disorder. Overanxious disorder and separation anxiety disorder were particularly associated with anorexia nervosa, and overanxious disorder and social phobia with bulimia (and with major depression). Many important risk factors for eating disorders may be rather general risk factors for psychiatric disorders, which operate by their effect on these associated personality and psychiatric characteristics, rather than on specific characteristics of eating disorders, such as dieting. A carefully conducted case control study, for example (Fairburn *et al.*, 1999), found a broad range of risk factors for anorexia nervosa and bulimia nervosa, but although they distinguished women with eating disorders from women who were well, most of them did not distinguish them from women with other psychiatric conditions (anxiety disorders and depression). The only risk factors specifically associated with anorexia nervosa were negative self-evaluation and perfectionism. Bulimia nervosa was specifically associated with childhood and parental obesity and an early menarche, at least as they were reported by the young women affected.

Many people believe that eating disorders became much more common in the second half of the twentieth century. Gordon's book, for example, is called *Eating Disorders: Anatomy of a Social Epidemic* and he refers to the 'explosive increase in anorexic and bulimic conditions in our times' (Gordon, 2000). The difficulty here, as with other psychiatric conditions such as autism, is in distinguishing a real rise in the incidence of the condition from a higher detection and treatment rate once it has come to public attention. Ideally one needs repeated community-based surveys, using the same case detection procedures, carried out in the same areas at different times. This requirement has been met to some extent for anorexia nervosa, and data of this kind are summarised by Russell (1995). He summarised a number of studies in which repeated surveys were carried out on the same populations at different times, in south Sweden,

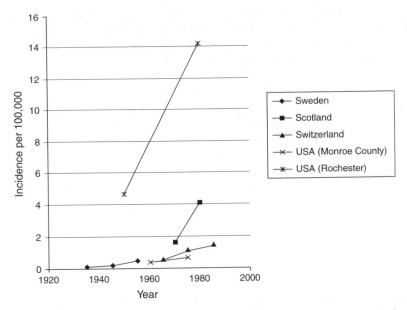

Figure 9.1 Secular trends in the incidence of anorexia nervosa in four countries. Data from Russell, 1995, Table 1.1.

north-east Scotland, Switzerland, and Monroe County and Rochester in the USA. The trends over time in these areas are shown in Figure 9.1. These data provide reasonable evidence for an increase in the incidence of anorexia nervosa over the period from the 1950s until the 1980s. A more recent summary of twelve population-based studies of the incidence of anorexia nervosa (Pawluck & Gorey, 1998) also found an increase, though it was restricted to women over 20. Russell (2004) offers a convincing case that bulimia nervosa is essentially a new disorder, arising in the period before 1972 when the first cases came to his attention. The evidence comes from the lack of references to such a disorder in the early psychiatric literature and in the archival medical records of the Mayo Clinic in Rochester, and from cohort studies interviewing people of different ages. Fombonne (1996) has reviewed studies of bulimia nervosa based on medical records and on community surveys, and found no solid evidence that the incidence of this condition rose further over the 1980s and 1990s, though more patients with the disorders were seen in specialist treatment centres.

Although it is difficult to be sure of the explanation of changes in the incidence of psychiatric disorders over time, there is some evidence that media influences of various kinds can influence the development of self-image problems that can play a role in the aetiology of eating disorders. Laboratory-based studies of effects of this kind were reviewed by Groetz et al. (2002), who summarised 25 studies involving controlled experiments that examined the immediate effect of images of slender models on the body image of women. These studies very consistently showed that thin media images had a negative effect on the body satisfaction of the observers. The effect was stronger in observers with a history of body image problems or eating disorders. An example of a population-based study showing this kind of media influence is the study of Martinéz-González and colleagues conducted in Navarra in northern Spain (Martínez-González et al., 2003). In this study a representative sample of the 12–21-year-old female population was recruited in 1997, and a two-stage procedure used to screen them for eating disorders. Firstly, they were given a Spanish version of the Eating Attitudes Test (EAT), and then high scorers on the test were examined by a psychiatrist using a semi-structured interview. At the initial examination 2862 girls were seen, and 119 cases of an eating disorder were identified (9 of anorexia nervosa, 22 of bulimia nervosa and 88 of eating disorder not otherwise specified). This comprises 4.15%. A group of 2509 girls who were initially free of eating disorders were followed up over 18 months. Over this period, 90 new cases arose (3.59%). The strongest predictors of the new development of an eating disorder were unmarried parents and eating alone at baseline. A less strong but statistically significant association was found with time spent listening to radio programmes, though associations were not found with television watching or magazine reading. Harrison (2000b) examined the role of television watching in 7–9-year-old children. She found that television watching did to some extent predict eating disorder symptoms as measured using the Children's Eating Attitudes Test (ChEAT), but it did not predict body shape standards favouring thinness, suggesting, unexpectedly, that the relationship between TV watching and eating disorder symptoms must be mediated in some other way. She examined the same relationships in older children and adolescents (Harrison, 2000a), and found no relationship between the extent of 'thin ideal' television exposure and eating disorder symptoms. An interesting natural experiment, however, is reported by Becker et al. (2002), who examined Eating Attitudes Test scores in the Nadroga province of Fiji in 1995, when television was introduced for the first time, and then three years later. Traditional Fijian body aesthetics do not emphasise slimness – rather the opposite – and only one case of anorexia nervosa had ever been reported on Fiji by the mid 1990s. The proportion of adolescent girls with EAT-26 scores above 20 was 12.7% in 1995, but had risen to 29.2% by 1998 after three years' exposure to television. Induced vomiting to control weight was completely absent in 1995, but was reported by 11.3% of the girls in 1998. The samples were quite small and obviously other aspects of the girls' environment may also have changed over this period, but narrative accounts from the young women involved testify to the influence of television viewing on thin body image ideals. One, for example, said 'When I look at the characters on TV, the way they act on TV and I just look at the body, the figure of that body, so I say, "look at them, they are thin and they all have this figure", so I myself want to become like that, to become thin' (p. 513). In another, prospective, study Field *et al.* (1999) examined the onset of purging over the following year in a group of about 7000 adolescent girls who were not purging at their first interview. Risk factors included reports by the girls, at their first interview, that they were 'trying to look like females on television, in movies, and in magazines'.

9.2   Body image and dieting

Although the eating disorders are clearly related to other affective disorders, especially those characterised by anxiety and depression, their more specific characteristic symptoms relate to eating behaviour and body image. In addition to young women with formally diagnosable eating disorders there are much larger numbers who report occasional self-induced vomiting or binge eating (10–50%) or have high scores on tests of abnormal eating attitudes or behaviour (up to 20%), and even more young women (50–60%) feel overweight and have dieted at some point in their lives (Fisher *et al.*, 1995). Young adolescents, especially girls, show more generally a remarkable level of dissatisfaction with their size and shape, a symptom which is central to the eating disorders. This dissatisfaction can be measured by verbal questions or graphically, using silhouettes. Silhouettes of people of different weights were first developed as a research tool by Stunkard *et al.* (Stunkard, Sørenson & Schulsinger, 1983), who used them during the course of genetic research to allow people to estimate the body build of their parents. Fallon and Rozin (1985) used these silhouettes in a study of undergraduate students in order to secure estimates not only of the actual body shape of the students as they perceived it, but also of their preferred (ideal) body shape. The difference between the two can then be used as a measure of body dissatisfaction. A version of this procedure using silhouettes of children rather than adults was produced by Collins, and used in a study of a large sample of preadolescent children around 8 years of age (Collins, 1991). Collins found that even in these young children both males and females preferred a thinner figure, with a bigger average discrepancy in girls.

Collins also found significant correlations between the child's assessment of their current body size and their actual measured BMI, but these correlations do not in themselves show how *accurate* the child's assessment of their own body size is, as the silhouettes used did not correspond to a known BMI. A high correlation simply shows that two variables are systematically related, and can be found even when body size is also systematically over- or underestimated. Truby and Paxton (2002), however, have developed a comparable scale (the Children's Body Image Scale) that was based on children of known BMI. Pre-pubescent children of varying BMIs were photographed in their underwear in a standard (anatomical) position. The BMIs of the children chosen corresponded closely to the 3rd, 10th, 25th, 75th, 90th and 97th centiles of the NCHS reference population (Hamill *et al.*, 1979). The same head was then substituted onto the bodies, and the figures adapted so that they were similar to one another except in respect of their BMIs. Using this scale with 7–12-year-old children, Truby and Paxton (2002) reported the mean discrepancy between the children's actual and perceived BMI as well as the correlation between the two. Girls of all ages matched themselves to a figure of lower BMI than their own – i.e. they significantly underestimated their body size. The correlation between their actual BMI and their perceived BMI was reasonably high (between .5 and .6) at all ages. In boys the same was true from 8 to 12, though the size of the discrepancy was smaller, and the correlations with actual weight were also smaller (.3 to .4). The youngest boys were unable to match their BMIs to that of the models at all.

We noted in Chapter 8 the difficulty presented for research studies by the lack of simple measures of adiposity that distinguish body fat from other contributors to body mass. Even a scale based on known BMIs incorporates the same fundamental problem of the BMI, which is that it reflects weight adjusted for height and not fatness *per se*. The same confusion is clearly present in the perception people have of their own fatness (Davis *et al.*, 1993). Davis *et al.* examined the relationship between different measures of body composition, weight dissatisfaction and dietary restraint in young women. The BMI was calculated from height and weight in the usual way. Frame size was calculated from measurements of a number of skeletal dimensions. Adiposity was estimated directly from skinfold measurements taken at four sites (biceps, triceps, subscapular and suprailiac). Davis *et al.* found that restrained eating and weight dissatisfaction were significantly associated with a higher BMI, as one would expect. When frame size and adiposity, two components of the BMI, were examined separately, however, restrained eating and weight dissatisfaction were strongly related to frame size, but were not related to adiposity at all – indeed, once frame size was taken into account the BMI itself did not predict restrained eating or weight dissatisfaction further at all. The implication is that the main source of body dissatisfaction in these young women comes not from how fat they are but from skeletal characteristics which no amount of restrained eating is going to alter.

How early does this body dissatisfaction arise? Wardle and Beales (1986) examined body image in 12–17-year-old London school children. The heights and weights of the children were measured, and the children were asked what weight they would like to be, and whether they felt themselves to be 'thin', 'slightly underweight', 'just right', 'slightly overweight' or 'fat'. Among the girls, 10% thought themselves underweight, 40% thought themselves slightly overweight and 12% thought themselves fat. Among the boys, on the other hand, 34% thought themselves underweight, 22% thought themselves slightly overweight and 5% thought themselves fat. Responses were related to the actual measured weights of the children: the more overweight they were, the bigger the difference between their actual and preferred body weight. Hill, Draper and Stack (1994) investigated these relationships in 9-year-old children. The weights and heights of the children were measured anthropometrically, and their body shape preferences measured using silhouettes. The results for body shape satisfaction are shown graphically in Figure 9.2. The overweight group had average BMIs of 21.7 in girls and 22.3 in boys, so both groups exceeded the more recently defined BMI criteria for overweight in children of this age (Cole *et al.*, 2000). Both overweight boys and overweight girls preferred to be thinner, and there was no obvious difference between them. Underweight boys and girls preferred to be heavier. In three groups of intermediate weight, however, the boys generally wanted to be heavier, and the girls thinner. Even a sample of 5-year-old girls showed some body dissatisfaction and weight concern (Davison, Markey & Birch, 2000).

Body dissatisfaction is of particular importance because there is reasonably good evidence that it is involved in the aetiology of eating disorders. Wardle and Beales (1986) examined dietary restraint as well as perceived overweight in their study, and found that there was a significant correlation between dietary restraint and perceived overweight even when its relationship with *actual* overweight was allowed for. Veron-Guidry and Williamson (1996) found a small but statistically significant correlation between body dissatisfaction scores and scores on the ChEAT, the children's version of the Eating Attitudes Test, in children 8–13 years old. In the study of Truby and Paxton (2002) the perceived-ideal body size discrepancy in 10–12-year-old children was

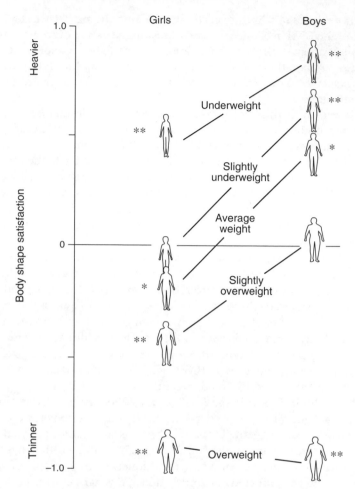

Figure 9.2 Body shape satisfaction in five groups of 9-year-old children of different BMIs (Hill, Draper & Stack, 1994). Body shape satisfaction is measured as the difference between current and preferred body shapes. A value of zero indicates satisfaction, while a negative value corresponds to a desire to be thinner and a positive value a desire to be fatter. Except in the most underweight group, the girls generally have a wish to be thinner. Significant differences between current and preferred shapes $*p < .05$, $**p < .01$. Reproduced by permission from Macmillan Publishers Ltd. *International Journal of Obesity*, *18*, 383–9. Copyright 1994.

significantly related to scores on the restraint scale of the Dutch Eating Behaviour Questionnaire, both in boys and girls. In a very careful systematic review Stice and Shaw (2002) have found consistent evidence for body dissatisfaction being a risk factor for eating disorder symptoms. A risk factor for an eating disorder here needs to be distinguished from a *symptom* of an eating disorder, and from an *effect* of an eating disorder. The key issue is whether evidence can be provided that the body dissatisfaction preceded the eating disorder symptoms. The evidence Stice and Shaw reviewed came from experimental studies or prospective longitudinal studies that allowed the temporal precedence of variables to be established. Although there have been isolated exceptions, eight independent studies have shown that elevations in body dissatisfaction does predict subsequent increases in eating disorder or bulimic symptoms; Stice (2002) describes body dissatisfaction as 'one of the most consistent and robust risk and maintenance factors for eating pathology' (p. 832). There are two possible pathways by which it might be having its effects, through effects on mood and through effects on dieting.

As regards effects on mood, Stice and his colleagues have shown in two independent longitudinal studies that body dissatisfaction predicts subsequent increases in depressive symptoms (Stice & Bearman, 2001; Stice et al., 2000). In the first of these studies (Stice et al., 2000) 1,124 girls between 13 and 17 years of age at study entry were studied over four years. Body dissatisfaction, dietary restraint, bulimic symptoms, depressive symptoms and major depression were examined at each time point. Participants who had ever met criteria for major depression when they entered the study were excluded from prospective analyses, which concentrated on the predictors of a major depression over the following three-year period in those who were not initially depressed. Body dissatisfaction, dietary restraint and bulimic symptoms were all associated with the subsequent development of a major depression. In the second study (Stice & Bearman, 2001) 231 young women from 13–17 years of age were followed up for 20 months. In this study depressive symptoms, rather than major depression per se, comprised the outcome variable. Again body dissatisfaction predicted increased levels of depression (and increased dieting and bulimic symptoms). In all the analyses there was careful control for initial levels of depression.

As regards effects on dieting, an example of a study relating body dissatisfaction to subsequent increases in dieting is the longitudinal study of college women by Cooley and Toray (2001). The young women were followed up over a three-year period, and dieting assessed at the beginning and the end of the period using a 10-item dietary restraint scale. Body image dissatisfaction in the young women was assessed at the beginning of this period, using a comparison of their perceived body weight, which was highly correlated with their actual BMI, and their ideal body weight. Body image dissatisfaction was the only significant predictor of increased dieting scores over this three-year period. This relationship was reported in the first longitudinal study in this area (Patton *et al.*, 1990) and has been a consistent finding since (Stice, 2002).

Dieting is very common, especially in young women. A study in 12–13-year-old girls found that 15.8% were dieting and 33.6% had dieted at some time (Roberts *et al.*, 2001). French *et al.* (1995) examined correlates of dieting in a large (>30,000) sample of 12–20-year-old school students in Minnesota. They were asked how often they had gone on a diet ('changing the way you eat so you can lose weight') in the last year and classified into five groups based on dieting frequency. 'Non-purgers' were separated from 'purgers'. About 62% of females and 21% of males reported dieting once or more often over the previous year, and 15% of females and 6.5% of males reported purging. There were striking associations between dieting and other generally problematic types of health-related behaviour, especially in females. The more frequent dieters, for example, used alcohol, tobacco and other drugs more, had a higher suicide risk and were more likely to have had sexual intercourse. They were also more likely to have been physically and sexually abused. All these associations remained statistically significant after control for age, socio-economic status, ethnicity, grade in school and BMI. Purging was independently associated with effects in the same direction. Statistically significant associations found in males after control for the same covariates were also in the same direction. French *et al.* did not examine the relationship between dieting and body size, but in a study of Australian adolescents (Patton *et al.*, 1997) a strong relationship between dieting and the BMI was found in both males and females, with dieting much more prevalent in those with higher BMIs. This study also found a higher rate of psychiatric morbidity among dieters, both in males and females, with particularly high rates in female extreme dieters. A strong and systematic relationship between dieting and the BMI was also found in another study of 14–16-year-old girls (Barker *et al.*, 2000), with every increase in BMI from under 19 to over $24 \, \text{kg/m}^2$ associated with an increased probability of dieting. Girls at the top of the range were 19 times as likely to diet as those at the bottom. So at least one of the risk factors for eating disorders is likely to become more common as overweight and obesity become more common. Dieting was associated with a reduced energy intake, as least according to the girls' own reports, but also with a greater consumption of green vegetables and brown bread. Some dissatisfaction with body weight was therefore also associated with a diet closer to current recommendations for healthy eating. As one might expect, there is a relationship between dieting and psychosexual maturity in young women. Cauffman and Steinberg (1996) found that dieting was more likely in girls who were dating boys, even when age and menarchial status were taken into account.

Much of the recent research work in this area has measured dietary restraint, rather than dieting *per se*. Dietary restraint is a more cognitive concept, implying the intention to restrict food intake to lose weight rather than simply dieting behaviour. It is, however, related to dieting itself. In two studies of adults more restrained eaters were found to eat less than less restrained eaters (Laessle *et al.*, 1989; Wardle & Beales, 1987). In both studies their average BMIs were slightly higher. As the nutritional data were collected by self-reporting methods, a possible interpretation of these studies is that they show a reporting bias, with restrained eaters underreporting their actual intake. However in a later study Tuschl *et al.* (1990) simultaneously examined energy intake assessed by food diaries over a 14-day period and energy expenditure measured by the doubly labelled water method. The restrained eaters had a significantly higher BMI, and again had a significantly lower energy intake as assessed from the 14-day diaries. Their energy expenditure was also significantly lower, by an amount that at least approximately matched their lower energy intake. This suggests that they were not underreporting their energy intake.

Like body dissatisfaction, dietary restraint develops quite early in the lives of young women. Hill, Oliver and Rogers investigated this in 9 and 14-year-old girls in the UK (Hill, Oliver & Rogers, 1992). In this study dietary restraint was measured using the Dutch Eating Behaviour Questionnaire (Van Strien *et al.*, 1986). The average restraint scores were as high in the 9 as in the 14-year-old girls. In a later study (Hill & Robinson, 1991) decreased energy intake was found in restrained 9-year-old girls, at least according to their own records. Carper, Fisher and Birch (2000), using an age-adapted version of the Dutch Eating Behaviour Questionnaire, found that one third of 5-year-olds reported some dietary restraint. At this age, however, 'talking the talk' about dieting (Carper, Fisher & Birch, 2000) does not correspond to actual dieting behaviour, a link which does, however, appear by the age of 7, at least according to the children's own reports (Shunk & Birch, 2004).

Does dieting lead to eating disorders? Longitudinal studies in which the relationship between self-reported dieting and subsequent increases in eating pathology are examined generally do show a relationship between the two. For example, Stice and Agras (1998) showed that dieting was the strongest predictor of the onset of binge eating and of compensatory behaviours over a nine-month period in 16–18-year-old women who were not bingeing when they were first assessed. Patton *et al.* (1999) examined predictors of eating disorders over a three-year period in a sample of just under 2000 school children who were 14–15 years old at the start of the study. The young women's heights and weights were measured, and their dieting, psychiatric morbidity and eating disorders assessed at the start of the study and then at six monthly intervals for three years. In this study there were two strong predictors of the development of eating disorders. Young women who dieted at a moderate level were five times more likely to develop them, and those who dieted at a severe level were 18 times more likely to do so. Independently, the young women in the highest category for psychiatric morbidity were almost seven times as likely to develop an eating disorder. The newly developing disorders in the study were partial syndromes of bulimia nervosa. Most other longitudinal studies of dieting show that it does predict the subsequent development of eating pathology (Hsu, 1997; Stice, 2002). There is some evidence that negative affect and dieting have synergistic effects, with high scores on both predicting a greater level of binge eating than would be expected from the additive effects of the two individual scores (Stice *et al.*, 2000).

9.3   Genetic and other risk factors

In spite of the strong cultural pressures they are subjected to, most young women do not develop eating disorders, and there is some evidence that the vulnerability in those who do is partly genetic in origin.

To begin with, it is clearly familial, with a higher risk of an eating disorder found in the relatives of known cases. This was established, for example, in a large-scale study of Strober *et al.* (2000). The study began with a sample of female probands 18–28 years old. Of these 152 were young women with the restricting sub-type of anorexia nervosa (i.e. without bulimic symptoms); 171 were young women with pure bulimia nervosa; and the remaining 181 had no history of a psychiatric illness. Relatives of the probands over 12 years of age were investigated using formal diagnostic interviews for eating disorders and for other psychiatric disorders. Of the female relatives of probands with anorexia nervosa, 6.8% had full or partial syndrome anorexia nervosa (equal numbers of each) and 7.2% had full or partial syndrome bulimia nervosa. Of the female relatives of probands with bulimia nervosa 7.1% had full or partial syndrome anorexia nervosa, and 7.7% had full or partial syndrome bulimia nervosa. The rates in the female relatives of the young women with no history of psychiatric illness were much lower (0.9% for anorexia nervosa and 2.2% for bulimia). Adjusted for age, the risk of anorexia nervosa was 11.4 times as high in the relatives of young women with anorexia nervosa, and the risk of bulimia 3.7 times as high in the female relatives of young women with bulimia nervosa. The risks across disorders were almost exactly the same: the risk of anorexia nervosa was 12.1 times as high in the relatives of young women with bulimia, and the risk of bulimia 3.5 times as high in the female relatives of young women with anorexia. The study was set up specifically to start with probands with the pure forms of anorexia and bulimia nervosa (i.e. without intermediate or mixed conditions) so these familial liabilities to the other eating disorders as well as to the one diagnosed in the proband do strongly suggest that the familial liability is to an eating disorder per se, rather than to one or other of the specific syndromes. Results of this kind provide additional grounds for Waller's (1993) argument that the general diagnosis of an eating disorder may be more significant psychologically than a differential diagnosis within the eating disorders.

To show more specifically that there are genetic influences on a disorder (rather than familial influences, which could be of other kinds) has generally depended on studies of twins. Twin studies are difficult to conduct in relation to eating disorders owing to their low prevalence, but the available data suggest that if one of a twin is diagnosed with anorexia nervosa the other twin has about a 50% probability of having the same disorder if the twins are monozygotic, and a less than 10% probability if they are dizygotic (Treasure & Holland, 1995). More recent summaries which deal with population-based twin studies as well as studies of treated patients generally confirm this genetic influence, though the exact size of the genetic contribution is hard to estimate owing to the small number of twin pairs available (Gorwood, Kipman & Foulon, 2003).

Genetic predispositions to eating disorders could operate in many different ways. They might influence associated personality traits, for example obsessive-compulsive traits or perfectionism, or associated psychopathological traits such as a tendency to anxiety or depression, or they might influence adiposity and weight loss (Hebebrand & Remschmidt, 1995). There is also evidence that the genetic influences may vary with age. Although their study did not deal specifically with diagnosable eating disorders, but with eating attitudes and behaviour recording on the Eating Disorder Inventory, Klump et al. found little genetic contribution to variability in weight preoccupation or eating abnormalities in 11-year-old twin pairs, but a quite strong (> 50%) genetic contribution in 17-year-old pairs (Klump, Kaye & Strober, 2001). They suggest a number of explanations by which genetic influences might come to operate over the adolescent period in this way. One is that a gene may be activated by hormonal or other changes taking place over puberty. Another involves a gene–environment correlation in which, for example, girls going into puberty are able to choose peer groups more similar to themselves in eating and dietary habits and so find social support for their own developing eating disorder.

Specific environmental risk factors in the personal histories of people with eating disorders have not been easy to identify. One possibility that has been given a good deal of attention is early sexual abuse (Connors & Morse, 1993; Everill & Waller, 1995; Waller, 1998; Wooley, 1994). Case histories and case series do show high levels of reported sexual abuse in young women with eating disorders. Unfortunately they are also quite common in other young women. In the Christchurch Health and Development Study (Fergusson, Horwood & Lynskey, 1996; Fergusson, Lynskey & Horwood, 1996), 10.4% of the study participants reported some kind of sexual abuse by the time they were 16 years old, and the rates were much higher in girls than in boys. Attempted sexual intercourse was reported by 5.6% of girls and 1.4% of boys. So more specific evidence is needed, and a recent prospective longitudinal study, in which 782 mothers and their offspring were interviewed when the offspring were children and again when they were adolescents and adults, did find that sexual abuse in childhood was a strong risk factor for self-induced vomiting, strict dieting and eating disorders (Johnson *et al.*, 2002). In this study rates of other psychiatric disorders were also considerably raised. For those reporting attempts at sexual intercourse as children major depression was about eight times as common and suicide attempts about twelve times as common. Other psychiatric problems (anxiety or conduct disorders or alcohol or other substance abuse or dependence) were three to five times as common. This suggests that a history of sexual abuse predisposes to a range of later psychiatric disorders, including the eating disorders, rather than predisposing to eating disorders specifically, which is consistent with an earlier, retrospective study. Welch and Fairburn (1994) compared the history of sexual abuse in four groups of women, comprising a group of clinic patients with bulimia nervosa, a second group in which bulimia nervosa was identified by screening a population through general practice registers, a third group identified in a similar way but with other psychiatric disorders (mostly with depression, but some with anxiety disorders), and a control group who were free from psychiatric disorders but were otherwise comparable to the community group with bulimia nervosa. The control group comprised 100 women, and the other three groups 50 each. The results were quite clear. A reported history of sexual abuse was significantly more common in the bulimic women than in otherwise comparable control women, with abuse involving physical contact being reported by 26% of the bulimic women and only 10% of the controls. But a history of sexual abuse was equally common in women with depression or anxiety disorders (24%). So although there is an association between sexual abuse and bulimia, it is part of a much more general association between sexual abuse and the later development of a range of psychiatric disorders. Similar associations were reported in respect of people with binge eating disorder: a history of physical and sexual abuse is more common when they are compared with healthy controls, but not when they are compared with general psychiatric controls (Fairburn *et al.*, 1998).

The incidence of formally diagnosed eating disorders increases markedly over the years around puberty. Two plausible developmental risk factors for eating disorders are increased adiposity at this time and the timing of puberty itself. Both can lead to increased body dissatisfaction, and they are also related to one another because greater adiposity leads to earlier puberty (Davison, Susman & Birch, 2003). The increase in adiposity before puberty is also greater in girls than boys (Figure 1.1). Dancyger and Garfinkel (1995) compared young women with full and partial syndrome eating disorders and found a personal history of overweight from 6 to 12 years of age in 37% of those with the full syndrome, 12% of those with the partial syndrome and 7% of a control group. The proportion overweight from 13 to 15 were 70%, 55% and 21% respectively. The personal histories came from the young women themselves, however, and distorted body image is a characteristic symptom of eating disorders. Longitudinal data with actual measurement of body size is needed to provide convincing evidence of an association. There is some evidence from longitudinal studies that higher relative weights do predict the development of eating disorder symptoms: this effect was found, for example, in the study of Gardner *et al.* (2000) described above. An overall quantitative summary of published studies showed that higher initial body mass does predict the development of eating pathology (Stice, 2002). The effect is a small one, though initial body mass is more strongly related to increases in body dissatisfaction and dieting of a more general kind. As regards the timing of puberty, although it is not very consistent, there is some evidence that earlier puberty is associated with higher rates of eating disorders (Graber *et al.*, 1997; Wichstrøm, 2000). Again a quantitative summary of the available studies showed that this was a statistically significant but very small association (Stice, 2002). Small though these associations are, it could be argued that increased obesity and earlier puberty might to some extent underlie the secular trend towards increased eating disorders seen in Western countries in recent years.

Because the incidence of clinically diagnosable eating disorders increases around the time of puberty, longitudinal research on the eating disorders has reasonably enough often started in the second decade (Attie & Brooks-Gunn, 1989; Calam & Waller, 1998; Cattarin & Thompson, 1994; Wichstrøm, 2000). The first of these longitudinal studies was by Attie and Brooks-Gunn (1989). The 193 children in the study were seen when they were 12–15 years old and then two years later. They were white children from academically oriented private schools in New York. The principal outcome measure at the two-year follow-up was the girls' score on the Eating Attitudes Test (EAT). An abbreviated version of this scale was also used when the children were initially seen. This design allows two types of analysis, firstly of the variables associated with high scores when the children were first seen, and secondly of the variables associated with change in their scores over the two year follow-up. When first seen, a range of different variables predicted EAT scores. EAT scores increased with the child's age (from 12 to 15). They were higher in fatter children. And they were strongly related to poorer body image and to a measure of psychopathology. Higher EAT scores at the later visit were predicted by higher EAT scores at the first visit (the raw correlation was 0.44). The only significant predictor of *change* in the scores among the variables measured at the first visit was body image; EAT scores increased more in children with a poorer body image at the first visit.

Cattarin and Thomson (1994) followed 210 female adolescents who were 10–15 years old at the start of the study over a period of three years. Eating disorder was assessed using two subscales of the Eating Disorder Inventory, the Drive for Thinness subscale and the Bulimia subscale. These measure restrictive and bulimic aspects of disordered eating respectively. For both scales the only significant predictor was the level of scores on the same scale at the start of the study. Similarly, in the study of Calam and Waller (1998) EAT and BITE scores measured at 12 years of age were the only significant predictors of EAT and BITE scores at 19 years. In the largest longitudinal study over the teenage years, Wichstrøm (2000) used a representative nationwide sample of 7751 Norwegian adolescents. They were 12–19 years old during the first wave of data collection, and they were studied again in a second wave of data collection two years later. Eating problems were assessed using a 12 item version of the EAT. Apart from gender, the strong predictor of disordered eating at the second time point was disordered eating at the first time point. There was no significant interaction with age; even in the youngest (12-year-old) children the best predictor of later high EAT scores was high EAT scores at the first measurement wave.

All these studies show, therefore, that high scores on the EAT by the age of 12, indicating abnormal eating attitudes, are the strongest predictor of later disordered eating scores – indeed it has been hard to identify any other consistent predictors of high later eating disorder scores. The implication is that although diagnosable eating disorders rise in incidence over the teenage years, the psychological characteristics associated with high eating disorder scores are substantially present in many young women by 12 years of age. We need, therefore, to consider whether there are any earlier predictors of these characteristics, which requires studies starting earlier in childhood. Three studies which start in early childhood are relevant here (Gardner *et al.*, 2000; Marchi & Cohen, 1990; Stice, Agras & Hammer, 1999).

In the study of Gardner *et al.* (Gardner, Stark, Friedman & Jackson, 2000) 216 children were recruited within six months of their 6th, 9th or 12th birthday, and examined annually for the next three years. Eating disorders were assessed using the Eating Disorder Inventory for Children (EDI-C) subscales for drive for thinness and bulimia from 6 to 8 years, and the children's version of the Eating Attitudes Test (ChEAT) from 9 to 14. Even at 6 years eating disorder symptoms were associated with low body esteem (and with teasing). At later ages (from 9 on) low body esteem, depression, body dissatisfaction, teasing and heavier weight were associated with higher eating disorder scores. Forward predictions over three years were also reported. In both boys and girls higher weight gain predicted higher scores. In girls increased body dissatisfaction also predicted high scores. Unfortunately forward prediction from earlier eating disorder scores was not examined.

Stice, Agras and Hammer (1999) examined the development of eating disturbances over the first five years. Just over 200 infants were recruited at birth and a range of measures recorded in the first year of life. These included the infant's BMI and a sucking measure from a feeding test at 2 and 4 weeks of age, and a range of eating disturbance measures relating to the child's mother taken from scales from the Three Factor Eating Questionnaire (Stunkard & Messick, 1985) and the Eating Disorder Inventory (Garner, Olmsted & Polivy, 1983). The mother's BMI was also measured. The outcome measures comprised answers to single questions to the child's mother concerning inhibited eating, secretive eating, overeating and overeating-induced vomiting in the child. These were intended to assess the kinds of behaviour in a child of 5 that might be manifestations of the bulimic or anorexic behaviour patterns seen later in adolescents or adults. Each of the four kinds of behaviour became progressively more common over the five-year period. Inhibited eating was more common in children with heavier mothers. It was not related to the child's own BMI though this was measured only at 1 month of age – it may have been related to their BMI when they were older. Secretive eating was associated with a number of measures recorded in the child's mother, including her BMI, body dissatisfaction and bulimic symptoms, though vomiting in the child was not. It would be very interesting to know to what extent these types of behaviour in 5-year-old children do relate to scores on more formal eating disorder scales of the kind that can be used in slightly older children (Maloney, McGuire & Daniels, 1988), and to dietary restraint, as the beginnings of dietary restraint can already be seen in 5-year-old children (Shunk & Birch, 2004). Using an adapted version of the restraint scale from the Dutch Eating Behaviour Questionnaire, Shunk and Birch found that dietary restraint in 5-year-old children was significantly related to weight concerns and to lower body esteem, though not to dieting itself at the time. Dietary restraint was, however, related to self-reported dieting by 7 years of age, and to self-reported dieting and to higher ChEAT score by 9.

In the study of Marchi and Cohen (1990) children were recruited when they were 1–10 years old, and followed up for a ten-year period and then later (Kotler *et al.*, 2001). The study sample was originally drawn as a representative random sample of families living in two upstate New York counties. Marchi and Cohen asked the children's mothers about their eating behaviour at three different ages, and the outcome data were reduced by factor analysis to give a limited number of scores. One of these concerned 'pickiness', which involved eating slowly, eating little and a low interest in food. Children who were picky eaters when 1–10 years old were more likely to show symptoms of anorexia nervosa ten years later. Pickiness from 8–18 years of age was also associated with anorexia symptoms two years later, though not subsequently (Kotler *et al.*, 2001; Marchi & Cohen, 1990). Pica (eating of substances that are not foods) was associated with bulimia symptoms. Eating conflicts, struggles around meals and unpleasant meals were related to anorexia nervosa symptoms at a later stage, but as they were assessed in early childhood over a wide age range (1 to 10) it is hard to know to what extent they might have resulted from initial stages of the development of disordered eating. Eating too little over the same age range protected against later bulimia nervosa.

These longitudinal studies suggest that there are developmental continuities in disordered eating attitudes and behaviour over the period from early adolescence, and give hints (perhaps not more) that there may be some relationship between early feeding behaviour and later eating disorder symptoms. Are there any other aspects of family life that can be linked with the development of eating disorders? If there are it has been very difficult to identify them. There are two problems in doing so. Prospective studies of eating disorders have been difficult to carry out because of the low rates of eating disorders in the population. Even if, say, 5% of young women eventually develop an eating disorder of some kind it would be very hard to carry out intensive family based investigation on the number of families required in childhood to give a group of affected young women later on of any reasonable size. So most research on family based risk factors has been retrospective (Fairburn et al., 1999; Karwautz et al., 2001; Murphy, Troop & Treasure, 2000). The difficulty with retrospective studies is that the earlier characteristics of the families generally have to be identified via the young women with the eating disorders, whose cognitive processes are likely to be distorted. It is quite possible, for example, that young women who develop anorexia nervosa have mothers who are more controlling (Murphy, Troop & Treasure, 2000) or parents with higher expectations (Karwautz et al., 2001) but it is hard to be sure without independent sources of evidence, which in relation to early family experiences tend not to be available. That is one problem. A second problem is that the behaviour of the parents in a family with a child with a psychological (or a physical) disorder can change as a response to the disorder. Blair, Freeman and Cull (1995), for example, compared the families of young women with anorexia and those of young women who were well, using self-reports from the young women and their siblings and parents. There were differences between them in a measure of 'expressed emotion'. Families with high expressed emotion were those in which parents made critical comments or were rated as hostile. Few of the families of well children showed high levels of expressed emotion (3%) while many more of the families of young women with anorexia nervosa did (42%). But this study also investigated a third group of families, in which the daughters had cystic fibrosis, and high expressed emotion was also found in 34% of these families. As we have seen, cystic fibrosis, like anorexia nervosa, is a life-threatening chronic illness that leads to malnutrition, poor growth and delayed puberty. But it is known to be a genetic disorder, so the high expressed emotion in the families in which a daughter had cystic fibrosis cannot possibly have caused the disorder, and presumably must have developed as a result of the illness in their child. Since living with a child with anorexia nervosa is likely to be as stressful, or even more stressful, this characteristic of the families of the young women with anorexia nervosa could also be a result rather than a cause of the condition.

9.4   Intergenerational aspects of eating disorders

Eating disorders are most common in women, and they mostly arise in the early reproductive years. They are familial, and their less than perfect concordance in monozygotic twins suggests a considerable environmental influence in their aetiology. The question therefore arises whether the development of young children is affected if their mother has an eating disorder, and if so how. Two approaches to the problem are possible. One can start with the mothers, and look for problems in the children of mothers with eating disorders. Or one can start with the children, and look for eating disorders in the mothers of children with feeding or growth problems.

In countries where malnutrition is common maternal malnutrition in pregnancy is an important cause of intra-uterine growth retardation, leading to infants born small for gestational age and, in some cases, preterm. Although malnutrition in pregnancy is not generally common in Western countries, the 'elective malnutrition' seen in some women with eating disorders can have the same effects as malnutrition caused in any other way. Using the first approach to the problem, Treasure and Russell (1988) recruited six women with long-standing anorexia nervosa and examined the pre- and postnatal growth of their infants. The average BMI of the women was 16.8 kg/m^2, and their average weight gain over the pregnancy was low (8 kg). Growth of the infants before birth was assessed by measuring their abdominal circumference using ultrasonography, and it was clearly delayed in the third trimester. In the period after birth, however, the growth of the infants 'caught up' over the first six months. A similar result has been reported by Waugh and Bulik (1999). They recruited ten women with an eating disorder and ten randomly selected controls, and showed a statistically significant reduction in the birth-weight of the infants of mothers with the eating disorders (of over half a kilogram), and in their birth length. Again the infants caught up and were very similar to the infants born to the control mothers by 3 months of age. Using the second approach to the problem, Conti, Abraham and Taylor (1998) compared the mothers of infants born preterm or small for gestational age and the mothers of control infants, using the Eating Disorder Inventory and Eating Disorder Examination to assess eating disorders and their symptoms. In the three months before the pregnancy, as assessed retrospectively, there was a considerably higher prevalence of DSM-IV diagnosable eating disorders in the mother of infants born SGA (32%) than in the mothers of infants born preterm (9%) or of normal weight at term (5%). Cigarette smoking is also associated with a lower birthweight (Kramer, 1987), and the mothers of the SGA infants smoked significantly more, but in multivariate analysis scores on the EDI bulimia subscale were significantly associated with an SGA birth after controlling for cigarette smoking. There is, therefore, good reason to think that eating disorders in the mother are associated with slow growth of the infant in late pregnancy and a low birthweight, an unhappy parallel with the widespread effects of malnutrition on birthweight in less developed countries.

The possibility that eating disorders in the mother might also adversely affect an infant's growth after birth arises because mothers with an eating disorder might restrict the food intake of their children as well as their own, especially, perhaps, if they are girls. Another possibility is that the depression that is often associated with eating disorders in the mother might adversely affect their interactions with the infant and so affect the infant's growth. Although the two studies cited above do not suggest that the infant's growth is affected in the period after birth, this possibility has been investigated more directly. Again, two approaches have been taken – first to start with mothers with eating disorders and to investigate how they feed their children and the way their children grow, and second to start with children who have eating problems or grow poorly and to investigate the possibility of eating disorders in their mothers.

Taking the first approach, suggestive evidence of a relationship was published by Brinch, Isager and Tolstrup (1988) and by van Wezel-Meijler and Wit (1989). In the study of Brinch *et al.* 140 women diagnosed with anorexia nervosa in the Rigshospitalet in Copenhagen were followed up on average 12.5 years later, when 50 of them had given birth, and they had 86 children between them. Of the infants, 14.3% were born below 2500 g, compared with 6.8% in the background population, reflecting the prenatal effects referred to above. The proportion dying in the first week of life was 81 per 1000, compared with a proportion of 14 per 1000 in the Danish population as a whole over the period in which the children were born. Of the seven children who died, five died due to complications of prematurity. Failure to thrive in the first year of life was reported in 17% of the infants. Unfortunately the criteria used to identify it were not very clear, and no comparisons are available with infants of similar birthweights and gestation from the same population.

In the first controlled investigation of failure to thrive in the infants of mothers with eating disorders, Stein *et al.* (1994) recruited two groups of mothers. The index group comprised 34 mothers who had had an eating disorder in the year after they gave birth. Of these, six met DSM-III-R diagnostic criteria for bulimia nervosa, 12 met them for an eating disorder not otherwise specified (EDNOS) and 16 were subthreshold cases. The controls comprised 24 mothers comparable in age and social class, but without a history of eating disorders. The mean birthweights of the infants born to the mothers in the two groups were very similar (3373 g for the index group and 3448 g for the controls). At 12–14 months the infants born to the mothers with eating disorders were relatively lighter than the infants born to the control mothers, though the difference was not quite statistically significant. In a later paper (Stein *et al.*, 1996) the same group of mothers was compared with two other groups, a group who were depressed in the post-natal year and a control group. The control group partly overlapped with those used in the earlier analysis, but was larger, and in this comparison the infants of the eating disordered group were significantly lighter than the infants in the other two groups. This is a suggestive but slightly equivocal result, and it was not replicated by Whitehouse and Harris (1998), who examined attained weight and height (and BMI) in children of a group of eating disordered mothers and matched controls. The groups were rather small, but no significant difference was found in the weights, heights or BMIs of the children when they were 31–60 months old. Agras *et al.* (1999) examined the early feeding of children of eating-disordered mothers and found no effect of the mothers' eating disorder on their children's BMI at any stage over the first five years, though the mothers were significantly more concerned about their children's weights. These authors used a mixed group with bulimia nervosa, binge eating disorder, anorexia nervosa and partial syndromes of each. Difficult though it would be, it might be necessary to examine more clearly differentiated groups of mothers, for example those with restricting and other forms of eating disorder, if the relationship between eating disorders in the mother and infant weight gain is to be clarified.

Stein *et al.* (1994) have also examined the actual behaviour of eating disordered mothers and their infants during mealtimes, and also during play sessions. They were more intrusive than the control mothers, both during mealtime interactions and during play, and expressed more negative emotion towards their infants during mealtimes. There was more marked conflict during mealtimes and the mood of the infants was rated as slightly less happy on average both during meals and at play. When considered simultaneously in regression analyses, infant weight was predicted by mothers' concerns about her own body shape and by conflict during mealtimes (after controlling for the infant's birthweight and the mother's height). This may mean that conflict interferes with the infants' food intake and slows growth, but as the mealtime measures were made when the infants were 12–14 months old it could alternatively mean that poor weight gain in the infants led to conflict during meals.

Taking the alternative approach, McCann *et al.* (1994) examined eating disorder symptoms in the mothers of children who failed to thrive. The children were identified from the patient lists of two Oxfordshire paediatricians; their weights at referral were on or below the 3rd centile. None of the mothers of these children fulfilled diagnostic criteria for anorexia nervosa or bulimia nervosa, but as a group they did score significantly higher on the restraint subscale of the Eating Disorder Examination. Eating disorder symptoms in mothers could be associated with feeding problems in their children even if their growth was not affected, since not all feeding problems are associated with growth problems. Stein *et al.* (1995) examined eating disorder symptoms in the mothers of 30 children (aged 2–12) with an ICD-10 (International Classification of Diseases, 10th revision) diagnosis of a feeding disorder. The criteria for this involved food refusal and extreme faddiness. They were compared with the mothers of an equal number of children with behavioural disturbances of other kinds, and with a bigger general community sample. The results showed that the mothers of the children with feeding disorders did have significantly elevated scores of all five subscales generated by the Eating Disorder Examination questionnaire – dietary restraint, bulimia, and concern about eating, body shape and weight – compared with the other mothers. This association could reflect ways in which mothers with eating disorders relate to their children, though it is also possible that they might reflect genetic associations. As noted earlier, Stice, Agras and Hammer (1999) have examined the same issue but in a longitudinal study in which they investigated the emergence of inhibited eating, secretive eating, overeating and vomiting in the first five years of life, using single questions to the mother. These measures were intended to assess eating disturbances in childhood that might be analogous to later eating disordered behaviour. All four kinds of behaviour emerged over the early years, with the highest risk of them emerging when the children were 5. Secretive eating and overeating were to some extent predicted by maternal eating behaviour as assessed using the Three-factor Eating Questionnaire, though inhibited eating and vomiting were not.

A more comprehensive discussion of this area can be found in the review of Patel, Wheatcroft, Park and Stein (2002). They comment that virtually all the published research in this area has concerned mothers and their daughters, with very little attention to fathers. Fathers may also, of course, have a role in the aetiology of eating disorders, though as they tend to be much less involved in the actual feeding of their children it might operate through mechanisms such as early sexual or physical abuse that predispose to psychopathology generally, rather than by influencing more directly their children's eating behaviour.

10   Some concluding thoughts

A woman in Madrid called the emergency services because her child wasn't eating his yoghurt (Corral, 2004). A father suffered a panic attack after accidentally giving his 11-month-old daughter a fruit smoothie that contained a tiny proportion of honey (Wilson, 2005). I dare say these are extreme cases, but parents do seem to show a remarkable degree of anxiety over the feeding and nutrition of their children, and not only parents. According to one recent report, poor nutrition may cause dyslexia, dyspraxia, autism, learning difficulties, irritability, anxiety, lethargy, insomnia, tiredness, depression, anti-social behaviour, reduced sense of smell and taste, cravings, mood swings, hyperactivity, poor concentration and tantrums (Purvis, 2005).

If only one thing is clear from this book, I hope it will be clear quite how difficult a task it would be to investigate all these possibilities. Effects of the principal known nutritional deficiencies on intellectual development in children have been of interest for at least 50 years, but it is very hard to be certain even of the significance of these. Iron deficiency is measurable and much of the biochemistry of iron is quite well understood. There are large numbers of iron-deficient children, and the prevention and treatment of iron deficiency is possible in principle, using procedures that are cheap and relatively safe, and can be implemented in double-blind trials so that investigators can test the children without knowing whether they have been given iron supplements or not. Yet a leading research worker in this field comments 'I have been working on iron deficiency for 25 years now, and really trying to do good studies. After all this effort, we still cannot give definite answers' (Lozoff, in discussion of Grantham-McGregor & Ani, 2001: 666s). The studies Lozoff has reported certainly are good, and there is, I think, reasonably good evidence that iron deficiency does have adverse effects on cognitive development, but it has been hard to demonstrate its effects unambiguously, and very hard to determine their magnitude and long-term significance. The same generalisations could be made about protein-energy malnutrition. And although there may well be many other candidates for important nutritional effects on psychological development, it will be a difficult job to investigate each of these thoroughly. In most of the areas we have looked at in this book there are reasonably well-conducted studies that nonetheless have given answers that appear to be contradictory. One obvious lesson is that a single study is never likely to produce a definitive answer. A number of well-conducted studies taken together may do so, or at least they may provide some reasonable limits for our anxieties.

Restricting ourselves to topics on which there is a substantial number of independent studies, the evidence that it is desirable for infants to be breastfed is strong. In parts of the world where people are poor and sanitation and water supplies are inadequate its benefits are huge. Not only does it reduce morbidity and mortality from diseases that are very common, but it also has important child spacing effects. Even in Western countries the health benefits of breast-feeding are important in relation to diarrhoeal disease in the first year, and there is also reasonably good evidence that breast-feeding protects against the subsequent development of obesity, though why it does so is not at all clear. The evidence for cognitive benefits of breast-feeding is also reasonably strong, though the benefits are probably quite small. The estimate from the meta-analysis of Anderson et al. (1999) suggests a benefit of about 3 IQ points. In spite of these benefits there is, unfortunately, still evidence of unacceptable attempts by commercial companies to promote the bottle-feeding of infants (Mayor, 2004).

An effect on IQ of a similar size (but an adverse effect) is also associated with failure to thrive in infancy, as identified by traditional anthropometric criteria. A substantial number of studies taken together suggest that children who fail to thrive in Western countries are slightly delayed developmentally, and that their later IQ is lower by an average of about 4 IQ points (Corbett & Drewett, 2004). This is probably an effect associated with malnutrition after birth, related to the effects of malnutrition on cognitive development found in less developed countries where malnutrition is more common. There is also some evidence for comparable effects associated with malnutrition before birth. Shenkin et al. suggest that IQ varies between children with the highest and lowest birthweights by about 10 IQ points, though this range was somewhat reduced by taking confounders into account (Shenkin, Starr & Deary, 2004), and it is not certain that this association between IQ and birthweight is a nutritional effect. It ought to be possible to improve the nutrition of young children before and after birth where it is necessary to do so. There is evidence, for example, that nutritional interventions with infants who fail to thrive can improve their weight gain (Wright et al., 1998). Whether their intellectual abilities can be improved in the same way is not yet clear.

How important, anyway, are relatively small differences in IQ of three or four points? That might depend on our point of view. In relation to the large effects of untreated phenylketonuria on intellectual ability these nutritional effects are quite small, or, as it is sometimes put, of 'doubtful clinical significance' (Rudolf & Logan, 2005). But what exactly does 'clinical significance' mean in relation to average differences in intelligence between populations of children? The importance of a child's intelligence lies in the relationship it has with the child's subsequent prospects in life, as reflected, for example, in their educational success and prospects for employment, and if we are concerned to optimise the welfare of all children, rather than just to avoid major sources of disability, it may be very important to take effects of this size seriously. Intellectual ability is the joint outcome of genetic and environmental factors, and a reasonable estimate would suggest that about half the variation in measured intelligence in Western populations today is of environmental origin (Devlin, Daniels & Roeder, 1997). More direct estimates of environmental influences are also available. The secular increase in IQ (the Flynn effect) suggests an increase of about 18 IQ points per generation (30 years). Schiff et al. examined the effects of moving children from working-class to middle-class families (Schiff et al., 1978). They found an increase in IQ of 16 points when they compared children who were moved and their siblings who were left in their original families. These are big effects, and suggest that substantial intellectual benefits could be brought about by appropriate modification of the environment in which children develop. But we do not know what environmental changes were responsible for the Flynn effect, and social class is not a single variable, but a marker associated with a large number of more specific economic, educational and health related variables. To decide what are appropriate modifications to the child's environment we would need to know exactly what features of the environment are important, and within the range of environments normally encountered by children in Western societies most of the environmental variables that have been shown to be specifically related to intelligence have relatively small effects.

Exposure to cocaine before birth, for example, is associated with an average reduction in IQ of 3.26 points (Lester, LaGasse & Selfer, 1998). Exposure to lead has effects that are dose dependent. An estimate from the meta-analysis of a large number of studies suggests that a typical doubling of body lead burden is associated with a reduction in IQ of 1 to 2 points, though there is some evidence that the effect is larger than this at low doses (Canfield et al., 2003). Domestic violence experienced by the mothers of young children is associated with a reduction of 5 IQ points in the child if it is at a medium level and 8 IQ points if it is more severe

(Koenen *et al.*, 2003). Being born preterm is associated with a difference of 10.2 IQ points (Bhutta *et al.*, 2002). The Abecedarian project, which involved an intensive educational intervention involving full-time educational child care of high quality from birth to 5 years, was associated with an IQ difference of 4.2 points at 21 years (Campbell *et al.*, 2001). A preventative intervention in preterm infants involving three years' home visits and centre-based schooling was associated with an improvement of 3.7 IQ points which was restricted to infants heavier at birth (Brooks-Gunn *et al.*, 1994). These are mostly effects of about the same order of magnitude as the nutritional effects we have been considering. So if we are to do good here, it looks as though we are going to have to do it in 'Minute Particulars', and try to deal with a range of environmental variables, each of which considered in isolation has only a small effect. In fact, as Lester *et al.* point out in relation to the effects of exposure to cocaine before birth, even a small average difference in IQ can have big economic implications, because a mean difference of 3.26 points implies an increase of 1.6% in the proportion of children with an IQ below 70, when they are generally provided with special educational services (at an additional cost of \$4–35 million, in the case they considered). In fact much higher costs are implied, because children with IQs in the 70–80 band will often also need additional services, and there will be more children in this band. As in other areas of health economics, the use of monetary figures here is not intended to imply that saving money would be the goal of the intervention. It is simply a way of providing an indication of the magnitude of the overall burden on children and their families of a failure to take these small environmental effects seriously, and of the resources that could be made available to children with other needs if they did not have to be used here.

The later effects of early nutrition and malnutrition on the development of children has been one of the main themes of this book. The other main theme has been the development of children's own behaviour, as it relates to their nutrition, and an important set of questions concerns continuities in feeding and other nutritionally related behaviour over the lifespan. At a behavioural level, there is a substantial difference between behaviour during the period of early infancy associated with milk feeding and behaviour in the childhood period after weaning, and although interesting possibilities are being investigated clear evidence for continuities of an important kind between children's behaviour across these two periods is not very strong. Many of the feeding problems in infancy, like the crying and sleeping problems, are problems more for the parents than for the developing child. The evidence that characteristics of feeding behaviour in the early years predict any of the adolescent eating disorders, for example, is not at the moment very strong. The main characteristics in childhood that are likely to be related to later eating disorders arise from 8 to 10 years of age and are a liability to the common psychiatric problems of late childhood and early adult life, especially anxiety and depression, and the body image problems that are now so widespread in young people.

It is possible that we have not looked in the right areas for continuities of other kinds. There are no real studies of continuities in individual differences in appetite over the childhood period, for example, and it is possible that individual differences of this kind could be related to lifetime risks for obesity. Even genetic effects can clearly operate via differences in appetite, as we saw in Chapter 7. A recent longitudinal study of early risk factors for obesity identified eight variables measured early in life that predicted obesity at 7 years (Reilly *et al.*, 2005). The variables were parental obesity, birthweight, weight at 8 and 18 months, weight gain in infancy, catch-up growth, early adiposity or body mass index, sleep duration and television viewing. Although the summary of the study states that 'the early life environment can determine later risk of obesity' most of the variables that were related to later obesity in this study reflect the early behaviour or somatic characteristics of the child, rather than aspects of the early environment. They suggest that individual differences related to later obesity develop early, but not necessarily that early environments are especially important in determining differences in later adiposity. Of course over recent years we have seen major increases in adiposity in children in Western countries, and changes in the environment are almost certain to have been responsible for these changes. But there is no reason why variation in averages in populations over time should have the same explanation as variation between individual members of a population at a particular time.

Although research seeking to identify factors underlying individual differences in adiposity is in its infancy, we know, in principle, why children become excessively fat. It is a consequence of an excess of energy intake over energy expenditure. How much is to be gained at a practical level by studies seeking to make this statement more precise seems to me rather uncertain. It must be clear to everybody that the measurement of energy intake and expenditure to the precision necessary to explain why some children store more fat than others would tax the most sophisticated study. And even if we had more precise information on this, it would not tell us what the possibilities for change are, and research dealing with everyday behavioural correlates and risk factors for adiposity and with what behaviour to target to reduce its prevalence may be more important practically.

The evidence that overweight and obesity in children has increased in recent years is incontrovertible, but the evidence that eating disorders have increased as well is also quite strong. The difference in bodily appearance between people with anorexia nervosa and people who are obese is stark, and might give the impression that these are completely different problems. But if we consider the eating disorders and obesity more generally we encounter a range of overlapping problems, including those associated with nutritional knowledge, with binge eating and other unhealthy eating practices, with dieting, purging and other unhealthy weight loss practices, with body image, and with self-esteem and depression. The overlap in these problems suggests that a good case can be made for seeking to integrate the prevention of obesity and the eating disorders within a single strategy, particularly when we are concerned with health education provided through schools or other communities of young people, and there are also good practical reasons for integrating the two (Irving & Neumark-Szainer, 2002). These include the relative costs of separate and integrated programmes (for example, of staff training and the provision of educational materials), the grounds for thinking that the prevention of both kinds of problem is best targeted at children and adolescents, and the need to avoid messages concerning eating disorders and obesity that taken together appear to be confusing or mutually contradictory.

Attempts at universal prevention for the eating disorders have been tried, almost always through schools (Pratt & Woolfenden, 2004), but there is currently no evidence available to suggest that they have any long-term effectiveness in preventing their development. An interesting possibility though, and one that gives some grounds for optimism, is that a school-based obesity prevention intervention programme (Planet Health) does appear to have reduced the use of purging and diet pills among girls (Austin et al., 2005), though not extreme dieting per se (Gortmaker et al., 1999). Although neither purging nor the use of diet pills was very common, the prevalence of these forms of weight control was halved in the schools provided with the intervention, which was focussed on improving nutrition, increasing physical activity and reducing television watching, and was successful in reducing adiposity in girls.

School-based health education programmes have a strikingly strong track record of evidence-based research, based on a strong commitment to randomised controlled trials. They provide an example of the use of methodologically strong designs in an educational context that would surely have been of benefit had they been used more extensively in other areas of educational research, giving us much more reliable information on whether 'Sure Start' programmes were effective, for example, or on how best to teach children to read (Tizard, Schofield & Hewison, 1982). The use of RCTs in health education has emphasised the randomising of groups rather than the randomising of individuals, because decisions concerning health-related behaviour are strongly influenced by groups (particularly, in children, their peer groups) so intervening with whole groups is more likely to be effective than intervening with individuals. Impressive though these studies have been methodologically, however, they have shown rather limited effectiveness in tackling the rise in obesity through health promotion in schools, probably because influences of other kinds reduce their effectiveness. What will be needed is a much more extensive range of social and political changes, and it may be virtually impossible to assess their effectiveness in systematically controlled ways. In a valuable review of lessons from controlling tobacco smoking that can be applied in the diet and activity area Yach *et al.* (2005) emphasise the importance of the comprehensiveness of intervention measures, and the need to avoid dissecting them into individual components in order to ascertain the effectiveness of each. This is partly because a range of measures introduced together may be effective even if each introduced in isolation is not. Bringing about a comprehensive social change for the benefits of future generations, as is certainly necessary in this area, may not be compatible with the needs of the most rigorous methods of evaluation. I am not, of course, saying that the most rigorous methods of evaluation should not be used when they usefully can.

References

Abbott, J., Conway, S., Etherington, C., *et al.* (2000). Perceived body image and eating behavior in young adults with cystic fibrosis and their healthy peers. *Journal of Behavioral Medicine, 23,* 501–17.

Abbott, R. D., White, L. R., Ross, G. W., *et al.* (1998). Height as a marker of childhood development and late-life cognitive function: the Honolulu-Asia aging study. *Pediatrics, 102,* 602–9.

ACC/SCN (2000). *Fourth Report on the World Nutrition Situation.* ACC/SCN in collaboration with IFPRI. Geneva: ACC/SCN.

Adamson, A., Rugg-Gunn, A., Butler, T., Appleton, D. & Hackett, A. (1992). Nutritional intake, height and weight of 11–12-year-old Northumbrian children in 1990 compared with information obtained in 1980. *British Journal of Nutrition, 68,* 543–63.

Addessi, E., Galloway, A. T., Visalberghi, E. & Birch, L. L. (2005). Specific social influences on the acceptance of novel foods in 2–5-year-old children. *Appetite, 45,* 264–71.

Agran, P. F., Anderson, C., Winn, D., *et al.* (2005). Rates of pediatric injuries by 3-month intervals for children 0 to 3 years of age. *Pediatrics, 111,* 683–92.

Agras, S., Hammer, L. & McNicholas, F. (1999). A prospective study of the influence of eating-disordered mothers on their children. *International Journal of Eating Disorders, 25,* 253–62.

Agras, W. S., Kraemer, H. C., Berkowitz, R. I., *et al.* (1987). Does a vigorous feeding style influence early development of adiposity? *Journal of Pediatrics, 110,* 799–804.

Ainsworth, M. D. S., Bell, S. M. & Stayton, D. J. (1974). Infant–mother attachment and social development: socialisation as a product of social responsiveness to signals. In M. Richards (ed.), *The Integration of a Child into a Social World* (pp. 99–135). Cambridge: Cambridge University Press.

Ainsworth, M. D. S., Blehar, M. C., Waters, E. & Wall, S. (1978). *Patterns of Attachment: Assessed in the Strange Situation and at Home.* Hillsdale, NJ: Lawrence Erlbaum.

Ainsworth, M. D. S. & Wittig, B. A. (1969). Attachment and exploratory behavior of one year olds in a strange situation. In B. Foss (ed.), *Determinants of Infant Behavior,* vol. IV (pp. 113–36). New York: Barnes & Noble.

221

222   References

Algarin, C., Peirano, P., Garrido, M., Pizarro, F. & Lozoff, B. (2003). Iron deficiency in infancy: long-lasting effects on auditory and visual system functioning. *Pediatric Research*, 53, 1–7.

Allison, D. B. (ed.) (1995). *Handbook of Asssessment Methods for Eating Behaviors and Weight-related Problems: Measures, Theory, and Research*. Thousand Oaks, CA: Sage Publications.

Allison, D. B., Kaprio, J., Korkeila, M., Koshenvuo, M. & Neale, M. C. (1996). The heritability of body mass index among an international sample of mono- zygotic twins reared apart. *International Journal of Obesity*, 20, 501–6.

Allison, D. B., Paultre, F., Heymsfield, S. B. & Pi-Sunyer, F. X. (1995). Is the intra-uterine period *really* a critical period for the development of adiposity? *International Journal of Obesity*, 19, 397–402.

Almroth, S. G. (1978). Water requirements of breast-fed infants in a hot climate. *American Journal of Clinical Nutrition*, 31, 1154–7.

Altemeier, W. O., Connor, S., Sherrod, K. & Vietze, P. (1985). Prospective study of antecedents for nonorganic failure to thrive. *Journal of Pediatrics*, 106, 360–5.

Amatayakul, K., Vutyavanich, T., Tanthayaphinant, O., *et al.* (1987). Serum prolactin and cortisol levels after suckling for varying periods of time and the effect of a nipple shield. *Acta Obstetrica Gynecologia Scandinavica*, 66, 47–51.

Andersen, R. E., Crespo, C. J., Bartlett, S. J., Cheskin, L. J. & Pratt, M. (1998). Relationship of physical activity and television watching with body weight and level of fatness among children: results from the Third National Health and Nutrition Examination Survey. *Journal of the American Medical Association*, 279, 938–42.

Anderson, J. W., Johnstone, B. M. & Remley, D. T. (1999). Breast-feeding and cognitive development: a meta-analysis. *American Journal of Clinical Nutrition*, 70, 525–35.

Andreson, G. V., Birch, L. L. & Johnson, P. A. (1990). The scapegoat effect on food aversions after chemotherapy. *Cancer*, 66, 1649–53.

Angelsen, N. K., Vik, T., Jacobsen, G. & Bakketeig, L. S. (2001). Breast feeding and cognitive development at age 1 and 5 years. *Archives of Disease in Childhood*, 85, 183–8.

Anliker, J. A., Laus, M. J., Samonds, K. W. & Beal, V. A. (1990). Parental mes- sages and the nutritional awareness of preschool children. *Journal of Nutrition Education*, 22, 24–9.

Anoop, S., Saravanan, B., Joseph, A., Cherian, A. & Jacob, K. S. (2004). Maternal depression and low maternal intelligence as risk factors for malnu- trition in children: a community based case-control study from South India. *Archives of Disease in Childhood*, 89, 325–9.

APA (1980). *Diagnostic and Statistical Manual of Mental Disorders* (3rd. edn). Washington, DC: American Psychiatric Association.
    (1994). *Diagnostic and Statistical Manual of Mental Disorders* (4th edn). Washington, DC: American Psychiatric Association.

Armstrong, J. A., Reilly, J. J. & Child Health Information Team (2003). Breast- feeding and lowering the risk of childhood obesity. *Lancet*, 359, 2003–4.

Ashraf, R. N., Jalil, F., Aperia A. & Lindblad, B. S. (1993). Additional water is not needed for healthy breast-fed babies in a hot climate. *Acta Paediatrica*, *82*, 1007–11.

Attie, I. & Brooks-Gunn, J. (1989). Development of eating problems in adolescent girls: a longitudinal study. *Developmental Psychology*, *25*, 70–9.

Auckett, M. A., Parks, Y. A., Scott, P. H. & Wharton, B. A. (1986). Treatment with iron increases weight gain and psychomotor development. *Archives of Disease in Childhood*, *61*, 849–57.

Auestad, N., Halter, R., Hall, R. T., *et al.* (2005). Growth and development in term infants fed long-chain polyunsaturated fatty acids: a double-masked, randomized, parallel, prospective, multivariate study. *Pediatrics*, *108*, 327–81.

Auestad, N., Montalto, M. B., Hall, R. T., *et al.* (1997). Visual acuity, erythrocyte fatty acid composition, and growth in term infants fed formulas with long chain polyunsaturated (LCP) fatty acids for one year. *Pediatric Research*, *41*, 1–10.

Austin, S. B., Field, A. E., Wiecha, J., Peterson, K. E. & Gortmaker, S. L. (2005). The impact of a school-based obesity prevention trial on disordered weight-control behaviors in early adolescent girls. *Archives of Pediatrics and Adolescent Medicine*, *159*, 225–30.

Aylward, G. P., Pfeiffer, S. I., Wright, A. & Verhulst, S. J. (1989). Outcome studies of low birth weight infants studied in the last decade: a metaanalysis. *Journal of Pediatrics*, *115*, 515–20.

Baddeley, A., Gardner, J. M. & Grantham-McGregor, S. (1995). Cross-cultural cognition: developing tests for developing countries. *Applied Cognitive Psychology*, *9*, S173–S195.

Bandini, L. G., Schoeller, D. A., Cyr, H. N. & Dietz, W. H. (1990). Validity of reported energy intake in obese and nonobese adolescents. *American Journal of Clinical Nutrition*, *52*, 421–5.

Barker, D. J. P. (1991). The foetal and infant origins of inequalities in health in Britain. *Journal of Public Health Medicine*, *13*, 64–8.

  (ed.). (1992). *Fetal and Infant Origins of Adult Disease*. London: British Medical Journal.

  (1994). *Mothers, Babies, and Disease in Later Life*. London: BMJ Publishing Group.

Barker, D. J. P., Hales, C. N., Fall, C. H. D., *et al.* (1993). Type 2 (non-insulin-dependent) diabetes mellitus, hypertension and hyperlipidaemia (syndrome X): relation to fetal growth. *Diabetologia*, *36*, 62–7.

Barker, D. J. P. & Osmond, C. (1986). Infant mortality, childhood nutrition, and ischaemic heart disease. *Lancet*, *1*, 1077–81.

Barker, D. J. P., Osmond, C., Rodin, I., Fall, C. H. D. & Winter, P. D. (1995). Low weight gain in infancy and suicide in adult life. *British Medical Journal*, *311*, 1203.

Barker, D. J. P., Winter, P. D., Osmond, C., Margetts, B. & Simmonds, S. J. (1989). Weight in infancy and death from ischaemic heart disease. *Lancet*, *II*, 578–80.

Barker, M., Robinson, S., Wilman, C. & Barker, D. J. P. (2000). Behaviour, body composition and diet in adolescent girls. *Appetite*, *35*, 161–70.

Barkham, P. (2005). Pandas at risk in bamboo crisis. *Guardian*, 29 March, p. 3.

Barr, R. G. (1990). The early crying paradox: a modest proposal. *Human Nature*, *1*, 355–89.

Barr, R. G., Hanley, J., Paterson, D. K. & Wooldridge, J. (1984). Breath hydrogen excretion in normal newborn infants in reponse to usual feeding patterns: evidence for 'functional lactase insufficiency' beyond the first month of life. *Journal of Pediatrics*, *104*, 527–33.

Barr, R. G., Pantel, M. A., Young, S. N., *et al.* (1999). The response of crying newborns to sucrose: is it a 'sweetness' effect? *Physiology and Behavior*, *66*, 409–17.

Basch, C. E., Zybert, P. & Shea, S. (1994). 5-A-DAY: dietary behavior and the fruit and vegetable intake of Latino children. *American Journal of Public Health*, *84*, 814–18.

Batchelor, J. & Kerslake, A. (1990). *Failure to Find Failure to Thrive: The Case for Improving Screening, Prevention and Treatment in Primary Care.* London: Whiting and Birch.

Batchelor, J. A. (1996). Has recognition of failure to thrive changed? *Child: Care Health and Development*, *22*, 235–40.

Bateson, P. (1979). How do sensitive periods arise and what are they for? *Animal Behaviour*, *27*, 470–86.

Baughcum, A. E., Powers, S. W., Johnson, S. B., *et al.* (2001). Maternal feeding practices and beliefs and their relationships to overweight in early childhood. *Developmental and Behavioral Pediatrics*, *22*, 391–408.

Bayley, N. (1969). *Bayley Scales of Infant Development.* New York: Psychological Corporation.

(1993). *Bayley Scales of Infant Development* (2nd edn). San Antonio, TX: Psychological Corporation.

Baylis, P. H. & Thompson, C. J. (1988). Osmoregulation of vasopressin secretion and thirst in health and disease. *Clinical Endocrinology*, *29*, 549–76.

Beauchamp, G. K. & Cowart, B. J. (1985). Congenital and experiential factors in the development of human flavour preferences. *Appetite*, *6*, 357–372.

Beauchamp, G. K., Cowart, B. J. & Moran, M. (1986). Developmental changes in salt acceptability in human infants. *Developmental Psychobiology*, *19*, 17–25.

Beauchamp, G. K. & Moran, M. (1984). Acceptance of sweet and salty tastes in 2-year-old children. *Appetite*, *5*, 291–305.

Becker, A. E., Burwell, R. A., Gilman, S. E., Herzog, D. B. & Hamburg, P. (2002). Eating behaviours and attitudes following prolonged exposure to television among ethnic Fijian girls. *British Journal of Psychiatry*, *180*, 509–14.

Bekhof, J., van Sprouson, F. J., Crone, M. R., *et al.* (2003). Influence of knowledge of the disease on metabolic control in phenylketonuria. *European Journal of Pediatrics*, *162*, 440–2.

Benoit, D., Zeanah, C. H. & Barton, M. L. (1989). Maternal attachment disturbances in failure to thrive. *Infant Mental Health Journal*, *10*, 185–202.

Bentley, M. E., Stallings, R. Y., Fukumoto, M. & Elder, J. A. (1991). Maternal feeding behavior and child acceptance of food during diarrhea, convalescence, and health in the Central Sierra of Peru. *American Journal of Public Health*, *81*, 43–7.

Berenson, G. S., Srinivasan, S. R., Hunter, S. M., *et al.* (1989). Risk factors in early life as predictors of adult heart disease: the Bogalusa Heart Study. *American Journal of Medical Sciences*, *298*, 141–51.

Berg, A. & Bracken, M. (1992). Measuring gestational age: an uncertain proposition. *British Journal of Obstetrics and Gynecology*, *99*, 280–2.

Bernstein, I. L. (1978). Learned taste aversions in children receiving chemotherapy. *Science*, *200*, 1302–3.

Berwick, D. M., Levy, J. C. & Kleinerman, R. (1982). Failure to thrive: diagnostic yield of hospitalisation. *Archives of Disease in Childhood*, *57*, 347–51.

Best, J. A., Flay, B. R., Towson, S. M. J., *et al.* (1984). Smoking prevention and the concept of risk. *Journal of Applied Social Psychology*, *14*, 257–73.

Beumont, P., Al-Alami, M. & Touyz, S. (1988). Relevance of a standard measurement of undernutrition to the diagnosis of anorexia nervosa: use of Quetelet's body mass index (BMI). *International Journal of Eating Disorders*, *7*, 399–405.

Bhutta, A. T., Cleves, M. A., Casey, P. H., Cradock, M. M. & Anand, K. J. S. (2002). Cognitive and behavioral outcome of school-aged children who were born preterm: a meta-analysis. *Journal of the American Medical Association*, *288*, 728–37.

Bickel, H. (1996). The first treatment of phenylketonuria. *European Journal of Pediatrics*, *155*, S2–S3.

Bingham, S. A. (1987). The dietary assessment of individuals; methods, accuracy, new techniques and recommendations. *Nutrition Abstract and Reviews (Series A)*, *57*, 705–42.

Birch, H. G. & Tizard, J. (1967). The dietary treatment of phenylketonuria: not proven? *Developmental Medicine and Child Neurology*, *9*, 9–12.

Birch, L. L., Gunder, L., Grimm-Thomas, K. & Laing, D. G. (1998). Infants' consumption of a new food enhances acceptance of similar foods. *Appetite*, *30*, 283–95.

Birch, L. L. (1979a). Dimensions of preschool children's food preferences. *Journal of Nutrition Education*, *11*, 77–80.

(1979b). Preschool children's food preferences and consumption patterns. *Journal of Nutrition Education*, *11*, 189–92.

Birch, L. L. & Deysher, M. (1986). Caloric compensation and sensory specific satiety: evidence for self regulation of food intake by young children. *Appetite*, *7*, 323–31.

Birch, L. L. & Fisher, M. S. (1995). Appetite and eating behaviour in children. *Pediatric Clinics of North America*, *42*, 931–53.

Birch, L. L., Fisher, J. O., Grimm-Thomas, K., *et al.* (2001). Confirmatory factor analysis of the Child Feeding Questionnaire: a measure of parental attitudes, beliefs and practices about child feeding and obesity proneness. *Appetite*, *36*, 201–10.

Birch, L. L. & Fisher, J. O. (2000). Mothers' child-feeding practices influence daughters' eating and weight. *American Journal of Clinical Nutrition*, *71*, 1054–61.

Birch, L. L., Johnson, S. L., Andresen, G., Peters, J. C. & Schulte, M. C. (1991). The variability of young children's energy intake. *New England Journal of Medicine*, *324*, 232–5.

Birch, L. L. & Marlin, D. W. (1982). I don't like it; I never tried it: effects of exposure on two-year-old children's food preferences. *Appetite*, *3*, 353–60.

Birch, L. L., McPhee, L., Steinberg, L. & Sullivan, S. (1990). Conditioned flavor preferences in young children. *Physiology and Behavior*, *47*, 501–5.

Birch, L. L., McPhee, L. S., Shoba, B. C., Pirok, E. & Steinberg, L. (1987). What kind of exposure reduces children's food neophobia? *Appetite*, *9*, 171–8.

Bishop, N., King, F. J. & Lucas, A. (1990). Linear growth in the early neonatal period. *Archives of Disease in Childhood*, *65*, 707–8.

Black, A. E., Cole, T. J., Wiles, S. & White, F. (1983). Daily variation in food intake of infants from 2 to 18 months. *Human Nutrition: Applied Nutrition*, *37A*, 448–58.

Black, A. E., Coward, W. A., Cole, T. J. & Prentice, A. M. (1996). Human energy expenditure in affluent societies: an analysis of 574 doubly-labelled water measurements. *European Journal of Clinical Nutrition*, *50*, 72–92.

Black, A. E., Prentice, A. M., Goldberg, G. R., et al. (1993). Measurements of total energy expenditure provide insights into the validity of dietary measurements of energy intake. *Journal of the American Dietetic Association*, *93*, 572–9.

Black, M., Hutcheson, J., Dubowitz, H. & Berenson-Howard, J. (1994). Parenting style and developmental status among children with nonorganic failure to thrive. *Journal of Pediatric Psychology*, *19*, 689–707.

Black, R. E., Brown, K. H. & Becker, S. (1984). Effects of diarrhea associated with specific enteropathogens on the growth of children in rural Bangladesh. *Journal of Pediatrics*, *73*, 799–805.

Black, R. E., Brown, K. H., Becker, S., Alim, A. R. M. A. & Merson, M. H. (1982). Contamination of weaning foods and transmission of enterotoxigenic Eschericia coli diarrhoea in children in rural Bangladesh. *Transaction of the Royal Society of Tropical Medicine and Hygiene*, *76*, 259–64.

Black, R. E., Williams, S. M., Jones, I. E. & Goulding, A. (2002). Children who avoid drinking cow milk have low dietary calcium intakes and poor bone health. *American Journal of Clinical Nutrition*, *76*, 675–80.

Blair, C., Freeman, C. & Cull, A. (1995). The families of anorexia nervosa and cystic fibrosis patients. *Psychological Medicine*, *25*, 985–93.

Blair, P. S., Drewett, R. F., Emmett, P. M., Ness, A., Emond, A. M. & ALSPAC study team (2004). Family, socioeconomic and prenatal factors associated with failure to thrive in the Avon Longitudinal Study of Parents and Children. *International Journal of Epidemiology*, *33*, 1–9.

Blass, E. M. & Hoffmeyer, L. B. (1991). Sucrose as an analgesic for newborn infants. *Pediatrics*, *87*, 215–18.

Blurton Jones, N. (1972). Comparative aspects of mother–child contact. In N. Blurton Jones (ed.), *Ethological Studies of Child Behaviour* (pp. 305–28). Cambridge: Cambridge University Press.

Boddy, J., Skuse, D. & Andrews, B. (2000). The developmental sequelae of non-organic failure to thrive. *Journal of Child Psychology and Psychiatry, 41*, 1003–14.

Bohler, E. & Bergstrom, S. (1996). Frequent diarrhoeas in early childhood have sustained effects on the height, weight and head circumference of children in East Bhutan. *Acta Paediatrica, 85*, 26–30.

Boomsma, D. I., van Beijsterveldt, C. E., Rietveld, M. J., Bartels, M. & van Baal, G. C. (2001). Genetics mediates relation of birth weight to childhood IQ. *British Medical Journal, 323*, 1426.

Booth, D. A. (1972). Conditioned satiety in the rat. *Journal of Comparative and Physiological Psychology, 81*, 457–71.

Booth, D. A., Lee, M. & McAleavey, C. (1976). Acquired sensory control of satiation in man. *British Journal of Psychology, 67*, 137–47.

Booth, D. A., Mather, P. & Fuller, J. (1982). Starch content of ordinary foods associatively conditions human appetite and satiation, indexed by intake and eating pleasantness of starch-paired flavours. *Appetite, 3*, 163–84.

Börjeson, M. (1976). The aetiology of obesity in children: a study of 101 twin pairs. *Acta Paediatric Scandinavica, 65*, 279–87.

Bornstein, M. H., Slater, A., Brown, E., Roberts, E. & Barrett, J. (1997). Stability of mental development from infancy to later childhood: three 'waves' of research. In G. Bremner, A. Slater & G. Butterworth (eds.), *Infant Development: Recent Advances* (pp. 191–215). Hove: Psychology Press.

Boskind-Lodahl, M. (1976). Cinderella's stepsisters: a feminist perspective on anorexia nervosa and bulimia. *Signs: Journal of Women in Culture and Society, 2*, 342–56.

Bouchard, C. & Pérusse, L. (1993). Genetics of obesity. *Annual Review of Nutrition, 13*, 337–54.

Bouchard, C., Pérusse, L., Leblanc, C., Tremblay, A. & Theriault, G. (1988). Inheritance of the amount and distribution of human body fat. *International Journal of Obesity, 12*, 205–15.

Bowman, R. L. & DeLucia, J. L. (1992). Accuracy of self-reported weight: a meta-analysis. *Behavior Therapy, 23*, 637–55.

Boynton-Jarrett, R., Thomas, T. N., Peterson, K. E., *et al.* (2003). Impact of television viewing patterns on fruit and vegetable consumption among adolescents. *Pediatrics, 112*, 1321–6.

Bracewell, M. & Marlow, N. (2002). Patterns of motor disability in very preterm children. *Mental Retardation and Developmental Disabilities, 8*, 241–8.

Braddon, F. E. M., Rodgers, B., Wadsworth, M. E. J. & Davies, J. M. C. (1986). Onset of obesity in a 36 year birth cohort study. *British Medical Journal, 292*, 299–303.

Brinch, M., Isager, T. & Tolstrup, K. (1988). Anorexia nervosa and motherhood: reproduction pattern and mothering behaviour of 50 women. *Acta Psychiatrica Scandinavica, 77*, 611–17.

Broberg, D. J. & Bernstein, I. L. (1987). Candy as a scapegoat in the prevention of food aversions in children receiving chemotherapy. *Cancer, 60*, 2344–7.

Broman, S. H., Nichols, P. L. & Kennedy, W. A. (1975). *Preschool IQ: Prenatal and Early Developmental Correlates*. Hillsdale, NJ: Lawrence Erlbaum.

Brook, G. C. D., Huntley, R. M. C. & Slack, J. (1975). Influence of hereditary and environment in determination of skinfold thicknesses in children. *British Medical Journal*, 2, 719–812.

Brooks-Gunn, J., Attie, I., Burrow, C., Rosso, J. T. & Warren, M. P. (1989). The impact of puberty on body and eating concerns in athletic and nonathletic contexts. *Journal of Early Adolescence*, 9, 269–90.

Brooks-Gunn, J., McCarton, C. M., Casey, P. H., *et al.* (1994). Early intervention in low-birth-weight premature infants: results through age 5 years from the Infant Health and Development Program. *Journal of the American Medical Association*, 272, 1257–62.

Brown, A. S., Susser, E. S., Lin, S. P., Neugebauer, R. & Gorman, J. M. (1995). Increased risk of affective disorders in males after second trimester prenatal exposure to the Dutch hunger winter of 1944–45. *British Journal of Psychiatry*, 166, 601–6.

Brown, A. S., van Os, J., Driessens, C., Hoek, H. W. & Susser, E. S. (2000). Further evidence of relation between prenatal famine and major affective disorder. *American Journal of Psychiatry*, 157, 190–5.

Brown, K. (1991). The importance of dietary quality versus dietary quantity for weanlings in less developed countries: a framework for discussion. *Food and Nutrition Bulletin*, 13, 86–94.

Brown, K. H., Peerson, J. M., Lopez de Romana, G., Creed de Kanashiro, H. & Black, R. E. (1995). Validity and epidemiology of reported poor appetite among Peruvian infants from a low-income, periurban community. *American Journal of Clinical Nutrition*, 61, 26–32.

Brown, K. H., Stallings, R. Y., Creed de Kanashiro, H., Lopez de Ramana, G. & Black, R. E. (1990). Effects of common illnesses on infants' energy intakes from breast milk and other foods during longitudinal community-based studies in Huascar (Lima), Peru. *American Journal of Clinical Nutrition*, 52, 1005–13.

Brown, R. T., Davis, P. C., Lambert, R., *et al.* (2000). Neurocognitive functioning and magnetic resonance imaging in children with sickle cell disease. *Journal of Pediatric Psychology*, 25, 503–13.

Bulik, C. M., Sullivan, P. F., Fear, J. L. & Joyce, P. R. (1997). Eating disorders and antecedent anxiety disorders: a controlled study. *Acta Psychiatrica Scandinavica*, 96, 101–7.

Bundred, P., Kitchener, D. & Buchan, I. (2001). Prevalence of overweight and obese children between 1989 and 1998: population based series of cross sectional studies. *British Medical Journal*, 322, 326–8.

Burgard, P. (2000). Development of intelligence in early treated phenylketonuria. *European Journal of Pediatrics*, 159, S74–S79.

Butte, N. (2001). The role of breastfeeding in obesity. *Pediatric Clinics of North America*, 48, 189–98.

Butte, N. F. (1996). Energy requirements of infants. *European Journal of Clinical Nutrition*, 50 Suppl 1, S24–S36.

Butte, N. F., Wong, W. W., Klein, P. D. & Garza, C. (1991). Measurement of milk intake: tracer-to-infant deuterium dilution method. *British Journal of Nutrition*, 65, 3–14.

Butterworth, G. & Hopkins, B. (1988). Hand-mouth co-ordination in the new-born baby. *British Journal of Developmental Psychology*, 6, 303–14.

Cachelin, F. M. & Maher, B. A. (1998). Is amenorrhea a critical criterion for anorexia nervosa? *Journal of Psychosomatic Research*, 44, 435–40.

Cadogan, J., Eastell, R., Jones, N. & Barker, M. E. (1997). Milk intake and bone mineral acquisition in adolescent girls: randomised, controlled intervention trial. *British Medical Journal*, 315, 1255–60.

Calam, R. & Waller, G. (1998). Are eating and psychosocial characteristics in early teenage years useful predictors of eating characteristics in early adult-hood? A 7-year longitudinal study. *International Journal of Eating Disorders*, 24, 351–62.

Cameron, N., Petifor, J., De Wet, T. & Norris, S. (2003). The relationship of rapid weight gain in infancy to obesity and skeletal maturity in childhood. *Obesity Research*, 11, 457–60.

Campbell, F. A., Pungello, E. P., Miller-Johnson, S., Burchinal, M. & Ramey, C. T. (2001). The development of cognitive and academic abilities: growth curves from an early childhood educational experiment. *Developmental Psychology*, 37, 231–42.

Campfield, L. A. (1997). Metabolic and hormonal control of food intake: high-lights of the last 25 years – 1972–1997. *Appetite*, 29, 135–52.

Campfield, L. A., Smith, F. J., Rosenbaum, M. & Hirsch, J. (1996). Human eating: evidence for a physiological basis using a modified paradigm. *Neuroscience and Biobehavioral Reviews*, 20, 133–7.

Canfield, R. L., Henderson, C. R., Cory-Schlecta, D. A., et al. (2003). Intellectual impairment in children with blood lead concentrations below 10 μg per deciliter. *New England Journal of Medicine*, 348, 500–2.

Capute, A. F., Shapiro, B. K., Palmer, F. B., Ross, A. & Wachtel, R. C. (1985). Normal gross motor development: the influence of race, sex and socioeco-nomic status. *Developmental Medicine and Child Neurology*, 27, 635–43.

Carlson, S. E., Werkman, S. H., Peeples, J. M. & Wilson, W. M. (1994). Long-chain fatty acids and early visual and cognitive development of preterm infants. *European Journal of Clinical Nutrition*, 48, S27–S30.

Carlson, S. E., Werkman, S. H. & Tolley, E. A. (1996). Effect of long-chain n-3 fatty acid supplementation on visual acuity and growth of preterm infants with and without bronchopulmonary dysplasia. *American Journal of Clinical Nutrition*, 63, 687–97.

Carper, J. L., Fisher, J. O. & Birch, L. L. (2000). Young girls' emerging dietary restraint and disinhibition are related to parental control in child feeding. *Appetite*, 35, 121–9.

Carruth, B. R. & Skinner, J. D. (2000). Revisiting the picky eater phenomenon: neophobic behaviors of young children. *Journal of the American College of Nutrition*, 19, 771–80.

Carruth, B. R., Skinner, J., Houck, K., et al. (1998). The phenomenon of the 'picky eater': a behavioral marker in eating patterns of toddlers. *Journal of the American College of Nutrition*, 17, 180–6.

Carruth, B. R., Ziegler, P. J., Gordon, A. & Barr, S. I. (2004). Prevalence of picky eaters among infants and toddlers and their caregivers' decisions about offering a new food. *Journal of the American Dietetic Association, 104,* S57–S64.

Casaer, P., Daniels, H., Devlieger, H., De Cock, P. & Eggermont, E. (1982). Feeding behaviour in preterm neonates. *Early Human Development, 7,* 331–46.

Casey, P. H. (1999). Diagnostic coding of children with failure to thrive. In D. Kessler & P. Dawson (eds.), *Failure to Thrive and Paediatric Undernutrition* (pp. 281–6). Baltimore, MD: Paul H. Brookes Publishing Co.

Casey, P. H., Kraemer, H. C., Bernbaum, J., Yogman, M. W. & Sells, J. C. (1991). Growth status and growth rates of a varied sample of low birthweight, preterm infants: a longitudinal cohort from birth to three years of age. *Journal of Pediatrics, 119,* 599–605.

Cass, H., Price, K., Reilly, S., Wisbeach, A. & McConachie, H. (1999). A model for the assessment and management of children with multiple disabilities. *Child: Care, Health and Development, 25,* 191–211.

Cattarin, J. A. & Thompson, J. K. (1994). A three-year longitudinal study of body image, eating disturbance, and general functioning in adolescent females. *Eating Disorders: Journal of Treatment and Prevention, 2,* 114–25.

Cauffman, E. & Steinberg, L. (1996). Interactive effects of menarchial status and dating on dieting and disordered eating in adolescent girls. *Developmental Psychology, 32,* 631–5.

Cavadini, C. C., Siega-Riz, A. M. & Popkin, B. M. (2000). US adolescent food intake trends from 1965 to 1996. *Archives of Disease in Childhood, 83,* 18–24.

Ceesay, S., Prentice, A. M., Cole, T. J., *et al.* (1997). Effects on birth weight and perinatal mortality of maternal dietary supplements in rural Gambia: 5 year randomised trial. *British Medical Journal, 315,* 786–90.

Chagnon, Y. C., Pérusse, L. & Bouchard, C. (1998). The human obesity gene map: the 1997 update. *Obesity Research, 6,* 76–92.

Champagne, C. M., Baker, N. B., DeLany, J. P., Harsha, D. W. & Bray, G. A. (1998). Assessment of energy intake underreporting by doubly labelled water and observations on reported nutrient intakes in children. *Journal of the American Dietetic Association, 98,* 426–30.

Charney, E., Chamblee Goodman, H., McBride, M., Lyon, B. & Pratt, R. (1976). Childhood antecedents of adult obesity: do chubby infants become obese adults? *New England Journal of Medicine, 295,* 6–9.

Chatoor, I., Ganiban, J., Colin, V., Plummer, N. & Harmon, R. (1998). Attachment and feeding problems: a reexamination of nonorganic failure to thrive and attachment insecurity. *Journal of the American Academy of Child and Adolescent Psychiatry, 37,* 1217–24.

Chavéz, A. & Martinez, C. (1975). Nutrition and development of children from poor rural areas. V. Nutrition and behavioural development. *Nutrition Reports International, 11,* 477–89.

Cheung, Y. B., Khoo, K. S., Karlberg, J. & Machin, D. (2002). Association between psychological symptoms in adults and growth in early life: longitudinal follow up study. *British Medical Journal, 325,* 749–51.

Clandinin, M. T., Van Aerde, J. E., Merkel, K. L., *et al.* (2005). Growth and development of preterm infants fed infant formulas containing docosahexaenoic acid and arachidonic acid. *Journal of Pediatrics, 146,* 461–8.

Clarke, A. M. & Clarke, A. D. B. (2000). *Early Experience and the Life Path.* London: Jessica Kingsley Publishers Ltd.

Clément, K., Vaisse, C., Lahlou, N., *et al.* (1998). A mutation in the human leptin receptor gene causes obesity and pituitary dysfunction. *Nature, 392,* 398–401.

Cockburn, F. (1994). Neonatal brain and dietary lipids. *Archives of Disease in Childhood, 70,* F1–F2.

Cohen, R., Brown, K. H., Canahuati, J., Rivers, L. L. & Dewey, K. G. (1994). Effects of age of introduction of complementary foods on infant breast milk intake, total energy intake, and growth: a randomised intervention study in the Honduras. *Lancet, 344,* 288–93.

Cole, T. J. (1989). Relating growth rate to environmental factors: methodological problems in the study of growth–infection interaction. *Acta Paediatrica Supplement, 350,* 12–20.

 (1990). The LMS method for constructing normalised growth standards. *European Journal of Clinical Nutrition, 44,* 45–60.

 (1993). The use and construction of anthropometric growth reference standards. *Nutrition Research Reviews, 6,* 19–50.

 (1994). Do growth chart centiles need a face lift? *British Medical Journal, 308,* 641–2.

 (1995). Conditional reference charts to assess weight gain in British infants. *Archives of Disease in Childhood, 73,* 8–16.

 (1996). Growth monitoring with the British 1990 growth reference. *Archives of Disease in Childhood, 76,* 47–9.

 (1998). Presenting information on growth distance and conditional velocity in one chart: practical issues of chart design. *Statistics in Medicine, 17,* 2697–707.

 (2004). Children grow and horses race: is the adiposity rebound a critical period for later obesity? *BMC Pediatrics 4-6* doi: 10.1186/1471-2431-4-6.

Cole, T. J., Bellizzi, M. C., Flegal, K. M. & Dietz, W. H. (2000). Establishing a standard definition for child overweight and obesity worldwide: international survey. *British Medical Journal, 320,* 1240–3.

Collins, M. E. (1991). Body figure perceptions and preferences among preadolescent children. *International Journal of Eating Disorders, 10,* 199–208.

Colom, R., Lluis-Font, J. M. & Andrés-Pueyo, A. (2004). The generational intelligence gains are caused by decreasing variance in the lower half of the distribution: supporting evidence for the nutrition hypothesis. *Intelligence, 33,* 83–91.

Connolly, K. & Dalgleish, M. (1989). The emergence of a tool-using skill in infancy. *Developmental Psychology, 25,* 894–912.

Connors, M. E. & Morse, W. (1993). Sexual abuse and eating disorders: a review. *International Journal of Eating Disorders, 13,* 1–11.

Considine, R. V., Sinha, M. K., Heiman, M. L., *et al.* (1996). Serum immunoreactive-leptin concentrations in normal-weight and obese humans. *New England Journal of Medicine, 334,* 292–5.

Conti, J., Abraham, S. & Taylor, A. (1998). Eating behavior and pregnancy outcome. *Journal of Psychosomatic Research*, 44, 465–77.

Cooke, L., Wardle, J. & Gibson, E. L. (2003). Relationship between parental reports of food neophobia and everyday food consumption in 2–6-year-old children. *Appetite*, 41, 205–6.

Cooke, R. W. I., Lucas, A., Yudkin, P. L. N. & Pryse-Davies, J. (1977). Head circumference as an index of brain weight in the fetus and newborn. *Early Human Development*, 1, 145–9.

Coolber, J. & Benoit, D. (1999). Failure to thrive: risk for clinical disturbance of attachment? *Infant Mental Health Journal*, 20, 87–104.

Cooley, E. & Toray, T. (2001). Body image and personality predictors of eating disorder symptoms during the college years. *International Journal of Eating Disorders*, 30, 28–36.

Cooper, Z. & Fairburn, C. G. (1987). The Eating Disorder Examination: a semistructured interview for the assessment of the specific psychopathology of eating disorders. *International Journal of Eating Disorders*, 6, 1–8.

Corbett, S. S. & Drewett, R. F. (2004). To what extent is failure to thrive in infancy associated with poorer cognitive development? A review and meta-analysis. *Journal of Child Psychology and Psychiatry*, 45, 641–54.

Corral, E. (2004). Erevigio Corral. *Observer Magazine*, 10 December, pp. 6–7.

Coward, W. A., Sawyer, M. B., Whitehead, R. G., Prentice, A. M. & Evans, J. (1979). New method for measuring milk intakes in breast-fed babies. *Lancet*, 2, 13–14.

Craft, S., Schatz, J., Glauser, T. A., Lee, B. & DeBaun, M. R. (1993). Neuropsychological effects of stroke in children with sickle cell anemia. *Journal of Pediatrics*, 123, 712–17.

  (1994). The effects of bifrontal stroke during childhood on visual attention: evidence from children with sickle cell anemia. *Developmental Neuropsychology*, 10, 285–97.

Crystal, S. R. (1995). Morning sickness: impact on offspring salt preference. *Appetite*, 25, 231–40.

Crystal, S. R. & Bernstein, I. L. (1998). Infant salt preference and mother's morning sickness. *Appetite*, 30, 297–307.

Curtis, V. (2003). Talking dirty: how to save a million lives. *International Journal of Environmental Health Research*, 13, S73–S79.

Curtis, V., Aunger, R. & Rabie, T. (2004). Evidence that disgust evolved to protect from risk of disease. *Proceedings of the Royal Society of London, B (Supplement)*, 271, S131–S133.

Curtis, V. & Biran, A. (2001). Dirt, disgust, and disease. *Perspectives in Biology and Medicine*, 44, 17–31.

Dahl, M., Eklund, G. & Sundelin, C. (1986). Early feeding problems in an affluent society II. Determinants. *Acta Paediatrica Scandinavica*, 75, 380–7.

Dahl, M. & Kristiansson, B. (1987). Early feeding problems in an affluent society IV. Impact on growth up to two years of age. *Acta Paediatrica Scandinavica*, 76, 881–8.

Dahl, M., Rydell, A.-M. & Sundelin, C. (1994). Children with early refusal to eat: follow-up during primary school. *Acta Paediatrica*, 83, 54–8.

Dahl, M. & Sundelin, C. (1992). Feeding problems in an affluent society: follow-up at four years of age in children with early refusal to eat. *Acta Paediatrica*, *81*, 575–9.

Daley, T. C., Whaley, S. E., Sigman, M. D., Espinosa, M. P. & Neumann, C. (2003). IQ on the rise: the Flynn effect in rural Kenyan children. *Psychological Science*, *14*, 215–19.

Daly, S. E. J., Owens, R. A. & Hartmann, P. E. (1993). The short-term synthesis and infant-regulated removal of milk in lactating women. *Experimental Physiology*, *78*, 209–20.

Dancyger, I. F. & Garfinkel, P. E. (1995). The relationship of partial syndrome eating disorders to anorexia nervosa and bulimia nervosa. *Psychological Medicine*, *25*, 1019–25.

Davies, D. P. (1979). Is inadequate breast-feeding an important cause of failure to thrive? *Lancet*, *1*, 541–2.

Davies, P. S. W., Coward, W. A., Gregory, J., White, A. & Mills, A. (1994). Total energy expenditure and energy intake in the pre-school child: a comparison. *British Journal of Nutrition*, *72*, 13–20.

Davies, S. W., Wells, J. C. K., Fieldhouse, C. A., Day, M. E. & Lucas, A. (1995). Parental body composition and infant energy expenditure. *American Journal of Clinical Nutrition*, *61*, 1026–9.

Davis, C., Durnin, J. V. G., Le Maire, A. & Dionne, M. (1993). Body composition correlates of weight dissatisfaction and dietary restraint in young women. *Appetite*, *20*, 197–207.

Davis, C. E., Hunsberger, S., Murray, D. M., *et al.* (1999). Design and statistical analysis for the Pathways study. *American Journal of Clinical Nutrition*, *69 Suppl*, 760S–3S.

Davison, K. K., Markey, C. N. & Birch, L. L. (2000). Etiology of body dissatisfaction and weight concerns among 5-year-old girls. *Appetite*, *35*, 143–51.

Davison, K. K., Susman, E. J. & Birch, L. L. (2003). Percent body fat at age 5 predicts earlier pubertal development among girls at age 9. *Pediatrics*, *111*, 815–21.

De Bruin, N. C., Degenhart, H. J., Gal, S., *et al.* (1998). Energy utilization and growth in breast-fed and formula-fed infants measured prospectively during the first year of life. *American Journal of Clinical Nutrition*, *67*, 885–96.

De Onis, M. & Blössner, M. (2000). Prevalence and trends of overweight among preschool children in developing countries. *American Journal of Clinical Nutrition*, *72*, 1032–9.

De Onis, M., Frongillo, E. A. & Blössner, M. (2000). Is malnutrition declining? An analysis of changes in levels of child malnutrition since 1980. *Bulletin of the World Health Organisation*, *78*, 1222–33.

De Wolff, M. S. & van IJzendoorn, M. H. (1997). Sensitivity and attachment: A meta-analysis on parental antecedents of infant attachment. *Child Development*, *68*, 571–91.

Deep, A., Nagy, L., Weltzin, T., Rao, R. & Kaye, W. (1995). Premorbid onset of psychopathology in long-term recovered anorexia nervosa. *International Journal of Eating Disorders*, *17*, 291–7.

DeFries, J. C., Plomin, R. & LaBuda, M. C. (1987). Genetic stability of cognitive development from childhood to adulthood. *Developmental Psychology, 23*, 4–12.

Delparigi, A., Tschöp, M., Heiman, M. L., *et al.* (2002). High circulating ghrelin: a potential cause for hyperphagia and obesity in Prader-Willi Syndrome. *Journal of Clinical Endocrinology and Metabolism, 87*, 5461–4.

DeMaeyer, E. & Adiels-Tegman, M. (1985). The prevalence of anaemia in the world. *World Health Organisation Statistical Quarterly, 38*, 302–12.

Dennison, B. A., Erb, T. A. & Jenkins, P. L. (2002). Television viewing and television in bedroom associated with overweight risk among low-income preschool children. *Pediatrics, 109*, 1028–35.

Desor, J. A., Maller, O. & Andrews, K. (1975). Ingestive response of human newborns to salty, sour, and bitter stimuli. *Journal of Comparative and Physiological Psychology, 89*, 966–70.

Desor, J. A., Maller, O. & Turner, R. E. (1973). Taste in acceptance of sugars by human newborns. *Journal of Comparative and Physiological Psychology, 84*, 496–501.

Devlin, B., Daniels, M. & Roeder, K. (1997). The heritability of IQ. *Nature, 388*, 468–71.

Dewey, K. G. (2003). Is breastfeeding protective against childhood obesity? *Journal of Human Lactation, 19*, 9–18.

Dewey, K. G., Cohen, R. J., Brown, K. H. & Rivera, L. L. (1999). Age of introduction of complementary foods and growth of term, low-birthweight, breast-fed infants: a randomised intervention study in Honduras. *American Journal of Clinical Nutrition, 69*, 679–86.

Dewey, K. G., Heinig, M. J., Nommsen, L. A. & Lönnerdal, B. (1991). Maternal versus infant factors related to breast milk intake and residual milk volume: the DARLING study. *Pediatrics, 87*, 829–37.

Dewey, K. G. & Lönnerdal, B. (1986). Infant self-regulation of breast milk intake. *Acta Paediatrica Scandinavica, 75*, 893–8.

Dewey, K. G., Nommsen-Rivers, L. A., Heinig, M. J. & Cohen, R. J. (2003). Risk factors for suboptimal infant breastfeeding behavior, delayed onset of lactation, and excessive neonatal weight loss. *Pediatrics, 112*, 607–19.

Diamond, A. & Herzberg, C. (1996). Impaired sensitivity to visual contrast in children treated early and continuously for phenylketonuria. *Brain, 119*, 523–38.

Diamond, A., Prevor, M. B., Callender, G. & Druin, D. (1997). Prefrontal cortex cognitive deficits in children treated early and continuously for PKU. *Monographs of the Society for Research in Child Development, 62 (4, Serial No 252)*.

Dickerson, J. W. T., Merat, A. & Yusuf, H. K. M. (1982). Effects of malnutrition on brain growth and development. In J. W. T. Dickerson & H. McGurk (eds.), *Brain and Behavioural Development* (pp. 73–108). London: Surrey University Press.

Dietz, W. H. (1997). Periods of risk in childhood for the development of adult obesity: what do we need to learn? *Journal of Nutrition, 127*, 1884S–6S.

(1998). Health consequences of obesity in youth: childhood predictors of adult disease. *Pediatrics, 101*, 518–25.

(2000). 'Adiposity rebound': reality or epiphenomenon? *Lancet*, *356*, 2027–8.

Dietz, W. H. & Gortmaker, S. L. (1985). Do we fatten our children at the television set? Obesity and television viewing in children and adolescents. *Pediatrics*, *75*, 807–12.

Dobson, J. C., Kushida, E., Williamson, M. & Friedman, E. G. (1976). Intellectual performance of 36 phenylketonuria patients and their nonaffected siblings. *Pediatrics*, *58*, 53–8.

Donnelly, J. E., Jacobsen, D. J., Whatley, J. E., *et al.* (1996). Nutrition and physical activity program to attenuate obesity and promote physical and metabolic fitness in elementary school children. *Obesity Research*, *4*, 229–43.

Dorosty, A. R., Emmett, P. M., Cowin, I. S., Reilly, J. J. & the ALSPAC study team (2000). Factors associated with early adiposity rebound. *Pediatrics*, *105*, 1115–18.

Dowdney, L., Skuse, D., Heptinstall, E., Puckering, C. & Zur-Szpiro, S. (1987). Growth retardation and development delay amongst inner-city children. *Journal of Child Psychology and Psychiatry*, *28*, 529–41.

Drewett, R., Amatayakul, K., Wongsawasdii, A., *et al.* (1993). Nursing frequency and the energy intake from breast milk and supplementary food in a rural Thai population: a longitudinal study. *European Journal of Clinical Nutrition*, *47*, 880–91.

Drewett, R., Wright, P. & Young, B. (1998). From feeds to meals: the development of hunger and food intake in infants and young children. In C. Niven & A. Walker (eds.), *Current Issues in Infancy and Parenthood* (pp. 204–17). Oxford: Butterworth Heinemann.

Drewett, R. F. (1978). The development of motivational systems. *Progress in Brain Research*, *48*, 407–17.

Drewett, R. F., Amatayakul, A., Baum, J. D., *et al.* (1989a). Nursing patterns and milk intake in Sanpatong. In E. V. van Hall & W. Everaerd (eds.), *The Free Woman: Women's Health in the 1990s* (pp. 359–66). Carnforth: The Parthenon Publishing Group.

Drewett, R. F., Blair, P., Emmett, P. & Emond, A. (2004). Failure to thrive in the term and preterm infants of mothers depressed in the postnatal period: a population-based birth cohort study. *Journal of Child Psychology and Psychiatry*, *45*, 359–66.

Drewett, R. F., Corbett, S. S. & Wright, C. M. (1999). Cognitive and educational attainment at school age of children who failed to thrive in infancy: a population based study. *Journal of Child Psychology and Psychiatry*, *40*, 551–61.

(2006). Physical and emotional development, appetite and body image in adolescents who failed to thrive as infants. *Journal of Child Psychology and Psychiatry*, *47*, 524–31.

Drewett, R. F., Kasese-Hara, M. & Wright, C. (2002). Feeding behaviour in young children who fail to thrive. *Appetite*, *40*, 55–60.

Drewett, R. F. & Woolridge, M. (1979). Sucking patterns of human babies on the breast. *Early Human Development*, *3*, 315–20.

(1981). Milk taken by human babies from the first and second breast. *Physiology and Behavior*, *26*, 327–9.

Drewett, R. F., Woolridge, M. W., Jackson, D. A., et al. (1989b). Relationships between nursing patterns, supplementary food intake and breast-milk intake in a rural Thai population. Early Human Development, 20, 13–23.

Drotar, D. (1990). Sampling issues in research with nonorganic failure-to-thrive children. Journal of Pediatric Psychology, 15, 255–72.

Drotar, D., Eckerle, D., Satola, J., Pallotta, J. & Wyatt, B. (1990). Maternal interactional behavior with nonorganic failure-to-thrive infants: a case comparison study. Child Abuse and Neglect, 14, 41–51.

Duke, R. E., Bryson, S., Hammer, L. D. & Agras, W. S. (2004). The relationship between parental factors at infancy and parent-reported control over children's eating at age 7. Appetite, 43, 247–52.

Eaton-Evans, J. & Dugdale, A. E. (1988). Sleep patterns of infants in the first year of life. Archives of Disease in Childhood, 63, 647–9.

Ehara, H., Ohno, K. & Takeshita, K. (1993). Growth and developmental patterns in Prader-Willi syndrome. Journal of Intellectual Disability Research, 37, 479–85.

Ellaway, A., Macintyre, S. & Bonnefoy, X. (2005). Graffiti, greenery and obesity in adults: secondary analysis of European cross sectional survey. British Medical Journal, 331, 611–12.

Emler, N. (2001). Self-esteem: The Causes and Consequences of Low Self-worth. York: Joseph Rowntree Foundation.

Emond, A. M., Hawkins, N., Pennock, C., Golding, J. & the ALSPAC Children in Focus Team (1996). Haemoglobin and ferritin concentrations in infants at 8 months of age. Archives of Disease in Childhood, 74, 36–9.

Engle, P. & Zeitlen, M. (1996). Active feeding behaviour compensates for low interest in food among young Nicaraguan children. Journal of Nutrition, 126, 1808–16.

Epstein, L. H., Valoski, A., Wing, R. R. & McCurley, J. (1990). Ten-year follow-up of behavioral, family-based treatment for obese children. Journal of the American Medical Association, 264, 2519–23.

(1994). Ten-year outcomes of behavioural family-based treatments for childhood obesity. Health Psychology, 13, 373–83.

Epstein, L. H., Wing, R. R., Koeske, R., Andrasik, F. & Ossip, D. J. (1981). Child and parent weight loss in family-based behavioral modification programs. Journal of Consulting and Clinical Psychology, 49, 674–85.

Epstein, L. H., Wing, R. R., Koeske, R. & Valoski, A. (1987). Long-term effects of family-based treatment of childhood obesity. Journal of Consulting and Clinical Psychology, 55, 91–5.

Ericksson, J. G., Forsén, T., Tuomilehto, J., Osmond, C. & Barker, D. J. P. (2001). Early growth and coronary heart disease in later life: longitudinal study. British Medical Journal, 322, 949–53.

Evans, K., Evans, R. & Simmer, K. (1995). Effect of the method of breast feeding on breast engorgement, mastitis and infantile colic. Acta Paediatrica, 84, 849–52.

Everill, J. & Waller, G. (1995). Reported sexual abuse and eating psychopathology: a review of the evidence for a causal link. International Journal of Eating Disorders, 18, 1–11.

Fairburn, C., Cooper, Z., Doll, H. & Welch, S. (1999). Risk factors for anorexia nervosa. Three integrated case-control comparisons. Archives of General Psychiatry, 56, 468–76.

Fairburn, C. G., Cooper, Z., Doll, H. A., Norman, P. & O'Connor, M. (2000). The natural course of bulimia nervosa and binge eating disorder in young women. *Archives of General Psychiatry*, *57*, 659–65.

Fairburn, C. G., Doll, H. A., Welch, S. L., *et al.* (1998). Risk factors for binge eating disorder: a community based, case-control study. *Archives of General Psychiatry*, *55*, 425–32.

Faith, M., Scanlon, K., Birch, L., Francis, L. & Sherry, B. (2004). Parent–child feeding strategies and their relationships to child eating and weight status. *Obesity Research*, *12*, 1711–22.

Faith, M. S., Berman, N., Heo, M., *et al.* (2001). Effects of contingent television on physical activity and television viewing in older children. *Pediatrics*, *107*, 1043–8.

Falgiglia, G. A., Couch, S. C., Gribble, L. S., Pabst, S. M. & Frank, R. (2000). Food neophobia in childhood affects dietary variety. *Journal of the American Dietetic Association*, *100*, 1474–81.

Fallon, A. E. & Rozin, P. (1985). Sex differences in perceptions of desirable body shape. *Journal of Abnormal Psychology*, *94*, 102–5.

Fallon, A. E., Rozin, P. & Pliner, P. (1984). The child's conception of food: the development of food rejections, with special reference to disgust and contamination sensitivity. *Child Development*, *55*, 566–75.

Farooqi, I. S., Jebb, S. A., Langmack, G., *et al.* (1999). Brief report: effects of recombinant leptin therapy in a child with congenital leptin deficiency. *New England Journal of Medicine*, *341*, 879–84.

Farooqi, I. S., Keogh, J. M., Yeo, G. S. H., *et al.* (2003). Clinical spectrum of obesity and mutations in the melanocortin 4 receptor gene. *New England Journal of Medicine*, *348*, 1085–95.

Farooqi, I. S. & O'Rahilly, S. O. (2005). Monogenic obesity in humans. *Annual Review of Medicine*, *56*, 443–58.

Farquarson, J., Cockburn, F., Patrick, W. A., Jamieson, E. C. & Logan, R. W. (1992). Infant cerebral cortex phospholipid fatty-acid composition and diet. *Lancet*, *340*, 810–13.

Feachem, R. G. & Koblinsky, M. A. (1984). Interventions for the control of diarrhoeal diseases among young children: promotion of breast-feeding. *Bulletin of the World Health Organization*, *62*, 271–91.

Feher, S. D. K., Berger, L. R., Johnson, J. D. & Wilde, J. B. (1989). Increasing breast milk production for premature infants with a relaxation/imagery audiotape. *Journal of Pediatrics*, *83*, 57–60.

Felt, B. T. & Lozoff, B. (1996). Brain iron and behavior of rats are not normalised by treatment of iron deficiency anemia during early development. *Journal of Nutrition*, *126*, 693–701.

Fergusson, D. M., Horwood, J. & Lynskey, M. T. (1996). Childhood sexual abuse and psychiatric disorder in young adulthood: II. Psychiatric outcome of childhood sexual abuse. *Journal of the American Academy of Child and Adolescent Psychiatry*, *34*, 1365–74.

Fergusson, D. M., Horwood, L. J. & Ridder, E. M. (2005). Show me the child at seven II: childhood intelligence and later outcomes in adolescence and young adulthood. *Journal of Child Psychology and Psychiatry*, *46*, 850–8.

Fergusson, D. M., Horwood, L. J. & Shannon, F. T. (1980). Length and weight gain in the first three months of life. *Human Biology*, *52*, 169–80.

Fergusson, D. M., Lynskey, M. T. & Horwood, J. (1996). Childhood sexual abuse and psychiatric disorder in young adulthood: I. Prevalence of sexual abuse and factors associated with sexual abuse. *Journal of the American Academy of Child and Adolescent Psychiatry*, *34*, 1355–64.

Fewtrell, M. S., Morley, R., Abbott, R. A., *et al.* (2002). Double-blind, randomised trial of long-chain polyunsaturated fatty acid supplementation in formula fed to preterm infants. *Pediatrics*, *110*, 73–82.

Field, A. E., Camargo, C. A., Taylor, C. B., Berkey, C. S. & Colditz, G. A. (1999). Relation of peer and media influences to the development of purging behaviors among preadolescent and adolescent girls. *Archives of Pediatrics and Adolescent Medicine*, *153*, 1184–9.

Finberg, L., Kiley, J. & Luttrell, C. N. (1963). Mass accidental salt poisoning in infancy. *Journal of the American Medical Association*, *184*, 187–224.

Fischhoff, J., Whitten, C. F. & Pettit, M. G. (1971). A psychiatric study of mothers of infants with growth failure secondary to maternal deprivation. *Journal of Pediatrics*, *79*, 209–15.

Fisher, J. O. & Birch, L. L. (2002). Eating in the absence of hunger and overweight in girls from 5 to 7 years of age. *American Journal of Clinical Nutrition*, *76*, 226–31.

Fisher, J. O., Mitchell, D. C., Smiciklas-Wright, H. & Birch, L. L. (2000). Maternal milk consumption predicts the tradeoff between milk and soft drinks in young girls' diet. *Journal of Nutrition*, *131*, 246–50.

Fisher, M., Golden, N. H., Katzman, D. K., *et al.* (1995). Eating disorders in adolescents: a background paper. *Journal of Adolescent Health*, *16*, 420–37.

Flay, B. R., Koepke, D., Thompson, S. J., *et al.* (1989). Six-year follow-up of the first Waterloo school smoking prevention trial. *American Journal of Public Health*, *79*, 1371–6.

Flay, B. R., Ryan, K. B., Best, J. A., *et al.* (1985). Are social-psychological smoking prevention programs effective? The Waterloo study. *Journal of Behavioural Medicine*, *8*, 37–59.

Flynn, J. R. (1987). Massive IQ gains in 14 nations: what IQ tests really measure. *Psychological Bulletin*, *101*, 171–91.

  (1998). IQ gains over time: toward finding the causes. In U. Neisser (ed.), *The Rising Curve: Long-term Gains in IQ and Related Measures* (pp. 25–66). Washington, DC: American Psychological Association.

  (1999). Searching for justice: the discovery of IQ gains over time. *American Psychologist*, *54*, 5–20.

Foerster, S. B., Kizer, K. W., Disorgra, L. K., *et al.* (1995). California's '5 a day – for better health!' campaign: an innovative population based effort to effect large-scale dietary change. *American Journal of Preventive Medicine*, *11*, 124–31.

Fombonne, E. (1996). Is bulimia nervosa increasing in frequency? *International Journal of Eating Disorders*, *19*, 287–96.

Fomon, S. J., Filer, L. J., Thomas, L. N., Anderson, T. A. & Nelson, S. E. (1975). Influence of formula concentration on caloric intake and growth of normal infants. *Acta Paediatrica Scandinavica*, *64*, 172–81.

Fomon, S. J., Filer, L. J., Thomas, L. N., Rogers, R. R. & Proksch, A. M. (1969). Relationship between formula concentration and rate of growth of normal infants. *Journal of Nutrition*, *98*, 241–54.

Fomon, S. J., Haschke, F., Ziegler, E. E. & Nelson, S. E. (1982). Body composition of reference children from birth to age 10 years. *American Journal of Clinical Nutrition*, *35*, 1169–75.

Fomon, S. J. & Nelson, S. E. (2002). Body composition of the male and female reference infants. *Annual Review of Nutrition*, *22*, 1–17.

Fomon, S. J., Owen, G. M. & Thomas, L. N. (1964). Milk or formula volume ingested by infants fed ad libitum. *American Journal of Diseases of Children*, *108*, 601–4.

Fomon, S. J., Thomas, L. N., Filer, L. J., Anderson, T. A. & Nelson, S. E. (1976). Influence of fat and carbohydrate content of diet on food intake and growth of male infants. *Acta Paediatrica Scandinavica*, *65*, 136–44.

Forsyth, B. W. C. (1989). Colic and the effect of changing formulas: a double-blind, multiple cross-over study. *Pediatrics*, *115*, 521–6.

Fowler, M. D., Johnson, M. P. & Atkinson, S. S. (1985). School achievement and absence in children with chronic health disease. *Journal of Pediatrics*, *106*, 683–7.

Frank, D. A. & Zeisel, S. H. (1988). Failure to thrive. *Pediatric Clinics of North America*, *35*, 1187–206.

Frankenburg, W. & Dodds, J. (1967). The Denver Developmental Screening Tests. *Journal of Pediatrics*, *71*, 181–91.

Freedman, D. S., Khan, L. K., Serdula, M. K., *et al.* (2005). The relation of childhood BMI to adult adiposity: the Bogalusa Heart Study. *Pediatrics*, *115*, 22–7.

Freedman, D. S., Srinivasan, S. R., Valdez, R. A., Williamson, D. F. & Berenson, G. S. (1997). Secular increases in relative weight and adiposity among children over two decades: the Bogalusa Heart Study. *Pediatrics*, *99*, 420–6.

Freeman, J., Cole, T., Chinn, S., *et al.* (1995). Cross sectional stature and weight reference curves for the UK, 1990. *Archives of Disease in Childhood*, *73*, 17–24.

French, S. A., Hannan, P. J. & Story, M. (2004). School soft drink intervention study: too good to be true? *British Medical Journal*, *329*, E315–E316 doi: 10.1136/bmj.329.7462.E315.

French, S. A., Perry, C. L., Leon, G. R. & Fulkerson, J. A. (1996). Self-esteem and change in body mass index over 3 years in a cohort of adolescents. *Obesity Research*, *4*, 27–33.

French, S. A., Story, M., Downes, B., Resnick, M. D. & Blum, R. W. (1995). Frequent dieting among adolescents: psychosocial and health behavior correlates. *American Journal of Public Health*, *85*, 695–701.

Friedman, J. M. (1997). Leptin, leptin receptors and the control of body weight. *European Journal of Medical Research*, *2*, 7–13.

Frost, R. O., Marten, P., Lahart, C. & Rosenblate, R. (1990). The dimensions of perfectionism. *Cognitive Therapy and Research*, *145*, 449–68.

Gale, C. R. & Martyn, C. N. (1996). Breastfeeding, dummy use and intelligence. *Lancet*, *347*, 1072–5.

Gale, C. R., Walton, S. & Martyn, C. N. (2003). Foetal and postnatal head growth and risk of cognitive decline in old age. *Brain*, *126*, 2273–8.

Galloway, A. T., Lee, Y. & Birch, L. L. (2003). Predictors and consequences of food neophobia and pickiness in young girls. *Journal of the American Dietetic Association*, *103*, 692–8.

Ganchrow, J. R. & Mennella, J. A. (2003). The ontogeny of human flavor perception. In R. L. Doty (ed.), *Handbook of Olfaction and Gustation* (pp. 823–46). New York: Marcel Dekker.

Garcia, S. E., Kaiser, L. L. & Dewey, K. G. (1990a). The relationship of eating frequency and caloric density to energy intake among rural Mexican pre-school children. *European Journal of Clinical Nutrition*, *44*, 381–7.

(1990b). Self-regulation of food intake among rural Mexican preschool children. *European Journal of Clinical Nutrition*, *44*, 371–80.

Gard, M. C. E. & Freeman, C. P. (1996). The dismantling of a myth: a review of eating disorders and socioeconomic status. *International Journal of Eating Disorders*, *20*, 1–12.

Gardner, J. M. M., Grantham-McGregor, S. M., Chang, S. M., Himes, J. H. & Powell, C. A. (1995). Activity and behavioral development in stunted and nonstunted children and response to nutritional supplementation. *Child Development*, *66*, 1785–97.

Gardner, R. M., Stark, K., Friedman, B. N. & Jackson, N. A. (2000). Predictors of eating disorder scores in children aged 6 through 14: a longitudinal study. *Journal of Psychosomatic Research*, *49*, 199–205.

Gardosi, J. O. (2005). Prematurity and fetal growth restriction. *Early Human Development*, *81*, 43–9.

Garfinkel, P. E., Kennedy, S. H. & Kaplan, A. S. (1995). Views on classification and diagnosis of eating disorders. *Canadian Journal of Psychiatry*, *40*, 445–56.

Garner, D. M. (1991). *Eating Disorder Inventory-2: Professional manual*. Odessa, FL: Psychological Assessment Resources.

Garner, D. M. & Garfinkel, P. E. (1979). The Eating Attitudes Test: an index of the symptoms of anorexia nervosa. *Psychological Medicine*, *9*, 273–9.

Garner, D. M., Olmsted, M. P., Bohr, Y. & Garfinkel, P. E. (1982). The Eating Attitudes Test: psychometric features and clinical correlates. *Psychological Medicine*, *12*, 871–8.

Garner, D. M., Olmsted, M. P. & Polivy, J. (1983). Development and validation of a multidimensional eating disorder inventory for anorexia nervosa and bulimia. *International Journal of Eating Disorders*, *2*, 15–34.

Geleijnse, J. M., Hofman, A., Witteman, J. C. M., *et al.* (1996). Long-term effects of neonatal sodium restriction on blood pressure. *Hypertension*, *29*, 913–17.

Gibson, E. L. & Wardle, J. (2003). Energy density predicts preferences for fruit and vegetables in 4-year-old children. *Appetite*, *41*, 97–8.

Gibson, E. L., Wardle, J. & Watts, C. J. (1998). Fruit and vegetable consumption, nutritional knowledge and beliefs in mothers and children. *Appetite*, *31*, 205–28.

Giglio, L., Cnadusso, M., Orazio, C., Mastella, G. & Faraguna, D. (1997). Failure to thrive: the earliest feature of cystic fibrosis in infants diagnosed by neonatal screening. *Acta Paediatrica*, *86*, 1162–5.

Gillman, M. W., Rifas-Shiman, S. I., Camargo, C. A. J., *et al.* (2001). Risk of overweight among adolescents who were breastfed as infants. *Journal of the American Medical Association*, 285, 2461–7.

Gilmour, J. & Skuse, D. (2003). Children with Prader-Willi syndrome and primary obesity: a comparison of appetite and psychosocial profiles. In U. Eiholzer, D. l'Allemand & W. B. Zipf (eds.), *Prader-Willi Syndrome as a Model for Obesity* (pp. 156–65). Basel: Karger.

Gilmour, J., Skuse, D. & Pembrey, M. (2001). Hyperphagic short stature and Prader-Willi syndrome: a comparison of behavioural phenotypes, genotypes and indices of stress. *British Journal of Psychiatry*, 179, 129–37.

Gisel, E. G. (1991). Effect of food texture on the development of chewing of children between six months and two years of age. *Developmental Medicine and Child Neurology*, 33, 69–79.

Gisel, E. G. & Patrick, J. (1988). Identification of childen with cerebral palsy unable to maintain a normal nutritional state. *Lancet*, 1, 283–6.

Glaser, H. H., Heagarty, M. C., Bullard, D. M. & Pivchick, E. C. (1968). Physical and psychological development of children with early failure to thrive. *Journal of Pediatrics*, 73, 690–8.

Golden, M. H. N. (1991). The nature of nutritional deficiency in relation to growth failure and poverty. *Acta Paediatrica Scandinavica Supplement*, 374, 95–110.

(1995). Specific deficiencies versus growth failure: Type 1 and Type 2 nutrients. *SCN News*, 12, 10–14.

Golding, J., Emmett, P. M. & Rogers, I. S. (1997). Gastroenteritis, diarrhoea and breast feeding. *Early Human Development*, 49 Suppl, S83–S103.

Golding, J., Rogers, I. S. & Emmett, P. M. (1997). Association between breast feeding, child development and behaviour. *Early Human Development*, 49 Suppl, S175–S184.

Goldstein, H. & Peckham, C. (1976). Birthweight, gestation, neonatal mortality and child development. In D. Roberts & A. Thompson (eds.), *The Biology of Human Fetal Growth* (pp. 81–102). London: Taylor & Francis.

Goran, M. I., Carpenter, W. H., McGloin, A., *et al.* (1995). Energy expenditure in children of lean and obese parents. *American Journal of Physiology*, 268 (Endocrinology and Metabolism 31), E917–E924.

Goran, M. I., Shewchuk, R., Gower, B. A., *et al.* (1998). Longitudinal changes in fatness in white children: no effect of childhood energy expenditure. *American Journal of Clinical Nutrition*, 67, 309–433.

Gordon, A. H. & Corcoran Jameson, J. (1979). Infant–mother attachment in patients with nonorganic failure to thrive syndrome. *Journal of the American Academic of Child Psychiatry*, 18, 251–9.

Gordon, R. (2000). *Eating Disorders: Anatomy of a Social Epidemic* (2nd edn). Oxford: Blackwell.

Gortmaker, S. L., Peterson, K., Wiccha, J., *et al.* (1999). Reducing obesity via a school-based interdisciplinary intervention among youth. *Archives of Pediatrics and Developmental Medicine*, 153, 409–18.

Gorwood, P., Kipman, A. & Foulon, C. (2003). The human genetics of anorexia nervosa. *European Journal of Pharmacology*, 480, 163–70.

Goulding, A., Rockell, J. E. P., Black, R. E., *et al.* (2004). Children who avoid drinking cow's milk are at increased risk for prepubertal bone fractures. *Journal of the American Dietetic Association, 104,* 250–3.

Graber, J. A., Lewinsohn, P. M., Seeley, J. R. & Brooks-Gunn, J. (1997). Is psychopathology associated with the timing of pubertal development? *Journal of the American Academy of Child and Adolescent Psychiatry, 36,* 1768–76.

Grantham-McGregor, S. & Ani, C. (2001). A review of studies on the effect of iron deficiency on cognitive development in children. *Journal of Nutrition, 131,* 649S–668S.

Grantham-McGregor, S., Stewart, M. & Powell, C. (1991). Behaviour of severely malnourished children in a Jamaican hospital. *Developmental Medicine and Child Neurology, 33,* 706–14.

Grantham-McGregor, S., Walker, S. P., Chang, S. M. & Powell, C. A. (1997). The effects of early childhood supplementation with and without stimulation on later development in stunted Jamaican children. *American Journal of Clinical Nutrition, 66,* 247–53.

Grantham-McGregor, S. M., Lira, P. I. C., Ashworth, A., Morris, S. S. & Assunçao, A. M. S. (1998). The development of low birth weight term infants and the effects of the environment in Northeast Brazil. *Journal of Pediatrics, 132,* 661–6.

Grantham-McGregor, S. M., Powell, C. A., Walker, S. P. & Himes, J. H. (1991). Nutritional supplementation, psychosocial stimulation, and mental development of stunted children: the Jamaican study. *Lancet, 338,* 1–5.

Graves, A. B., Mortimer, J. A., Larson, E. B., *et al.* (1996). Head circumference as a measure of cognitive reserve: association with severity of impairment in Alzheimer's disease. *British Journal of Psychiatry, 169,* 86–92.

Greeves, L. G., Patterson, C. C., Carson, D. J., *et al.* (2000). Effect of genotype on changes in intelligence quotient after dietary relaxation in phenylketonuria. *Archives of Disease in Childhood, 82,* 216–21.

Griffiths, P. (2000). Neuropsychological approaches to treatment policy issues in phenylketonuria. *European Journal of Pediatrics, 159* [Suppl 2], S82–S86.

Gringras, P. & Chen, W. (2001). Mechanisms for differences in monozygotic twins. *Early Human Development, 64,* 105–17.

Groetz, L. M., Levine, M. P. & Murnen, S. K. (2002). The effects of experimental presentation of thin media images on body dissatisfaction: a meta-analytic review. *International Journal of Eating Disorders, 31,* 1–16.

Groner, J. A., Holzman, N. A., Charney, E. & Mellitts, D. E. (1986). A randomized trial of oral iron on tests of short-term memory and attention span in young pregnant women. *Journal of Adolescent Health Care, 7,* 44–8.

Grudnik, J. L. & Kranzler, J. H. (2001). Meta-analysis of the relationship between intelligence and inspection time. *Intelligence, 29,* 523–35.

Guillaume, M. & Lissau, I. (2002). Epidemiology. In W. Burniat, T. J. Cole, I. Lissau & E. M. E. Poskitt (eds.), *Child and Adolescent Obesity* (pp. 28–49). Cambridge: Cambridge University Press.

Gunnarsdottir, I. & Thorsdottir, I. (2003). Relationship between growth and feeding in infancy and body mass index at the age of 6 years. *International Journal of Obesity, 27,* 1523–7.

Gunnell, D., Magnusson, P. K. E. & Rasmussen, F. (2005). Low intelligence test scores in 18 year old men and risk of suicide: cohort study. *British Medical Journal, 330,* 167–71.

Gunther, M. (1945). Sore nipples: cause and prevention. *Lancet, 2,* 590–3.

Gustafson, G. E., Woods, R. & Green, J. A. (2000). Can we hear the causes of infants' crying? In R. Barr, B. Hopkins & J. Green (eds.), *Crying as a Sign, a Symptom, and a Signal* (pp. 8–22). London: MacKeith Press.

Habbick, B. F. & Gerrard, J. W. (1984). Failure to thrive in the contented breast-fed baby. *Canadian Medical Association Journal, 131,* 765–8.

Habicht, J. P., DaVanzo, J. & Butz, W. P. (1988). Mother's milk and sewage: their interactive effects on infant mortality. *American Academy of Pediatrics, 81,* 456–61.

Habicht, J. P., Martorell, R., Yarbrough, C., Malina, R. M. & Klein, R. E. (1974). Height and weight standards for preschool children. How relevant are ethnic differences in growth potential? *Lancet, 2,* 611–15.

Hall, W. G. & Williams, C. L. (1983). Suckling isn't feeding is it? A search for developmental continuities. *Advances in the Study of Behavior, 13,* 219–54.

Halmi, K. A., Sunday, S. R., Strober, M., *et al.* (2000). Perfectionism in anorexia nervosa: variation by clinical subtype, obsessionality and pathological eating behaviour. *American Journal of Psychiatry, 157,* 1799–805.

Hambidge, K. M. (1986). Zinc deficiency in the weanling – how important? *Acta Paediatrica Scandinavica, 323,* 52–8.

Hamill, P. V. V., Drizd, T. A., Johnson, C. L., *et al.* (1979). Physical growth: National Center for Health Statistics percentiles. *American Journal of Clinical Nutrition, 32,* 607–29.

Hamlyn, B., Brooker, S., Oleinikova, K. & Wands, S. (2002). *Infant Feeding 2000.* London: The Stationery Office.

Hanson, R., Smith, J. A. & Hume, W. (1985). Achievements of infants in items of the Griffiths scales: 1980 compared to 1950. *Child: Care, Health and Development, 11,* 91–104.

Haouari, N., Wood, C., Griffiths, G. & Levene, M. (1995). The analgesic effect of sucrose in full term infants: a randomised controlled trial. *British Medical Journal, 310,* 1498–500.

Harris, G. (1988). Determinants of the introduction of solid food. *Journal of Reproductive and Infant Psychology, 6,* 241–9.

Harris, G., Blissett, J. & Johnson, R. (2000). Food refusal associated with illness. *Child Psychology and Psychiatry Reviews, 5,* 48–56.

Harris, G. & Booth, D. A. (1987). Infants' preference for salt in food: its dependence upon recent dietary experience. *Journal of Reproductive and Infant Psychology, 5,* 97–104.

Harris, G., Thomas, A. & Booth, D. A. (1990). Development of salt taste in infancy. *Developmental Psychology, 26,* 534–8.

Harrison, K. (2000a). Television viewing, fat stereotyping, body shape standards, and eating disorder symptomatology in grade school children. *Communication Research, 27,* 617–40.

(2000b). The body electric: thin-ideal media and eating disorders in adolescence. *Journal of Communication, 50,* 119–43.

Harter, S. (1982). The perceived competance scale for children. *Child Development*, *53*, 87–97.

Harvey, D., Prince, J., Bunton, J., Parkinson, C. & Campbell, S. (1982). Abilities of children who were small-for-gestational-age babies. *Pediatrics*, *69*, 296–300.

Hastings, G., Stead, M., McDermott, L., et al. (2003). *Review of Research on the Effects of Food Promotion to Children*. Centre for Social Marketing, University of Strathclyde.

Hawdon, J. M., Beauregard, N., Slattery, J. & Kennedy, G. (2000). Identification of neonates at risk of developing feeding problems in infancy. *Developmental Medicine and Child Neurology*, *42*, 235–9.

Healy, M. J. R. (1978). Notes on the statistics of growth standards. *Annals of Human Biology*, *1*, 41–6.

Hebebrand, J. & Remschmidt, H. (1995). Anorexia nervosa viewed as an extreme weight condition: genetic implications. *Human Genetics*, *95*, 1–11.

Helps, S., Fuggle, P., Udwin, O. & Dick, M. (2003). Psychosocial and neurocognitive aspects of sickle cell disease. *Child and Adolescent Mental Health*, *8*, 11–17.

Heptinstall, E., Puckering, C., Skuse, D., et al. (1987). Nutrition and mealtime behaviour in families of growth-retarded children. *Human Nutrition: Applied Nutrition*, *41A*, 390–402.

Herzog, D. B. & Delinsky, S. S. (2001). Classification of the eating disorders. In R. Striegel-Moore & L. Smolak (eds.), *Eating Disorders: Innovative Directions in Research and Practice* (pp. 31–50). Washington, DC: American Psychological Association.

Heyman, M. B., Vichinsky, E., Katz, R., et al. (1985). Growth retardation in sickle-cell disease treated by nutritional support. *Lancet*, *1*, 903–6.

Hill, A., Draper, E. & Stack, J. (1994). A weight on children's minds: body shape dissatisfactions at 9-years old. *International Journal of Obesity*, *18*, 383–9.

Hill, A. J., Oliver, S. & Rogers, P. J. (1992). Eating in the adult world: the rise of dieting in childhood and adolescence. *British Journal of Clinical Psychology*, *31*, 95–105.

Hill, A. J. & Robinson, A. (1991). Dieting concerns have a functional effect on the behaviour of nine-year-old girls. *British Journal of Clinical Psychology*, *30*, 265–7.

Hillervik-Lindquist, C. (1991). Studies on perceived breast milk insufficiency. *Acta Paediatrica Scandinavica*, *376*, 8–27.

Hillervik-Lindquist, C., Hofvander, Y. & Sjölin, S. (1991). Studies on perceived breast-milk insufficiency 111: consequences for breastmilk consumption and growth. *Acta Paediatrica Scandinavica*, *80*, 297–303.

Himms-Hagen, J. (1995a). Does thermoregulatory feeding occur in newborn infants? A novel view of the role of brown adipose tissue thermogenesis in control of food intake. *Obesity Research*, *3*, 361–9.

   (1995b). Role of brown adipose tissue thermogenesis in control of thermoregulatory feeding in rats: a new hypothesis that links thermostatic and glucostatic hypotheses for control of food intake. *Proceedings of the Society for Experimental Society and Medicine*, *208*, 159–69.

Holland, A., Treasure, J., Coskeran, P., et al. (1993). Measurement of excessive appetite and metabolic changes in Prader-Willi syndrome. *International Journal of Obesity*, *17*, 527–32.

Holland, A. J., Treasure, J., Coskeran, P. & Dallow, J. (1995). Characteristics of the eating disorder in Prader-Willi syndrome: implications for treatment. *Journal of Intellectual Disability Research, 39*, 373–81.

Holland, B., Welch, A. A., Unwin, I. D., et al. (1991). *McCance and Widdowson's The Composition of Foods* (5th revised and extended edn). Cambridge: The Royal Society of Chemistry and Ministry of Agriculture, Fisheries and Food.

Horne, P. J., Lowe, C. F., Bowdery, M. & Egerton, C. (1998). The way to healthy eating for children. *British Food Journal, 100*, 133–40.

Horne, P. J., Lowe, C. F., Fleming, P. F. J. & Dowey, A. J. (1995). An effective procedure for changing food preferences in 5–7-year-old children. *Proceedings of the Nutrition Society, 54*, 441–52.

Howard, R. W. (2005). Objective evidence of rising population ability: a detailed examination of longitudinal chess data. *Personality and Individual Differences, 38*, 347–63.

Howie, P. W., Forsyth, J. S., Ogston, S. A., Clark, A. & Florey, C. D. (1990). Protective effect of breast-feeding against infection. *British Medical Journal, 300*, 11–16.

Hsu, L. K. G. (1997). Can dieting cause an eating disorder? *Psychological Medicine, 27*, 509–13.

Hughes, J. M., Li, L., Chinn, S. & Rona, R. J. (1997). Trends in growth in England and Scotland, 1972 to 1994. *Archives of Disease in Childhood, 76*, 182–9.

Hursti, U. K. & Sjödén, P. (1997). Food and general neophobia and their relationship with self-reported food choice: familial resemblance in Swedish families with children of ages 7–17 years. *Appetite, 29*, 89–103.

Huttenlocher, P. R. (1999). Synaptogenesis in the human cerebral cortex and the concept of critical periods. In N. Fox, L. Leavitt & J. Warhol (eds.), *The Role of Experience in Infant Development* (pp. 15–28). New York: Johnson & Johnson Consumer Companies Ltd.

Hytten, F. A. (1954). Clinical and chemical studies of human lactation II. Variations in major constituents during a feeding. *British Medical Journal, 1*, 176–9.

Hytten, F. E. (1959). Differences in yield and composition between first and second lactations. *British Journal of Nutrition, 18*, xxi–xxii.

Idjradinata, P. & Pollitt, E. (1993). Reversal of developmental delays in iron-deficient anaemic infants treated with iron. *Lancet, 341*, 1–4.

Irving, L. M. & Neumark-Szainer, D. (2002). Integrating the prevention of eating disorders and obesity: feasible or futile? *Preventive Medicine, 34*, 299–309.

Iwaniec, D. & Herbert, M. (1982). The assessment and treatment of children who fail to thrive. *Social Work Today, 13*, 8–12.

Iwaniec, D., Herbert, M. & McNeish, A. S. (1985). Social work with failure-to-thrive children and their families. Part I. *British Journal of Social Work, 15*, 243–59.

Jacobi, C., Agras, W. S., Bryson, S. & Hammer, L. D. (2003). Behavioral validation, precursors, and concomitants of picky eating in childhood. *Journal of the American Academy of Child and Adolescent Psychiatry, 42*, 76–84.

Jain, A., Sherman, S. N., Chamberlin, L. A., et al. (2005). Why don't low-income mothers worry about their preschoolers being overweight? *Pediatrics, 107*, 1138–46.

James, J., Thomas, P., Cavan, D. & Kerr, D. (2004). Preventing childhood obesity by reducing the consumption of carbonated drinks: cluster randomised trial. *British Medical Journal*, *328*, 1237–42.

James, W. H. (1982). The IQ advantage of the heavier twin. *British Journal of Psychology*, *73*, 513–17.

Janovský, M., Martínek, J. & Stanincová, V. (1967). The distribution of sodium, chloride and fluid in the body of young infants with increased intake of NaCl. *Biologia Neonatorium*, *11*, 261–72.

Jefferis, B. J. M. H., Power, C. & Hertzman, C. (2002). Birth weight, childhood socioeconomic environment, and cognitive development in the 1958 British birth cohort study. *British Medical Journal*, *325*, 305–10.

Jeffrey, A. N., Voss, L. D., Metcalf, B. S., Alba, S. & Wilkin, T. J. (2005). Parents' awareness of overweight in themselves and their children: cross-sectional study within a cohort (EarlyBird21). *British Medical Journal*, *330*, 23–4.

Johnson, J., Cohen, P., Kasen, S. & Brook, J. S. (2002). Childhood adversities associated with risk for eating disorders or weight problems during adolescence or early adulthood. *American Journal of Psychiatry*, *159*, 394–400.

Johnson, S. L. (2000). Improving preschoolers' self-regulation of energy intake. *Pediatrics*, *106*, 1429–35.

Johnson, S. L. & Birch, L. L. (1994). Parents' and children's adiposity and eating style. *Pediatrics*, *94*, 653–61.

Johnson, S. L., McPhee, L. & Birch, L. L. (1991). Conditioned preferences: young children prefer flavors associated with high dietary fat. *Physiology and Behavior*, *50*, 1245–51.

Jotangia, D., Moody, A., Stamatakis, E. & Wardle, H. (2005). *Obesity Among Children under 11*. National Centre for Social Research, Department of Epidemiology and Public Health at the Royal Free and University College Medical School.

Kagan, J., Reznick, J. S. & Snidman, N. (1988). Biological bases of childhood shyness. *Science*, *240*, 167–71.

Kaplan, K. & Wadden, T. (1986). Childhood obesity and self-esteem. *Journal of Pediatrics*, *109*, 367–70.

Karlberg, J. (1987). On the modelling of human growth. *Statistics in Medicine*, *6*, 185–92.

  (1989). A biologically-oriented mathematical model (ICP) for human growth. *Acta Paediatrica Scandinavica Supplement*, *350*, 70–94.

Karlberg, J. & Albertsson-Wikland, K. (1995). Growth in full-term small-for-gestational-age infants: from birth to final height. *Pediatric Research*, *38*, 733–9.

Karwautz, A., Rabe-Hesheth, X. H., Zhao, J., *et al.* (2001). Individual-specific risk factors for anorexia nervosa: a pilot study using a discordant sister-pair design. *Psychological Medicine*, *31*, 317–29.

Kasese-Hara, M., Wright, C. & Drewett, R. F. (2002). Energy compensation in young children who fail to thrive. *Journal of Child Psychology and Psychiatry*, *43*, 449–56.

Kearney, P. J., Malone, A. J., Hayes, T., Cole, M. & Hyland, M. (1998). A trial of lactase in the management of infant colic. *Journal of Human Nutrition and Dietetics*, *11*, 281–5.

Keim, N. L., Stern, J. S. & Havel, P. J. (1998). Relation between circulating leptin concentrations and appetite during a prolonged, moderate energy deficit in women. *American Journal of Clinical Nutrition*, 68, 794–801.

Kelleher, K. J., Casey, P. H., Bradley, R., *et al*. (1993). Risk factors and outcomes for failure to thrive in low birth weight preterm infants. *Pediatrics*, 91, 941–8.

Kerwin, M. E. (1999). Empirically supported treatments in pediatric psychology: severe feeding problems. *Journal of Pediatric Psychology*, 24, 193–214.

Kessler, D. B. (1999). Failure to thrive and pediatric undernutrition: historical and theoretical context. In D. B. Kessler and P. Dawson (eds.), *Failure to Thrive and Pediatric Undernutrition: A Transdisciplinary Approach* (pp. 3–17). Baltimore, MD: Paul H. Brookes Publishing Co.

Kessler, D. B. & Dawson, P. (1999). *Failure to Thrive and Pediatric Undernutrition: A Transdisciplinary Approach*. Baltimore, MD: Paul H. Brookes Publishing Co.

Kessler, R. C., McGonagle, K. A., Zhao, S., *et al*. (1994). Lifetime and 12-month prevalence of DSM-III-R psychiatric disorders in the United States. *Archives of General Psychiatry*, 51, 8–19.

Key, T. J. A., Thorogood, M., Appleby, P. & Burr, M. L. (1996). Dietary habits and mortality in 11000 vegetarians and health conscious people: results of a 17 year follow-up. *British Medical Journal*, 313, 775–8.

Khan, M. U. & Ahmad, K. (1986). Withdrawal of food during diarrhoea: major mechanism of malnutrition following diarrhoea in Bangladesh children. *Journal of Tropical Pediatrics*, 32, 57–61.

Klesges, R. C., Haddock, C. K., Stein, R. J., *et al*. (1992). Relationship between psychosocial functioning and body fat in preschool children: a longitudinal investigation. *Journal of Consulting and Clinical Psychology*, 60, 793–6.

Klump, K. L., Kaye, W. H. & Strober, M. (2001). The evolving genetic foundations of eating disorders. *Psychiatric Clinics of North America*, 24, 215–25.

Knight, S., Singhal, A., Thomas, P. & Serjeant, G. (1995). Factors associated with lowered intelligence in homozygous sickle cell disease. *Archives of Disease in Childhood*, 73, 316–20.

Knobloch, H., Pasamanick, B. & Sherard, E. S. (1966). A developmental screening inventory for infants. *Pediatrics*, 38, 1095–8.

Koch, R., Azen, C., Friedman, E. G. & Williamson, M. L. (1984). Paired comparisons between early treated PKU children and their matched sibling controls on intelligence and school achievement test results at eight years of age. *Journal of Inherited Metabolic Disease*, 7, 86–90.

Koenen, K. C., Moffitt, T. E., Caspi, A., Taylor, A. & Purcell, S. (2003). Domestic violence is associated with environmental suppression of IQ in young children. *Development and Psychopathology*, 15, 297–311.

Koeppen-Schomerus, G., Wardle, J. & Plomin, R. (2001). A genetic analysis of weight and overweight in 4-year-old twin pairs. *International Journal of Obesity*, 25, 838–44.

Kolb, B. (1999). Neuroanatomy and development overview. In N. Fox, L. Leavitt & J. Warhol (eds.), *The Roles of Early Experience in Infant Development* (pp. 5–14). New York: Johnson & Johnson Consumer Companies.

Konner, M. & Worthman, C. (1980). Nursing frequency, gonadal function, and birth spacing among !Kung hunter-gatherers. *Science*, *207*, 788–91.

Kopp, C. B. & McCall, R. B. (1982). Predicting later mental performance for normal, at-risk, and handicapped infants. In P. Baltes & O. G. J. Brim (eds.), *Life-span Development and Behavior*, vol. IV (pp. 33–61). New York: Academic Press.

Korndörfer, S. R., Lucas, A. R., Suman, V. R., *et al.* (2003). Long-term survival of patients with anorexia nervosa: a population-based study in Rochester, Minn. *Mayo Clinic Proceedings*, *78*, 278–84.

Kostanski, M. & Gullone, E. (1998). Adolescent body image dissatisfaction: relationships with self-esteem, anxiety and depression controlling for body mass. *Journal of Child Psychology and Psychiatry*, *39*, 255–62.

Kotelchuck, M. (1980). Non-organic failure to thrive: the status of interactional and environmental etiological theories. *Advances in Behavioral Pediatrics*, *1*, 29–51.

Kotelchuck, M. & Newberger, E. H. (1983). Failure to thrive: a controlled study of familial characteristics. *Journal of the American Academy of Child Psychiatry*, *22*, 322–8.

Kotler, L. A., Cohen, P., Davies, M., Pine, D. S. & Walsh, B. T. (2001). Longitudinal relationships between childhood, adolescent, and adult eating disorders. *Journal of the American Academy of Child and Adolescent Psychiatry*, *40*, 1434–40.

Kraemer, H. C., Berkowitz, R. I. & Hammer, D. L. (1990). Methodological difficulties in studies of obesity: I. Measurement issues. *Annals of Behavioral Medicine*, *12*, 112–18.

Kramer, M. S. (1987). Determinants of low birth weight: methodological assessment and meta-analysis. *Bulletin of the World Health Organization*, *65*, 663–737.

  (1993). Effects of energy and protein intakes on pregnancy outcome: an overview of the research evidence from controlled clinical trials. *American Journal of Clinical Nutrition*, *58*, 627–35.

Kramer, M. S., Barr, R. G., Leduc, D. G., Biosjoly, C. & Pless, I. B. (1983). Maternal psychological determinants of infant obesity. *Journal of Chronic Disease*, *36*, 329–35.

Kramer, M. S., Barr, R. G., Leduc, D. G., *et al.* (1985). Determinants of weight and adiposity in the first year of life. *Journal of Pediatrics*, *106*, 10–14.

Kramer, M. S., Chalmers, B., Hodnet, E. D., *et al.* (2001). Promotion of breastfeeding intervention trial (PROBIT). *Journal of the American Medical Association*, *285*, 413–20.

Kramer, M. S., Guo, T., Platt, R. W., *et al.* (2002). Breastfeeding and infant growth: biology or bias? *Pediatrics*, *110*, 343–7.

Kramer, M. S. & Kakuma, R. (2002). *The Optimal Duration of Exclusive Breastfeeding: A Systematic Review*. Geneva: World Health Organisation.

Kramer, M. S., McClean, F. H., Boyd, M. E. & Usher, R. H. (1988). The validity of gestational age estimation by menstrual dating in term, preterm, and postterm gestations. *Journal of the American Medical Association*, *260*, 3306–8.

Kramer, M. S., Platt, R., Yang, H., McNemara, H. & Usher, R. H. (1999). Are all growth-restricted newborns created equal(ly)? *Pediatrics*, *103*, 599–602.

Krebs, N. F., Hambridge, K. M. & Walravens, P. A. (1984). Increased food intake of young children receiving a zinc supplement. *American Journal of Diseases of Children*, *138*, 270–3.

Krebs-Smith, S. M., Cook, A., Subar, A., *et al.* (1996). Fruit and vegetable intakes of children and adolescents in the United States. *Archives of Pediatrics and Adolescent Medicine*, *150*, 81–6.

Krebs-Smith, S. M., Heimendiner, J., Patterson, B. H., *et al.* (1995). Psychosocial factors associated with fruit and vegetable consumption. *American Journal of Health Promotion*, *10*, 98–104.

Kron, R. E., Johannes, I. & Goddard, K. E. (1968). Consistent individual differences in the nutritive sucking behavior of the human newborn. *Psychosomatic Medicine*, *30*, 151–61.

Kumar, V., Clements, C., Marwah, K. & Diwedi, P. (1985). Beliefs and therapeutic preferences of mothers in management of acute diarrhoeal disease in children. *Journal of Tropical Pediatrics*, *31*, 109–12.

Kurlak, L. O. & Stephenson, T. J. (1999). Plausible explanations for effects of long chain polyunsaturated fatty acids (LCPUFA) on neonates. *Archives of Disease in Childhood Fetal and Neonatal Edition*, *80*, F148–F154.

Lachenmeyer, J. R. & Davidovicz, H. (1987). Failure to thrive: A critical review. In B. B. Lahey & A. E. Kasdin (eds.), *Advances in Clinical Child Psychology*, vol. X (pp. 335–58). New York and London: Plenum Press.

Laessle, R. G., Tuschl, R. J., Kotthaus, B. C. & Pirke, K. M. (1989). Behavioral and biological correlates of dietary restraint in normal life. *Appetite*, *12*, 83–94.

Laitinen, S., Rasanen, L., Viikari, J. & Akerblom, H. K. (1995). Diet of Finnish children in relation to the family's socio-economic status. *Scandinavian Journal of Social Medicine*, *23*, 88–94.

Lansdown, R. G., Goldstein, H., Shah, P. M., *et al.* (1996). Culturally appropriate measures for monitoring child development at family and community level: a WHO collaborative study. *Bulletin of the World Health Organization*, *74*, 283–90.

Launer, L. J., Forman, M. R., Hundt, G. L., *et al.* (1992). Maternal recall of infant feeding events is accurate. *Journal of Epidemiology and Community Health*, *46*, 203–6.

Lawrence, M., Lawrence, F., Durnin, J. V. G. A. & Whitehead, R. G. (1991). A comparison of physical activity in Gambian and UK children aged 6–18 months. *European Journal of Clinical Nutrition*, *45*, 243–52.

Lazarus, R., Baur, L., Webb, K. & Blyth, F. (1996). Adiposity and body mass indices in children: Benn's index and other weight for height indices as measures of relative adiposity. *International Journal of Obesity*, *20*, 406–12.

Lee, K. (1994). The crying of Korean infants and related factors. *Developmental Medicine and Child Neurology*, *36*, 601–7.

Lee, S., Chiu, H. F. K. & Chen, C. (1989). Anorexia nervosa in Hong Kong: why not more in Chinese? *British Journal of Psychiatry*, *154*, 683–8.

Lee, S., Ho, T. P. & Hsu, L. K. G. (1993). Fat phobic and non-fat phobic anorexia nervosa: a comparative study of 70 Chinese patients in Hong Kong. *Psychological Medicine*, *23*, 999–1017.

Leshem, M. (1998). Salt preference in adolescence is predicted by common prenatal and infantile mineralofluid loss. *Physiology and Behaviour*, *63*, 699–704.

Lester, B. M., LaGasse, L. L. & Selfer, R. (1998). Cocaine exposure and children: the meaning of subtle effects. *Science*, *282*, 633–4.

Levitsky, D. A. & Barnes, R. H. (1972). Nutritional and environmental interactions in the behavioral development of the rat: long-term effects. *Science*, *176*, 68–71.

Lew, A. R. & Butterworth, G. (1995). The effects of hunger on hand–mouth co-ordination in newborn infants. *Developmental Psychology*, *31*, 456–63.

Lindberg, L., Bohlin, G. & Hagekull, B. (1991). Early feeding problems in a normal population. *International Journal of Eating Disorders*, *10*, 395–405.

Linden, W. (1981). Exposure treatments for focal phobias. *Archives of General Psychiatry*, *38*, 769–75.

Lissa-Lund-Sørensen, I. & Sørensen, T. I. A. (1992). Prospective study of the influence of social factors in childhood on overweight in young adulthood. *International Journal of Obesity*, *16*, 169–75.

Liu, J., Raine, A., Venables, P. H., Dalais, C. & Mednick, S. A. (2003). Malnutrition at age 3 years and lower cognitive ability at age 11 years: independence from psychosocial adversity. *Archives of Pediatric and Adolescent Medicine*, *157*, 593–600.

Liu, J., Raine, A., Venables, P. H. & Mednick, S. A. (2004). Malnutrition at age 3 years and externalising behavior problems at ages 8, 11, and 17 years. *American Journal of Psychiatry*, *161*, 2005–13.

Lohman, T. G., Going, S., Stewart, D., et al. (2001). The effect of Pathways obesity prevention study on body composition in American children. *FASEB*, A1093.

Looker, A. C., Daliman, P. R., Carroll, M. D., Gunter, E. W. & Johnson, C. L. (1997). Prevalence of iron deficiency in the United States. *Journal of the American Medical Association*, *277*, 973–6.

Lothe, L., Ivarsson, S. A., Ekman, R. & Lindberg, T. (1990). Motilin and infantile colic. *Acta Paediatrica Scandinavica*, *79*, 410–16.

Lothe, L. & Lindberg, T. (1989). Cow's milk whey protein elicits symptoms of infantile colic in colicky formula-fed infants: a double-blind crossover study. *Journal of Pediatrics*, *83*, 262–6.

Lozoff, B., De Andraca, L., Walter, T. & Pino, P. (1997). Does preventing iron-deficiency anemia (IDA) improve developmental test scores? *Pediatric Research*, *A 39*, 136A.

Lozoff, B., Jimenez, E., Hagen, J., Mollen, E. & Wolf, A. W. (2000). Poorer behavioral and developmental outcome more than 10 years after treatment for iron deficiency in infancy. *Pediatrics*, *105*, 51–62.

Lozoff, B., Jimenez, E. & Wolf, A. W. (1991). Long-term developmental outcome of infants with iron deficiency. *New England Journal of Medicine*, *325*, 687–94.

Lozoff, B., Klein, N. K., Nelson, E. C., et al. (1998). Behavior of infants with iron-deficiency anemia. *Child Development*, *69*, 24–36.

Lozoff, B., Klein, N. K. & Prabucki, K. M. (1986). Iron-deficient anemic infants at play. *Developmental and Behavioral Pediatrics*, *7*, 152–8.

Lozoff, B. G., Wolf, A. W., McClish, D. K., *et al.* (1987). Iron deficiency anemia and iron therapy: effects on infant developmental test performance. *Pediatrics*, *79*, 981–95.

Lubrano-Berthelier, C., Le Stunff, C., Bougnères, P. & Vaisse, C. (2004). A homozygous null mutation delineates the role of the melanocortin-4 receptor in humans. *Journal of Clinical Endocrinology and Metabolism*, *89*, 2028–32.

Lucas, A., Fewtrell, M. S., Morley, R., *et al.* (1996). Randomized outcome trial of human milk fortification and developmental outcome in preterm infants. *American Journal of Clinical Nutrition*, *64*, 142–51.

Lucas, A., Gore, S. M., Cole, T. J., *et al.* (1986). Multicentre trial on feeding low birthweight infants: effects of diet on early growth. *Archive of Disease in Childhood*, *61*, 849–57.

Lucas, A., Morley, R. & Cole, T. J. (1998). Randomised trial of early diet in preterm babies and later intelligence quotient. *British Medical Journal*, *317*, 1481–7.

Lucas, A., Morley, R., Cole, T. J., *et al.* (1989). Early diet in preterm babies and developmental status in infancy. *Archives of Disease in Childhood*, *64*, 1570–8.
(1990). Early diet in preterm babies and developmental status at 18 months. *Lancet*, *335*, 1477–81.

Lucas, A., Stafford, M., Morley, R., *et al.* (1999). Efficacy and safety of long-chain polyunsaturated fatty acid supplementation of infant-formula milk: a randomised trial. *Lancet*, *354*, 1948–54.

Lucas, A. & St James-Roberts, I. (1998). Crying, fussing and colic behaviour in breast- and bottle-fed infants. *Early Human Development*, *53*, 9–18.

Lucas, A. R., Beard, C. M., O'Fallon, W. M. & Kurland, L. T. (1991). 50-year trends in the incidence of anorexia nervosa in Rochester, Minn.: a population-based study. *American Journal of Psychiatry*, *148*, 917–22.

Lucassen, P. L. B. J., Assendelft, W. J. J., van Eijk, J. T. M., *et al.* (2005). Systematic review of the occurrence of infantile colic in the community. *Archives of Disease in Childhood*, *84*, 398–403.

Luciana, M., Sullivan, J. & Nelson, C. A. (2001). Associations between phenylalanine-to-tyrosin ratios and performances on tests of neuropsychological function in adolescents treated early and continuously for phenylketonuria. *Child Development*, *72*, 1637–52.

Lundgren, E. M., Cnattingius, S., Jonsson, B. & Tuvemo, T. (2001). Intellectual and psychological performance in males born small for gestational age with and without catch-up growth. *Pediatric Research*, *50*, 91–6.

Lynn, R. (1990). The role of nutrition in secular increases in intelligence. *Personality and Individual Differences*, *11*, 273–85.

Lynn, R. & Hampson, S. (1986). The rise of national intelligence: evidence from Britain, Japan and the USA. *Personality and Individual Differences*, *7*, 23–32.

Lynn, R. & Harland, P. (1998). A positive effect of iron supplementation on the IQs of iron deficient children. *Personality and Individual Differences*, *24*, 883–5.

MacDonald, A. (2000). Diet and compliance in phenylketonuria. *European Journal of Pediatrics*, *159* [Suppl 2], S136–S141.

MacDonald, A., Harris, G., Rylance, G., Asplin, D. & Booth, I. W. (1997). Abnormal feeding behaviours in phenylketonuria. *Journal of Human Nutrition and Dietetics*, *10*, 163–70.

MacDonald, A., Holden, C. & Harris, G. (1991). Nutritional strategies in cystic fibrosis: current issues. *Journal of the Royal Society of Medicine*, *84*, 28–35.

Maes, H., Neale, M. & Eaves, L. (1997). Genetic and environmental factors in relative body weight and human adiposity. *Behaviour Genetics*, *27*, 325–51.

Makrides, M., Newman, M., Simmer, K., Pater, J. & Gibson, R. (1995). Are long-chain polyunsaturated fatty acids essential nutrients in infancy? *Lancet*, *345*, 1463–8.

Maloney, M. J., McGuire, J. B. & Daniels, S. R. (1988). Reliability testing of a children's version of the Eating Attitude Test. *Journal of the American Academy of Child and Adolescent Psychiatry*, *27*, 541–3.

Marchi, M. & Cohen, P. (1990). Early childhood eating behaviors and adolescent eating disorders. *Journal of the American Academy of Child and Adolescent Psychiatry*, *29*, 112–17.

Marlier, L. & Schaal, B. (2005). Human newborns prefer human mik: conspecific milk odor is attractive without postnatal experience. *Child Development*, *76*, 155–68.

Martin, S., Housely, K., McKoy, H., *et al.* (1988). Self-esteem of adolescent girls as related to weight. *Perceptual and Motor Skills*, *67*, 119–29.

Martínez-González, M. A., Gual, P., Lahortiga, F., *et al.* (2003). Parental factors, mass media influences, and the onset of eating disorders in a prospective population-based cohort. *Pediatrics*, *111*, 315–20.

Martorell, R. (1998). Nutrition and the worldwide rise in IQ scores. In U. Neisser (ed.), *The Rising Curve: Long-term Gains in IQ and Related Measures* (pp. 183–206). Washington, DC: American Psychological Association.

Mathisen, B., Skuse, D., Wolke, D. & Reilly, S. (1989). Oral-motor dysfunction and failure to thrive among inner-city infants. *Developmental Medicine and Child Neurology*, *31*, 293–302.

Mathisen, B., Worrall, L., Masel, J., Wall, C. & Shepherd, R. W. (1999). Feeding problems in infants with gastro-oesophageal disease: a controlled study. *Journal of Paediatrics and Child Health*, *35*, 163–9.

Matte, T., Bresnahan, M., Begg, M. & Susser, E. (2001). Influence of variation in birth weight within normal range and within sibships on IQ at age 7 years: cohort study. *British Medical Journal*, *323*, 310–14.

Matthiesen, A.-S., Ransjö-Arvidson, A.-B., Nissen, E. & Uvnäs-Moberg, K. (2001). Postpartum maternal oxytocin release by newborns: effects of infant hand massage and sucking. *Birth*, *28*, 13–19.

Mayor, S. (2004). Report warns of continuing violations of code on breast milk substitute marketing. *British Medical Journal*, *328*, 1218.

McCall, R. B. (1977). Childhood IQs as predictors of adult educational and occupational status. *Science*, *197*, 482–3.

McCall, R. B. & Carriger, M. S. (1993). A meta-analysis of infant habituation and recognition memory performance as predictors of later IQ. *Child Development*, *64*, 57–79.

McCann, J. B., Stein, A., Fairburn, C. G. & Dunger, D. B. (1994). Eating habits and attitudes of mothers of children with non-organic failure to thrive. *Archives of Disease in Childhood*, *70*, 234–6.

McCarthy, H. D., Ellis, S. M. & Cole, T. J. (2003). Central overweight and obesity in British youth aged 11–16 years: cross sectional surveys of waist circumference. *British Medical Journal, 326,* 624–7.

McCoy, R., Kadowaki, C., Wilks, S., Engstrom, J. & Meier, P. (1988). Nursing management of breast feeding for preterm infants. *Journal of Perinatal and Neonatal Nursing, 2,* 42–55.

Mehta, K. C., Specker, B. L., Bartholmey, S., Giddens, J. & Ho, M. L. (1998). Trial on timing of introduction of solids and food type on infant growth. *Pediatrics, 102,* 569–73.

Meier, P. (1988). Bottle- and breast-feeding: effects on transcutaneous oxygen pressure and temperature in preterm infants. *Nursing Research, 37,* 36–41.

Melhuish, E. C. (1987). Socio-emotional behaviour at 18 months as a function of daycare experience, temperament, and gender. *Infant Mental Health Journal, 8,* 364–73.

   (1993). A measure of love? An overview of the assessment of attachment. *ACPP Newsletter and Review, 15,* 269–75.

Mendelson, B. K. & White, D. R. (1982). Relation between body-esteem and self-esteem of obese and normal children. *Perceptual and Motor Skills, 54,* 899–905.

Mendez, M. A. & Adair, L. S. (1999). Severity and timing of stunting in the first two years of life affect performance on cognitive tests in late childhood. *Journal of Nutrition, 129,* 1555–62.

Menella, J. A. (1997). The human infant's suckling responses to the flavor of alcohol in human milk. *Alcoholism: Clinical and Experimental Research, 21,* 581–5.

   (1998). Short-term effects of maternal alcohol consumption on lactation performance. *Alcoholism: Clinical and Experimental Research, 22,* 1389–92.

Mennella, J. A. & Beauchamp, G. K. (1991a). Maternal diet alters the sensory qualities of human milk and the nursling's behavior. *Pediatrics, 88,* 737–44.

   (1991b). The transfer of alcohol to human milk. *New England Journal of Medicine, 325,* 981–4.

   (1993a). Beer, breast feeding and folklore. *Developmental Psychobiology, 26,* 459–66.

   (1993b). The effects of repeated exposure to garlic-flavored milk on the nursling's behaviour. *Pediatric Research, 34,* 805–8.

   (1996). The human infant's response to vanilla flavors in mother's milk and formula. *Infant Behavior and Development, 19,* 13–19.

   (2002). Flavor experiences during formula feeding are related to preferences during childhood. *Early Human Development, 68,* 71–82.

Midence, K., McManus, C., Fuggle, P. & Davies, S. (1996). Psychological adjustment and family functioning in a group of British children with sickle cell disease: preliminary empirical findings and a meta-analysis. *British Journal of Clinical Psychology, 35,* 439–50.

Miller, A. R. & Barr, R. G. (1991). Infantile colic: is it a gut issue? *Pediatric Clinics of North America, 38,* 1407–23.

Miller, J. J., McVeagh, P., Fleet, G. H., Petocz, P. & Brand, J. C. (1989). Breath hydrogen secretion in infants with colic. *Archives of Disease in Childhood, 64,* 725–9.

Miller-Loncar, C., Bigsby, R., High, P., Wallach, M. & Lester, B. (2004). Infant colic and feeding difficulties. *Archives of Disease in Childhood*, *89*, 908–12.

Mingroni, M. A. (2004). The secular rise in IQ: giving heterosis a closer look. *Intelligence*, *32*, 65–83.

Mitchell, J. E., Crow, S., Peterson, C. B., Wonderlich, S. & Crosby, R. D. (1998). Feeding laboratory studies in patients with eating disorders: a review. *International Journal of Eating Disorders*, *24*, 115–24.

Mitchell, W., Gorrell, R. W. & Greenberg, R. A. (1980). Failure-to-thrive: a study in a primary care setting. Epidemiology and follow-up. *Pediatrics*, *65*, 971–7.

Moffatt, M. E. K., Longstaffe, S., Besant, J. & Dureski, C. (1994). Prevention of iron deficiency and psychomotor decline in high-risk infants through use of iron-fortified formula: a randomised controlled trial. *Journal of Pediatrics*, *125*, 527–34.

Montague, C. T., Farooqi, I. S., Whitehead, J. P., *et al.* (1997). Congenital leptin deficiency is associated with severe early onset obesity in humans. *Nature*, *387*, 903–8.

Moore, L. L., Gao, D., Bradlee, M. L., *et al.* (2003). Does physical activity predict body fat change throughout childhood? *Preventive Medicine*, *37*, 10–17.

Moore, L. L., Lombardi, D. A., White, M. J., *et al.* (1991). Influence of parents' physical activity levels on activity levels of young children. *Journal of Pediatrics*, *118*, 215–19.

Moore, L. L., Singer, M. R., Bradlee, M. L., *et al.* (2005). Intake of fruits, vegetables, and dairy products in early childhood and subsequent blood pressure change. *Epidemiology*, *16*, 4–11.

Morison, S., Dodge, J. A., Cole, T. J., *et al.* (1997). Height and weight in cystic fibrosis: a cross sectional study. *Archives of Disease in Childhood*, *77*, 497–500.

Morrow, A. L., Guerrero, M. L., Shults, J., *et al.* (1999). Efficacy of home-based peer counselling to promote exclusive breast-feeding: a randomized controlled trial. *Lancet*, *353*, 1226–31.

Mortensen, E. L., Michaelsen, K. F., Sanders, S. A. & Reinisch, J. M. (2005). A dose-response relationship between maternal smoking during late pregnancy and adult intelligence in male offspring. *Paediatric and Perinatal Epidemiology*, *19*, 4–11.

Motarjemi, Y., Kaferstein, F., Moy, G. & Quevedo, F. (1993). Contaminated weaning food: a major risk factor for diarrhoea and associated malnutrition. *Bulletin of the World Health Organization*, *71*, 79–92.

Motion, S., Northstone, K., Emond, A., Stucke, S. & Golding, J. (2002). Early feeding problems in children with cerebral palsy: weight and neuro-developmental outcomes. *Developmental Medicine and Child Neurology*, *44*, 40–3.

Motion, S., Northstone, K., Emond, A. & the ALSPAC study team (2001). Persistent early feeding difficulties and subsequent growth and developmental outcomes. *Ambulatory Child Health*, *7*, 231–7.

Mrdjenovic, G. & Levitsky, D. A. (2005). Children eat what they are served: the imprecise regulation of energy intake. *Appetite*, *44*, 273–82.

Müller, M. J., Asbeck, I., Mast, M., Langnäse, K. & Grund, A. (2001). Prevention of obesity – more than an intention: concept and first results of the Kiel Obesity Prevention Study (KOPS). *International Journal of Obesity*, *25* Suppl 1, S66–S74.

Murphy, F., Troop, N. A. & Treasure, J. L. (2000). Differential environmental factors in anorexia nervosa. *British Journal of Clinical Psychology*, *39*, 193–203.

Murray, L. & Carothers, A. D. (1990). The validation of the Edinburgh Post-natal Depression Scale on a community sample. *British Journal of Psychiatry*, *157*, 288–90.

Must, A. & Strauss, R. (1999). Risks and consequences of childhood and adolescent obesity. *International Journal of Obesity*, *23* Suppl 2, S2–S11.

Mustillo, S., Worthman, C., Rekanli, A., Keeler, G., Angold, A. & Costello, E. J. (2003). Obesity and psychiatric disorder: developmental trajectories. *Pediatrics*, *111*, 851–9.

Negayama, K. (1993). Weaning in Japan: a longitudinal study of mother and child behaviours during milk- and solid-feeding. *Early Development and Parenting*, *2*, 29–37.

Neifert, M. R., Seacat, J. M. & Jobe, W. E. (1985). Lactation failure due to insufficient glandular development of the breast. *Pediatrics*, *76*, 823–8.

Nelson, M. C., Gordon-Larsen, P. & Adair, L. S. (2005). Are adolescents who were breast-fed less likely to be overweight? Analyses of sibling pairs to reduce confounding. *Epidemiology*, *16*, 247–53.

Nettelbeck, T. (2001). Correlation between inspection time and psychometric abilities. *Intelligence*, *29*, 459–74.

Nettelbeck, T. & Wilson, C. (2004). The Flynn effect: smarter not faster. *Intelligence*, *32*, 85–93.

Neville, M. C., Keller, R., Seacat, J., *et al.* (1988). Studies in human lactation: milk volumes in lactating women during the onset of lactation and full lactation. *American Journal of Clinical Nutrition*, *48*, 1375–86.

Newton, M. & Newton, N. R. (1948). The let-down reflex in human lactation. *Journal of Pediatrics*, *33*, 698–704.

Nicolaïdis, S., Galaverna, O. & Metzler, C. H. (1990). Extra cellular dehydration during pregnancy increases salt appetite of offspring. *American Journal of Physiology*, *258*, R281–3.

Nisbett, R. E. & Gurwitz, S. B. (1970). Weight, sex and the eating behaviour of human newborns. *Journal of Comparative and Physiological Psychology*, *73*, 245–53.

Noel, G. L., Suh, H. K. & Frantz, A. G. (1974). Prolactin release during nursing and breast stimulation in postpartum and nonpostpartum subjects. *Journal of Clinical Endocrinology and Metabolism*, *38*, 413–23.

Oates, R. K., Peacock, A. & Forrest, D. (1985). Long term effects of nonorganic failure to thrive. *Pediatrics*, *75*, 36–40.

O'Brien, K. M. & Vincent, N. K. (2003). Psychiatric comorbidity in anorexia and bulimia nervosa: nature, prevalence, and causal relationships. *Clinical Psychology Review*, *23*, 57–74.

O'Brien, L. M., Heycock, E. G., Hanna, M., Jones, P. W. & Cox, J. L. (2004). Postnatal depression and faltering growth: a community study. *Pediatrics*, *113*, 1242–7.

O'Brien, R. W., Smith, S. A., Bush, P. J. & Peleg, E. (1990). Obesity, self-esteem, and health locus of control in black youths during transition to adolescence. *American Journal of Health Promotion*, 5, 133–9.

Oddy, W. H., Kendall, G. E., Blair, E., *et al.* (2003). Breast feeding and cognitive development in childhood: a prospective birth cohort study. *Paediatric and Perinatal Epidemiology*, 17, 81–90.

Os, J. van, Jones, P., Wadsworth, M. & Murray, R. (1997). Developmental precursors of affective illness in a general population birth cohort. *Archives of General Psychiatry*, 54, 625–31.

Osmond, C., Barker, D. J. P., Winter, P. D., Fall, C. H. D. & Simmonds, S. J. (1993). Early growth and death from cardiovascular disease in women. *British Medical Journal*, 307, 837–40.

Ostrander, C. R., Cohen, R. S., Hopper, A. O., *et al.* (1983). Breath hydrogen analysis: a review of the methodologies and clinical applications. *Journal of Pediatric Gastroenterology and Nutrition*, 2, 525–33.

Ounstead, M., Moar, V. A. & Scott, A. (1985). Head circumference charts updated. *Archives of Disease in Childhood*, 60, 936–9.

Parkinson, K. N. & Drewett, R. F. (2001). Feeding behaviour in the weaning period. *Journal of Child Psychology and Psychiatry*, 42, 971–8.

Parkinson, K. N., Wright, C. M. & Drewett, R. F. (2004). Mealtime energy intake and feeding behaviour in children who fail to thrive: a population-based case-control study. *Journal of Child Psychology and Psychiatry*, 45, 1030–5.

Parkinson, K. W. (1998). *Feeding Behaviour in Late Infancy*. Ph.D. thesis, University of Durham.

Patel, P., Wheatcroft, R., Park, R. J. & Stein, A. (2002). The children of mothers with eating disorders. *Clinical Child and Family Psychology Review*, 5, 1–19.

Patel, V., DeSouza, N. & Rodrigues, M. (2003). Postnatal depression and infant growth and development in low income countries: a cohort study from Goa, India. *Archives of Disease in Childhood*, 88, 34–7.

Patel, V. & Prince, M. (2006). Maternal psychological morbidity and low birth weight in India. *British Journal of Psychiatry*, 188, 284–5.

Patton, G. C., Carlin, J. B., Shao, Q., *et al.* (1997). Adolescent dieting: healthy weight control or borderline eating disorders? *Journal of Child Psychology and Psychiatry*, 38, 299–306.

Patton, G. C., Johnson-Sabine, E., Wood, K., Mann, A. H. & Wakeling, A. (1990). Abnormal eating attitudes in London schoolgirls – a prospective epidemiological study: outcome at twelve month follow-up. *Psychological Medicine*, 20, 383–94.

Patton, G. C., Selzer, R., Coffey, G., Carlin, J. B. & Wolfe, R. (1999). Onset of adolescent eating disorders: population based cohort study over 3 years. *British Medical Journal*, 318, 765–8.

Pawluck, D. E. & Gorey, K. M. (1998). Secular trend in the incidence of anorexia nervosa: integrative review of population-based studies. *International Journal of Eating Disorders*, 23, 347–52.

Pearson, H. A. (1990). Prevention of iron-deficiency anemia: iron fortification of infant foods. In J. Dobbing (ed.), *Brain, Behaviour and Iron in the Infant Diet* (pp. 177–87). London: Springer-Verlag.

Pelchat, M. L. & Pliner, P. (1986). Antecedents and correlates of feeding problems in young children. *Journal of Nutrition Education*, *18*, 23–9.

Pelletier, D. L., Frongillo, E. A. & Habicht, J. P. (1993). Epidemiologic evidence for a potentiating effect of malnutrition on child mortality. *American Journal of Public Health*, *83*, 1130–3.

Pelletier, D. L., Frongillo, E. A., Schroeder, D. G. & Habicht, J. P. (1995). The effects of malnutrition on child mortality in developing countries. *Bulletin of the World Health Organization*, *73*, 443–8.

Pennington, B. F., Van Doornick, W. J., McCabe, L. L. & McCabe, E. R. B. (1985). Neuropsychological deficits in early-treated phenylketonuric children. *American Journal of Mental Deficiency*, *89*, 476–4.

Perry, C. L., Bishop, D. B., Taylor, G., *et al.* (1998). Changing fruit and vegetable consumption among children: the 5-a-day power program in St Paul, Minnesota. *American Journal of Public Health*, *84*, 603–9.

Perry, C. L., Kelder, S. H. & Klepp, K.-I. (1994). Community-wide cardiovascular disease prevention with young people: long-term outcomes in the Class of 1989 study. *European Journal of Public Health*, *4*, 188–94.

Pettitt, D. J., Baird, H. R., Aleck, K. A., Bennett, P. A. & Knowler, W. C. (1983). Excessive obesity in offspring of Pima Indian women with diabetes during pregnancy. *New England Journal of Medicine*, *308*, 242–5.

Phillips, D. I. W., Handelsman, D. J., Eriksson, J. G., *et al.* (2001). Prenatal growth and subsequent marital status: longitudinal study. *British Medical Journal*, *322*, 771.

Phillips, R. G. & Hill, A. J. (1998). Fat, plain but not friendless: self-esteem and peer acceptance of obese pre-adolescent girls. *International Journal of Obesity*, *22*, 287–93.

Pinelli, J. & Symington, A. (2005). Non-nutritive sucking for promoting physiological stability and nutrition in preterm infants (Cochrane Review). *The Cochrane Library*, *Issue 2* (pp. 1–21). Oxford: Update Software.

Pinilla, T. & Birch, L. L. (1993). Help me make it through the night: behavioral entrainment of breast-fed infants' sleep patterns. *Pediatrics*, *91*, 436–44.

Pliner, P. (1982). The effects of mere exposure on liking for edible substances. *Appetite*, *3*, 283–90.

Pliner, P., Eng, A. & Krishnan, K. (1995). The effects of fear and hunger on food neophobia in humans. *Appetite*, *25*, 77–87.

Pliner, P. & Hobden, K. (1992). Development of a scale to measure the trait of food neophobia in humans. *Appetite*, *19*, 105–20.

Pliner, P. & Loewen, E. R. (1997). Temperament and food neophobia in children and their mothers. *Appetite*, *28*, 239–54.

Pliner, P., Pelchat, M. & Grabski, M. (1993). Reduction of neophobia in humans by exposure to novel foods. *Appetite*, *20*, 111–23.

Poelmann, J. & Fiese, B. H. (2001). The interaction of maternal and infant vulnerabilities on developing attachment relationships. *Development and Psychopathology*, *13*, 1–11.

Polan, H. J., Kaplan, M. D., Kessler, D. B., *et al.* (1991). Psychopathology in mothers of children who fail to thrive. *Infant Mental Health Journal*, *12*, 55–64.

Pollitt, E. (1975). Failure to thrive: socioeconomic, dietary intake and mother–child interaction data. *Federation Proceedings*, *34*, 1593–7.

(1993). Iron deficiency and cognitive function. *Annual Review of Nutrition*, *13*, 521–37.

(1995). Functional significance of the covariance between protein energy malnutrition and iron deficiency anemia. *Journal of Nutrition*, *125*, 2272S–7S.

Pollitt, E. & Eichler, A. (1976). Behavioral disturbances among failure-to-thrive children. *American Journal of Diseases of Children*, *130*, 24–9.

Pollitt, E., Eichler, A. W. & Chan, C. K. (1975). Psychosocial development and behaviour of mothers of failure-to-thrive children. *American Journal of Orthopsychiatry*, *45*, 525–37.

Pollitt, E., Gorman, K., Engle, P., Martorell, R. & Rivera, J. (1993). Early supplementary feeding and cognition. *Monographs of the Society for Research in Child Development*, *58*, 1–118.

Pond, C. M. (1977). The significance of lactation in the evolution of mammals. *Evolution*, *31*, 177–99.

(1983). Parental feeding as a determinant of ecological relationships in Mesozoic terrestrial ecosystems. *Palaeontologica*, *28*, 215–23.

(1998). *The Fats of Life*. Cambridge: Cambridge University Press.

Poskitt, E. M. E. & Cole, T. J. (1977). Do fat babies stay fat? *British Medical Journal*, *1*, 7–9.

Poustie, V. J. & Rutherford, P. (2003). Dietary interventions for phenylketonuria (Cochrane Review). *The Cochrane Library, Issue 2*. Oxford: Update Software.

Power, C., Lake, J. K. & Cole, T. J. (1997). Measurement and long-term health risks of child and adolescent fatness. *International Journal of Obesity*, *21*, 507–26.

Powers, S. W., Patton, S. R., Byars, K. C., *et al.* (2002). Caloric intake and eating behaviour in infants and toddlers with cystic fibrosis. *Pediatrics*, *109*, 1–10.

Pratt, B. M. & Woolfenden, S. R. (2004). Interventions for preventing eating disorders in children and adolescents (Cochrane Review). *The Cochrane Library, Issue 3*. Chichester, UK: John Wiley.

Prechtl, H. F. R. (1958). The directed head turning response and allied movements of the human baby. *Behaviour*, *13*, 212–42.

Preece, M. A., Freeman, J. V. & Cole, T. J. (1996). Sex differences in weight in infancy: published centile charts have been updated. *British Medical Journal*, *313*, 1486.

Prentice, A. M. (2002). Measurement of energy expenditure. In C. Fairburn & K. Brownell (eds.), *Eating Disorders and Obesity: A Comprehensive Handbook* (pp. 131–5). New York: Guilford Press.

Prentice, A. M. & Jebb, S. A. (1995). Obesity in Britain: gluttony or sloth? *British Medical Journal*, *311*, 437–9.

Prentice, A. M. & Moore, S. E. (2005). Early programming of adult diseases in resource poor countries. *Archives of Disease in Childhood*, *90*, 429–32.

Price, R. A. & Gottesman, I. I. (1991). Body fat in identical twins reared apart: roles for genes and environment. *Behavior Genetics*, *21*, 1–7.

Purvis, A. (2005). What's for tea? *The Observer Food Monthly*, April, 11–20.

Rahman, A., Lovel, H., Bunn, J., Iqbal, Z. & Harrington, R. (2004). Mothers' mental health and infant growth: a case-control study from Rawalpindi, Pakistan. *Child: Care, Health and Development*, *30*, 21–7.

Ramenghi, L. A., Evans, D. J. & Levene, M. I. (1999). 'Sucrose analgesia': absorptive mechanism or taste perception? *Archives of Disease in Childhood Fetal and Neonatal Edition*, *80*, F146–F147.

Ramenghi, L. A., Griffith, G. C., Wood, C. M. & Levine, M. I. (1996). Effect of non-sucrose sweet tasting solution on neonatal heel prick responses. *Archives of Disease in Childhood*, *74*, F129–F131.

Ramenghi, L. A., Wood, C. M., Griffith, G. C. & Levene, M. I. (1996). Reduction of pain response in premature infants using intraoral sucrose. *Archives of Disease in Childhood*, *74*, F126–F128.

Ramsay, D. T., Kent, J. C., Owens, R. A. & Hartmann, P. E. (2004). Ultrasound imaging of milk ejection in the breast of lactating women. *Pediatrics*, *113*, 361–7.

Ramsay, M., Gisel, E. G. & Boutry, M. (1993). Non-organic failure to thrive: growth failure secondary to feeding-skills disorder. *Developmental Medicine and Child Neurology*, *35*, 285–97.

Ransjö-Arvidson, A.-B., Matthiesen, A.-S., Lilja, G., *et al.* (2001). Maternal analgesia during labor disturbs newborn behaviour: effects on breastfeeding, temperature, and crying. *Birth*, *28*, 5–12.

Rasmussen, K. M. (2001). The 'fetal origins' hypothesis: challenges and opportunities for maternal and child nutrition. *Annual Review of Nutrition*, *21*, 73–95.

Råstam, M. (1992). Anorexia nervosa in 51 Swedish adolescents: premorbid problems and comorbidity. *Journal of the American Academy of Child and Adolescent Psychiatry*, *31*, 819–29.

Rattigan, S., Ghisalberti, A. V. & Hartmann, P. E. (1981). Breast-milk production in Australian women. *British Journal of Nutrition*, *45*, 243–9.

Ravelli, G., Stein, Z. A. & Susser, M. W. (1976). Obesity in young men after famine exposure in utero and early infancy. *New England Journal of Medicine*, *295*, 349–53.

Record, R. G., McKeown, T. & Edwards, J. H. (1969). The relation of measured intelligence to birth weight and duration of gestation. *Annals of Human Genetics*, *33*, 71–9.

Reilly, J. R., Armstrong, J., Dorosty, A. R., *et al.* (2005). Early life risk factors for obesity in childhood: cohort study. *British Medical Journal*, *330*, 1357–63.

Reilly, S. & Skuse, D. (1992). Characteristics and management of feeding problems of young children with cerebral palsy. *Developmental Medicine and Child Neurology*, *34*, 379–88.

Reilly, S., Skuse, D. & Poblete, X. (1996). Prevalence of feeding problems and oral motor dysfunction in children with cerebral palsy: a community survey. *Journal of Pediatrics*, *129*, 877–82.

Reilly, S. M., Skuse, D. H., Wolke, D. & Stevenson, J. (1999). Oral-motor dysfunction in children who fail to thrive: organic or non-organic? *Developmental Medicine and Child Neurology*, *41*, 115–22.

Resnicow, K., Smith, P., Baranowski, T., Baranowski, J., Vaughan, R. & Davis, M. (1998). 2-year tracking of children's fruit and vegetable intake. *Journal of the American Dietetic Association*, *98*, 785–9.

Reynolds, O. (1996). Causes and outcome of perinatal brain injury. In D. Magnusson (ed.), *The Lifespan Development of Individuals: Behavioral, Neurobiological, and Psychosocial Perspectives* (pp. 52–75). Cambridge: Cambridge University Press.

Rider, E. A. & Bithoney, W. G. (1999). Medical asssessment and management and the organization of medical services. In D. B. Kessler & P. Dawson (eds.), *Failure to Thrive and Pediatric Undernutrition: A Transdisciplinary Approach* (pp. 173–93). Baltimore, MD: Paul H. Brookes Publishing Co.

Roberts, S. J., Maxwell, S. M., Bagnall, G. & Bilton, R. (2001). The incidence of dieting amongst adolescent girls: a question of interpretation. *Journal of Human Nutrition and Dietetics, 14,* 103–9.

Robinson, T. N. (1999). Reducing children's television viewing to prevent obesity: a randomised controlled trial. *Journal of the American Medical Association, 282,* 1561–7.

Robinson, T. N., Hammer, L. D., Killen, J. D., *et al.* (1993). Does television viewing increase obesity and reduce physical activity? Cross-sectional and longitudinal analyses among adolescent girls. *Pediatrics, 91,* 273–80.

Robinson, T. N., Kiernan, M., Matheson, D. M. & Haydel, K. F. (2001). Is parental control over children's eating associated with childhood obesity? Results from a population-based sample of third graders. *Obesity Research, 9,* 306–12.

Rodgers, J. L., Cleveland, H. H., van den Oord, E. & Rowe, D. C. (2000). Resolving the debate over birth order, family size and intelligence. *American Psychologist, 55,* 599–612.

Rogers, I. (2003). The influence of birthweight and the intrauterine environment on adiposity and fat distribution in later life. *International Journal of Obesity, 27,* 755–77.

Rogers, I. S., Emmett, P. M. & Golding, J. (1997). The incidence and duration of breastfeeding. *Early Human Development, 49* Suppl, S45–S74.

Rolland-Cachera, M. F., Deheeger, M., Bellisele, F., *et al.* (1984). Adiposity rebound in children: a simple indicator for predicting obesity. *American Journal of Clinical Nutrition, 39,* 129–35.

Rolls, B. J., Engell, D. & Birch, L. L. (2000). Serving portion size influences 5-year-old but not 3-year-old children's food intakes. *Journal of the American Dietetic Association, 100,* 232–4.

Roncagliolo, M., Garrido, M., Walter, T., Peirano, P. & Lozoff, B. (1998). Evidence of altered central nervous system development in infants with iron deficient anemia a 6 mo: delayed maturation of auditory brainstem responses. *American Journal of Clinical Nutrition, 68,* 683–6.

Rose, S. A. & Feldman, J. F. (2000). The relation of very low birthweight to basic cognitive skills in infancy and childhood. In C. Nelson (ed.), *The Effects of Early Adversity on Neurobehavioural Development* (pp. 31–59). Mahwah, NJ: Lawrence Erlbaum Associates.

Rosenfeld, M., Davis, R., FitzSimmons, S., Pepe, M. & Ramsey, B. (1997). Gender gap in cystic fibrosis mortality. *American Journal of Epidemiology, 145,* 794–803.

Rosenstein, D. & Oster, H. (1988). Differential facial responses to four basic tastes in newborns. *Child Development, 59,* 1555–68.

Rowland, M. G. M., Barrell, R. A. E. & Whitehead, R. G. (1978). Bacterial contamination in traditional Gambian weaning foods. *Lancet*, *1*, 136–8.

Rowlands, A. V., Ingledew, D. K., Powell, S. M. & Eston, R. G. (2004). Interactive effects of habitual physical activity and calcium intake on bone density in boys and girls. *Journal of Applied Physiology*, *97*, 1203–8.

Rozin, P. (1976). The selection of foods by rats, humans and other animals. In J. S. Rosenblatt, R. A. Hinde, E. Shaw & C. Beer (eds.), *Advances in the Study of Behavior*, vol. VI (pp. 21–76). New York: Academic Press.

Rozin, P., Dow, S., Moscovitch, M. & Rajaram, S. (1998). What causes humans to begin and end a meal? A role for memory for what has been eaten, as evidenced by a study of multiple meal eating in amnesic patients. *Psychological Science*, *9*, 392–6.

Rozin, P., Fallon, A. & Augustoni-Ziskind, M. (1985). The child's conception of food: the development of contamination sensitivity to 'disgusting' substances. *Developmental Psychology*, *21*, 1075–9.

Rozin, P., Hammer, L., Oster, H., Horowitz, T. & Marmora, V. (1986). The child's conception of food: differentiation of catagories of rejected substances in the 16 months to 5 year age range. *Appetite*, *7*, 141–51.

Rozin, P. & Millman, L. (1987). Family environment, not heredity, accounts for family resemblances in food preferences and attitudes: a twin study. *Appetite*, *8*, 125–34.

Rudolf, M. C. J. & Logan, S. (2005). What is the long term outcome for children who fail to thrive? A systematic review. *Archives of Disease in Childhood*, *90*, 925–31.

Russell, G. (1979). Bulimia nervosa: an ominous variant of anorexia nervosa. *Psychological Medicine*, *9*, 429–48.

Russell, G. F. M. (1995). Anorexia nervosa through time. In G. Szmukler, C. Dare & J. Treasure (eds.), *Handbook of Eating Disorders* (pp. 5–17). Chichester: Wiley.

  (2004). Thoughts on the 25th anniversary of bulimia nervosa. *European Eating Disorders Review*, *12*, 139–52.

Russell, H. & Oliver, C. (2003). The assessment of food-related problems in individuals with Prader-Willi syndrome. *British Journal of Clinical Psychology*, *42*, 379–92.

Rutter, M., Caspi, A. & Moffitt, T. E. (2003). Using sex differences in psychopathology to study causal mechanisms: unifying issues and research strategies. *Journal of Child Psychology and Psychiatry*, *44*, 1092–115.

Rutter, M., Tizard, J. & Whitmore, K. (1970). *Education, Health and Behaviour*. London: Longman Group Ltd.

Rydell, A.-M., Dahl, M. & Sundelin, C. (1995). Characteristics of school children who are choosy eaters. *Journal of Genetic Psychology*, *156*, 217–29.

Sachdev, H. P. S., Krishna, J., Puri, R. K., Satyanarayana, L. & Kumar, S. (1991). Water supplementation in exclusively breastfed infants during summer in the tropics. *Lancet*, *337*, 929–33.

Saelens, B. E., Ernst, M. M. & Epstein, L. H. (2000). Maternal child feeding practices and obesity: a discordant sibling analysis. *International Journal of Eating Disorders*, *27*, 459–63.

Sahota, P., Rudolf, M. C. J., Dixey, R., *et al.* (2004a). Evaluation of implementation and effect of primary school based intervention to reduce risk factors for obesity. *British Medical Journal, 323,* 1027–9.

Sahota, P., Rudolf, M. C. J., Dixey, R., *et al.* (2004b). Randomised controlled trial of primary school based intervention to reduce risk factors for obesity. *British Medical Journal, 323,* 1029–34.

Saint, L., Maggiore, P. & Hartmann, P. E. (1986). Yield and nutrient content of milk in eight women breast-feeding twins and one woman breast-feeding triplets. *British Journal of Nutrition, 56,* 49–58.

Sallade, A. (1973). A comparison of psychological adjustment of obese vs non-obese children. *Journal of Psychosomatic Research, 17,* 89–96.

Sanchez-Grinan, M. I., Peerson, J. M. & Brown, K. H. (1991). Effect of dietary energy density on total ad-libitum energy consumption by recovering malnourished children. *European Journal of Clinical Nutrition, 46,* 197–204.

Satter, E. M. (1996). Internal regulation and the evolution of normal growth as the basis for prevention of obesity in children. *Journal of the American Dietetic Association, 96,* 860–4.

Saxena, S., Ambler, G., Cole, T. J. & Majeed, A. (2004). Ethnic group differences in overweight and obese children and young people in England: cross sectional survey. *Archives of Disease in Childhood, 89,* 30–6.

Scarr, S., Weinberg, R. A. & Waldman, I. D. (1993). IQ correlations in transracial adoptive families. *Intelligence, 17,* 541–55.

Schiff, M., Duyme, M., Dumaret, A., *et al.* (1978). Intellectual status of working-class children adopted early into upper middle-class families. *Science, 200,* 1503–4.

Schnittker, J. (2005). Chronic illness and depressive symptoms in late life. *Social Science and Medicine, 60,* 13–23.

Sclafani, A. (1997). Learned control of ingestive behaviour. *Appetite, 29,* 153–8.

Scott, J. A. & Binns, C. W. (1999). Factors associated with the initiation and duration of breastfeeding: a review of the literature. *Breastfeeding Reviews, 7,* 5–16.

Scriver, C. R., & Clow, C. L. (1980a). Phenylketonuria: epitome of human biochemical genetics. (First of two parts.) *New England Journal of Medicine, 303,* 1336–42.

  (1980b). Phenylketonuria: epitome of human biochemical genetics. (Second of two parts.) *New England Journal of Medicine, 303,* 1394–400.

Seidman, D. S., Laor, A., Gale, R., Stevenson, D. K. & Danon, Y. L. (1991). A longitudinal study of birthweight and being overweight in late adolescence. *American Journal of Diseases of Children, 145,* 782–5.

Shaoul, R., Kessel, A., Toubi, E., *et al.* (2003). Leptin and cytokines levels in children with failure to thrive. *Journal of Pediatric Gastroenterology and Nutrition, 37,* 487–91.

Shea, S., Stein, A., Basch, C., Contento, I. & Zybert, P. (1992). Variability and self-regulation of energy intake in young children in their everyday environment. *Pediatrics, 90,* 542–6.

Shenkin, S., Starr, J. M. & Deary, I. J. (2004). Birth weight and cognitive ability in childhood: a systematic review. *Psychological Bulletin, 130,* 989–1013.

Shenkin, S., Starr, J. M., Rush, M. A., Whalley, L. J. & Deary, I. J. (2001). Birth weight and cognitive function at age 11 years: the Scottish Mental Survey 1932. *Archives of Disease in Childhood*, 85, 189–97.

Sherriff, A., Emond, A., Bell, J. C., Golding, G. & the ALSPAC study team. (2001). Should infants be screened for anaemia? A prospective study investigating the relation between haemoglobin at 8, 12, and 18 months and development at 18 months. *Archives of Disease in Childhood*, 84, 480–5.

Sherry, B. (1999). Epidemiology of inadequate growth. In D. B. Kessler & P. Dawson (eds.), *Failure to Thrive and Pediatric Undernutrition: A Transdisciplinary Approach* (pp. 19–36). Baltimore, MD: Paul H. Brookes Publishing Co.

Shields, J. (1962). *Monozygotic Twins: Brought up Apart and Brought up Together*. London: Oxford University Press.

Shunk, J. A. & Birch, L. L. (2004). Validity of dietary restraint among 5- to 9-year old girls. *Appetite*, 42, 241–7.

Siegal, M. (1988). Children's knowledge of contagion and contamination as causes of illness. *Child Development*, 59, 1353–9.

(1997). *Knowing Children: Experiments in Conversation and Cognition* (2nd edn). Hove: Psychology Press Ltd.

Sigman, M., McDonald, M. A., Newmann, C. & Bwibo, N. (1991). Prediction of cognitive competence in Kenyan children from toddler nutrition, family characteristics and abilities. *Journal of Child Psychology and Psychiatry*, 32, 307–20.

Sigman, M., Neumann, C., Baksh, M., Bwibo, M. & McDonald, M. A. (1989). Relations between nutrition and development in Kenyan toddlers. *Journal of Pediatrics*, 115, 357–64.

Sigman, M., Neumann, C., Carter, E., *et al.* (1988). Home interactions and the development of Embu toddlers in Kenya. *Child Development*, 59, 1251–61.

Signorelli, N. & Lears, M. (1992). Television and children's conceptions of nutrition. *Health Communication*, 4, 245–57.

Silverstein, B., Perdue, L., Peterson, B., Vogel, L. & Fantini, D. A. (1986). Possible causes of the thin standard of bodily attractiveness for women. *International Journal of Eating Disorders*, 5, 907–16.

Silverstein, B., Peterson, B. & Perdue, L. (1986). Some correlates of the thin standard of body attractiveness for women. *International Journal of Eating Disorders*, 5, 895–905.

Simeon, D. T. & Grantham-McGregor, S. M. (1990). Nutritional deficiencies and children's behaviour and mental development. *Nutrition Research Reviews*, 3, 1–24.

Simpson, C., Schanler, R. J. & Lau, C. (2002). Early introduction of oral feeding in preterm infants. *Pediatrics*, 110, 517–22.

Simpson, J. & Stephenson, T. (1993). Regulation of extracellular fluid volume in neonates. *Early Human Development*, 34, 179–90.

Singer, M. R., Moore, L. L., Garrahie, E. J. & Ellison, R. C. (1995). The tracking of nutrient intake in young children: the Framingham children's study. *American Journal of Public Health*, 85, 1673–7.

Skuse, D. (1993). Epidemiological and definitional issues in failure to thrive. *Child and Adolescent Psychiatric Clinics*, 2, 37–59.

Skuse, D., Gill, D., Reilly, S., Wolke, D. & Lynch, M. (1995). Failure to thrive and the risk of child abuse: a prospective population study. *Journal of Medical Screening*, 2, 145–9.

Skuse, D., Pickles, A., Wolke, D. & Reilly, S. (1994). Postnatal growth and mental development: evidence for a 'sensitive period'. *Journal of Child Psychology and Psychiatry*, 35, 521–45.

Skuse, D., Stevenson, J., Reilly, S. & Mathisen, B. (1995). Schedule for oral-motor assessment (SOMA): methods of validation. *Dysphagia*, 10, 192–202.

Skuse, D., Wolke, D. & Reilly, S. (1992). Failure to thrive: clinical and developmental aspects. In H. Remschmidt & M. Schmidt (eds.), *Developmental Psychopathology* (pp. 46–71). Lewiston, NY: Hogrefe & Huber.

Slater, A. (1995). Individual differences in infancy and later IQ. *Journal of Child Psychology and Psychiatry*, 36, 69–112.

Smith, I., Beasley, M. G. & Ades, A. E. (1990a). Effect on intelligence of relaxing the low phenylalanine diet in phenylketonuria. *Archives of Disease in Childhood*, 65, 311–16.

(1990b). Intelligence and quality of dietary treatment in phenylketonuria. *Archives of Disease in Childhood*, 65, 472–8.

Smith, I. & Knowles, J. (2000). Behaviour in early treated phenylketonuria: a systematic review. *European Journal of Pediatrics*, 159 [Suppl 2], S89–S93.

Smith, M. L., Hanley, W. B., Clarke, J. T. R., *et al.* (1998). Randomised controlled trial of tyrosine supplementation on neuropsychological performance in phenylketonuria. *Archives of Disease in Childhood*, 78, 116–21.

Sobal, J. & Stunkard, A. J. (1989). Socioeconomic status and obesity: a review of the literature. *Psychological Bulletin*, 105, 260–75.

Sørenson, H. T., Sabroe, S., Olsen, J., Rothman, K. J., Gillman, M. W. & Fisher, P. (1997). Birth weight and cognitive function in young adult life: historical cohort study. *British Medical Journal*, 315, 401–3.

Spitzer, R. L., Devlin, M., Walsh, B. T., *et al.* (1992). Binge eating disorder: a multisite field trial of the diagnostic criteria. *International Journal of Eating Disorders*, 11, 191–203.

Spitzer, R. L., Yanovski, S., Wadden, T. A. & Wing, R. (1993). Binge eating disorder: its further validation in a multisite study. *International Journal of Eating Disorders*, 13, 137–53.

Spooner, B. & Roberts, P. (2005). *Fungi*. London: HarperCollins.

Spruijt-Metz, D., Lindquist, C. H., Birch, L. L., Fisher, J. O. & Goran, M. I. (2002). Relation between mothers' child-feeding practices and children's adiposity. *American Journal of Clinical Nutrition*, 75, 581–6.

Stamatakis, E., Primatesta, P., Chinn, S., Rona, R. & Falacheti, E. (2005). Overweight and obesity trends from 1974 to 2003 in English children: what is the role of socioeconomic factors? *Archives of Disease in Childhood*, 90, 999–1004.

Stark, L. (2003). Can nutritional counselling be more behavioural? Lessons learned fron dietary management of cystic fibrosis. *Proceedings of the Nutrition Society*, 62, 793–9.

Stark, L. J., Jelalian, E., Powers, S. W., et al. (2000). Parent and child mealtime behaviors in families of children with cystic fibrosis. *Journal of Pediatrics*, *136*, 195–200.

Stark, L. J., Mulvihill, M. M., Jelalian, E., et al. (1997). Descriptive analysis of eating behavior in school-age children with cystic fibrosis and healthy control children. *Pediatrics*, *99*, 665–71.

Stein, A., Murray, L., Cooper, P. & Fairburn, C. G. (1996). Infant growth in the context of maternal eating disorders and maternal depression: a comparative study. *Psychological Medicine*, *26*, 569–74.

Stein, A., Stein, J., Walters, E. A. & Fairburn, C. G. (1995). Eating habits and attitudes among mothers of children with feeding disorders. *British Medical Journal*, *310*, 228.

Stein, A., Woolley, H., Cooper, S. D. & Fairburn, C. G. (1994). An observational study of mothers with eating disorders and their infants. *Journal of Child Psychology and Psychiatry*, *35*, 733–48.

Stein, Z., Susser, M., Saenger, G. & Marolla, F. (1972). Nutrition and mental performance: prenatal exposure to the Dutch famine of 1944–1945 seems not to be related to mental performance at age 19. *Science*, *178*, 708–13.

Steiner, J. E. (1973). The gusto-facial response: observations on normal and anencephalic newborn infants. In J. F. Bosma (ed.), *Oral Sensation and Perception* (pp. 254–78). Bethesda: US Dept H.E.W. Publications.

Stephenson, D. M., Gardner, J. M. M., Walker, S. P. & Ashworth, A. (1994). Weaning-food viscosity and energy density: their effects on ad libitum consumption and energy intakes in Jamaican children. *American Journal of Clinical Nutrition*, *60*, 465–9.

Stevenson, R. D. & Allaire, J. H. (1991). The development of normal feeding and swallowing. *Pediatric Clinics of North America*, *38*, 1439–53.

Stevenson, R. D., Roberts, C. D. & Vogle, L. (1995). The effects of non-nutritional factors on growth in cerebral palsy. *Developmental Medicine and Child Neurology*, *37*, 124–30.

Stice, E. (2002). Risk and maintenance factors for eating disorders. *Psychological Bulletin*, *128*, 825–48.

Stice, E. & Agras, W. S. (1998). Predicting onset and cessation of bulimic behaviors during adolescence: a longitudinal grouping analysis. *Behavior Therapy*, *29*, 257–76.

Stice, E., Agras, W. S. & Hammer, L. D. (1999). Risk factors for the emergence of childhood eating disturbances: a five-year prospective study. *International Journal of Eating Disorders*, *25*, 375–87.

Stice, E., Akutagawa, D., Gaggar, A. & Agras, W. S. (2000). Negative affect moderates the relationship between dieting and binge eating. *International Journal of Eating Disorders*, *27*, 218–29.

Stice, E. & Bearman, S. K. (2001). Body-image and eating disturbances prospectively predict growth in depressive symptoms in adolescent girls. *Developmental Psychology*, *37*, 597–607.

Stice, E., Hayward, C., Cameron, R., Killen, J. D. & Taylor, C. B. (2000). Body image and eating disturbances predict onset of depression in female adolescents: a longitudinal study. *Journal of Abnormal Psychology*, *109*, 438–44.

Stice, E. & Shaw, H. E. (2002). Role of body dissatisfaction in the onset and maintenance of eating pathology: a synthesis of research findings. *Journal of Psychosomatic Research*, *53*, 985–93.

Stoltzfus, R. J., Kvalsvig, J. D., Chwaya, H. M., *et al.* (2001). Effects of iron supplementation and anti-helmintic treatment on motor and language development of preschool children in Zanzibar: double blind, placebo controlled study. *British Medical Journal*, *323*, 1–8.

Story, M. (1999). School-based approaches for preventing and treating obesity. *International Journal of Obesity*, *23* Suppl 2, S43–S51.

Strauss, R. S. (2000). Childhood obesity and self-esteem. *Pediatrics*, *105*, 15–19.

Strauss, R. S. & Dietz, W. H. (1998). Growth and development of term children born with low birth weight: effects of genetic and environmental factors. *Journal of Pediatrics*, *133*, 67–72.

Striegel-Moore, R. H., Dohm, F. A., Solomon, E. E., Fairburn, C. G., Pike, K. M. & Wifley, D. E. (2000). Subthreshold binge eating disorder. *International Journal of Eating Disorders*, *27*, 270–8.

Strien, T. van, Frijters, J. E. R., Bergers, G. P. A. & Defares, P. B. (1986). The Dutch Eating Behavior Questionnaire (DEBQ) for assessment of restrained, emotional, and external eating behavior. *International Journal of Eating Disorders*, *5*, 295–315.

Strobel, A., Issad, T., Camoin, L., Ozata, M. & Strosberg, A. D. (1998). A leptin missense mutation associated with hypogonadism and morbid obesity. *Nature Genetics*, *18*, 213–15.

Strober, M., Freeman, R., Lampert, C., Diamond, J. & Kaye, W. (2000). Controlled family study of anorexia nervosa and bulimia nervosa: evidence of shared liability and transmission of partial syndromes. *American Journal of Psychiatry*, *157*, 393–401.

Strupp, B. & Levitsky, D. (1995). Enduring cognitive effects of early malnutrition: a theoretical reappraisal. *Journal of Nutrition*, *125*, 2221S–32S.

Stunkard, A., Berkowitz, R., Stallings, V. & Schoeller, D. (1999). Energy intake, not energy output, is a determinant of body size in infants. *American Journal of Clinical Nutrition*, *69*, 524–30.

Stunkard, A. J., Harris, J. R., Pedersen, N. L. & McClearn, G. E. (1990). The body-mass index of twins who have been reared apart. *New England Journal of Medicine*, *322*, 1483–7.

Stunkard, A. J. & Messick, S. (1985). The three-factor eating questionnaire to measure dietary restraint, disinhibition and hunger. *Journal of Psychosomatic Research*, *29*, 71–83.

Stunkard, A. J., Sørenson, T. & Schulsinger, F. (1983). Use of the Danish adoption register for the study of obesity and thinness. In S. Kety, L. Rowland, R. Sidman & S. Matthysse (eds.), *The Genetics of Neurological and Psychiatric Disorders* (pp. 115–20). New York: Raven Press.

Sullivan, P. B., Juszczak, E., Lambert, B. R., *et al.* (2002). Impact of feeding problems on nutritional intake and growth: Oxford Feeding Study II. *Developmental Medicine and Child Neurology*, *44*, 461–7.

Sullivan, P. B., Lambert, B., Rose, M., *et al.* (2000). Prevalence and severity of feeding and nutritional problems in children with neurological impairment:

Oxford Feeding Study. *Developmental Medicine and Child Neurology*, *42*, 674–80.

Sullivan, S. A. & Birch, L. L. (1990). Pass the sugar, pass the salt: experience dictates preference. *Developmental Psychobiology*, *26*, 546–51.

(1994). Infant dietary experience and acceptance of solid foods. *Pediatrics*, *93*, 271–7.

Sutton, A. J., Abrams, K. R., Jones, D. R., Sheldon, T. A. & Song, F. (2000). *Methods for Meta-analysis in Medical Research*. Chichester: John Wiley & Sons.

Swift, A. V., Cohen, M. J., Hynd, G. W., *et al.* (1989). Neuropsychological impairment in children with sickle cell anemia. *Pediatrics*, *84*, 1077–85.

Tanner, J. M. (1989). *Foetus into Man* (2nd edn). Ware: Castlemead Publications.

Tanner, J. M. & Thompson, A. M. (1970). Standards for birthweight at gestation periods from 32 to 42 weeks, allowing for maternal height and weight. *Archives of Disease in Childhood*, *45*, 566–9.

Taras, H. L., Sallis, J. F., Patterson, T. L., Nader, P. R. & Nelson, J. A. (1989). Television's influence on children's diet and physical activity. *Journal of Developmental and Behavioral Pediatrics*, *10*, 176–80.

Taveras, E. M., Scanlon, K. S., Birch, L., *et al.* (2004). Association of breast-feeding with maternal control of infant feeding at age 1 year. *Pediatrics*, *114*, 577–83.

Teasdale, T. W. & Owen, D. R. (1989). Continuing secular increases in intelligence and a stable prevalence of high intelligence levels. *Intelligence*, *13*, 255–62.

Thommessen, M., Heiberg, A., Kase, B. F., Larsen, S. & Riis, G. (1991). Feeding problems, height and weight in different groups of disabled children. *Acta Paediatrica Scandinavica*, *80*, 527–33.

Thompson, C., Syddall, H., Rodin, I., Osmond, C. & Barker, D. J. P. (2001). Birth weight and the risk of depressive disorder in late life. *British Journal of Psychiatry*, *179*, 450–5.

Tinsley, B. J. (2003). *How Children Learn to be Healthy*. Cambridge: Cambridge University Press.

Tizard, J., Schofield, W. N. & Hewison, J. (1982). Collaboration between teachers and parents in assisting children's reading. *British Journal of Educational Psychology*, *52*, 1–15.

Toates, F. (2001). *Biological Psychology: An Integrative Approach*. Harlow: Prentice Hall.

Tolia, V. (1995). Very early onset nonorganic failure to thrive in infants. *Journal of Pediatric Gastroenterology and Nutrition*, *20*, 73–80.

Torun, B., Davies, P. S. W., Livingstone, M. B. E., *et al.* (1996). Energy requirements and dietary recomendations for children and adolescents 1 to 18 years old. *European Journal of Clinical Nutrition*, *50* Suppl 1, S37–S81.

Toschke, A. M., Vignerova, J., Lhotska, L., *et al.* (2002). Overweight and obesity in 6- to 14-year-old Czech children in 1991: protective effect of breast-feeding. *Journal of Pediatrics*, *141*, 764–9.

Treasure, J. & Holland, A. (1995). Genetic factors in eating disorders. In G. Szmukler, C. Dare & J. Treasure (eds.), *Handbook of Eating Disorders* (pp. 65–81). Chichester: John Wiley & Sons.

Treasure, J. L. & Russell, G. M. F. (1988). Intrauterine growth and neonatal weight gain in babies of women with anorexia nervosa. *British Medical Journal*, *296*, 1038.

Troiano, R. P., Briefel, R. R., Carroll, M. D. & Bialostosky, K. (2000). Energy and fat intakes of children and adolescents in the United States: data from the National Health and Nutrition Examination Surveys. *American Journal of Clinical Nutrition*, *72* (Suppl), 1343S–53S.

Troiano, R. P. & Flegal, K. M. (1998). Overweight children and adolescents: description, epidemiology, and demographics. *Pediatrics*, *101* Suppl, 497–504.

Troiano, R. P., Frongillo, E. A. J., Sobal, J. & Levitsky, D. A. (1996). The relationship between body weight and mortality: a quantitative analysis of combined information from existing studies. *International Journal of Obesity*, *20*, 63–75.

Truby, H. & Paxton, S. J. (2001). Body image and dieting behavior in cystic fibrosis. *Pediatrics*, *107*, 1–7.

(2002). Development of the children's body image scale. *British Journal of Clinical Psychology*, *41*, 185–203.

Tuschl, R. J., Platte, P., Laessle, R. G., Stichler, W. & Pirke, K. (1990). Energy expenditure and everyday eating behavior in healthy young women. *American Journal of Clinical Nutrition*, *52*, 81–6.

Vågerö, D. & Modin, B. (2002). Prenatal growth, subsequent marital status, and mortality: longitudinal study. *British Medical Journal*, *324*, 398.

Vaisse, C., Clément, K., Guy-Grand, B. & Froguel, P. (1998). A frameshift mutation in human *MC4R* is associated with a dominant form of obesity. *Nature Genetics*, *20*, 113–14.

Valenzuela, M. (1990). Attachment in chronically underweight young children. *Child Development*, *61*, 1984–90.

(1997). Maternal sensitivity in a developing society: the context of urban poverty and infant chronic undernutrition. *Developmental Psychology*, *33*, 845–55.

Varendi, H., Porter, R. H. & Winberg, J. (1994). Does the newborn baby find the nipple by smell? *Lancet*, *344*, 989–90.

Vernon, P. A., Wickett, J. C., Bazana, P. G. & Stelmack, R. M. (2000). The neuropsychology and psychophysiology of human intelligence. In R. Sternberg (ed.), *Handbook of Intelligence* (pp. 245–64). Cambridge: Cambridge University Press.

Veron-Guidry, S. & Williamson, D. A. (1996). Development of a body image assessment procedure for children and preadolescents. *International Journal of Eating Disorders*, *20*, 287–93.

Villar, J. & Belizan, J. M. (1982). The relative contribution of prematurity and fetal growth retardation to low birth weight in developing and developed countries. *American Journal of Obstetrics and Gynecology*, *143*, 793–8.

Vobecky, J. S., Vobecky, J. & Froda, S. (1988). The reliability of the maternal memory in a retrospective assessment of nutritional status. *Journal of Clinical Epidemiology*, *41*, 261–5.

Von Kries, R., Koletzko, B., Sauerwald, T., *et al.* (1999). Breast feeding and obesity: cross-sectional study. *British Medical Journal*, *319*, 147–50.

Wadden, T. A., Foster, G. D., Brownell, K. D. & Filey, E. (1984). Self-concept in obese and normal-weight children. *Journal of Consulting and Clinical Psychology*, *52*, 1104–5.

Wadden, T. A., Foster, G. D., Stunkard, A. J. & Linowitz, J. R. (1989). Dissatisfaction with weight and figure in obese girls: discontent but not depression. *International Journal of Obesity*, *13*, 89–97.

Wailoo, M. P., Peterson, S. A. & Whittaker, H. (1990). Disturbed nights in 3–4 month old infants: the effects of feeding and thermal environment. *Archives of Disease in Childhood*, *65*, 499–501.

Waisbren, S. E. & Azen, C. (2005). Cognitive and behavioral development in maternal phenylketonuria offspring. *Pediatrics*, *112*, 1544–7.

Walker, A. F. (1990). The contribution of weaning foods to protein-energy malnutrition. *Nutrition Research Reviews*, *3*, 25–49.

Walker, S. P., Grantham-McGregor, S. M., Himes, J. H., Powell, C. A. & Chang, S. M. (1996). Early childhood supplementation does not benefit the long-term growth of stunted children in Jamaica. *Journal of Nutrition*, *126*, 3017–24.

Walker, S. P., Grantham-McGregor, S. M., Powell, C. A. & Chang, S. M. (2000). Effects of growth restriction in early childhood on growth, IQ, and cognition at age 11 to 12 years and the benefits of nutritional supplementation and psychosocial stimulation. *Journal of Pediatrics*, *137*, 36–41.

Walker, S. P., Powell, C. A., Grantham-McGregor, S. M., Himes, J. H. & Chang, S. M. (1991). Nutritional supplementation, psychosocial stimulation, and mental development of stunted children: the Jamaican study. *American Journal of Clinical Nutrition*, *54*, 642–8.

Wallace, J. P., Inbar, G. & Ernsthausen, K. (1992). Infant acceptance of post-exercise breast milk. *Pediatrics*, *89*, 1245–7.

Waller, G. (1993). Why do we diagnose different types of eating disorder? Arguments for a change in research and clinical practice. *Eating Disorders Review*, *1*, 74–89.

  (1998). Perceived control in eating disorders: relationship with reported sexual abuse. *International Journal of Eating Disorders*, *23*, 213–16.

Walter, T., De Andraca, I., Chadud, P. & Perales, C. G. (1989). Iron deficiency anemia: adverse effects on infant psychomotor development. *Pediatrics*, *84*, 7–16.

Wang, Y. (2001). Cross-national comparison of childhood obesity: the epidemic and the relationship between obesity and socioeconomic status. *International Journal of Epidemiology*, *30*, 1129–36.

Ward, M., Kessler, D. & Altman, S. (1993). Infant-mother attachment in children with failure to thrive. *Infant Mental Health Journal*, *14*, 208–20.

Ward, M., Lee, S. & Lipper, E. (2000). Failure-to-thrive is associated with disorganized infant-mother attachment and unresolved maternal attachment. *Infant Mental Health Journal*, *21*, 428–42.

Wardle, J. & Beales, S. (1986). Restraint, body image and food attitudes in children from 12 to 18 years. *Appetite*, *7*, 209–17.

  (1987). Restraint and food intake: an experimental study of eating patterns in the laboratory and in normal life. *Behaviour Research and Therapy*, *25*, 179–85.

Wardle, J., Herrera, M.-L., Cooke, L. & Gibson, E. L. (2003). Modifying children's food preferences: the effects of exposure and reward on acceptance of an unfamiliar vegetable. *European Journal of Clinical Nutrition*, 57, 341–8.

Wardle, J., Parmenter, K. & Waller, J. (2000). Nutrition knowledge and food intake. *Appetite*, 34, 269–75.

Warshaw, J. B. (1985). Intrauterine growth retardation: adaptation or pathology? *Pediatrics*, 76, 998–9.

Wasz-Höckert, O., Lind, J., Vuorenkoski, V., Partanen, T. & Valanne, E. (1968). *The Infant Cry: A Spectrographic and Auditory Analysis*. London: Spastics International Medical Publications.

Waterlow, J. C. (1981). Observations on the suckling's dilemma: a personal view. *Journal of Human Nutrition*, 35, 85–98.

Waterlow, J. C., Buzina, R., Keller, W., et al. (1977). The presentation and use of height and weight data for comparing the nutritional status of groups of children under the age of 10 years. *Bulletin of the World Health Organisation*, 55, 489–98.

Waterlow, J. C. & Thomson, A. M. (1979). Observations on the adequacy of breast-feeding. *Lancet*, 2, 238–41.

Watkins, W. E. & Pollitt, E. (1997). 'Stupidity or worms': Do intestinal worms impair mental performance? *Psychological Bulletin*, 121, 171–91.

Waugh, E. & Bulik, C. M. (1999). Offspring of women with eating disorders. *International Journal of Eating Disorders*, 25, 123–33.

Weglage, J., Grenzebach, M., Pietsch, M., et al. (2000). Behavioural and emotional problems in early-treated adolescents with phenylketonuria in comparison with diabetic patients and healthy controls. *Journal of Inherited Metabolic Disease*, 23, 487–96.

Welch, S. & Fairburn, C. G. (1994). Sexual abuse and bulimia nervosa: three integrated case control comparisons. *American Journal of Psychiatry*, 151, 402–7.

Wells, J. C., Stanley, M., Laidlaw, A. S., et al. (1997). Investigation of the relationship between infant temperament and later body composition. *International Journal of Obesity*, 21, 400–6.

Wells, J. C. K., Coward, W. A., Cole, T. J. & Davies, P. S. W. (2002). The contribution of fat and fat-free tissue to body mass index in contemporary children and the reference child. *International Journal of Obesity*, 26, 1323–8.

Wells, J. C. K. & Davies, P. S. W. (1996). Relationship between behavior and energy expenditure in 12-week-old infants. *American Journal of Human Biology*, 8, 465–72.

Wells, J. C. K., Fuller, N. J., Dewit, O., Fewtrell, M. S., Elia, M. & Cole, T. J. (1999). Four-component model of body composition in children: density and hydration of fat-free mass and comparison with simpler models. *American Journal of Clinical Nutrition*, 69, 904–12.

Welsh, M. C., Pennington, B. F., Ozonoff, S., Rouse, B. & McCabe, E. R. B. (1990). Neuropsychology of early-treated phenylketonuria: specific executive function deficits. *Child Development*, 61, 1697–713.

Wessel, M. A., Cobb, J. C., Jackson, E. B., Harris, G. S. & Detwiler, A. C. (1954). Paroxysmal fussing in infancy, sometimes called 'colic'. *Pediatrics*, 14, 421–34.

Wezel-Meijler, G. van, & Wit, J. M. (1989). The offspring of mothers with anorexia nervosa: a high-risk group for under nutrition and stunting? *European Journal of Pediatrics*, 149, 130–5.

Whitaker, R. C., Pepe, M. S., Wright, J. A., Seidel, K. D. & Dietz, W. H. (1998). Early adiposity rebound and the risk of adult obesity. *Pediatrics*, 101, e5: DOI: 10.1542/peds.101.3.e5.

White, A., Freeth, S. & O'Brien, M. (1992). *Infant Feeding 1990*. London: HMSO.

White, D. A. & DeBaun, M. (1998). Cognitive and behavioral function in children with sickle cell disease: a review and discussion of methodological issues. *Journal of Pediatric Hematology/Oncology*, 20, 458–62.

Whitehouse, P. J. & Harris, G. (1998). The inter-generational transmission of eating disorders. *European Eating Disorders Review*, 6, 238–54.

Whitten, C. F., Pettit, M. G. & Fischhoff, J. (1969). Evidence that growth failure from maternal deprivation is secondary to undereating. *Journal of the American Medical Association*, 209, 1675–80.

WHO (1981). *Contemporary Patterns of Breast-feeding: Report on the WHO Collaborative Study of Breast-Feeding*. Geneva: World Health Organisation.

(1986). Use and interpretation of anthropometric indicators of nutritional status. *Bulletin of the World Health Organisation*, 64, 929–41.

(1995). An evaluation of infant growth: the use and interpretation of anthropometry. *Bulletin of the World Health Organisation*, 73, 165–74.

(1997). *Obesity: Preventing and Managing the Global Epidemic*. Geneva: World Health Organisation.

WHO Collaborative Study Team on the Role of Breastfeeding on the Prevention of Infant Mortality (2000). Effect of breastfeeding on infant and child mortality due to infectious diseases in less developed countries: a pooled analysis. *Lancet*, 355, 451–5.

Wichstrøm, L. (2000). Psychological and behavioral factors unpredictive of disordered eating: a prospective study of the general adolescent population in Norway. *International Journal of Eating Disorders*, 28, 33–42.

Wilde, C. J., Prentice, A. & Peaker, M. (1995). Breast-feeding: matching supply with demand in human lactation. *Proceedings of the Nutritional Society*, 54, 401–6.

Wilensky, D. S., Ginsberg, G., Altman, M., Tulchinsky, T. H., Ben Yishay, F. & Auerbach, J. (1996). A community based study of failure to thrive in Israel. *Archives of Disease in Childhood*, 75, 145–8.

Willats, P., Forsyth, J. S., DiModugno, M. K., Varma, S. & Colvin, M. (1998). Effect of long-chain polyunsaturated fatty acids in infant formula on problem solving at 10 months of age. *Lancet*, 352, 688–91.

Williamson, D. A., Anderson, D. A., Jackman, L. P. & Jackson, S. R. (1995). Assessment of eating disordered thoughts, feelings, and behaviors. In D. B. Allison (ed.), *Handbook of Assessment Methods for Eating Behaviors and Weight-Related Problems: Measures, Theory, and Research* (pp. 347–86). Thousand Oaks, CA: SAGE Publications.

Williamson, D. A., Ravussin, E., Wong, M., *et al.* (2005). Microanalysis of eating behavior of three leptin deficient adults treated with leptin therapy. *Appetite*, 45, 75–80.

Wilson, B. (2005). Honey, I poisoned the kids. *The Guardian*, 25 August, Life, p. 6.

Wilson, N., Quigley, R. & Mansoor, O. (1999). Food ads on TV: a health hazard for children? *Australian and New Zealand Journal of Public Health*, *23*, 647–50.

Winick, M., Meyer, K. K. & Harris, R. C. (1975). Malnutrition and environmental enrichment by early adoption. *Science*, *190*, 1173–5.

Wolff, P. H. (1968a). The serial organization of sucking in the young infant. *Pediatrics*, *42*, 943–56.

(1968b). Sucking patterns of infant mammals. *Brain Behavior and Evolution*, *1*, 354–67.

Wolke, D. (1998). Premature babies and the Special Care Baby Unit (SCBU)/ Neonatal Intensive Care Unit (NICU): environmental, medical and developmental considerations. In C. W. Niven (ed.), *Current Issues in Infancy and Parenthood*, vol. III (pp. 255–81). Oxford: Butterworth Heinemann.

Wolke, D., Skuse, D. & Mathisen, B. (1989). Behavioural style in failure-to-thrive infants: a preliminary communication. *Journal of Pediatric Psychology*, *15*, 237–53.

Wolke, D., Söhne, B., Ohrt, B. & Riegel, K. (1995). Follow-up of preterm children: important to document drop-outs. *Lancet*, *345*, 447.

Woods, S. C., Schwartz, M. W., Baskin, D. G. & Seeley, R. J. (2000). Food intake and the regulation of body weight. *Annual Review of Psychology*, *51*, 255–77.

Wooley, S. (1994). Sexual abuse and eating disorders: the concealed debate. In P. Fallon, M. A. Katzman & S. C. Wooley (eds.), *Feminist Perspectives on Eating Disorders* (pp. 171–211). New York: Guilford Press.

Woolf, L. I. (1986). The heterozygote advantage in phenylketonuria. *American Journal of Human Genetics*, *38*, 773–5.

Woolridge, M. W. & Fisher, C. (1988). Colic, 'overfeeding', and symptoms of lactose malabsorption in the breast-fed baby: a possible artifact of feed management? *Lancet*, *2*, 382–4.

Wright, C. & Birks, E. (2000). Risk factors for failure to thrive: a population based survey. *Child: Care, Health and Development*, *26*, 5–16.

Wright, C., Waterston, A. & Aynsley-Greene, A. (1994). Effect of deprivation on weight gain in infancy. *Acta Paediatrica*, *83*, 357–9.

Wright, C. M., Callum, J., Birks, E. & Jarvis, S. (1998). Effect of community based management in failure to thrive: randomised controlled trial. *British Medical Journal*, *317*, 571–4.

Wright, C. M., Matthews, J. N. S., Waterston, A. & Aynsley-Green, A. (1994). What is a normal rate of weight gain in infancy? *Acta Paediatrica*, *83*, 351–6.

Wright, C. M., Parker, L., Lamont, D. & Craft, A. W. (2001). Implication of childhood obesity for adult health: findings from thousand families cohort study. *British Medical Journal*, *323*, 1280–4.

Wright, P. (1987). Mothers' assessment of hunger in relation to meal size in breastfed infants. *Journal of Reproductive and Infant Psychology*, *5*, 173–81.

Wright, P. & Deary, I. J. (1992). Breastfeeding and intelligence. *Lancet*, *339*, 612.

Wright, P., Fawcett, J. & Crow, R. (1980). The development of differences in the feeding behaviour of bottle and breast fed human infants from birth to two months. *Behavioural Processes*, *5*, 1–20.

Wright, P., Macleod, H. A. & Cooper, M. J. (1983). Waking at night: the effect of early feeding experience. *Child: Care, Health and Development*, *9*, 309–19.

Wyly, M. V. (1997). *Infant Assessment*. Oxford: Westview Press.

Wyshak, G. (2000). Teenaged girls, carbonated beverage consumption, and bone fractures. *Archive of Pediatric and Adolescent Medicine*, *154*, 610–13.

Wyshak, G. & Frish, R. E. (2000). Carbonated beverages, dietary calcium, the dietary calcium/phosphorus ratio, and bone fracture in girls and boys. *Journal of Adolescent Health*, *15*, 210–15.

Yach, D., McKee, M., Lopez, A. D. & Novotny, T. (2005). Improving diet and physical activity: 12 lessons from controlling tobacco smoking. *British Medical Journal*, *330*, 989–1000.

Yeo, G. S. H., Farooqi, I. S., Aminian, S., *et al.* (1998). A frameshift mutation in MC4R associated with dominantly inherited human obesity. *Nature Genetics*, *20*, 111–12.

Yip, Y. (1990). The epidemiology of childhood iron deficiency: evidence for improving iron nutrition among US children. In J. Dobbing (ed.), *Brain, Behaviour, and Iron in the Infant Diet* (pp. 27–39). London: Springer-Verlag.

Young, B. & Drewett, R. F. (2000). Eating behaviour and its variability in one-year-old children. *Appetite*, 171–7.

Index

278   Index